CRITICAL ESSAYS

AND

LITERARY FRAGMENTS

AN ENGLISH GARNER

CRITICAL ESSAYS
AND
LITERARY FRAGMENTS

WITH AN INTRODUCTION BY
J. CHURTON COLLINS

NEW YORK
COOPER SQUARE PUBLISHERS, INC.
1964

PUBLISHERS' NOTE

THE texts contained in the present volume are reprinted with very slight alterations from the *English Garner* issued in eight volumes (1877-1890, London, 8vo) by Professor Arber, whose name is sufficient guarantee for the accurate collation of the texts with the rare originals, the old spelling being in most cases carefully modernised. The contents of the original *Garner* have been rearranged and now for the first time classified, under the general editorial supervision of Mr. Thomas Seccombe. Certain lacunae have been filled by the interpolation of fresh matter. The Introductions are wholly new and have been written specially for this issue. The references to volumes of the *Garner* (other than the present volume) are for the most part to the editio princeps, 8 vols. 1877-90.

Published by
Cooper Square Publishers, Inc.
59 Fourth Avenue, New York, N. Y. 10003
Library of Congress Catalog Card No. 64-16741
Printed in the United States of America

51163

CONTENTS

INTRODUCTION

THE miscellaneous pieces comprised in this volume are of interest and value, as illustrating the history of English literature and of an important side of English social life, namely, the character and status of the clergy in the seventeenth and early eighteenth centuries. They have been arranged chronologically under the subjects with which they are respectively concerned. The first three—the excerpt from Wilson's *Art of Rhetoric*, Sir Philip Sidney's *Letter* to his brother Robert, and the dissertation from Meres's *Palladis Tamia*—are, if minor, certainly characteristic examples of pre-Elizabethan and Elizabethan literary criticism. The next three—the *Dedicatory Epistle to the Rival Ladies*, Howard's *Preface to Four New Plays*, and the *Essay of Dramatic Poesy*—not only introduce us to one of the most interesting critical controversies of the seventeenth century, but present us, in the last work, with an epoch-marking masterpiece, both in English criticism and in English prose composition. Bishop Copleston's brochure brings us to the early days of the *Edinburgh Review*, and to the dawn of the criticism with which we are, unhappily, only too familiar in our own time. From criticism we pass, in the extract from Ellwood's life of himself, to biography and social history, to the most vivid account we have of Milton as a personality and in private life. Next comes a series of pamphlets illustrating social and literary history in the reigns of Anne and George I.,

opening with the pamphlets bearing on Swift's inimitable
Partridge hoax, now for the first time collected and reprinted, and preceding Gay's *Present State of Wit*, which
gives a lively account of the periodic literature current
in 1711. Next comes Tickell's valuable memoir of his
friend Addison, prefixed, as preface, to his edition of
Addison's works, published in 1721, with Steele's singularly
interesting strictures on the memoir, being the dedication
of the second edition of the *Drummer* to Congreve. The
reprint of Eachard's *Grounds and Occasions of the Contempt
of the Clergy and Religion Enquired into*, with the preceding
extract from Chamberlayne's *Angliæ Notitia* and the succeeding papers of Steele's in the *Tatler* and *Guardian*,
throws light on a question which is not only of great interest
in itself, but which has been brought into prominence
through the controversies excited by Macaulay's famous
picture of the clergy of the seventeenth and eighteenth
centuries. Last comes what is by general consent acknowledged to be one of the most valuable contributions ever
made to the literature of proverbs, Franklin's summary
of the maxims in *Poor Richard's Almanack*.

Our first excerpt is the preface to a work which is entitled
to the distinction of being the first systematic contribution
to literary criticism written in the English language. It
appeared in 1553, and was entitled *The Art of Rhetorique,
for the use of all suche as are studious of eloquence, sette
foorthe in Englishe by Thomas Wilson*, and it was dedicated
to John Dudley, Earl of Warwick. Thomas Wilson—
erroneously designated Sir Thomas Wilson, presumably
because he has been confounded with a knight of that
name—was born about 1525, educated at Eton and subsequently at King's College, Cambridge, whence he gradu-

ated B.A. in 1549. In life he played many parts, as tutor to distinguished pupils, notably Henry and Charles Brandon, afterwards Dukes of Suffolk, as diplomatist and ambassador to various countries, as a Secretary of State and a Privy Councillor, as one of the Masters of Requests, and as Master of St. Catherine's Hospital at the Tower, at which place and in which capacity he terminated a very full and busy life on June 16th, 1581. The pupil of Sir John Cheke and of Sir Thomas Smith, and the intimate friend of Roger Ascham, Wilson was one of the most accomplished scholars in England, being especially distinguished by his knowledge of Greek. He is the author of a translation, of a singularly vigorous translation, of the *Olynthiacs* and *Philippics* of Demosthenes, published in 1570. His most popular work, judging at least from the quickly succeeding editions, appears to have been his first, *The Rule of Reason, conteinynge the Art of Logique set forth in Englishe*, published by Grafton in 1551, and dedicated to Edward VI. *The Art of Rhetorique* is said to have been published at the same time, but the earliest known copy is dated January 1553. The interest of this Art of Rhetoric is threefold. It is the work of a writer intelligently familiar with the Greek and Roman classics, and it thus stands beside Elyot's *Governour*, which appeared two years before, as one of the earliest illustrations of the influence of the Renaissance on our vernacular literature. It is one of the earliest examples, not only of the employment of the English language in the treatment of scholastic subjects, but of the vindication of the use of English in the treatment of such subjects ; and, lastly, it is remarkable for its sound and weighty good sense. His friend, Ascham, had already said : 'He that wyll wryte well in any tongue muste folowe thys councel of Aristotle, to speake as the common people do, to think as wise men do, and so shoulde every man understande hym. Many English writers have not done so, but usinge straunge words, as Latin, French, and Italian, do make all thinges darke and harde.' And it is indeed by no means improbable that this work, which is written to inculcate all that Ascham upheld, may have been suggested by Ascham. It is in three books, and draws largely on Quintilian, the first two books being substantially little more than a compilation, but a very judicious one, from the *Institutes of Oratory*. But Wilson is no pedant, and has many excellent remarks on the nature of the influence which the classics should exercise on English composition. One passage is worth transcribing—

'Among all other lessons, this should first be learned, that we never affect any straunge ynkhorne termes, but to speake as is commonly received, neither seeking to be over fine, nor yet being over carelesse, using our speeche as most men doe, and ordering our wittes as the fewest have done. Some seke so far outlandishe English, that thei forget altogether their mothers language. And I dare sweare this, if some of their mothers were alive, thei were not able to tell what thei saie; and yet these fine English clerkes will saie thei speake in their mother tongue—if a man should charge them for counterfeityng the kinges Englishe. . . . The unlearned or foolish phantasicalle that smelles but of learnyng (suche fellowes as have seen learned men in their daies) will so Latin their tongues that the simple can not but wonder at their talke, and thinke surely thei speake by some revelation. I know them that thinke Rhetorique to stand wholie upon darke woordes; and he that can catche an ynke horne terme by the taile him thei coumpt to bee a fine Englisheman and a good Rhetorician.'

In turning to Wilson's own style, we are reminded of Butler's sarcasm—

> 'All a rhetorician's rules
> Teach nothing but to name his tools.'

He is not, indeed, deficient, as the excerpt given shows, in dignity and weightiness, but neither there nor elsewhere has he any of the finer qualities of style, his rhythm being harsh and unmusical, his diction cumbrous and diffuse.

The excerpt which comes next in this miscellany is by the author of that treatise which is, with the exceptions, perhaps, of George Puttenham's *Art of English Poesie* and Ben Jonson's *Discoveries*, the most precious contribution to criticism made in the Elizabethan age; but, indeed, the *Defence of Poesie* stands alone: alone in originality, alone in inspiring eloquence. The letter we print is taken from Arthur Collins's *Sydney Papers*, vol. i. pp. 283-5, and was written by Sir Philip Sidney to his brother Robert, afterwards (August 1618) second Earl of Leicester, then at Prague. From letters of Sir Henry Sidney in the same collection (see letters dated March 25th and October 1578) we learn that Robert, then in his eighteenth year, had been sent abroad to see the world and to acquire foreign languages, that he was flighty and extravagant, and had in consequence greatly annoyed his father, who had threatened to recall him home. 'Follow,' Sir Henry had written, 'the direction of your most loving brother. Imitate his virtues, exercyses, studyes and accyons, hee ys a rare ornament of thys age.' This letter was written at a critical time in Sidney's life. With great courage and with the noblest intentions, though with extraordinary want of tact, for he was only in his twenty-sixth year, he had presumed to dissuade Queen Elizabeth from marrying the Duke of Anjou. The Queen had been greatly offended, and he had had to retire from Court. The greater part of the year 1580 he spent at Wilton with his sister Mary, busy with the *Arcadia*. In August he had, through the influence of his uncle Leicester, become reconciled with the Queen, and a little later took up his residence at Leicester House, from which this letter is dated. It is a mere trifle, yet it illustrates very strikingly and even touchingly Sidney's serious, sweet, and beautiful character. The admirable remarks on the true use of the study of history, such as 'I never require great study in Ciceronianism, the chief abuse of Oxford, *qui dum verba sectantur, res ipsas negligunt*,' remind us of the author of the *Defence*; while the 'great part of my comfort is in you,' 'be careful of yourself, and I shall never have cares,' and the 'I write this to you as one that for myself have given over the delight in the world,' show that he had estimated royal reconciliations at their true value, and anticipate the beautiful and pathetic words with which he is said to have taken leave of the world. Short and hurried as this letter is, we feel it is one of those trifles which, as Plutarch observes, throw far more light on character than actions of importance often do.

Between 1580 and the appearance of Meres's work in 1598 there was much activity in critical literature. Five years before the date of Sidney's letter George Gascogne had published his *Certayne Notes of Instruction concerning the makyng of Verse in Rhyme*. This was succeeded in 1584 by James I.'s *Ane Short Treatise conteining some rewles and cautelis to be observit*. Then came William Webbe's *Discourse of English Poesie*, 1586, which had been preceded by Sidney's charming *Defence of Poetry*, composed in or about 1579, but not published till 1595. This and Puttenham's elaborate treatise, *The Art of English Poesie contrived into three books* (1589), had indeed marked an epoch in the history of criticism. Memorable, too, in this branch of literature is Harington's *Apologie for Poetry*

(1591), prefixed to his translation of the *Orlando Furioso*. But it was not criticism only which had been advancing. The publication of the first part of Lyly's *Euphues* and of Spenser's *Shepherd's Calendar* in 1579 may be said to have initiated the golden age of our literature. The next twenty years saw Marlowe, Greene, Peele, Kyd, Shakespeare, Chapman, Decker, and Ben Jonson at the head of our drama; Spenser, Warner, Daniel, and Drayton leading narrative poetry; the contributors to *England's Helicon*, published a year later, at the head of our sonneteers and lyric poets; and Sidney, Lyly, Greene, and Hooker in the van of our prose literature. The history of Meres's work, a dissertation from which is here extracted, is curious. In or about 1596, Nicholas Ling and John Bodenham conceived the idea of publishing a series of volumes containing proverbs, maxims, and sententious reflections on religion, morals, and life generally. Accordingly in 1597 appeared a small volume containing various apothegms, extracted principally from the Classics and the Fathers, compiled by Nicholas Ling and dedicated to Bodenham. It was entitled *Politeuphuia: Wits Commonwealth*. In the following year appeared ' *Palladis Tamia, Wits Treasury: Being the Second Part of Wits Commonwealth*. By Francis Meres, Maister of Arts in both Universities.' On the title-page is the motto ' *Vivitur ingenio, cetera mortis erunt.*' It was printed by P. Short for Cuthbert Burbie. From the address to the reader, which does not appear in the first edition, though it was apparently intended for that edition, we learn that it had been undertaken because of the extraordinary popularity of *Wits Commonwealth*, which 'thrice within one year had runne thorough the Presse.' Meres's work differs importantly from *Wits Commonwealth*. It is not merely a compilation, but contains original matter, generally by way of commentary. The extracts are much fuller, many being taken from modern writers, notably Robert Greene, Lyly, Warner, and Sir Philip Sidney. In 1634 the work was re-issued under another title, *Wits Commonwealth, The Second Part: A Treasurie of Divine, Moral, and Phylosophical Similes and Sentences generally useful. But more particular published for the Use of Schools.* In 1636 it was again reprinted. The only part of Meres's work which is of interest now is what is here reprinted. It belongs to that portion of his compilation which treats of studies and reading, the preceding sections discussing respectively of 'books,' of 'reading of books,' of 'choice to be had in reading of books,' of 'the use of reading many books,' of 'philosophers,' of 'poetry,' of 'poets,' consisting for the most part of remarks compiled from Plutarch, and in one or two instances from Sir Philip Sidney's *Defence of Poetry.* A portion of the passage which immediately precedes the *Discourse* may be transcribed because of its plain speaking about the indifference of Elizabeth and her ministers to the fortune of poets; though this, with curious inconsistency, is flatly contradicted, probably for prudential reasons, in the *Discourse* itself—

'As the Greeke and Latin Poets have wonne immortal credit to their native speech, being encouraged and graced by liberal patrones and bountiful benefactors; so our famous and learned Lawreate masters of England would entitle our English to far greater admired excellency, if either the Emperor Augustus or Octavia his sister or noble Mæcenas were alive to reward and countenance them; or if witty Comedians and stately Tragedians (the glorious and goodlie representers of all fine witte, glorified phrase and great action) bee still supported and uphelde, by which meanes (O ingrateful and damned age) our Poets are soly or chiefly maintained, countenanced and patronized.'

Of the author of this work, Francis Meres or Meers, comparatively little is known. He sprang from an old and highly respectable family in Lincolnshire, and was born in 1565, the son of Thomas Meres, of Kirton in Holland in that county. After graduating from Pembroke College, Cambridge, in 1587, proceeding M.A. in 1591 at his own University, and subsequently by *ad eundem* at Oxford, he settled in London, where in 1597, having taken orders, he was living in Botolf Lane. He was presented in July 1602 to the rectory of Wing in Rutland, keeping a school there. He remained at Wing till his death, in his eighty-first year, January 29, 1646-7. As Charles FitzGeoffrey, in a Latin poem in his *Affaniæ* addressed to Meres, speaks of him as '*Theologus et poeta*,' it is possible that the 'F. M.' who was a contributor to the *Paradise of Dainty Devices* is to be identified with Meres. In addition to the *Palladis Tamia*, Meres was the author of a sermon published in 1597, a copy of which is in the Bodleian, and of two translations from the Spanish, neither of which is of any interest.

Meres's *Discourse* is, like the rest of his work, mainly a compilation, with additions and remarks of his own. Much of it is derived from the thirty-first chapter of the first book of Puttenham; with these distinctions, that Meres's includes the poets who had come into prominence between 1589 and 1598, and instituted parallels, biographical and critical, between them and the ancient Classics. It is the notices of these poets, and more particularly the references to Shakespeare's writings, which make this treatise so invaluable to literary students. Thus we are indebted to Meres for a list of the plays which Shakespeare had produced by 1598, and for a striking testimony to his eminence at that date as a dramatic poet, as a narrative poet, and as a writer of sonnets. The perplexing reference to *Love's Labour's Won* has never been, and perhaps never will be, satisfactorily explained. To assume that it is another title for *All's Well that Ends Well* in an earlier form is to cut rather than to solve the knot. It is quite possible that it refers to a play that has perished. The references to the imprisonment of Nash for writing the *Isle of Dogs*, to the unhappy deaths of Peele, Greene, and Marlowe, and to the high personal character of Drayton are of great interest. Meres was plainly a man of muddled and inaccurate learning, of no judgment, and of no critical power, a sort of Elizabethan Boswell without Boswell's virtues, and it is no paradox to say that it is this which gives his *Discourse* its chief interest. It probably represents not his own but the judgments current on contemporary writers in Elizabethan literary circles. And we cannot but be struck with their general fairness. Full justice is done to Shakespeare, who is placed at the head of the dramatists; full justice is done to Spenser, who is styled divine, and placed at the head of narrative poets; to Sidney, both as a prose writer and as a poet; to Drayton, to Daniel, and to Hall, Lodge, and Marston, as satirists. We are surprised to find such a high place assigned to Warner, 'styled by the best wits of both our universities the English Homer,' and a modern critic would probably substitute different names, notably those of Lodge and Campion, for those of Daniel and Drayton in a list of the chief lyric poets then in activity. In Meres's remarks on painters and musicians, there is nothing to detain us.

Of a very different order is the important critical treatise which comes next, Dryden's *Essay of Dramatic Poesy*, to which are prefixed as prolegomena Dryden's *Dedicatory Epistle to The Rival Ladies*, Sir Robert Howard's *Preface to*

Four New Plays, and, as supplementary, Howard's *Preface to The Duke of Lerma*, and Dryden's *Defence of the Essay of Dramatic Poesy*. As Dryden's *Essay*, like almost all his writings, both in verse and prose, was of a more or less occasional character, it will be necessary to explain at some length the origin of the controversy out of which it sprang, as well as the immediate object with which it was written.

The Restoration found Dryden a literary adventurer, with a very slender patrimony and with no prospects. Poetry was a drug in the market; hack-work for the booksellers was not to his taste; and the only chance of remunerative employment open to him was to write for the stage. To this he accordingly betook himself. He began with comedy, and his comedy was a failure. He then betook himself to a species of drama, for which his parts and accomplishments were better fitted. Dryden had few or none of the qualifications essential in a great dramatist; but as a rhetorician, in the more comprehensive sense of the term, he was soon to be unrivalled. In the rhymed heroic plays, as they were called, he found just the sphere in which he was most qualified to excel. The taste for these dramas, which owed most to France and something to Italy and Spain, had come in with the Restoration. Their chief peculiarities were the complete subordination of the dramatic to the rhetorical element, the predominance of pageant, and the substitution of rhymed for blank verse. Dryden's first experiment in this drama was the *Rival Ladies*, in which the tragic portions are composed in rhyme, blank verse being reserved for the parts approaching comedy. In his next play, the *Indian Queen*, written in conjunction with Howard, blank verse is wholly discarded. The dedication of the *Rival Ladies* to Orrery is appro-

priate. Roger Boyle, Baron Broghill, and first Earl of
Orrery, was at this time Lord President of Munster, and
it was he who had revived these rhymed plays in his
Henry V., which was brought out in the same year as
Dryden's comedy. Whoever has read this drama and
Orrery's subsequent experiments, *Mustapha* (1665), the
Black Prince (1667), *Tryphon* (1668), will be able to estimate
Dryden's absurd flattery at its proper value.

But these dramatic innovations were sure not to pass without protest, though the protest came from a quarter where it
might least have been expected. Sir Robert Howard was
the sixth son of Thomas, first Earl of Berkshire. He had
distinguished himself on the Royalist side in the Civil
War, and had paid the penalty for his loyalty by an imprisonment in Windsor Castle during the Commonwealth.
At the Restoration he had been made an Auditor of the
Exchequer. Dryden seems to have made his acquaintance
shortly after arriving in London. In 1660 Howard published a collection of poems and translations, to which
Dryden prefixed an address 'to his honoured friend' on
'his excellent poems.' Howard's rank and position made
him a useful friend to Dryden, and Dryden in his turn was
no doubt of much service to Howard. Howard introduced
him to his family, and in December 1663 Dryden married
his friend's eldest sister, the Lady Elizabeth Howard. In
the following year Dryden assisted his brother-in-law in
the composition of the *Indian Queen*. There had probably been some misunderstanding or dispute about the
extent of the assistance which Dryden had given, which
accounts for what follows. In any case Howard published
in 1665, professedly under pressure from Herringman, four
plays, two comedies, *The Surprisal* and *The Committee*, and

two tragedies, the *Vestal Virgin* and *Indian Queen*; and to
the volume he prefixed the preface, which is here reprinted.
It will be seen that though he makes no reference to
Dryden, he combats all the doctrines laid down in the
preface to the *Rival Ladies*. He exalts the English drama
above the French, the Italian, and the Spanish; and vindicates blank verse against rhymed, making, however, a
flattering exception of Orrery's dramas. If Dryden was
not pleased, he appears to have had the grace to conceal
his displeasure. For he passed the greater part of 1666 at
his father-in-law's house, and dedicated to Howard his
Annus Mirabilis. But Howard was to have his answer. In
the *Essay of Dramatic Poesy* he is introduced in the person
of Crites, and in his mouth are placed all the arguments
advanced in the *Preface* that they may be duly refuted and
demolished by Dryden in the person of Neander. At this
mode of retorting Howard became really angry; and in the
Preface to the Duke of Lerma, published in the middle of
1668, he replied in a tone so contemptuous and insolent
that Dryden, in turn, completely lost his temper. The sting
of Howard's *Preface* lies, it will be seen, in his affecting the
air of a person to whom as a statesman and public man the
points in dispute are mere trifles, hardly worth consideration,
and in the patronising condescension with which he descends
to a discussion with one to whom as a mere *litterateur* such
trifles are of importance. The *Defence of the Essay of
Dramatic Poesy* Dryden prefixed to the second edition of
the *Indian Emperor*, one of the best of his heroic plays.
The seriously critical portion of this admirable little treatise
deals with Howard's attacks on the employment of rhyme
in tragedy, on the observance of strict rules in dramatic
composition, and on the observance of the unities. But

irritated by the tone of Howard's tract, Dryden does not
confine himself to answering his friend's arguments. He
ridicules, what Shadwell had ridiculed before, Howard's
coxcombical affectation of universal knowledge, makes
sarcastic reference to an absurdity of which his opponent
had been guilty in the House of Commons, mercilessly
exposes his ignorance of Latin, and the uncouthness and
obscurity of his English. The brothers-in-law afterwards
became reconciled, and in token of that reconciliation
Dryden cancelled this tract.

The *Essay of Dramatic Poesy* was written at Charleton
Park in the latter part of 1665, and published by Herringman
in 1668. It was afterwards carefully revised, and republished
with a dedication to Lord Buckhurst in 1684. Dryden
spent more pains than was usual with him on the composition of this essay, though he speaks modestly of it
as 'rude and indigested,' and it is indeed the most elaborate
of his critical disquisitions. It was, he said, written 'chiefly
to vindicate the honour of our English writers from the
censure of those who unjustly prefer the French before
them.' Its more immediate and particular object was to
regulate dramatic composition by reducing it to critical
principles, and these principles he discerned in a judicious
compromise between the licence of romantic drama as
represented by Shakespeare and his School, and the austere
restraints imposed by the canons of the classical drama.
Assuming that a drama should be 'a just and lively image
of human nature, representing its passions and humours,
and the changes of fortune to which it is subject, for the
delight and instruction of mankind,' it is shown that this
end can only be attained in a drama founded on such a
compromise; that the ancient and modern classical drama

fails in nature; that the Shakespearian drama fails in art.
At the conclusion of the essay he vindicates the employment of rhyme, a contention which he afterwards abandoned. The dramatic setting of the essay was no doubt
suggested by the Platonic *Dialogues*, or by Cicero, and the
essay itself may have been suggested by Flecknoe's short
Discourse of the English Stage, published in 1664.

The *Essay of Dramatic Poesy* may be said to make an era
in the history of English criticism, and to mark an era in the
history of English prose composition. It was incomparably
the best purely critical treatise which had hitherto appeared
in our language, both synthetically in its definition and
application of principles, and particularly in its lucid,
exact, and purely discriminating analysis. It was also the
most striking and successful illustration of what may be
called the new prose style, or that style which, initiated by
Hobbes and developed by Sprat, Cowley, and Denham[1]
blended the ease and plasticity of colloquy with the solidity
and dignity of rhetoric, of that style in which Dryden was
soon to become a consummate master.

The *Advice to a Young Reviewer* brings us into a
very different sphere of criticism, and has indeed a direct
application to our own time. It was written by Edward
Copleston, afterwards Dean of St. Paul's and Bishop of
Llandaff. Born in February 1776 at Offwell, in Devonshire,
Copleston gained in his sixteenth year a scholarship at
Corpus Christi College, Oxford. After carrying off the prize
for Latin verse, he was elected in 1795 Fellow of Oriel. In
1800, having been ordained priest, he became Vicar of St.
Mary's. In 1802 he was elected Professor of Poetry, in
which capacity he delivered the lectures subsequently pub-
lished under the title of *Prælectiones Academicæ*—a favourite

---

[1] See his Preface to his version of part of Virgil's second *Aeneid*.

book of Cardinal Newman's. In 1814 he succeeded Dr. Eveleigh as Provost of Oriel. In 1826 he was made Dean of Chester, in 1828 Bishop of Llandaff and Dean of St. Paul's. He died at Llandaff, on October 14th, 1849. Copleston is one of the fathers of modern Oxford, and from his provostship date many of the reforms which transformed the University of Gibbon and Southey into the University of Whateley, of Newman, of Keble, and of Pusey. The brochure which is printed here was written when Copleston was Fellow and Tutor of Oriel. It was immediately inspired, not, as is commonly supposed, by the critiques in the *Edinburgh Review*, but by the critiques in the *British Critic*, a periodical founded in 1793, and exceedingly influential between that time and about 1812. Archbishop Whateley, correcting a statement in the *Life* of Copleston by W. J. Copleston, says that it was occasioned by a review of Mant's poems in the *British Critic*.[1] But on referring to the review of these poems, which appeared in the November number of 1806, plainly the review referred to, we find nothing in it to support Whateley's assertion. That the reviews in the *British Critic* are, however, what Copleston is parodying in the critique of *L'Allegro* is abundantly clear, but what he says about voyages and travels and about science and recondite learning appear to have reference to articles particularly characteristic of the *Edinburgh Review*. It was not, however, till after the date of Copleston's parody that the *Edinburgh Review* began conspicuously to illustrate what Copleston here satirises; it was not till a time more recent still that periodical literature generally exemplified in literal seriousness what Copleston intended as extravagant irony. It is interesting to compare with Copleston's

---

[1] Whateley's *Reminiscences of Bishop Copleston*, p. 6.

remarks what Thackeray says on the same subjects in the twenty-fourth chapter of *Pendennis*, entitled 'The Pall Mall Gazette.' This brochure is evidently modelled on Swift's 'Digression Concerning Critics' in the third section of the *Tale of a Tub*, and owes something also to the *Treatise on the Bathos* in Pope's and Swift's *Miscellanies*, as the title may have been suggested by Shaftesbury's *Advice to an Author*. The *Advice* itself and the supplementary critique of Milton are clever and have good points, but they will not bear comparison with the satire of Swift and Pope.

The excerpt which comes next in this Miscellany links with the name of the author of the *Essay of Dramatic Poesy* the name of the most illustrious of his contemporaries. The difference, indeed, between Milton and Dryden is a difference not in degree merely, but in kind, so immeasurably distant and alien is the sphere in which they moved and worked both as men and as writers. It has sometimes been questioned whether Dryden is a poet. Few would dispute that Milton divides with Shakespeare the supremacy in English poetry. In Dryden as a man there is little to attract or interest us. In character and in private life he appears to have been perfectly commonplace. We close his biography, and our curiosity is satisfied. With Milton it is far otherwise. We feel instinctively that he belongs to the demi-gods of our race. We have the same curiosity about him as we have about Homer, Æschylus, and Shakespeare, so that the merest trifles which throw any light on his personality assume an interest altogether out of proportion to their intrinsic importance. Our debt to Ellwood is, it must be admitted, much less than it might have been, if he had thought a little more of Milton and a little less of his somewhat stupid self

and the sect to which he belonged. But, as the proverb says, we must not look a gift-horse in the mouth, and
we are the richer for the Quaker's reminiscences. With
Ellwood's work, the *History of Thomas Ellwood, written
by Himself,* we are only concerned so far as it bears on his
relation with Milton. Born in 1639, the son of a small
squire and justice of the peace at Crowell in Oxfordshire,
Ellwood had, in 1659, been persuaded by Edward Burrough,
one of the most distinguished of Fox's followers, to join
the Quakers. He was in his twenty-fourth year when he
first met Milton. Milton was then living in Jewin Street,
having removed from his former lodging in Holborn, most
probably in the autumn of 1661. The restoration had
terminated his work as a controversialist and politician.
For a short time his life had been in peril, but he had
received a pardon, and could at least live in peace. He
could no longer be of service as a patriot, and was now
occupied with the composition of *Paradise Lost.* Since
1650 he had been blind, and for study and recreation was
dependent on assistance. Having little domestic comfort
as a widower, he had just married his third wife.

Ellwood's narrative tells its own story. What especially
strikes us in it, and what makes it particularly interesting, is
that it presents Milton in a light in which he is not presented
elsewhere. Ellwood seems to have had the same attraction
for him as Bonstetten had for Gray. No doubt the simplicity,
freshness, and enthusiasm of the young Quaker touched
and interested the lonely and world-wearied poet who,
when Ellwood first met him, had entered on his fifty-fifth
year; he had no doubt, too, the scholar's sympathy with a
disinterested love of learning. In any case, but for Ellwood,
we should never have known the softer side of Milton's

character, never have known of what gentleness, patience,
and courtesy he was capable. And, indeed, when we
remember Milton's position at this time, as tragical as that
of Demosthenes after Chæronea, and of Dante at the Court
of Verona, there is something inexpressibly touching in
the picture here given with so much simplicity and with
such evident unconsciousness on the part of the painter
of the effect produced. There is one passage which is quite
delicious, and yet its point may be, as it commonly is, easily
missed. It illustrates the density of Ellwood's stupidity,
and the delicate irony of the sadly courteous poet. Milton
had lent him, it will be seen, the manuscript of *Paradise
Lost*; and on Ellwood returning it to him, 'he asked me
how I liked it, and what I thought of it, which I modestly
but freely told him, and after some further discourse about
it I pleasantly said to him, "Thou has said much here of
Paradise Lost, but what has thou to say of Paradise
Found?"' Now the whole point and scope of Paradise
Lost is Paradise Found — the redemption — the substitution of a spiritual Eden within man for a physical Eden
without man, a point emphasised in the invocation, and
elaborately worked out in the closing vision from the
Specular Mount. It is easy to understand the significance
of what follows: 'He made me no answer, but sat sometime in a muse; then broke off that discourse, and fell
upon another subject.' The result no doubt of that
'muse' was the suspicion, or, perhaps, the conviction, that
the rest of the world would, in all probability, be as obtuse
as Ellwood; and to that suspicion or conviction we appear
to owe *Paradise Regained.* The Plague over, Milton
returned to London, settling in Artillery Walk, Bunhill
Fields. 'And when afterwards I went to wait on him there

. . . he shewed me his second poem, called *Paradise
Regained*, and in a pleasant tone said to me, " This is owing
to you, for you put it into my head by the question you put
to me at Chalfont, which before I had not thought of." ' In
' the pleasant tone' more, and much more, is implied, of that
we may be very sure, than meets the ear. We should like
to have seen the expression on Milton's face both on this
occasion and also when, on Dryden requesting his permission to turn *Paradise Lost* into an opera, he replied, ' Oh,
certainly, you may tug my verses if you please, Mr.
Dryden.' It may be added that *Paradise Lost* was not
published till 1667, and *Paradise Regained* did not see
the light till 1671. Ellwood seems to imply that *Paradise
Regained* was composed between the end of August or the
beginning of September 1665, and the end of the autumn
of the same year, which is, of course, incredible and quite
at variance with what Phillips tells us. Ellwood is, no
doubt, expressing himself loosely, and his ' afterwards'
need not necessarily relate to his first, or to his second, or
even to his third visit to Milton after the poet's return to
Artillery Walk, but refers vaguely to one of those ' occasions which drew him to London.' When he last saw
Milton we have no means of knowing. He never refers to
him again. His autobiography closes with the year 1683.

For the rest of his life Ellwood was engaged for the most
part in fighting the battles of the Quakers—esoterically in
endeavouring to compose their internal feuds, exoterically
in defending them and their tenets against their common
enemies—and in writing poetry, which it is to be hoped he
did not communicate to his ' master.' After the death of
his father in 1684 he lived in retirement at Amersham. His
most important literary service was his edition of George
Fox's *Journal*, the manuscript of which he transcribed and

published. He died at his house on Hunger Hill, Amersham, in March 1714, and lies with Penn in the Quaker's burying-ground at New Jordan, Chalfont St. Giles.

We have now arrived at the pamphlets in our Miscellany bearing on the reign of Queen Anne. First come the Partridge tracts. The history of the inimitable hoax of which they are the record is full of interest. In November 1707 Swift, then Vicar of Laracor, came over to England on a commission from Archbishop King. His two satires, the *Battle of the Books* and the *Tale of a Tub*, published anonymously three years before, had given him a foremost place among the wits, for their authorship was an open secret. Though he was at this time principally engaged in the cause of the Established Church, in active opposition to what he considered the lax latitudinarianism of the Whigs on the one hand and the attacks of the Freethinkers on the other, he found leisure for doing society another service. Nothing was more detestable to Swift than charlatanry and imposture. From time immemorial the commonest form which quackery has assumed has been associated with astrology and prophecy. It was the frequent theme or satire in the New Comedy of the Greeks and in the Comedy of Rome ; it has fallen under the lash of Horace and Juvenal ; nowhere is Lucian more amusing than when dealing with this species of roguery. Chaucer with exquisite humour exposed it and its kindred alchemy in the fourteenth century, and Ben Jonson and the author of *Albumazar* in the seventeenth. Nothing in *Hudibras* is more rich in wit and humour than the exposure of Sidrophel, and one of the best of Dryden's comedies is the *Mock Astrologer*. But it was reserved for Swift to produce the most amusing satire which has ever gibbeted these mischievous mountebanks.

John Partridge, whose real name is said to have been

Hewson, was born on the 18th of January 1644. He began life, it appears, as a shoemaker; but being a youth of some abilities and ambition, had acquired a fair knowledge of Latin and a smattering of Greek and Hebrew. He had then betaken himself to the study of astrology and of the occult sciences. After publishing the *Nativity of Lewis XIV.* and an astrological essay entitled *Prodromus*, he set up in 1680 a regular prophetic almanac, under the title of *Merlinus Liberatus.* A Protestant alarmist, for such he affected to be, was not likely to find favour under the government of James II., and Partridge accordingly made his way to Holland. On his return he resumed his Almanac, the character of which is exactly described in the introduction to the *Predictions*, and it appears to have had a wide sale. Partridge, however, was not the only impostor of his kind, but had, as we gather from notices in his Almanac and from his other pamphlets, many rivals. He was accordingly obliged to resort to every method of bringing himself and his Almanac into prominence, which he did by extensive and impudent advertisements in the newspapers and elsewhere. In his Almanac for 1707 he issues a notice warning the public against impostors usurping his name. It was this which probably attracted Swift's attention and suggested his mischievous hoax.

The pamphlets tell their own tale, and it is not necessary to tell it here. The name, Isaac Bickerstaff, which has in sound the curious propriety so characteristic of Dickens's names, was, like so many of the names in Dickens, suggested by a name on a sign-board, the name of a locksmith in Long Acre. The second tract, purporting to be written by a revenue officer, and giving an account of Partridge's death, was, of course, from the

pen of Swift.   The verses on Partridge's death appeared
anonymously on a separate sheet as a broadside. It is
amusing to learn that the tract announcing Partridge's
death, and the approaching death of the Duke of Noailles,
was taken quite seriously, for Partridge's name was struck
off the rolls of Stationers' Hall, and the Inquisition in
Portugal ordered the tract containing the treasonable prediction to be burned. As Stationers' Hall had assumed
that Partridge was dead—a serious matter for the prospects
of his Almanac—it became necessary for him to vindicate his
title to being a living person. Whether the next tract,
Squire Bickerstaff Detected, was, as Scott asserts, the result
of an appeal to Rowe or Yalden by Partridge, and they,
under the pretence of assisting him, treacherously making a
fool of him, or an independent *jeu d'esprit*, is not quite
clear. Nor is it easy to settle with any certainty the
authorship. In the Dublin edition of Swift's works, it is
attributed to Nicholas Rowe; Scott assigns it to Thomas
Yalden, the preacher of Bridewell and a well-known poet.
Congreve is also said to have had a hand in it.   It would
have been well for Partridge had he allowed matters to rest
here, but unhappily he inserted in the November issue of his
Almanac another solemn assurance to the public that he was
still alive ; and was fool enough to add, that he was not only
alive at the time he was writing, but was also alive on the
day on which Bickerstaff had asserted that he was dead.
Swift saw his opportunity, and in the most amusing of this
series of tracts proceeded to prove that Partridge, under
whatever delusions as to his continued existence he might
be labouring, was most certainly dead and buried.

The tracts here printed by no means exhaust the literature of the Partridge hoax, but nothing else which appeared

is worth reviving. It is surprising that Scott should include in Swift's works a vapid and pointless contribution attributed to a 'Person of Quality.' The effect of all this on poor Partridge was most disastrous; for three years his Almanac was discontinued. When it was revived, in 1714, he had discovered that his enemy was Swift. What comments he made will be found at the end of these tracts. Partridge did not long survive the resuscitation of his Almanac. What had been fiction became fact on June 24th, 1715, and his virtues and accomplishments, delineated by a hand more friendly than Swift's, were long decipherable, in most respectable Latin, on his tomb in Mortlake Churchyard.

The Partridge hoax has left a permanent trace in our classical literature. When, in the spring of 1709, Steele was about to start the *Tatler*, he thought he could best secure the ear of the public by adopting the name with which Englishmen were then as familiar as a century and a half afterwards they became with the name of Pickwick. It was under the title of the *Lucubrations of Isaac Bickerstaff* that the essays which initiated the most attractive and popular form of our periodical literature appeared.

The next tract, Gay's *Present State of Wit*, takes up the history of our popular literature during the period which immediately succeeded the discomfiture of poor Partridge. Its author, John Gay, who is, as we need scarcely add, one of the most eminent of the minor poets of the Augustan age, was at the time of its appearance almost entirely unknown. Born in September 1685, at Barnstaple, of a respectable but decayed family, he had received a good education at the free grammar school of that place. On leaving school he had been apprenticed to a silk mercer in London. But he had polite tastes, and employed his leisure time in scribbling

verses and in frequenting with his friend, Aaron Hill, the
literary coffee-houses. In 1708 he published a vapid and
stupid parody, suggested by John Philip's *Splendid Shilling*
and *Cider*, entitled *Wine*. His next performance was the
tract which is here printed, and which is dated May 3rd,
1711. It is written with skill and sprightliness, and
certainly shows a very exact and extensive acquaintance
with the journalistic world of those times. And it is this
which gives it its value. The best and most useful form,
perhaps, which our remarks on it can take will be to furnish
it with a running commentary explaining its allusions both
to publications and to persons. It begins with a reference
to the unhappy plight of Dr. King. This was Dr. William
King, who is not to be confounded with his contemporaries
and namesakes, the Archbishop of Dublin or the Principal
of St. Mary Hall, Oxford, but who may be best, perhaps,
described as the Dr. William King 'who could write verses
in a tavern three hours after he could not speak.' He had
long been a prominent figure among wits and humorists.
His most important recent performances had been his *Art of
Cookery* and his *Art of Love*, published respectively in 1708
and in 1709. In the latter year he had, much to the disgust
of Sir John Soames, issued some very amusing parodies of
the *Philosophical Transactions*, which he entitled *Useful
Transactions in Philosophy and other sorts of Learning*, to
be continued as long as it could find buyers. It ceased
apparently to find buyers, and after reaching three numbers
had collapsed. When the *Examiner* was started in August
1710, King was one of the chief contributors. Latterly,
however, things had been going very badly with this 'poor
starving wit,' as Swift called him. He was either imprisoned
or on the point of being imprisoned in the Fleet, but death

freed him from his troubles at the end of 1712. John Ozell
was, perhaps, the most ridiculous of the scribblers then
before the public, maturing steadily for the *Dunciad*, where,
many years afterwards, he found his proper place.   He
rarely aspired beyond 'translations,' and the *Monthly
Amusement* referred to is not, as might be supposed, a
periodical, but simply his frequent appearances as a
translator. Gay next passes to periodicals and newspapers.
De Foe is treated as he was always treated by the wits.
Pope's lines are well known, and the only reference to him
in Swift is: ' The fellow who was pilloried—I forget his
name.' Posterity has done him more justice. The 'poor
Review' is of course the *Weekly Review*, started by De Foe
in 1704, the first number of which appeared on Saturday,
February 19th of that year. It had been continued weekly,
and still continued, till 1712, extending to nine volumes,
eight of which are extant.[1] The *Observator*, which is also
described as in its decline, had been set up by John Tutchin
in imitation of the paper issued by Sir Roger L'Estrange in
1681, its first number appearing April 1st, 1702. Tutchin,
dying in 1707, the paper was continued for the benefit of his
widow, under the management of George Ridpath, the editor
of the *Flying Post*, and it continued to linger on till 1712,
when it was extinguished by the Stamp Tax.   The first
number of the *Examiner* appeared on the 3rd of August
1710, and it was set up by the Tories to oppose the *Tatler*,
the chief contributors to it being Dr. King, Bolingbroke,
then Henry St. John, Prior, Atterbury, and Dr. Freind.
With No. 14 (Thursday, October 26th, 1710), Swift
assumed the management, and writing thirty-two papers
successively, made it the most influential political journal

[1] See *Late Stuart Tracts.*

in the kingdom. The 'Letter to Crassus' appeared on February 1st, 1711, and was written by Swift. To oppose the *Examiner*, the Whigs set up what, after the second number, they called the *Whig Examiner*, the first number of which appeared on September 14th, 1710. It was continued weekly till October 12th, five numbers appearing, all of which were, with one exception, perhaps, written by Addison, so that Gay's conjecture—if Bickerstaff may be extended to include Addison—was correct. The *Medley*, to which Gay next passes, was another Whig organ. The first number appeared on August 5th, 1710, and it was continued weekly till August 6th, 1711. It was conducted by Arthur Mainwaring, a man of family and fortune, and an ardent Whig, with the assistance of Steele, Anthony Henley, and Oldmixon.

With the reference to the *Tatler*, we pass from obscurity into daylight. Since April 12th, 1709, that delightful periodical had regularly appeared three times a week. With the two hundredth and seventy-first number on January 2nd, 1711, it suddenly ceased. Of the great surprise and disappointment caused by its cessation, of the causes assigned for it, and of the high appreciation of all it had effected for moral and intellectual improvement and pleasure, Gay gives a vivid picture. What he says conjecturally about the reasons for its discontinuance is so near the truth that we may suspect he had had some light on the subject from Steele himself. It was, of course, from the preface to the edition of the first three volumes of the collected *Tatlers*, published in 1710, that Gay derived what he says about the contributions of Addison (though Steele had not mentioned him by name, in accordance, no doubt, with Addison's request) and about the verses of Swift. In all probability this was the first public association of Addison's name with the *Tatler*. The Mr. Henley referred to was Anthony Henley, a man of family and fortune, and one of the most distinguished of the wits of that age, to whom Garth dedicated *The Dispensary*. In politics he was a rabid Whig, and it was he who described Swift as 'a beast for ever after the order of Melchisedec.' Gay had not been misinformed, for Henley was the author of the first letter in No. 26 and of the letter in No. 193, under the character of Downes.

The cessation of the *Tatler* had been the signal for the appearance of several spurious papers purporting to be new numbers. One entitling itself No. 272 was published by one John Baker; another, purporting to be No. 273, was by 'Isaac Bickerstaff, Junior.' Then, on January 6th, appeared what purported to be Nos. 272 and 273 of the original issue, with a letter from Charles Lillie, one of the publishers of the original *Tatler*. Later in January, William Harrison, a *protégé* of Swift, a young man whose name will be familiar to all who are acquainted with Swift's *Journal to Stella*, was encouraged by Swift to start a new *Tatler*, Swift liberally assisting him with notes, and not only contributing himself but inducing Congreve also to contribute a paper. And this new *Tatler* actually ran to fifty-two numbers, appearing twice a week between January 13th and May 19th, 1711, but, feeble from the first, it then collapsed. Nor had the *Tatler* been without rivals. In the two hundred and twenty-ninth number of the *Tatler*, Addison, enumerating his antagonists, says, 'I was threatened to be answered weekly *Tit for Tat*, I was undermined by the *Whisperer*, scolded at by a *Female Tatler*, and slandered by another of the same character under the title of *Atalantis*.' To confine ourselves, however, to the publications mentioned by Gay. The *Growler* appeared on the 27th of January 1711, on the discontinuance of the *Tatler*. The *Whisperer* was first published on October 11th, 1709, under the character of ' Mrs. Jenny Distaff, half-sister to Isaac Bickerstaff.' The *Tell Tale* appears to be a facetious title for the *Female Tatler*, the first number of which appeared on July 8th, 1709, and was continued for a hundred and eleven numbers, under the editorship of Thomas Baker, till March 3rd, 1710. The allusion in the postscript to the *British Apollo* is to a paper entitled *The British Apollo: or Curious Amusements for the Ingenious*, the first number of which appeared on Friday, March 13th, 1708, the paper regularly continuing on Wednesdays and Fridays till March 16th, 1711. Selections from this curious miscellany were afterwards printed in three volumes, and ran into three editions. Gay does not appear to be aware that this periodical had ceased. The reference in ' the two statesmen of the last reign whose characters are well expressed in their mottoes' are to Lord Somers and the Earl of Halifax, as what follows refers respectively to Addison and Steele. The tract closes with a reference to the *Spectator*, the first number of which had appeared on the first of the preceding March.

Gay's brochure attracted the attention of Swift, who thus refers to it in his *Journal to Stella*, May 14th, 1711 : ' Dr. Freind was with me and pulled out a two-penny pamphlet just published called *The State of Wit*. The author seems to be a Whig, yet he speaks very highly of a paper called the *Examiner*, and says the supposed author of it is Dr. Swift, but above all he praises the *Tatler* and *Spectator*.'

The two tracts which follow consist of the Life of Addison, which forms the preface to Addison's collected works, published by Tickell in 1721, and of the Dedicatory

Epistle prefixed by Steele to an edition of Addison's *Drummer* in 1722. To the student of the literary history of those times they are of great interest and importance. Of all Addison's friends, Steele had long been the most intimate of the younger men whom he had taken under his patronage. Tickell was the most loyal and the most attached. While still at Oxford he had expressed his admiration of Addison in extravagant terms: on arriving in London he made his acquaintance. Tickell was an accomplished poet and man of letters, and though not a profound a graceful scholar. Addison was pleased with a homage which was worth accepting. As he rose, his *protégé* rose with him. On his appointment as Chief Secretary in Ireland he took Tickell with him. When he was appointed Secretary of State he chose him as Under Secretary, and shortly before his death made him his literary executor, instructing him to collect his writings in a final and authentic edition. This, for reasons which will be explained directly, was a task of no small difficulty, but to this task Tickell loyally addressed himself. In the spring of 1721 appeared, in four sumptuous quartos, the collected edition of Addison's works. It was prefaced by the biography which is here reprinted, and to the biography was appended that noble and pathetic elegy which will make Tickell's name as immortal as Addison's.

There can be very little doubt that Steele had been greatly distressed and hurt by the rupture of the friendship which had so long existed between himself and Addison, but that Tickell should have taken his place in Addison's affections must have been inexpressibly galling to him. Naturally irritated, his irritation had no doubt been intensified by Addison appointing Tickell Under Secretary of State, and

still more by his making him his literary executor—offices
which Steel might naturally have expected, had all gone
well, to fill himself. It would not have been in human nature
that he could regard Tickell with any other feelings than
hostility and jealousy. Tickell's omission of the *Drummer*
from Addison's works was, in all probability—such at least
is the impression which the letter makes on me—a mere
pretext for the gratification of personal spite. There is
nothing to justify the interpretation which he puts on
Tickell's words. All that Steele here says about Addison
he had said publicly and quite as emphatically before, as
Tickell had recorded. As Steele had, in Tickell's own
words, given to Addison 'the honour of the most applauded
pieces,' it is absurd to accuse Tickell of insinuating that
Addison wished his papers to be marked because he was
afraid Steele would assume the credit of these pieces. In
one important particular he flatly contradicts himself.
At the beginning he asks 'whether it was a decent and
reasonable thing that works written, as a great part of
Mr. Addison's were, in correspondence with me, ought to
have been published without my review of the catalogue
of them.' Three pages afterward, it appears that, in compliance with the request of Addison delivered to him by
Tickell, he did mark with his own hand those *Tatlers* which
were inserted in Addison's works—a statement of Tickell's,
but a statement to which Steele takes no exception. So
far from attempting to disparage Steele, Tickell does
ample justice to him ; and to accuse him of insensibility
to Addison's virtues, and of cold indifference to him personally, is a charge refuted not only by all we know of
Tickell, but by every page in the tract itself. Many of the
objections which he makes to Tickell's remarks are too

absurd to discuss. From nothing indeed which Tickell
says, but from one of Steele's own admissions, it is
impossible not to draw a conclusion very derogatory to
Steele's honesty, and to make us suspect that his sensitive-
ness was caused by his own uneasy conscience : 'What I
never did declare was Mr. Addison's I had his direct injunctions to hide.' This certainly seems to imply that
Steele had allowed himself to be credited with what really
belonged to his friend. A month after Addison's death he
had written in great alarm to Tonson, on hearing that it
had been proposed to separate Addison's papers in the
Tatler from his own. He bases his objection, it is true, on
the pecuniary injury which he and his family would suffer,
but this is plainly mere subterfuge. The truth probably is,
that Steele wished to leave as undefined as possible what
belonged to Addison and what belonged to himself ; that
he was greatly annoyed when he found that their respective shares were by Addison's own, or at least his alleged,
request to be defined ; that in his assignation of the papers
he had not been quite honest ; and that, knowing this, he
suspected that Tickell knew it too. There is nothing to
support Steele's assertion that it was at his instigation that
Addison distinguished his contributions to the *Spectator*
and the *Guardian*. Addison, as his last injunctions
showed, must have contemplated a collective edition of his
works, and must have desired therefore that they should
be identified. Steele's ambition, no doubt, was that he
and his friend should go down to posterity together, but
the appointment of Tickell instead of himself as Addison's
literary executor dashed this hope to the ground.

Few things in literary biography are more pathetic than
the estrangement between Addison and Steele. They had

played as boys together; they had, for nearly a quarter of
a century, shared each other's burdens, and the burdens had
not been light; in misfortune and in prosperity, in business
and in pleasure, they had never been parted. The wisdom
and prudence of Addison had more than once been the
salvation of Steele; what he knew of books and learning
had been almost entirely derived from Addison's conversation; what moral virtue he had, from Addison's influence.
And he had repaid this with an admiration and affection
which bordered on idolatry. A more generous and genial,
a more kindly, a more warm-hearted man than Steele never
lived, and it is easy to conceive what his feelings must
have been when he found his friend estranged from him
and a rival in his place. There is much to excuse what
this letter to Congreve plainly betrays; but excuse is not
justification. Tickell had a delicate and difficult task to
perform: a duty to his dead friend, which was paramount,
a duty to Steele, and a duty to himself, and he succeeded
in performing each with admirable tact. Whether Tickell
ever made any reply to Steele's strictures, I have not been
able to discover.

We pass now from the literary pamphlets to the extract
and excerpts illustrating the condition of the Church and
the clergy at the end of the seventeenth and about the first
half of the eighteenth century. They are of particular
interest, not only in themselves, but in their relation to
Swift and Macaulay—to Swift as a Church reformer, to
Macaulay as a social historian. Few historical questions
in our own time provoked more controversy than the
famous pages delineating the clergy who, according to
Macaulay, were typical of their order about the time of the
Restoration. The first excerpt is from Chamberlayne's

Angliæ Notitia. The author of that work, Edward Chamberlayne, was born on the 13th of December 1616. He was educated at Oxford, where he graduated as B.A. in April 1638. For a short time he was Reader in Rhetoric to the University, but on the breaking out of the Civil War he left for the Continent, where he visited nearly every country in Europe. At the Restoration he returned; and about 1675, after having been secretary to the Earl of Carlisle, he became tutor to the King's natural son, Henry Fitzroy, afterwards Duke of Grafton, and subsequently instructor in English to Prince George of Denmark. He was also one of the earliest Fellows of the Royal Society. He died at Chelsea in May 1703. In 1669 he published anonymously *Angliæ Notitia, or the Present State of England with Divers Reflection upon the Ancient State therefor*, a work no doubt suggested by and apparently modelled on the well-known *L'Estat Nouveau de la France*. The work contains more statistics than reflections, and is exactly what its title implies—a succinct account of England, beginning with its name, its climate, its topography, and giving information, now invaluable, about everything included in its constitution and in its economy. The extract printed here is, as is indicated, from pp. 383-389 and p. 401. The work passed through two editions in the year of its appearance, the second bearing the author's name, and at the time of Chamberlayne's death it had, with successive amplifications, reached its twentieth edition.

Of a very different order to Chamberlayne's work is the remarkable tract which follows. The author, John Eachard, was born about 1636, at what date is doubtful, but he was admitted into Catherine Hall, Cambridge, in May 1653. Becoming Fellow of the Hall in 1658, he was chosen, on

the death of Dr. Lightfoot, Master. His perfectly unevent-
ful life closed on the 7th of July 1697. Personally he was
a facetious and agreeable man, and had the reputation of
being rather a wit and humorist than a divine and scholar.
Baker complained of his inferiority as a preacher; and
Swift, observing 'that men who are happy enough at ridicule are sometimes perfectly stupid upon grave subjects,'
gives Eachard as an instance. *The Grounds and Occasions of
the Contempt of the Clergy and Religion enquired into, In a
letter written to R. L.*, appeared anonymously in 1670.
This anonymity Eachard carefully preserved during the
controversies which it occasioned. It is difficult to understand how any one after reading the preface could have
misunderstood the purpose of the book. But Eachard's
fate was Swift's fate afterwards, though there was more
excuse for the High Church party missing the point of
the *Tale of a Tub* than for the clergy generally missing
that of Eachard's plea for them. Ridicule is always a
dangerous ally, especially when directed against an institution or community, for men naturally identify themselves
with the body of which they are members, and resent as
individuals what reflects on them collectively. When one
of the opponents of Barnabus Oley in his preface to Herbert's
Country Parson observed: 'The pretence of your book
was to *show* the occasions, your book is *become* the occasion of the contempt of God's ministers,' he expressed what
the majority of the clergy felt. The storm burst at once,
and the storm raged for months. 'I have had,' wrote
Eachard in one of his many rejoinders, 'as many several
names as the Grand Seignior has titles of honour; for
setting aside the vulgar and familiar ones of Rogue, Rascal,
Dog, and Thief (which may be taken by way of endear-

ment as well as out of prejudice and offence), as also
those of more certain signification, as Malicious Rogue,
Ill-Natured Rascal, Lay Dog, and Spiteful Thief.' He had
also, he said, been called Rebel, Traitor, Scot, Sadducee,
and Socinian. Among the most elaborate replies to his
work were: *An Answer to a Letter of Enquiry into the
Ground*, etc., 1671 ; *A Vindication of the Clergy from the
Contempt imposed upon them*, By the author of the
Grounds, etc., 1672; *Hieragonisticon, or Corah's Doom,
being an Answer to*, etc., 1672 ; *An Answer to two Letters of
T. B.*, etc., 1673. The occasional references to it in the
theological literature of these times are indeed innumerable.
Many affected to treat him as a mere buffoon—the con-
coctor, as one bitterly put it, of 'a pretty fardle of tales
bundled together, and they have had the hap to fall into
such hands as had rather lose a friend, not to say their
country, than a jest.' Anthony Wood, writing at the time
of its appearance, classes it with 'the fooleries, playes,
poems, and drolling books,' with which, as he bitterly complains, people were 'taken with,' coupling with it Marvell's
Rehearsal Transposed and Butler's *Hudibras*.[1]

To some of his opponents Eachard replied. Of his method
of conducting controversy, in which it is clear that he
perfectly revelled, I give a short specimen. It is from his
letter to the author of *Hieragonisticon* :—

'You may possibly think, sir, that I have read your book,
but if you do you are most mistaken. For as long as I
can get Tolambu's *History of Mustard*, Frederigo *Devasta-
tion of Pepper*, *The Dragon*, with cuts, Mandringo's *Pismires
rebuffeted* and *retro-confounded, Is qui me dubitat, or a flap
against the Maggot of Heresie, Efflorescentina Flosculorum,*

[1] Wood's *Life and Times*, Clark's Ed. vol. ii. p. 240.

or a choice collection of F. (*sic*) Withers *Poems* or the like, I
do not intend to meddle with it.   Alas, sir, I am as unlikely
to read your book that I can't get down the title no more
than a duck can swallow a yoked heifer'—and then follows
an imitation of gulps straining at the divided syllables
of Hieragonisticon.

There is no reason to suspect the sincerity of Eachard,
or to doubt that he was, in his own words, an honest
and hearty wisher that 'the best of the clergy might for
ever continue, as they are, rich and learned, and that
the rest might be very useful and well esteemed in their
profession.'   To describe the work as 'a series of jocose
caricatures — as Churchill Babington in his animadversions on Macaulay's *History* does—is absurd.   Eachard
was evidently a man of strong common sense, of much
shrewdness, a close observer, and one who had acquainted
himself exactly and extensively with the subject which he
treats.   But he was a humorist, and, like Swift, sometimes
gave the reins to his humour.   It must be remembered that
his remarks apply only to the inferior clergy, and there can
be no doubt that since the Reformation they had, as a
body, sunk very low.   Chamberlayne had no motive for
exaggeration, but the language he uses in describing them
is stronger even than Eachard's.   Swift had no motive for
exaggeration, and yet his pictures of Corusodes and Eugenio
in his *Essay on the Fates of Clergymen*, and what we gather
from his *Project for the Advancement of Religion*, his *Letter
to a Young Clergyman*, and what may be gathered generally
from his writings, very exactly corroborate Eachard's
account.   The lighter literature of the later seventeenth
and of the first half of the eighteenth century teems with
proofs of the contempt to which their ignorance and

poverty exposed them. To the testimonies of Oldham and Steele, and to the authorities quoted by Macaulay and Mr. Lecky, may be added innumerable passages from the *Observator*, from De Foe's *Review*, from Pepys,[1] from Baxter's *Life* of himself, from Archbishop Sharp's *Life*, from Burnet, and many others.

It is remarkable that Eachard says nothing about two causes which undoubtedly contributed to degrade the Church in the eyes of the laity: its close association with party politics, and the spread of latitudinarianism, a conspicuous epoch in which was marked some twenty-six years later in the Bangorian controversy.

The appearance of the first volume of Macaulay's *History* in 1848 again brought Eachard's work into prominence. Macaulay's famous description of the clergy of the seventeenth century in his third chapter was based mainly on Eachard's account. The clergy and orthodox laity of our own day were as angry with Eachard's interpreter as their predecessors, nearly two centuries before, had been with Eachard himself. The controversy began seriously, after some preliminary skirmishing in the newspapers and lighter reviews, with Mr. Churchill Babington's *Mr. Macaulay's Characters of the Clergy in the Latter Part of the Seventeenth Century Considered*, published shortly after the appearance of the *History*. What Mr. Babington and those whom he represented forgot was precisely what Eachard's opponents had forgotten, that it was not the clergy universally who had been described, for Macaulay, like Eachard, had distinguished, but the clergy as represented by its proletariat.

---

[1] See, for example, *Diary*, February 16th, 1668: 'Much discourse about the bad state of the Church, and how the clergy are come to be men of no worth in the world, and, as the world do now generally discourse, they must be reformed.'

If Eachard had occasionally given the reins to humour,
Macaulay had occasionally perhaps given them to rhetoric.
But of the substantial accuracy of both there can be no
doubt at all.

On the intelligent, discriminating friends of the Church,
Eachard's work had something of the same effect as Jeremy
Collier's *Short View of the Profaneness and Immorality of
the English Stage* had in another sphere. It directed serious
attention to what all thoughtful and right-feeling people
must have felt to be a national scandal. It was an appeal
to sentiment and reason on matters with respect to which,
in this country at least, such appeals are seldom made in
vain. It did not, indeed, lead immediately to practical
reform, but it advanced the cause of reform by inspiring and
bringing other initiators into the field. And pre-eminent
among these was Swift. Swift was evidently well acquainted
with Eachard's work. In the apology prefixed to the
fourth edition of the *Tale of a Tub* in 1710, he speaks of
Eachard with great respect. Contemptuously explaining
that he has no intention of answering the attacks which had
been made on the *Tale*, he observes: 'When Dr. Eachard
wrote his book about the *Contempt of the Clergy*, numbers of
these answerers immediately started up, whose memory, if he
had not kept alive by his replies, it would now be utterly
unknown that he were ever answered at all.' No one who
is familiar with Swift's tracts on Church reform can doubt
that he had read Eachard's work with minute attention,
and was greatly influenced by it. In his *Project for
the Advancement of Religion*, he largely attributed the
scandalous immorality everywhere prevalent to the insufficiency of religious instruction, and to the low character
of the clergy, the result mainly of their ignorance and

poverty. His *Letter to a Young Clergyman* is little more than a didactic adaptation of that portion of Eachard's work which deals with the character and education of the clergy. The *Essay on the Fates of Clergymen* is another study from the *Contempt*, while the fragment of the tract which he had begun, *Concerning that Universal Hatred which prevails against the Clergy*, brings us still more closely to Eachard. The likeness between them cannot be traced further; they were both, it is true, humorists, but there is little in common between the austere and bitter, yet, at the same time, delicious flavour of the one, and the trenchant and graphic, but coarse and rollicking, humour of the other.

The essays reprinted from the *Tatler* give humorous expression to a grievance which not only wounded the pride of the clergy, but touched them on an equally sensitive part—the stomach. It was not usual for the chaplain in great houses to remain at table for the second course. When the sweets were brought in, he was expected to retire. As Macaulay puts it: 'He might fill himself with the corned beef and carrots; but as soon as the tarts and cheese-cakes made their appearance, he quitted his seat and stood aloof till he was summoned to return thanks for the repast, from a great part of which he had been excluded.' Gay refers to this churlish custom in the second book of *Trivia* :—

> 'Cheese that the table's closing rites denies,
> And bids me with th' unwilling chaplain rise.'

Possibly the custom originally arose, not from any wish to mark the social inferiority of the chaplain, but because his presence was a check on conversation. It must be owned, however, that this would have been more intelligible had he retired, not with the corned beef and carrots, but with the ladies. The passage quoted by Steele from Oldham is from his *Satire, addressed to a Friend that is about to Leave the University and come Abroad in the World*, not the only poem in which Oldham has thrown light on the degraded profession of the clergy. See the end of his *Satire, spoken in the person of Spenser.*

The last piece in this Miscellany has no connection with what precedes it, but it has an interest of its own. Among the many services of one of the purest and most indefatigable of philanthropists to his fellow-citizens was the establishment of what is commonly known as *Poor Richard's Almanack.* Of this periodical, and of the particular number of it which is here reprinted, Franklin gives the following account in his autobiography :—

'In 1732 I first published an Almanack, under the name of *Richard Saunders*; it was continued by me about twenty-five years, and commonly called *Poor Richard's Almanack.* I endeavoured to make it both entertaining and useful, and it accordingly came to be in such demand that I reaped considerable profit from it, vending annually near ten thousand. And observing that it was generally read (scarce any neighbourhood in the province being without it), I considered it as a proper vehicle for conveying instruction among the common people, who bought scarcely any other books. I therefore filled all the little spaces that occurred between the remarkable days in the calendar with proverbial sentences, chiefly such as inculcated industry and frugality as the means of procuring wealth and thereby securing virtue, it being more difficult for a man in want to act always honestly, as, to use here one of these proverbs, "it is hard for an empty sack to stand upright." These proverbs, which contained the wisdom of many ages and nations, I assembled and formed into a connected discourse prefixed to the *Almanack* of 1757, as the harangue of a wise

old man to the people attending an auction. The bringing all
these scattered counsels thus into a focus enabled them to make
a greater impression.   The piece being universally approved, was
copied in all the newspapers of the American Continent, reprinted
in Britain on a large sheet of paper to be stuck up in houses ; two
translations were made of it in France, and great numbers bought
by the clergy to distribute gratis among their poor parishioners and
tenants.   In Pennsylvania, as it discouraged useless expense in
foreign superfluities, some thought it had its share of influence in
producing that growing plenty of money which was observable for
several years after its publication.'—*Memoirs of Benjamin Franklin*,
Part II., Works Edit. 1833, vol. ii. pp. 146-148.

Reprinted innumerable times while Franklin was alive, this
paper has, since his death, passed through seventy editions
in English, fifty-six in French, eleven in German, and nine
in Italian.   It has been translated into nearly every language
in Europe: into French, German, and Italian, as we have seen;
into Spanish, Danish, Swedish, Polish, Bohemian, Dutch,
Welsh, and modern Greek; it has also been translated into
Chinese.[1]   In the edition of *Franklin's Works*, printed in
London in 1806, it appears under the title of *The Way to
Wealth, as clearly shown in the Preface to an old Pennsylvanian
Almanack, entitled Poor Richard Improved*, and under this title
it was usually printed when detached from the Almanack.

As Franklin himself owns, the maxims have little pre-
tension to originality.   It is evident that he had laid under
contribution such collections as Clerk's *Adagia Latino-
Anglica*, Herbert's *Jacula Prudentum*, James Howell's
collection of proverbs, David Ferguson's *Scotch Proverbs*
(with the successively increasing editions between 1641 and
1706), Ray's famous *Collection of English Proverbs*, William

---

[1] For this information I am indebted to Mr. Paul Leicester Ford's interesting
monograph on the sayings of Poor Richard, prefixed to his selections from the
Almanack, privately printed at Brooklyn in 1890.

Penn's *Maxims*, and the like.   A few are probably original, and many have been re-minted and owe their form to him.

The first number of the famous *Almanack* from which they are extracted was published at the end of 1732, just after Franklin had set up as a printer and stationer for himself, its publication being announced in the *Pennsylvania Gazette* of December 9th, 1732; and for twenty-five years it continued regularly to appear, the last number being that for the year 1758, and having for preface the discourse which became so extraordinarily popular.   The name assumed by Franklin was no doubt borrowed from that of Richard Saunders, a well-known astrologer of the seventeenth century, of whom there is a notice in the *Dictionary of National Biography*. But Mr. Leicester Ford[1] says that it was the name of 'a chyrurgeon' of the eighteenth century who for many years issued a popular almanac entitled *The Apollo Anglicanus*. Of this publication I know nothing, and can discover nothing. The probability is that its compiler, whoever he was, anticipated Franklin in assuming the name of John Saunders. He is most certainly not to be identified with Saunders the astrologer, who died in, or not much later than, 1687.

It remains to add that no pains have been spared to make the texts of the excerpts and tracts in this Miscellany as accurate as possible—indeed, Mr. Arber's name is a sufficient guarantee of the efficiency with which this important part of the work has been done.   For the modernisation of the spelling, which some readers may perhaps be inclined to regret, and for the punctuation, as well as for the elucidatory notes within brackets, Mr. Arber is solely responsible.

J. CHURTON COLLINS.

[1] Introduction to his selections from the *Almanack*.

THOMAS WILSON.

*Eloquence first given by GOD,
after lost by man, and last
repaired by GOD again.*

Thomas Wilson.

❡ *Eloquence first given by GOD, after lost by man, and last repaired by GOD again.*

[*The Art of Rhetoric.*]

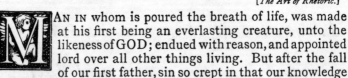

MAN IN whom is poured the breath of life, was made at his first being an everlasting creature, unto the likeness of GOD; endued with reason, and appointed lord over all other things living. But after the fall of our first father, sin so crept in that our knowledge was much darkened, and by corruption of this our flesh, man's reason and entendment [*intellect*] were both overwhelmed. At what time, GOD being sore grieved with the folly of one man; pitied, of His mere goodness, the whole state and posterity of mankind. And therefore whereas through the wicked suggestion of our ghostly enemy, the joyful fruition of GOD's glory was altogether lost; it pleased our heavenly Father to repair mankind of his free mercy and to grant an everlasting inheritance unto such as would by constant faith seek earnestly thereafter.

Long it was, ere that man knew; himself being destitute of GOD's grace, so that all things waxed savage, the earth untilled, society neglected, GOD's will not known, man against man, one against another, and all against order. Some lived by spoil, some like brute beasts grazed upon the ground, some went naked, some roamed like woodwoses [*mad wild men*], none did anything by reason, but most did what they could by manhood. None almost considered the everliving GOD; but all lived most commonly after their own lust. By death, they thought that all things ended; by life, they looked for none other living. None remembered the true observation of wedlock, none tendered the education

of their children; laws were not regarded, true dealing
was not once used.   For virtue, vice bare place; for right
and equity, might used authority.   And therefore whereas
man through reason might have used order, man through
folly fell into error.   And thus for lack of skill and want of
grace, evil so prevailed that the devil was most esteemed:
and GOD either almost unknown among them all or else
nothing feared among so many.   Therefore—even now when
man was thus past all hope of amendment—GOD still
tendering his own workmanship; stirred up his faithful and
elect, to persuade with reason all men to society: and gave
his appointed ministers knowledge both to see the natures of
men; and also granted to them the gift of utterance, that
they might with ease win folk at their will, and frame them
by reason to all good order.

And therefore whereas men lived brutishly in open fields
having neither house to shroud [cover] them in, nor attire to
clothe their backs; nor yet any regard to seek their best
avail [interest]: these appointed of GOD, called them together
by utterance of speech; and persuaded with them what was
good, what was bad, and what was gainful for mankind.
And although at first the rude could hardly learn, and either
for the strangeness of the thing would not gladly receive the
offer or else for lack of knowledge could not perceive the
goodness: yet being somewhat drawn and delighted with the
pleasantness of reason and the sweetness of utterance, after
a certain space, they became through nurture and good
advisement, of wild, sober; of cruel, gentle; of fools, wise;
and of beasts, men.   Such force hath the tongue, and such
is the power of Eloquence and Reason that most men are
forced, even to yield in that which most standeth against
their will.   And therefore the poets do feign that HERCULES,
being a man of great wisdom, had all men linked together by
the ears in a chain, to draw them and lead them even as he
listed.   For his wit so great, his tongue so eloquent, and his
experience such that no man was able to withstand his
reason: but every one was rather driven to do that which he
would, and to will that which he did; agreeing to his advice
both in word and work, in all that ever they were able.

Neither can I see that men could have been brought by
any other means to live together in fellowship of life, to

maintain cities, to deal truly, and willingly to obey one another: if men, at the first, had not by art and eloquence persuaded that which they full oft found out by reason. For what man, I pray you, being better able to maintain himself by valiant courage than by living in base subjection, would not rather look to rule like a lord, than to live like an underling; if by reason he were not persuaded that it behoveth every man to live in his own vocation, and not to seek any higher room than that whereunto he was at the first, appointed? Who would dig and delve from morn till evening? Who would travail and toil with the sweat of his brows? Yea, who would, for his King's pleasure, adventure and hazard his life, if wit had not so won men that they thought nothing more needful in this world nor anything whereunto they were more bounden than here to live in their duty and to train their whole life, according to their calling. Therefore whereas men are in many things weakly by nature, and subject to much infirmity; I think in this one point they pass all other creatures living, that they have the gift of speech and reason.

And among all other, I think him of most worthy fame, and amongst men to be taken for half a god that therein doth chiefly and above all other excel men; wherein men do excel beasts. For he that is among the reasonable, of all the most reasonable; and among the witty, of all the most witty; and among the eloquent, of all the most eloquent: him, think I, among all men, not only to be taken for a singular man, but rather to be counted for half a god. For in seeking the excellency hereof, the sooner he draweth to perfection the nigher he cometh to GOD, who is the chief Wisdom: and therefore called GOD because He is the most wise, or rather wisdom itself.

Now then seeing that GOD giveth heavenly grace unto such as called unto him with outstretched hands and humble heart; never wanting to those that want not to themselves: I purpose by His grace and especial assistance, to set forth such precepts of eloquence, and to show what observation the wise have used in handling of their matters: that the unlearned by seeing the practice of others, may have some knowledge themselves; and learn by their neighbours' device what is necessary for themselves in their own case.

Sir PHILIP SIDNEY.

Letter to his brother ROBERT, then in Germany, 18 October 1580.

Sir PHILIP SIDNEY to his brother, ROBERT SIDNEY, who was the first Earl of LEICESTER of that familiar name.

MY DEAR BROTHER,

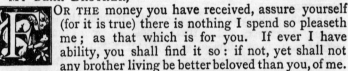 OR THE money you have received, assure yourself (for it is true) there is nothing I spend so pleaseth me; as that which is for you. If ever I have ability, you shall find it so: if not, yet shall not any brother living be better beloved than you, of me. I cannot write now to N. WHITE. Do you excuse me! For his nephew, they are but passions in my father; which we must bear with reverence: but I am sorry he should return till he had the circuit of his travel; for you shall never have such a servant, as he would prove. Use your own discretion!

For your countenance, I would (for no cause) have it diminished in Germany. In Italy, your greatest expense must be upon worthy men, and not upon householding. Look to your diet, sweet ROBIN! and hold up your heart in courage and virtue. Truly, great part of my comfort is in you! I know not myself what I meant by bravery in you; so greatly you may see I condemn you. Be careful of yourself, and I shall never have cares.

I have written to Master SAVELL. I wish you kept still together. He is an excellent man. And there may, if you list, pass good exercises betwixt you and Master NEVELL. There is great expectation of you both.

For method of writing history, BODEN hath written at large. You may read him, and gather out of many words, some matter.

This I think, in haste. A Story is either to be considered as a Story; or as a Treatise, which, besides that, addeth many things for profit and ornament. As a Story, he is nothing, but a narration of things done, with the beginnings, causes, and appendices thereof. In that kind, your method must be to have *seriem temporum* very exactly, which the chronologies of MELANCTHON, TARCHAGNORA, LANGUET and such others will help you to.

Then to consider by that . . . . as you note yourself, XENOPHON to follow THUCYDIDES, so doth THUCYDIDES follow HERODOTUS, and DIODORUS SICULUS follow XENOPHON. So generally, do the Roman stories follow the Greek; and the particular stories of the present monarchies follow the Roman.

In that kind, you have principally to note the examples of virtue and vice, with their good or evil success; the establishment or ruins of great Estates, with the causes, the time, and circumstances of the laws then written of; the enterings and endings of wars; and therein, the stratagems against the enemy, and the discipline upon the soldier.

And thus much as a very historiographer.

Besides this, the Historian makes himself a Discourser for profit; and an Orator, yea, a Poet sometimes, for ornament. An Orator; in making excellent orations, *è re nata*, which are to be marked, but marked with the note of rhetorical remembrances: a Poet; in painting for the effects, the motions, the whisperings of the people, which though in disputation, one might say were true—yet who will mark them well shall find them taste of a poetical vein, and in that kind are gallantly to be marked — for though perchance, they were not so, yet it is enough they might be so. The last point which tends to teach profit, is of a Discourser; which name I give to whosoever speaks *non simpliciter de facto, sed de qualitatibus et circumstantiis facti*: and that is it which makes me and many others, rather note much with our pen than with our mind.

Because we leave all these discourses to the confused trust of our memory ; because they be not tied to the tenour of a question : as Philosophers use sometimes, places; the Divine, in telling his opinion and reasons in religion; sometimes the Lawyer, in showing the causes and benefits of laws; sometimes a Natural Philosopher, in setting down the causes of any strange thing which the Story binds him to speak of; but most commonly a Moral Philosopher, either in the ethic part, where he sets forth virtues or vices and the natures of passions; or in the politic, when he doth (as often he doth) meddle sententiously with matters of Estate. Again, sometimes he gives precept of war, both offensive and defensive. And so, lastly, not professing any art as his matter leads him, he deals with all arts; which—because it carrieth the life of a lively example — it is wonderful what light it gives to the arts themselves; so as the great Civilians help themselves with the discourses of the Historians. So do Soldiers ; and even Philosophers and Astronomers.

But that I wish herein is this, that when you read any such thing, you straight bring it to his head, not only of what art; but by your logical subdivisions to the next member and parcel of the art. And so—as in a table—be it witty words, of which TACITUS is full; sentences, of which LIVY; or similitudes, whereof PLUTARCH : straight to lay it up in the right place of his storehouse—as either military, or more specially defensive military, or more particularly, defensive by fortification—and so lay it up. So likewise in politic matters. And such a little table you may easily make wherewith I would have you ever join the historical part; which is only the example of some stratagem, or good counsel, or such like.

This write I to you, in great haste, of method, without method : but, with more leisure and study—if I do not find some book that satisfies—I will venture to write more largely of it unto you.

Master SAVELL will, with ease, help you to set down such a table of remembrance to yourself; and for your sake I perceive he will do much; and if ever I be able, I will deserve it of him. One only thing, as it comes into my mind, let me remember you of, that you consider wherein the Historian excelleth, and that to note: as DION NICÆUS in the searching the secrets of government; TACITUS, in the pithy opening of the venom of wickedness; and so of the rest.

My time—exceedingly short—will suffer me to write no more leisurely. STEPHEN can tell you who stands with me, while I am writing.

Now, dear brother! take delight likewise in the mathematicals. Master SAVELL is excellent in them. I think you understand the sphere. If you do, I care little for any more astronomy in you. Arithmetic and Geometry, I would wish you well seen in: so as both in matter of number and measure, you might have a feeling and active judgment. I would you did bear the mechanical instruments, wherein the Dutch excel.

I write this to you as one, that for myself have given over the delight in the world; but wish to you as much, if not more, than to myself.

So you can speak and write Latin, not barbarously; I never require great study in Ciceronianism, the chief abuse of Oxford, *qui dum verba sectantur, res ipsas negligunt.*

My toyful books I will send—with GOD's help—by February [1581]; at which time you shall have your money. And for £200 [*nearly £2,000 at the present day*] a year, assure yourself! If the estates of England remain, you shall not fail of it. Use it to your best profit!

My Lord of LEICESTER sends you £40, as I understand, by STEPHEN; and promiseth he will continue that stipend yearly at the least. Then that is above commons. In any case, write largely and diligently unto him: for, in truth, I have good proof that he means to be every way good unto you. The odd £30 shall come with the £100, or else my father and I will jarle.

Now, sweet Brother, take a delight to keep and increase your music. You will not believe what a want I find of it, in my melancholy times.

At horsemanship; when you exercise it, read CRISON CLAUDIO, and a book that is called *La Gloria de l' Cavallo* withal: that you may join the thorough contemplation of it with the exercise: and so shall you profit more in a month, than others in a year.   And mark the bitting, saddling, and cur[ry]ing of horses.

I would, by the way, your Worship would learn a better hand.   You write worse than I: and I write evil enough. Once again, have a care of your diet; and consequently of your complexion.   Remember *gratior est veniens in pulchro corpore virtus.*

Now, Sir, for news; I refer myself to this bearer.   He can tell you how idly we look on our neighbour's fires: and nothing is happened notable at home; save only DRAKE'S return.   Of which yet, I know not the secret points: but about the world he hath been, and rich he is returned. Portugal, we say, is lost.   And to conclude, my eyes are almost closed up, overwatched with tedious business.

God bless you, sweet Boy! and accomplish the joyful hope I conceive of you.   Once again commend me to Master NEVELL, Master SAVELL, and honest HARRY WHITE, and bid him be merry.

When you play at weapons; I would have you get thick caps and bracers [*gloves*], and play out your play lustily; for indeed, ticks and dalliances are nothing in earnest: for the time of the one and the other greatly differs.   And use as well the blow as the thrust.   It is good in itself; and besides increaseth your breath and strength, and will make you a strong man at the tourney and barriers.   First, in any case, practise the single sword; and then, with the dagger.   Let no day pass without an hour or two of such exercise.   The rest, study; or confer diligently: and so shall you come home to my comfort and credit.

Lord! how I have babbled! Once again, farewell, dearest Brother!

Your most loving and careful brother
PHILIP SIDNEY.

At Leicester House
this 18th of October 1580.

FRANCIS MERES, M.A.

Sketch of English Literature, Painting, and Music, up to September 1598.

A comparative Discourse of our English Poets [Painters and Musicians] with the Greek, Latin, and Italian Poets [Painters and Musicians].

AS GREECE had three poets of great antiquity, ORPHEUS, LINUS, and MUSÆUS; and Italy, other three ancient poets, LIVIUS ANDRONICUS, ENNIUS, and PLAUTUS: so hath England three ancient poets, CHAUCER, GOWER, and LYDGATE.

As HOMER is reputed the Prince of Greek poets; and PETRARCH of Italian poets: so CHAUCER is accounted the god of English poets.

As HOMER was the first that adorned the Greek tongue with true quantity: so [WILLIAM LANGLAND, the author of] *PIERS PLOWMAN* was the first that observed the true quantity of our verse without the curiosity of rhyme.

OVID writ a Chronicle from the beginning of the world
to his own time; that is, to the reign of AUGUSTUS the
Emperor: so hath HARDING the Chronicler (after his manner
of old harsh rhyming) from ADAM to his time; that is, to
the reign of King EDWARD IV.

As SOTADES Maronites, the Iambic poet, gave himself
wholly to write impure and lascivious things: so SKELTON
(I know not for what great worthiness, surnamed the
Poet Laureate) applied his wit to scurrilities and ridiculous
matters; such [as] among the Greeks were called *Pantomimi*,
with us, buffoons.

As CONSALVO PEREZ, that excellent learned man, and
secretary to King PHILIP [II.] of Spain, in translating the
"Ulysses" [*Odyssey*] of HOMER out of Greek into Spanish,
hath, by good judgement, avoided the fault of rhyming,
although [he hath] not fully hit perfect and true versifying:
so hath HENRY HOWARD, that true and noble Earl of SURREY,
in translating the fourth book of VIRGIL's *Æneas*: whom
MICHAEL DRAYTON in his *England's Heroical Epistles* hath
eternized for an *Epistle to his fair GERALDINE*.

As these Neoterics, JOVIANUS PONTANUS, POLITIANUS,
MARULLUS TARCHANIOTA, the two STROZÆ the father and the
son, PALINGENIUS, MANTUANUS, PHILELPHUS, QUINTIANUS
STOA, and GERMANUS BRIXIUS have obtained renown, and
good place among the ancient Latin poets: so also these
Englishmen, being Latin poets; WALTER HADDON,
NICHOLAS CARR, GABRIEL HARVEY, CHRISTOPHER OCKLAND,
THOMAS NEWTON, with his *LELAND*, THOMAS WATSON,
THOMAS CAMPION, [JOHN] BRUNSWERD, and WILLEY have
attained [a] good report and honourable advancement in the
Latin empire [of letters].

As the Greek tongue is made famous and eloquent by
HOMER, HESIOD, EURIPIDES, ÆSCHYLUS, SOPHOCLES, PIN-
DARUS, PHOCYLIDES, and ARISTOPHANES; and the Latin
tongue by VIRGIL, OVID, HORACE, SILIUS ITALICUS, LUCANUS,
LUCRETIUS, AUSONIUS, and CLAUDIANUS: so the English
tongue is mightily enriched, and gorgeously invested in rare

ornaments and resplendent habiliments by Sir PHILIP
SYDNEY, SPENSER, DANIEL, DRAYTON, WARNER, SHAKE-
SPEARE, MARLOW, and CHAPMAN.

As XENOPHON, who did imitate so excellently as to give
us *effigiem justi imperii*, "the portraiture of a just empire"
under the name of CYRUS, (as CICERO saith of him) made
therein an absolute heroical poem; and as HELIODORUS
wrote in prose, his sugared invention of that picture of love in
THEAGINES *and* CARICLEA; and yet both excellent admired
poets: so Sir PHILIP SIDNEY writ his immortal poem, *The
Countess of* PEMBROKE's "*Arcadia*" in prose; and yet our
rarest poet.

As SEXTUS PROPERTIUS said, *Nescio quid magis nascitur
Iliade* : so I say of SPENSER's *Fairy Queen*; I know not what
more excellent or exquisite poem may be written.

As ACHILLES had the advantage of HECTOR, because it
was his fortune to be extolled and renowned by the heavenly
verse of HOMER: so SPENSER's *ELIZA, the Fairy Queen*, hath
the advantage of all the Queens in the world, to be eternized
by so divine a poet.

As THEOCRITUS is famoused for his *Idyllia* in Greek, and
VIRGIL for his *Eclogues* in Latin: so SPENSER their imitator
in his *Shepherds Calendar* is renowned for the like argument;
and honoured for fine poetical invention, and most exquisite wit.

As PARTHENIUS Nicæus excellently sang the praises of
ARETE: so DANIEL hath divinely sonnetted the matchless
beauty of DELIA.

As every one mourneth, when he heareth of the lamentable
plangors [*plaints*] of [the] Thracian ORPHEUS for his dearest
EURYDICE: so every one passionateth, when he readeth the
afflicted death of DANIEL's distressed ROSAMOND.

As LUCAN hath mournfully depainted the Civil Wars of
POMPEY and CÆSAR: so hath DANIEL, the Civil Wars of
York and Lancaster; and DRAYTON, the Civil Wars of
EDWARD II. and the Barons.

As VIRGIL doth imitate CATULLUS in the like matter of
ARIADNE, for his story of Queen DIDO: so MICHAEL
DRAYTON doth imitate OVID in his *England's Heroical
Epistles.*

As SOPHOCLES was called a Bee for the sweetness of his
tongue: so in CHARLES FITZ-GEFFRY's *DRAKE*, DRAYTON is

termed "golden-mouthed," for the purity and preciousness of his style and phrase.

As ACCIUS, MARCUS ATILIUS, and MILITHUS were called *Tragaediographi* ; because they writ tragedies : so we may truly term MICHAEL DRAYTON, *Tragaediographus* : for his passionate penning [*the poem of*] the downfalls of valiant ROBERT of NORMANDY, chaste MATILDA, and great GAVESTON.

As JOANNES HONTERUS, in Latin verse, wrote three books of Cosmography, with geographical tables; so MICHAEL DRAYTON is now in penning in English verse, a poem called *Poly-olbion* [which is] geographical and hydrographical of all the forests, woods, mountains, fountains, rivers, lakes, floods, baths [*spas*], and springs that be in England.

As AULUS PERSIUS FLACCUS is reported, among all writers to [have] been of an honest life and upright conversation : so MICHAEL DRAYTON, *quem toties honoris et amoris causa nomino*, among scholars, soldiers, poets, and all sorts of people, is held for a man of virtuous disposition, honest conversation, and well governed carriage : which is almost miraculous among good wits in these declining and corrupt times; when there is nothing but roguery in villainous man, and when cheating and craftiness are counted the cleanest wit and soundest wisdom.

As DECIUS AUSONIUS Gallus, *in libris Fastorum*, penned the occurrences of the world from the first creation of it to this time ; that is, to the reign of the Emperor GRATIAN : so WARNER, in his absolute *Albion's England*, hath most admirably penned the history of his own country from NOAH to his time, that is, to the reign of Queen ELIZABETH. I have heard him termed of the best wits of both our Universities, our English HOMER.

As EURIPIDES is the most sententious among the Greek poets : so is WARNER among our English poets.

As the soul of EUPHORBUS was thought to live in PYTHAGORAS : so the sweet witty soul of OVID lives in mellifluous and honey-tongued SHAKESPEARE. Witness his *VENUS and ADONIS*; his *LUCRECE*; his sugared *Sonnets*, among his private friends ; &c.

As PLAUTUS and SENECA are accounted the best for Comedy and Tragedy among the Latins : so SHAKESPEARE among the English is the most excellent in both kinds for the stage.

For Comedy: witness his *Gentlemen of Verona*; his [*Comedy of*] *Errors*; his *Love's Labour's Lost*; his *Love's Labour's Won* [? *All's Well that Ends Well*] his *Midsummer Night's Dream*; and his *Merchant of Venice*.

For Tragedy: his RICHARD II., RICHARD III., HENRY IV., *King* JOHN, TITUS ANDRONICUS, and his ROMEO *and* JULIET.

As EPIUS STOLO said that the Muses would speak with PLAUTUS'S tongue, if they would speak Latin: so I say that the Muses would speak with SHAKESPEARE'S fine filed phrase; if they would speak English.

As MUSÆUS, who wrote the love of HERO and LEANDER, had two excellent scholars, THAMYRAS and HERCULES; so hath he [*MUSÆUS*] in England, two excellent poets, imitators of him in the same argument and subject, CHRISTOPHER MARLOW and GEORGE CHAPMAN.

As OVID saith of his work,

> *Jamque opus exegi, quod nec JOVIS ira, nec ignis,*
> *Nec poterit ferrum, nec edax abolere vetustas;*

And as HORACE saith of his,

> *Exegi monumentum œre perennius*
> *Regalique situ pyramidum altius,*
> *Quod non imber edax, non Aquilo impotens*
> *Possit diruere, aut innumerabilis*
> *Annorum series, et fuga temporum :*

So I say, severally, of Sir PHILIP SIDNEY's, SPENSER's DANIEL's, DRAYTON's, SHAKESPEARE's, and WARNER's works,

> *Non JOVIS ira : imbres : MARS : ferrum : flamma : senectus :*
> *Hoc opus unda : lues : turbo : venena ruent.*
> *Et quanquam ad pulcherrimum hoc opus evertendum, tres illi Dii*
> *conspirabunt, CHRONUS, VULCANUS, et PATER ipse gentis.*
> *Non tamen annorum series, non flamma, nec ensis ;*
> *Æternum potuit hoc abolere Decus.*

As Italy had DANTE, BOCCACE [*BOCCACIO*], PETRARCH, TASSO, CELIANO, and ARIOSTO: so England had MATTHEW ROYDON, THOMAS ATCHELOW, THOMAS WATSON, THOMAS KYD, ROBERT GREENE, and GEORGE PEELE.

As there are eight famous and chief languages; Hebrew,
Greek, Latin, Syriac, Arabic, Italian, Spanish, and French;
so there are eight notable several kinds of poets, [1] Heroic,
[2] Lyric, [3] Tragic, [4] Comic, [5] Satiric, [6] Iambic,
[7] Elegiac, and [8] Pastoral.

[1] As HOMER and VIRGIL among the Greeks and Latins
are the chief Heroic poets: so SPENSER and WARNER be our
chief heroical "makers."

[2] As PINDARUS, ANACREON, and CALLIMACHUS, among the
Greeks; and HORACE and CUTALLUS among the Latins
are the best Lyric poets: so in this faculty, the best among
our poets are SPENSER, who excelleth in all kinds; DANIEL,
DRAYTON, SHAKESPEARE, BRETON.

[3] As these Tragic poets flourished in Greece: ÆSCHYLUS,
EURIPIDES, SOPHOCLES, ALEXANDER Ætolus; ACHÆUS
ERITHRIŒUS, ASTYDAMAS Atheniensis, APOLLODORUS Tar-
sensis, NICOMACHUS Phrygius, THESPIS Atticus, and TIMON
APOLLONIATES; and these among the Latins, ACCIUS,
MARCUS ATILIUS, POMPONUS SECUNDUS, and SENECA: so
these are our best for Tragedy; The Lord BUCKHURST,
Doctor LEG, of Cambridge, Doctor EDES, of Oxford, Master
EDWARD FERRIS, the author[s] of the *Mirror for Magis-
trates*, MARLOW, PEELE, WATSON, KYD, SHAKESPEARE,
DRAYTON, CHAPMAN, DECKER, and BENJAMIN JOHNSON.

As MARCUS ANNEUS LUCANUS writ two excellent tragedies;
one called *MEDEA*, the other *De incendio Trojæ cum PRIAMI
calamitate*: so Doctor LEG hath penned two famous tragedies;
the one of *RICHARD III.*, the other of *The Destruction of
Jerusalem*.

[4] The best poets for Comedy among the Greeks are these:
MENANDER, ARISTOPHANES, EUPOLIS Atheniensis, ALEXIS
Terius, NICOSTRATUS, AMIPSIAS Atheniensis, ANAXANDRIDES
Rhodeus, ARISTONYMUS, ARCHIPPUS Atheniensis, and CALLIAS
Atheniensis; and among the Latins, PLAUTUS, TERENCE,
NÆVIUS, SEXTUS TURPILIUS, LICINIUS IMBREX, and
VIRGILIUS Romanus: so the best for Comedy amongst us be
EDWARD [VERE], Earl of OXFORD; Doctor GAGER, of Oxford;
Master ROWLEY, once a rare scholar of learned Pembroke
Hall in Cambridge; Master EDWARDES, one of Her Majesty's
Chapel; eloquent and witty JOHN LILLY, LODGE, GASCOIGNE,
GREENE, SHAKESPEARE, THOMAS NASH, THOMAS HEYWOOD,

ANTHONY MUNDAY, our best plotter; CHAPMAN, PORTER, WILSON, HATHWAY, and HENRY CHETTLE.

[5] As HORACE, LUCILIUS, JUVENAL, PERSIUS, and LUCUL-LUS are the best for Satire among the Latins : so with us, in the same faculty, these are chief [WILLIAM LANGLAND, the author of] *PIERS PLOWMAN*, [T.] LODGE, [JOSEPH] HALL of Emmanuel College in Cambridge [*afterwards Bishop of NORWICH*]; [JOHN MARSTON] the Author of *PYGMALION's Image, and certain Satires* ; the Author of *Skialetheia*.

[6] Among the Greeks, I will name but two for Iambics, ARCHILOCHUS Parius and HIPPONAX Ephesius : so amongst us, I name but two Iambical poets; GABRIEL HARVEY and RICHARD STANYHURST, because I have seen no more in this kind.

[7] As these are famous among the Greeks for Elegies, MELANTHUS, MYMNERUS Colophonius, OLYMPIUS Mysius, PARTHENIUS Nicœus, PHILETAS Cous, THEOGENES Megaren-sis, and PIGRES Halicarnassœus; and these among the Latins, MÆCENAS, OVID, TIBULLUS, PROPERTIUS, C. VALGIUS, CASSIUS SEVERUS, and CLODIUS Sabinus : so these are the most passionate among us to bewail and bemoan the per-plexities of love, HENRY HOWARD, Earl of SURREY, Sir THOMAS WYATT the Elder, Sir FRANCIS BRYAN, Sir PHILIP SIDNEY, Sir WALTER RALEIGH, Sir EDWARD DYER, SPENSER, DANIEL, DRAYTON, SHAKESPEARE, WHETSTONE, GASCOIGNE, SAMUEL PAGE sometime Fellow of Corpus Christi College in Oxford, CHURCHYARD, BRETON.

[8] As THEOCRITUS in Greek; VIRGIL and MANTUAN in Latin, SANNAZAR in Italian, and [THOMAS WATSON] the Author of *AMINTÆ Gaudia* and *WALSINGHAM's MELIBŒUS* are the best for Pastoral : so amongst us the best in this kind are Sir PHILIP SIDNEY, Master CHALLONER, SPENSER, STEPHEN GOSSON, ABRAHAM FRAUNCE, and BARNFIELD.

These and many other Epigrammatists, the Latin tongue hath ; Q. CATULLUS, PORCIUS LICINIUS, QUINTUS CORNI-FICIUS, MARTIAL, CNŒUS GETULICUS, and witty Sir THOMAS MORE : so in English we have these, HEYWOOD, DRANT, KENDAL, BASTARD, DAVIES.

As noble MÆCENAS, that sprang from the Etruscan Kings, not only graced poets by his bounty, but also by being a poet himself; and as JAMES VI., now King of Scotland, is not only a favourer of poets, but a poet; as my friend Master RICHARD BARNFELD hath in this distich passing well recorded,

> The King of Scots now living is a poet,
> As his *Lepanto* and his *Furies* show it :

so ELIZABETH, our dread Sovereign and gracious Queen, is not only a liberal Patron unto poets, but an excellent poet herself; whose learned, delicate and noble Muse surmounteth, be it in Ode, Elegy, Epigram; or in any other kind of poem, Heroic or Lyric.

OCTAVIA, sister unto AUGUSTUS the Emperor, was exceeding[ly] bountiful unto VIRGIL, who gave him for making twenty-six verses, £1,137, to wit, ten *sestertiæ* for every verse (which amounted to above £43 for every verse) : so learned MARY, the honourable Countess of PEMBROKE [and] the noble sister of the immortal Sir PHILIP SIDNEY, is very liberal unto poets. Besides, she is a most delicate poet, of whom I may say, as ANTIPATER Sidonius writeth of SAPPHO :

> *Dulcia Mnemosyne demirans carmina Sapphus,*
> *Quæsivit decima Pieris unde foret.*

Among others, in times past, poets had these favourers; AUGUSTUS, MÆCENAS, SOPHOCLES, GERMANICUS; an Emperor, a Nobleman, a Senator, and a Captain: so of later times, poets have [had] these patrons; ROBERT, King of Sicily, the great King FRANCIS [I.] of France, King JAMES of Scotland, and Queen ELIZABETH of England.

As in former times, two great Cardinals, BEMBA and BIENA did countenance poets : so of late years, two great Preachers, have given them their right hands in fellowship; BEZA and MELANCTHON.

As the learned philosophers FRACASTORIUS and SCALIGER have highly prized them: so have the eloquent orators, PONTANUS and MURETUS very gloriously estimated them.

As GEORGIUS BUCHANANUS' *JEPTHÆ*, amongst all modern

tragedies, is able to abide the touch of ARISTOTLE's precepts and EURIPIDES's examples: so is Bishop WATSON's *ABSALOM*.

As TERENCE for his translations out of APOLLODORUS and MENANDER, and AQUILIUS for his translation out of MENANDER, and C. GERMANICUS AUGUSTUS for his out of ARATUS, and AUSONIUS for his translated *Epigrams* out of [the] Greek, and Doctor JOHNSON for his *Frog-fight* out of HOMER, and WATSON for his *ANTIGONE* out of SOPHOCLES, have got good commendations : so these versifiers for their learned translations, are of good note among us ; PHAER for VIRGIL's *Æneid*, GOLDING for OVID's *Metamorphosis*, HARINGTON for his *ORLANDO Furioso*, the Translators of SENECA's *Tragedies*, BARNABE GOOGE for PALINGENIUS's [*Zodiac of Life*], TURBERVILLE for OVID's *Epistles* and MANTUAN, and CHAPMAN for his inchoate HOMER.

As the Latins have these Emblematists, ANDREAS ALCIATUS, REUSNERUS, and SAMBUCUS: so we have these, GEFFREY WHITNEY, ANDREW WILLET, and THOMAS COMBE.

As NONNUS PANAPOLYTA wrote the *Gospel* of Saint JOHN in Greek hexameters: so GERVASE MARKHAM hath written SOLOMON's *Canticles* in English verse.

As CORNELIUS PLINIUS writ the life of POMPONUS SECUNDUS : so young CHARLES FITZ-GEFFERY, that high towering falcon, hath most gloriously penned *The honourable Life and Death of worthy Sir FRANCIS DRAKE*.

As HESIOD wrote learnedly of husbandry in Greek: so TUSSER [hath] very wittily and experimentally written of it in English.

As ANTIPATER Sidonius was famous for extemporal verse in Greek, and OVID for his

Quicquid conabar dicere versus erat :

so was our TARLETON, of whom Doctor CASE, that learned physician, thus speaketh in the Seventh Book and 17th chapter of his *Politics*.

ARISTOTLES suum THEODORETUM laudavit quendam peritum Tragædiarum actorem, CICERO suum ROSCIUM : nos Angli TARLETONUM, in cujus voce et vultu omnes jocosi affectus, in cujus cerebroso capite lepidæ facetiæ habitant.

And so is now our witty [THOMAS] WILSON, who, for

learning and extemporal wit in this faculty, is without compare or compeer ; as to his great and eternal commendations,
he manifested in his challenge at the *Swan*, on the Bank
Side.

As ACHILLES tortured the dead body of HECTOR; and as
ANTONIUS and his wife FULVIA tormented the lifeless corpse
of CICERO ; so GABRIEL HARVEY hath showed the same
inhumanity to GREENE, that lies full low in his grave.

As EUPOLIS of Athens used great liberty in taxing the vices
of men : so doth THOMAS NASH. Witness the brood of the
HARVEYS !

As ACTÆON was worried of his own hounds : so is TOM NASH
of his *Isle of Dogs*. Dogs were the death of EURIPIDES ; but
be not disconsolate, gallant young JUVENAL ! LINUS, the son of
APOLLO, died the same death. Yet GOD forbid that so brave
a wit should so basely perish ! Thine are but paper dogs,
neither is thy banishment like OVID's, eternally to converse
with the barbarous *Getæ*. Therefore comfort thyself, sweet
TOM ! with CICERO's glorious return to Rome ; and with the
counsel ÆNEAS gives to his seabeaten soldiers, *Lib 1, Æneid*.

Pluck up thine heart ! and drive from thence both fear
    and care away !
To think on this, may pleasure be perhaps another day.
    Durato, et temet rebus servato secundis.

As ANACREON died by the pot : so GEORGE PEELE, by the
pox.

As ARCHESILAUS PRYTANŒUS perished by wine at a drunken
feast, as HERMIPPUS testifieth in *DIOGENES* : so ROBERT
GREENE died by a surfeit taken of pickled herrings and
Rhenish wine; as witnesseth THOMAS NASH, who was at the
fatal banquet.

As JODELLE, a French tragical poet, being an epicure
and an atheist, made a pitiful end : so our tragical poet
MARLOW, for his Epicurism and Atheism, had a tragical death;
as you may read of this MARLOW more at large, in the *Theatre
of GOD's judgments*, in the 25th chapter, entreating of *Epicures
and Atheists*.

As the poet LYCOPHRON was shot to death by a certain rival
of his : so CHRISTOPHER MARLOW was stabbed to death by
a baudy Servingman, a rival of his, in his lewd love.

PAINTERS.

PELLES painted a mare and a dog so lively [*lifelike*], that horses and dogs passing by would neigh and bark at them.   He grew so famous for his excellent art, that great ALEXANDER came often to his shop to visit him, and commanded that none other should paint him. At his death, he left *VENUS* unfinished; neither was any [one] ever found, that durst perfect what he had begun.

ZEUXIS was so excellent in painting, that it was easier for any man to view his pictures than to imitate them; who, to make an excellent table [*picture*], had five Agrigentine virgins naked by him.   He painted grapes so lively, that birds did fly to eat them.

PARRHASIUS painted a sheet [*curtain*] so artificially, that ZEUXIS took it for a sheet indeed; and commanded it to be taken away, to see the picture that he thought it had veiled.

As learned and skilful Greece had these excellently renowned for their limning; so England hath these: HILIARD, ISAAC OLIVER, and JOHN DE CREETES, very famous for their painting.

As Greece moreover had these painters, TIMANTES, PHIDIAS, POLIGNOTUS, PANEUS, BULARCHUS, EUMARUS, CIMON CLEONŒUS, PYTHIS, APPOLLODORUS Atheniensis, ARISTIDES Thebanus, NICOPHANES, PERSEUS, ANTIPHILUS, and NICEARCHUS: so in England, we have also these; WILLIAM and FRANCIS SEGAR, brethren; THOMAS and JOHN BETTES; LOCKEY, LYNE, PEAKE, PETER COLE, ARNOLDE, MARCUS, JACQUES DE BRAY, CORNELIUS, PETER GOLCHIS, HIERONIMO and PETER VAN DE VELDE.

As LYSIPPUS, PRAXITELES, and PYRGOTELES were excellent engravers: so we have these engravers; ROGERS, CHRISTOPHER SWITSER, and CURE.

MUSIC.

HE LOADSTONE draweth iron unto it, but the stone of Ethiopia called *Theamedes* driveth it away: so there is a kind of music that doth assuage and appease the affections, and a kind that doth kindle and provoke the passions.

As there is no law that hath sovereignty over love ; so there is no heart that hath rule over music, but music subdues it.

As one day takes from us the credit of another : so one strain of music extincts [*extinguishes*] the pleasure of another.

As the heart ruleth over all the members : so music overcometh the heart.

As beauty is not beauty without virtue : so music is not music without art.

As all things love their likes : so the more curious ear, the delicatest music.

As too much speaking hurts, too much galling smarts ; so too much music gluts and distempereth.

As PLATO and ARISTOTLE are accounted Princes in philosophy and logic ; HIPPOCRATES and GALEN, in physic ; PTOLOMY in astromony ; EUCLID in geometry ; and CICERO in eloquence : so BOËTIUS is esteemed a Prince and captain in music.

As Priests were famous among the Egyptians ; Magi among the Chaldeans, and Gymnosophists among the Indians ; so Musicians flourished among the Grecians : and therefore EPAMINONDAS was accounted more unlearned than THEMISTOCLES, because he had no skill in music.

As MERCURY, by his eloquence, reclaimed men from their barbarousness and cruelty : so ORPHEUS, by his music, subdued fierce beasts and wild birds.

As DEMOSTHENES, ISOCRATES, and CICERO, excelled in oratory : so ORPHEUS, AMPHION, and LINUS surpassed in music.

As Greece had these excellent musicians, ARION, DORCEUS, TIMOTHEUS Milesius, CHRYSOGONUS, TERPANDER, LESBIUS, SIMON Magnesius, PHILAMON, LINUS, STRATONICUS, ARISTONUS, CHIRON, ACHILLES, CLINIAS, EUMONIUS, DEMODOCHUS, and RUFFINUS : so England hath these, Master COOPER, Master FAIRFAX, Master TALLIS, Master TAVERNER, Master BLITHMAN, Master BYRD, Doctor TIE, Doctor DALLIS, Doctor BULL, Master THOMAS MUD, sometime Fellow of Pembroke Hall in Cambridge, Master EDWARD JOHNSON, Master BLANKES, Master RANDALL, Master PHILIPS, Master DOWLAND, and Master MORLEY.

A Choice is to be had in Reading of Books.

S THE Lord DE LA NOUE in the sixth Discourse of his *Politic and Military Discourses*, censureth the books of *AMADIS de Gaul*; which, he saith, are no less hurtful to youth than the works of MACHIAVELLI to age: so these books are accordingly to be censured of, whose names follow.

BEVIS *of Hampton*.

GUY *of Warwick*.

ARTHUR *of the Round Table*.

HUON *of Bordeaux*.

OLIVER *of Castile*.

The Four Sons of AYMON.

GARGANTUA.

GIRELEON.

The Honour of Chivalry.

PRIMALEON *of Greece*.

PALERMIN DE OLIVA.

The Seven Champions [*of Christendom*].

The Mirror of Knighthood.

BLANCHARDINE.

MERVIN.

OWLGLASS.

The Stories of PALLADIN *and* PALMENDOS.

The Black Knight.

The Maiden Knight.

The History of CÆLESTINA.

The Castle of Fame.

GALLIAN *of France*.

ORNATUS *and* ARTESIA.

&c.

Poets.

S THAT ship is endangered where all lean to one side; but is in safety, one leaning one way and another another way: so the dissensions of Poets among themselves, doth make them, that they less infect their readers. And for this purpose, our Satirists [JOSEPH] HALL [*afterwards Bishop of* NORWICH], [JOHN MARSTON] the Author of PYGMALION's *Image and Certain Satires*, [JOHN] RANKINS, and such others, are very profitable.

John Dryden.

Dedicatory Epistle to *The Rival Ladies*.

[Printed in 1664.]

To the Right Honourable Roger, Earl of Orrery.

My Lord,

This worthless present was designed you, long before it was a Play; when it was only a confused mass of thoughts tumbling over one another in the dark: when the Fancy was yet in its first work, moving the sleeping Images of Things towards the light, there to be distinguished; and then, either chosen or rejected by the Judgement. It was yours, my Lord! before I could call it mine.

And I confess, in that first tumult of my thoughts, there appeared a disorderly kind of beauty in some of them; which gave me hope, something worthy of my Lord of Orrery might be drawn from them: but I was then, in that eagerness of Imagination, which, by over pleasing Fanciful Men, flatters them into the danger of writing; so that, when I had moulded it to that shape it now bears, I looked with such disgust upon it, that the censures of our severest critics are charitable to what I thought, and still think of it myself.

'Tis so far from me, to believe this perfect; that I am apt to conclude our best plays are scarcely so. For the Stage being the Representation of the World and the actions in it; how can it be imagined that the Picture of Human Life can be more exact than Life itself is?

He may be allowed sometimes to err, who undertakes to move so many Characters and Humours (as are requisite in a Play) in those narrow channels, which are proper to each of them; to conduct his Imaginary Persons through so many various intrigues and chances, as the labouring Audience shall think them lost under every billow: and then, at length, to work them so naturally out of their distresses, that when the whole Plot is laid open, the Spectators may rest satisfied that every Cause was powerful enough to produce the Effect it had; and that the whole Chain of them was, with such due order, linked together, that the first Accident [*Incident*] would, naturally, beget the second, till they All rendered the Conclusion necessary.

These difficulties, my Lord! may reasonably excuse the errors of my Undertaking: but for this confidence of my Dedication, I have an argument, which is too advantageous for me not to publish it to the World. 'Tis the kindness your Lordship has continually shown to all my writings. You have been pleased, my Lord! they should sometimes cross the Irish seas, to kiss your hands; which passage, contrary to the experience of others, I have found the least dangerous in the world. Your favour has shone upon me, at a remote distance, without the least knowledge of my person: and, like the influence of the heavenly bodies, you have done good, without knowing to whom you did it. 'Tis this virtue in your Lordship, which emboldens me to this attempt. For did I not consider you as my Patron, I have little reason to desire you for my Judge: and should appear, with as much awe before you, in the Reading; as I had, when the full theatre sate upon the Action.

For who so severely judge of faults, as he who has given testimony he commits none? Your excellent *Poems* having afforded that knowledge of it to the World, that your enemies are ready to upbraid you with it as a crime, for a Man of Business to write so well. Neither durst I have justified your Lordship in it, if examples of it had not been in the world before you: if XENOPHON had not written a Romance; and a certain Roman, called AUGUSTUS CÆSAR, a Tragedy and Epigrams. But their writing was the entertainment of their pleasure; yours is only a diversion of your pain. The Muses have seldom employed your thoughts, but when some violent fit of the gout has snatched you from Affairs of State: and, like the priestess of APOLLO, you never come to deliver his oracles, but unwillingly, and in torment. So that we are obliged to your Lordship's misery, for our delight. You treat us with the cruel pleasure of a Turkish triumph, where those who cut and wound their bodies, sing songs of victory as they pass; and divert others with their own sufferings. Other men endure their diseases, your Lordship only can enjoy them!

Plotting and Writing in this kind, are, certainly, more troublesome employments than many which signify more, and are of greater moment in the world. The Fancy, Memory, and Judgement are then extended, like so many limbs, upon the rack; all of them reaching, with their utmost stress, at Nature: a thing so almost infinite and boundless, as can never fully be comprehended but where the Images of all things are always present.

Yet I wonder not your Lordship succeeds so well in this attempt. The knowledge of men is your daily practice in the world. To work and bend their stubborn minds; which go not all after the same grain, but, each of them so particular a way, that the same common humours, in several persons, must be wrought upon by several means.

Thus, my Lord! your sickness is but the imitation of your health; the Poet but subordinate to the Statesman in you. You still govern men with the same address, and manage business with the same prudence: allowing it here, as in the world, the due increase and growth till it comes to the just height; and then turning it, when it is fully ripe, and Nature calls out (as it were) to be delivered. With this only advantage of ease to you, in your Poetry: that you have Fortune, here, at your command: with which, Wisdom does often unsuccessfully struggle in the world. Here is no Chance, which you have not foreseen. All your heroes are more than your subjects, they are your creatures: and, though they seem to move freely, in all the sallies of their passions; yet, you make destinies for them, which they cannot shun. They are moved, if I may dare to say so, like the rational creatures of the Almighty Poet; who walk at liberty, in their own opinion, because their fetters are invincible: when, indeed, the Prison of their Will is the more sure, for being large; and instead of an Absolute Power over their actions, they have only a Wretched Desire of doing that, which they cannot choose but do.

I have dwelt, my Lord! thus long, upon your Writing; not because you deserve not greater and more noble commendations, but because I am not equally able to express them in other subjects. Like an ill swimmer, I have willingly stayed long in my own depth; and though I am eager of performing more, yet I am loath to venture out beyond my knowledge. For beyond your Poetry, my Lord! all is Ocean to me.

To speak of you as a Soldier, or a Statesman, were only

to betray my own ignorance: and I could hope no better success from it, than that miserable Rhetorician had, who solemnly declaimed before HANNIBAL "of the Conduct of Armies, and the Art of War." I can only say, in general, that the Souls of other men shine out at little cranies; they understand some one thing, perhaps, to admiration, while they are darkened on all the other parts: but your Lordship's Soul is an entire Globe of Light, breaking out on every side; and if I have only discovered one beam of it, 'tis not that the light falls unequally, but because the body which receives it, is of unequal parts.

The acknowledgement of which, is a fair occasion offered me, to retire from the consideration of your Lordship to that of myself. I here present you, my Lord! with that in Print, which you had the goodness not to dislike upon the Stage; and account it happy to have met you here in England: it being, at best, like small wines, to be drunk out upon the place [*i.e., of vintage, where produced*]; and has not body enough to endure the sea.

I know not, whether I have been so careful of the Plot and Language, as I ought: but for the latter, I have endeavoured to write English, as near as I could distinguish it from the tongue of pedants, and that of affected travellers. Only, I am sorry that, speaking so noble a language as we do, we have not a more certain Measure of it, as they have in France: where they have an "Academy" erected for that purpose, and endowed with large privileges by the present King [*LOUIS XIV.*]. I wish, we might, at length, leave to borrow words from other nations; which is now a wantonness in us, not a necessity: but so long as some affect to speak them, there will not want others who will have the boldness to write them.

But I fear, lest defending the received words; I shall be accused for following the New Way: I mean, of writing Scenes in Verse; though, to speak properly, 'tis no so much a New Way amongst us, as an Old Way new revived. For, many years [*i.e.,* 1561] before SHAKESPEARE's Plays, was the Tragedy of *Queen* [or rather *King*] GORBODUC [*of which, however, the authentic title is* "FERREX *and* PORREX"] in English Verse; written by that famous Lord BUCKHURST, afterwards Earl of DORSET, and progenitor to that excellent Person,

[Lord *BUCKHURST, see p.* 503] who, as he inherits his Soul and Title, I wish may inherit his good fortune!

But supposing our countrymen had not received this Writing, till of late! Shall we oppose ourselves to the most polished and civilised nations of Europe? Shall we, with the same singularity, oppose the World in this, as most of us do in pronouncing Latin? Or do we desire, that the brand which BARCLAY has, I hope unjustly, laid upon the English, should still continue? *Angli suos ac sua omnia impense mirantur; cœteras nationes despectui habent.* All the Spanish and Italian Tragedies I have yet seen, are writ in Rhyme. For the French, I do not name them: because it is the fate of our countrymen, to admit little of theirs among us, but the basest of their men, the extravagancies of their fashions, and the frippery of their merchandise.

SHAKESPEARE, who (with some errors, not to be avoided in that Age) had, undoubtedly, a larger Soul of Poesy than ever any of our nation, was the First, who (to shun the pains of continual rhyming) invented that kind of writing which we call Blank Verse [*DRYDEN is here wrong as to fact, Lord SURREY wrote the earliest* printed *English Blank Verse in his Fourth Book of the Æneid, printed in* 1548]; but the French, more properly *Prose Mesurée*: into which, the English Tongue so naturally slides, that in writing Prose, 'tis hardly to be avoided. And, therefore, I admire [*marvel that*] some men should perpetually stumble in a way so easy: and, inverting the order of their words, constantly close their lines with verbs. Which, though commended, sometimes, in writing Latin; yet, we were whipt at Westminster, if we used it twice together.

I know some, who, if they were to write in Blank Verse *Sir, I ask your pardon!* would think it sounded more heroically to write   *Sir, I, your pardon ask!*

I should judge him to have little command of English, whom the necessity of a *rhyme* should force upon this rock; though, sometimes, it cannot be easily avoided.

And, indeed, this is the only inconvenience with which Rhyme can be charged. This is that, which makes them say, "Rhyme is not natural. It being only so, when the Poet either makes a vicious choice of words; or places them, for Rhyme's sake, so unnaturally, as no man would, in ordinary speaking." But when 'tis so judiciously ordered, that the first word in the verse seems to beget the second; and that, the next; till that becomes the last word in the line, which, in the negligence of Prose, would be so: it must, then, be granted, Rhyme has all advantages of Prose, besides its own.

But the excellence and dignity of it, were never fully known, till Mr. WALLER taught it. He, first, made writing easily, an Art: first, showed us to conclude the Sense, most commonly in distiches; which in the Verse of those before him, runs on for so many lines together, that the reader is out of breath, to overtake it.

This sweetness of Mr. WALLER's Lyric Poesy was, afterwards, followed in the Epic, by Sir JOHN DENHAM, in his *Cooper's Hill*; a Poem which, your Lordship knows! for the majesty of the style, is, and ever will be the Exact Standard of Good Writing.

But if we owe the invention of it to Mr. WALLER; we are acknowledging for the noblest use of it, to Sir WILLIAM D'AVENANT; who, at once, brought it upon the Stage, and made it perfect in *The Siege of Rhodes*.

The advantages which Rhyme has over Blank Verse, are so many that it were lost time to name them.

Sir PHILIP SIDNEY, in his *Defence of Poesy*, gives us one, which, in my opinion, is not the least considerable: I mean, *the Help it brings to Memory*; which Rhyme so knits up by the Affinity of Sounds, that by remembering the last word in one line, we often call to mind both the verses.

Then, in the Quickness of Repartees, which in Discoursive Scenes fall very often: it has so particular a grace, and is so aptly suited to them, that *the Sudden Smartness of the Answer, and the Sweetness of the Rhyme set off the beauty of each other*.

But that benefit, which I consider most in it, because I have not seldom found it, is that *it Bounds and Circumscribes the Fancy*. For Imagination in a Poet, is a faculty so wild and lawless, that, like a high ranging spaniel, it must have clogs tied to it, lest it outrun the Judgement. The great easiness of Blank Verse renders the Poet too luxuriant. He is tempted to say many things, which might better be omitted, or, at least, shut up in fewer words.

But when the difficulty of artful Rhyming is interposed,

where the Poet commonly confines his Sense to his Couplet ;
and must contrive that Sense into such words that the
Rhyme shall naturally follow them, not they the Rhyme [*pp.*
571 581]: the Fancy then gives leisure to the Judgement to
come in ; which, seeing so heavy a tax imposed, is ready to
cut off all unnecessary expenses.

This last consideration has already answered an objection,
which some have made, that " Rhyme is only an Em-
broidery of Sense ; to make that which is ordinary in itself,
pass for excellent with less examination." But, certainly,
that which most regulates the Fancy, and gives the Judgement its busiest employment, is like[ly] to bring forth the
richest and clearest thoughts. The Poet examines that
most which he produceth with the greatest leisure, and
which, he knows, must pass the severest test of the audience,
because they are aptest to have it ever in their memory :
as the stomach makes the best concoction when it strictly
embraces the nourishment, and takes account of every little
particle as it passes through.

But, as the best medicines may lose their virtue, by being ill
applied ; so is it with Verse, if a fit Subject be not chosen for
it. Neither must the Argument alone, but the Characters
and Persons be great and noble : otherwise, as SCALIGER
says of CLAUDIAN, the Poet will be *Ignobiliore materia
depressus.* The Scenes which (in my opinion) most commend it, are those of Argumentation and Discourse, on the
result of which, the doing or not doing [of] some considerable
Action should depend.

But, my Lord ! though I have more to say upon this subject ; yet, I must remember, 'tis your Lordship, to whom I
speak : who have much better commended this Way by your
writing *in* it ; than I can do, by writing *for* it. Where my
Reasons cannot prevail, I am sure your Lordship's Example
must. Your Rhetoric has gained my cause ; as least, the
greatest part of my design has already succeeded to my wish :
which was, to interest so noble a Person in the Quarrel ;
and withal, to testify to the World, how happy I esteem
myself in the honour of being, My Lord,

Your Lordship's most humble, and most obedient servant,

JOHN DRYDEN.

The Honourable Sir ROBERT HOWARD, Auditor of the Exchequer.

Preface to *Four new Plays*.

[Licensed 7 March 1665, Printed the same year.]

TO THE READER.

THERE is none more sensible than I am, how great a charity the most Ingenious may need, that expose their private wit to a public judgement : since the same Phancy from whence the thoughts proceed, must probably be kind to its own issue. This renders men no perfecter judges of their own writings, than fathers are of their own children : who find out that wit in them, which another discerns not ; and see not those errors, which are evident to the unconcerned. Nor is this Self Kindness more fatal to men in their writings, than in their actions ; every man being a greater flatterer to himself, than he knows how to be to another : otherwise, it were impossible that things of such distant natures, should find their own authors so equally kind in their affections to them ; and men so different in parts and virtues, should rest equally contented in their own opinions.

This apprehension, added to that greater [one] which I have of my own weakness, may, I hope, incline the Reader to believe me, when I assure him that these follies were made public, as much against my inclination as judgement. But, being pursued with so many solicitations of Mr. HERRING-MAN's [*the Publisher*], and having received civilities from him, if it were possible, exceeding his importunities : I, at last, yielded to prefer that which he believed his interest ; before that, which I apprehended my own disadvantage. Considering withal, that he might pretend, It would be a real loss to him : and could be but an imaginary prejudice to me : since things of this nature, though never so excellent, or never so mean, have seldom proved the foundation of men's

new built fortunes, or the ruin of their old. It being the fate
of Poetry, though of no other good parts, to be wholly separated from Interest : and there are few that know me but
will easily believe, I am not much concerned in an unprofitable
Reputation.

This clear account I have given the Reader, of this seeming
contradiction, to offer that to the World which I dislike myself : and, in all things, I have no greater an ambition than
to be believed [to be] a Person, that would rather be unkind
to myself, than ungrateful to others.

I have made this excuse for myself. I offer none for my
writings ; but freely leave the Reader to condemn that which
has received my sentence already.

Yet, I shall presume to say something in the justification
of our nation's Plays, though not of my own : since, in my
judgement, without being partial to my country, I do really
prefer our Plays as much before any other nation's ; as I do the
best of ours before my own.

The manner of the Stage Entertainments has differed in
all Ages ; and, as it has increased in use, it has enlarged itself
in business. The general manner of Plays among the
Ancients we find in SENECA's Tragedies, for serious subjects ;
and in TERENCE and PLAUTUS, for the comical. In which
latter, we see some pretences to Plots ; though certainly short
of what we have seen in some of Mr. [BEN.] JOHNSON's Plays.
And for their Wit, especially PLAUTUS, I suppose it suited
much better in those days, than it would do in ours. For
were their Plays strictly translated, and presented on our
Stage ; they would hardly bring as many audiences as they
have now admirers.

The serious Plays were anciently composed of Speeches
and Choruses ; where all things are Related, but no matter of
fact Presented on the Stage. This pattern, the French do,
at this time, nearly follow : only leaving out the Chorus,
making up their Plays with almost Entire and Discoursive
Scenes ; presenting the business in Relations [*p*. 535]. This
way has very much affected some of our nation, who possibly
believe well of it, more upon the account that what the French
do ought to be a fashion, than upon the reason of the thing.

It is first necessary to consider, Why, probably, the compositions of the Ancients, especially in their serious Plays were after this manner? And it will be found, that the subjects they commonly chose, drave them upon the necessity; which were usually the most known stories and Fables [*p.* 522]. Accordingly, SENECA, making choice of MEDEA, HYPPOLITUS, and HERCULES Œtæus, it was impossible to *show* MEDEA throwing old mangled Æson into her age-renewing caldron, or to *present* the scattered limbs of HYPPOLITUS upon the Stage, and *show* HERCULES burning upon his own funeral pile.

And this, the judicious HORACE clearly speaks of, in his *Arte Poetica* ; where he says

Non tamen intus
Digna geri, promes in scenam : multaque tolles
Ex oculis, quæ mox narret facundia præsens.
Nec pueros coram populo MEDEA trucidet   [*p.* 537.]
Aut humana palam coquat extra nefarius ATREUS,
Aut in avem PROGNE vertatur, CADMUS in anguem.
Quodcunque ostendit mihi sic, incredulus odi.

So that it appears a fault to chose such Subjects for the Stage; but much greater, to affect that Method which those subjects enforce: and therefore the French seem much mistaken, who, without the necessity, sometimes commit the error. And this is as plainly decided by the same author, in his preceding words

Aut agitur res in Scenis aut acta refertur :
Segnius irritant animos demissa per aurem ;
Quam quæ sunt oculis subjecta fidelibus, et quæ
Ipse sibi tradit spectator.

By which, he directly declares his judgement, " That every thing makes more impression Presented, than Related." Nor, indeed, can any one rationally assert the contrary. For, if they affirm otherwise, they do, by consequence, maintain, That a whole Play might as well be Related, as Acted.

Therefore whoever chooses a subject, that enforces him to RELATIONS, is to blame; and he that does it without the necessity of the subject, is much more.

If these premises be granted, 'tis no partiality to conclude, That our English Plays justly challenge the preeminence.

Yet, I shall as candidly acknowledge, that our best Poets have differed from other nations, though not so happily [*felicitously*], in usually mingling and interweaving Mirth and Sadness, through the whole course of their Plays. BEN. JOHNSON only excepted; who keeps himself entire to one Argument. And I confess I am now convinced in my own judgement, that it is most proper to keep the audience in one entire disposition both of Concern and Attention: for when Scenes of so different natures, immediately succeed one another; 'tis probable, the audience may not so suddenly recollect themselves, as to start into an enjoyment of Mirth, or into the concern for the Sadness. Yet I dispute not but the variety of this world may afford pursuing accidents of such different natures; but yet, though possible in themselves to be, they may not be so proper to be Presented. An Entire Connection being the natural beauty of all Plays: and Language, the Ornament to dress them in; which, in serious Subjects, ought to be great and easy, like a high born Person that expresses greatness without pride or affection.

The easier dictates of Nature ought to flow in Comedy; yet separated from obsceneness. There being nothing more impudent than the immodesty of words. Wit should be chaste; and those that have it, can only write well

> *Si modo*
> *Scimus in urbanum Lepido se ponere dicto.*

Another way of the Ancients, which the French follow, and our Stage has, now lately, practised; is to write in Rhyme. And this is the dispute betwixt many ingenious persons, *Whether Verse in Rhyme; or Verse without the Sound, which may be called Blank Verse* (though a hard expression) *is to be preferred?*

But take the question, largely, and it is never to be decided

C   7

[*p.* 512]; but, by right application, I suppose it may. For, in the general, they are both proper: that is, one for a Play; the other for a Poem or Copy of Verses: as Blank Verse being as much too low for one [*i.e., a Poem or Verses*]; as Rhyme is unnatural for the other [*i.e., a Play*].

A Poem, being a premeditated Form of thoughts, upon designed occasions: ought not to be unfurnished of any Harmony in Words or Sound. The other [*a Play*] is presented as the *present effect* of accidents not thought of. So that, 'tis impossible, it should be equally proper to both these; unless it were possible that all persons were born so much more than Poets, that verses were not to be composed by them, but already made in them.

Some may object "That this argument is trivial; because, whatever is showed, 'tis known still to be but a Play." But such may as well excuse an ill scene, that is not naturally painted; because they know 'tis only a scene, and not really a city or country.

But there is yet another thing which makes Verse upon the Stage appear more unnatural, that is, when a piece of a verse is made up by one that knew not what the other meant to say; and the former verse answered as perfectly in Sound as the last is supplied in Measure. So that the smartness of a Reply, which has its beauty by coming from sudden thoughts, seems lost by that which rather looks like a Design of two, than the Answer of one.

It may be said, that "Rhyme is such a confinement to a quick and luxuriant Phancy, that it gives a stop to its speed, till slow Judgement comes in to assist it [*p.* 492];" but this is no argument for the question in hand. For the dispute is not which way a man may write best in; but which is most proper for the subject he writes upon. And if this were let pass, the argument is yet unsolved in itself; for he that wants Judgement in the liberty of his Phancy, may as well shew the defect of it in its confinement: and, to say truth, he that has judgement will avoid the errors, and he that wants it, will commit them both.

It may be objected, " 'Tis improbable that any should speak *ex tempore*, as well as BEAUMONT and FLETCHER makes them; though in Blank Verse." I do not only acknowledge

that, but that 'tis also improbable any will write so well that
way.   But if that may be allowed improbable; I believe it
may be concluded impossible that any should speak as good
Verses in Rhyme, as the best Poets have writ : and therefore,
that which seems *nearest* to what he intends is ever to be
preferred.

Nor are great thoughts more adorned by Verse; than
Verse unbeautified by mean ones.   So that Verse seems
not only unfit in the best use of it, but much more in the
worst, when " a servant is called," or " a door bid to be shut "
in Rhyme [*p.* 569].   Verses, I mean good ones, do, in their
height of Phancy, declare the labour that brought them
forth ! like Majesty that grows with care : and Nature, that
made the Poet capable, seems to retire, and leave its offers to
be made perfect by pains and judgement.

Against this, I can raise no argument, but my Lord of
ORRERY's writings.   In whose Verse, the greatness of the
Majesty seems unsullied with the cares, and his inimitable
Phancy descends to us in such easy expressions, that they
seem as if neither had ever been added to the other : but
both together flowing from a height; like birds got so high
that use no labouring wings, but only, with an easy care,
preserve a steadiness in motion.   But this particular happiness, among those multitudes which that excellent Person
is owner of, does not convince my reason, but employ my
wonder.   Yet, I am glad such Verse has been written for our
Stage; since it has so happily exceeded those whom we
seemed to imitate.

But while I give these arguments against Verse, I may
seem faulty, that I have not only writ ill ones, but writ any.
But since it was the fashion; I was resolved, as in all indifferent things, not to appear singular: the danger of the
vanity being greater than the error.   And therefore, I followed it as a fashion; though very far off.

For the Italian plays; I have seen some of them, which
have been given me as the best : but they are so inconsiderable that the particulars of them are not at all worthy to
entertain the Reader.   But, as much as they are short of
others, in this; they exceed in their other performances on
the Stage.   I mean their Operas : which, consisting of
Music and Painting; there's none but will believe it as

much harder to equal them in that way, than 'tis to excel
them in the other.

The Spanish Plays pretend to more ; but, indeed, are not
much : being nothing but so many novels put into Acts and
scenes, without the least attempt or design of making the
Reader more concerned than a well-told tale might do.
Whereas, a Poet that endeavours not to heighten the accidents which Fortune seems to scatter in a well-knit Design,
had better have told his tale by a fireside, than presented it
on a Stage.

For these times, wherein we write. I admire to hear the
Poets so often cry out upon, and wittily (as they believe)
threaten their judges ; since the effects of their mercy has so
much exceeded their justice, that others with me, cannot but
remember how many favourable audiences, some of our ill
plays have had : and, when I consider how severe the former
Age has been to some of the best of Mr. JOHNSON's never to
be equalled Comedies ; I cannot but wonder why any Poet
should speak of former Times, but rather acknowledge that
the want of abilities in this Age are largely supplied with the
mercies of it.

I deny not, but there are some who resolve to like nothing,
and such, perhaps, are not unwise ; since, by that general
resolution, they may be certainly in the right sometimes :
which, perhaps, they would seldom be, if they should venture
their understandings in different censures ; and, being forced
to a general liking or disliking (lest they should discover too
much their own weakness), 'tis to be expected they would
rather choose to pretend to Judgement than Good Nature,
though I wish they could find better ways to shew either.

But I forget myself ; not considering that while I entertain
the Reader, in the entrance, with what a good play should
be : when he is come beyond the entrance, he must be treated
with what ill plays are. But in this, I resemble the greatest
part of the World, that better know how to talk of many things,
than to perform them ; and live short of their own discourses.

And now, I seem like an eager hunter, that has long pursued a chase after an inconsiderable quarry ; and gives over,
weary : as I do.

OF

Dramatic Poesy,

AN

ESSAY.

By *JOHN DRYDEN* Esq.;

Fungar vice cotis, acutum
Reddere quæ ferrum valet, exors ipsa secandi.
Horat. De Arte Poet.

LONDON,
Printed for *Henry Herringman*, at the sign of the
Anchor, on the Lower-walk of the New-
Exchange. 1668.

To the Right Honourable
CHARLES Lord BUCKHURST.

M y   L o r d,

S I WAS *lately reviewing my loose papers, amongst the rest I found this Essay, the writing of which, in this rude and indigested manner wherein your Lordship now sees it, served as an amusement to me in the country* [*in* 1665], *when the violence of the last Plague had driven me from the town. Seeing, then, our theatres shut up; I was engaged in these kind*[s] *of thoughts with the same delight with which men think upon their absent mistresses.*

I confess I find many things in this Discourse, which I do not now approve; my judgement being a little altered since the writing of it: but whether for the better or worse, I know not. Neither indeed is it much material in an Essay, *where all I have said is problematical.*

For the way of writing Plays in Verse, which I have seemed to favour[*p.* 561]; *I have, since that time, laid the practice of it aside till I have more leisure, because I find it troublesome and slow. But I am no way altered from my opinion of it, at least, with any reasons which have opposed it. For your Lordship may easily observe that none are very violent against it; but those who either have not attempted it, or who have succeeded ill in their attempt. 'Tis enough for me, to have your Lordship's example for my excuse in that little which I have done in it: and I am sure my adversaries can bring no such arguments against Verse, as the Fourth Act of* POMPEY *will furnish me with in its defence.*

Yet, my Lord! you must suffer me a little to complain of you! that you too soon withdraw from us a contentment, of which we expected the continuance, because you gave it us so early. 'Tis a revolt without occasion from your Party! where your merits had already raised you to the highest commands: and where you have not the excuse of other men that you have been ill used and therefore laid down arms. I know no other quarrel you can have to Verse, than that which SPURINA *had to his beauty; when he tore and mangled the features of his face, only because they pleased too well the lookers on. It was an honour which seemed to wait for you, to lead out a New Colony of Writers from the Mother Nation; and, upon the first spreading of your ensigns, there had been many in a readiness to have followed so fortunate a Leader ; if not all, yet the better part of writers.*

> Pars, indocili melior grege, mollis et expes
> Inominata perprimat cubilia.

I am almost of opinion that we should force you to accept of the command ; as sometimes the Prætorian Bands have compelled their Captains to receive the Empire.   The Court, which is the best and surest judge of writing, has generally allowed of Verse ; and in the Town, it has found favourers of Wit and Quality.

As for your own particular, my Lord ! you have yet youth and time enough to give part of it to the Divertisement of the of the Public, before you enter into the serious and more unpleasant Business of the World.

That which the French Poet said of the Temple of Love, may be as well applied to the Temple of Muses.   The words, as near[ly] as I can remember them, were these—

> La jeunesse a mauvaise grace
> N'ayant pas adoré dans le Temple d'Amour ;
> Il faut qu'il entre : et pour le sage ;
> Si ce n'est son vrai sejour,
> Ce'st un gîte sur son passage.

I leave the words to work their effect upon your Lordship, in their own language ; because no other can so well express the nobleness of the thought : and wish you may be soon called to bear a part in the affaires of the Nation, where I know the World expects you, and wonders why you have been so long forgotten ; there being no person amongst our young nobility, on whom the eyes of all men are so much bent.   But, in the meantime, your Lordship may imitate the Course of Nature, which gives us the flower before the fruit ; that I may speak to you in the language of the Muses, which I have taken from an excellent Poem to the King [i.e., CHARLES II.]

> As Nature, when she fruit designs, thinks fit
> By beauteous blossoms to proceed to it,
> And while she does accomplish all the Spring,
> Birds, to her secret operations sing.

I confess I have no greater reason in addressing this Essay to your Lordship, than that it might awaken in you the desire of writing something, in whatever kind it be, which might be an honour to our Age and country. And, methinks, it might have the same effect upon you, which, HOMER tells us, the fight of the Greeks and Trojans before the fleet had on the spirit of ACHILLES; who, though he had resolved not to engage, yet found a martial warmth to steal upon him at the sight of blows, the sound of trumpets, and the cries of fighting men.

For my own part, if in treating of this subject, I sometimes dissent from the opinion of better Wits, I declare it is not so much to combat their opinions as to defend mine own, which were first made public. Sometimes, like a scholar in a fencing school, I put forth myself, and show my own ill play, on purpose to be better taught. Sometimes, I stand desperately to my arms, like the Foot, when deserted by their Horse; not in hope to overcome, but only to yield on more honourable terms.

And yet, my Lord! this War of Opinions, you well know, has fallen out among the Writers of all Ages, and sometimes betwixt friends: only it has been persecuted by some, like pedants, with violence of words; and managed, by others, like gentlemen, with candour and civility. Even TULLY had a controversy with his dear ATTICUS; and in one of his Dialogues, makes him sustain the part of an enemy in Philosophy, who, in his Letters, is his confident of State, and made privy to the most weighty affairs of the Roman Senate: and the same respect, which was paid by TULLY to ATTICUS; we find returned to him, afterwards, by CÆSAR, on a like occasion: who, answering his book in praise of CATO, made it not so much his business to condemn CATO, as to praise CICERO.

But that I may decline some part of the encounter with my adversaries, whom I am neither willing to combat, nor well able to resist; I will give your Lordship the relation of a dispute betwixt some of our wits upon this subject: in which, they did not only speak of Plays in Verse, but mingled, in the freedom of discourse, some things of the Ancient, many of the Modern Ways of Writing; comparing those with these, and the Wits of our Nation with those of others. 'Tis true, they differed in their opinions, as 'tis probable they would; neither do I take upon me to reconcile, but to relate them, and that, as TACITUS professes of himself, sine studio partium aut ira, "without passion or interest": leaving your Lordship to decide it in favour of which part, you shall judge most reasonable! And withal, to pardon the many errors of

Your Lordship's most obedient humble servant,

JOHN DRYDEN.

42

TO THE READER.

HE drift of the ensuing Discourse was chiefly to vindicate the honour of our English Writers from the censure of those who unjustly prefer the French before them. This I intimate, lest any should think me so exceeding vain, as to teach others an Art which they understand much better than myself. But if this incorrect Essay, written in the country, without the help of books or advice of friends, shall find any acceptance in the World: I promise to myself a better success of the Second Part, wherein the virtues and faults of the English Poets who have written, either in this, the Epic, or the Lyric way, will be more fully treated of; and their several styles impartially imitated.

AN ESSAY
OF
Dramatic Poesy.

IT was that memorable day [*3rd of June* 1665] in the first summer of the late war, when our Navy engaged the Dutch; a day, wherein the two most mighty and best appointed Fleets which any Age had ever seen, disputed the command of the greater half of the Globe, the commerce of Nations, and the riches of the Universe. While these vast floating bodies, on either side, moved against each other in parallel lines; and our countrymen, under the happy conduct of His Royal Highness [*the Duke of YORK*], went breaking by little and little, into the line of the enemies: the noise of the cannon from both navies reached our ears about the City; so that all men being alarmed with it, and in a dreadful suspense of the event which we knew was then deciding, every one went following the sound as his fancy [*imagination*] led him. And leaving the Town almost empty, some took towards the Park; some cross the river, others down it: all seeking the noise in the depth of silence.

Among the rest, it was the fortune of EUGENIUS, CRITES, LISIDEIUS and NEANDER to be in company together: three of them persons whom their Wit and Quality have made known to all the Town; and whom I have chosen to hide under these borrowed names, that they may not suffer by so ill a Relation as I am going to make, of their discourse.

Taking then, a barge, which a servant of LISIDEIUS had provided for them, they made haste to shoot the Bridge [*i.e.*, *London Bridge*] : and [so] left behind them that great fall of waters, which hindered them from hearing what they desired.

After which, having disengaged themselves from many vessels which rode at anchor in the Thames, and almost blocked up the passage towards Greenwich : they ordered the watermen to let fall their oars more gently ; and then, every one favouring his own curiosity with a strict silence, it was not long ere they perceived the air break about them, like the noise of distant thunder, or of swallows in a chimney. Those little undulations of sound, though almost vanishing before they reached them ; yet still seeming to retain somewhat of their first horror, which they had betwixt the fleets.

After they had attentively listened till such time, as the sound, by little and little, went from them ; EUGENIUS [*i.e.*, *Lord BUCKHURST*] lifting up his head, and taking notice of it, was the first to congratulate to the rest, that happy Omen of our nation's victory : adding, "we had but this to desire, in confirmation of it, that we might hear no more of that noise, which was now leaving the English coast."

When the rest had concurred in the same opinion, CRITES [*i.e.*, *Sir ROBERT HOWARD*] (a person of a sharp judgment, and somewhat a too delicate a taste in wit, which the World have mistaken in him for ill nature) said, smiling, to us, "That if the concernment of this battle had not been so exceeding[ly] great, he could scarce have wished the victory at the price, he knew, must pay for it; in being subject to the reading and hearing of so many ill verses, he was sure would be made upon it." Adding, "That no argument could 'scape some of those eternal rhymers, who watch a battle with more diligence than the ravens and birds of prey; and the worst of them surest to be first in upon the quarry : while the better able, either, out of modesty, writ not at all; or set that due value upon their poems, as to let them be often called for, and long expected."

"There are some of those impertinent people you speak of," answered LISIDEIUS [*i.e.*, *Sir CHARLES SEDLEY*], "who, to my knowledge, are already so provided, either way, that

they can produce not only a Panegyric upon the Victory : but,
if need be, a Funeral Elegy upon the Duke, and, after they
have crowned his valour with many laurels, at last, deplore
the odds under which he fell ; concluding that his courage
deserved a better destiny." All the company smiled at the
conceipt of LISIDEIUS.

But CRITES, more eager than before, began to make particular exceptions against some writers, and said, "The
Public Magistrate ought to send, betimes, to forbid them : and
that it concerned the peace and quiet of all honest people, that
ill poets should be as well silenced as seditious preachers."

"In my opinion" replied EUGENIUS, "you pursue your point
too far ! For, as to my own particular, I am so great a lover
of Poesy, that I could wish them all rewarded, who attempt
but to do well. At least, I would not have them worse used
than SYLLA the Dictator did one of their brethren heretofore.
Quem in concione vidimus (says TULLY, speaking of him) *cum
ei libellum malus poeta de populo subjecisset, quod epigramma in
eum fecisset tantummodo alternis versibus longiusculis, statim ex iis
rebus quæ tunc vendebat jubere ei præmium tribui, sub ea conditione
ne quid postea scriberet.*"

"I could wish, with all my heart," replied CRITES, "that
many whom we know, were as bountifully thanked, upon the
same condition, that they would never trouble us again.
For amongst others, I have a mortal apprehension of two
poets, whom this Victory, with the help of both her wings,
will never be able to escape."

"'Tis easy to guess, whom you intend," said LISIDEIUS,
"and without naming them, I ask you if one [*i.e.*, GEORGE
WITHER] of them does not perpetually pay us with clenches
upon words, and a certain clownish kind of raillery? If, now
and then, he does not offer at a catachresis [*which* COTGRAVE
*defines as ' the abuse, or necessary use of one word, for lack of
another more proper* '] or Clevelandism, wresting and torturing
a word into another meaning? In fine, if be not one of those
whom the French would call *un mauvais buffon*; one that is
so much a well willer to the Satire, that he spares no man : and
though he cannot strike a blow to hurt any, yet ought to be
punished for the malice of the action ; as our witches are justly
hanged, because they think themselves so, and suffer deservedly for believing they did mischief, because they meant it."

"You have described him," said CRITES, "so exactly, that I
am afraid to come after you, with my other Extremity of
Poetry. He [*i.e.*, *FRANCIS QUARLES*] is one of those, who, having had some advantage of education and converse [*i.e., conversation, in the sense of Culture through mixture with society*], knows
better than the other, what a Poet should be; but puts it into
practice more unluckily than any man. His style and matter
are everywhere alike. He is the most calm, peaceable writer
you ever read. He never disquiets your passions with the
least concernment; but still leaves you in as even a temper
as he found you. He is a very Leveller in poetry; he creeps
along, with ten little words in every line, and helps out his
numbers with *For to*, and *Unto*, and all the pretty expletives
he can find, till he drags them to the end of another line:
while the Sense is left, tired, halfway behind it. He doubly
starves all his verses; first, for want of Thought, and then, of
Expression. His poetry neither has wit in it, nor seems to have
it; like him, in MARTIAL,

> *Pauper videri* CINNA *vult, et est pauper.*

He affects plainness, to cover his Want of Imagination.
When he writes in the serious way; the highest flight of his
Fancy is some miserable *antithesis* or seeming contradiction:
and in the comic; he is still reaching at some thin conceit,
the ghost of a jest, and that too flies before him, never to be
caught. These swallows, which we see before us on the
Thames, are the just resemblance of his Wit. You may observe how near the water they stoop! how many proffers they
make to dip, and yet how seldom they touch it! and when
they do, 'tis but the surface! they skim over it, but to catch a
gnat, and then mount in the air and leave it!"

"Well, gentlemen!" said EUGENIUS, "you may speak
your pleasure of these authors; but though I and some few
more about the Town, may give you a peaceable hearing:
yet, assure yourselves! there are multitudes who would think
you malicious, and them injured; especially him whom you
first described, he is the very *Withers* of the City. They have
bought more Editions of his works, than would serve to lay
under all their pies at the Lord Mayor's Christmas. When
his famous poem [*i.e., Speculum Speculativium; Or, A Considering Glass. Being an Inspection into the present and late*

sad condition of these Nations. . . . London. Written June xiii. XDCLX, and there imprinted the same year] first came out in the year 1660, I have seen them read it in the midst of Change time. Nay, so vehement were they at it, that they lost their bargain by the candles' ends! But what will you say, if he has been received among the Great Ones? I can assure you, he is, this day, the envy of a Great Person, who is Lord in the Art of Quibbling; and who does not take it well, than any man should intrude so far into his province."

"All I would wish," replied CRITES, "is that they who love his writings, may still admire him and his fellow poet. *Qui Bavium non odit &c.*, is curse sufficient."

"And farther," added LISIDEIUS; "I believe there is no man who writes well; but would think himself very hardly dealt with, if their admirers should praise anything of his. *Nam quos contemnimus eorum quoque laudes contemnimus.*"

"There are so few who write well, in this Age," said CRITES, "that methinks any praises should be welcome. They neither rise to the dignity of the last Age, nor to any of the Ancients: and we may cry out of the Writers of this Time, with more reason than PETRONIUS of his, *Pace vestra liceat dixisse, primi omnium eloquentiam perdidistis!* 'You have debauched the true old Poetry so far, that Nature (which is the Soul of it) is not in any of your writings!'"

"If your quarrel," said EUGENIUS, "to those who now write, be grounded only upon your reverence to Antiquity; there is no man more ready to adore those great Greeks and Romans than I am: but, on the other side, I cannot think so contemptibly of the Age I live in, or so dishonourably of my own Country as not to judge [that] we equal the Ancients in most kinds of Poesy, and in some, surpass them; neither know I any reason why I may not be as zealous for the reputation of our Age, as we find the Ancients themselves, in reference to those who lived before them. For you hear HORACE saying

> *Indignor quidquam reprehendi, non quia crasse*
> *Compositum, ille pide've putetur, sed quia nuper.*

And, after,

> *Si meliora dies, ut vina, poemata reddit,*
> *Scire velim pretium chartis quotus arroget annus?*

But I see I am engaging in a wide dispute, where the arguments are not like[ly] to reach close, on either side [*p*. 497]: for Poesy is of so large extent, and so many (both of the Ancients and Moderns) have done well in all kinds of it, that, in citing one against the other, we shall take up more time this evening, than each man's occasions will allow him.   Therefore, I would ask CRITES to what part of Poesy, he would confine his arguments? and whether he would defend the general cause of the Ancients against the Moderns; or oppose any Age of the Moderns against this of ours?

CRITES, a little while considering upon this demand, told EUGENIUS, he approved of his propositions; and, if he pleased, he would limit their dispute to Dramatic Poesy: in which, he thought it not difficult to prove, either that the Ancients were superior to the Moderns; or the last Age to this of ours.

EUGENIUS was somewhat surprised, when he heard CRITES make choice of that subject.   "For ought I see," said he, "I have undertaken a harder province than I imagined.   For though I never judged the plays of the Greek and Roman poets comparable to ours: yet, on the other side, those we now see acted, come short of many which were written in the last Age.   But my comfort is, if we were o'ercome, it will be only by our own countrymen; and if we yield to them in this one part of Poesy, we [the] more surpass them in all the other[s].

For in the Epic, or Lyric way, it will be hard for them to shew us one such amongst them, as we have many now living, or who lately were so.   They can produce nothing so Courtly writ, or which expresses so much the conversation of a gentleman, as Sir JOHN SUCKLING; nothing so even, sweet, and flowing, as Mr. WALLER; nothing so majestic, so correct, as Sir JOHN DENHAM; nothing so elevated, so copious, and full of spirit, as Mr. COWLEY.   As for the Italian, French, and Spanish plays, I can make it evident, that those who now write, surpass them; and that the Drama is wholly ours."

All of them were thus far of EUGENIUS his opinion, that "the sweetness of English Verse was never understood or practised by our fathers"; even CRITES himself did not much oppose it: and every one was willing to acknowledge how much our Poesy is improved by the happiness of some writers yet living, who first taught us to mould our thoughts into easy and significant words; to retrench the superfluities of expression; and to make our Rhyme so properly a part of the Verse, that it should never mislead the Sense, but itself be led and governed by it.

EUGENIUS was going to continue this discourse, when LISIDEIUS told him, that "it was necessary, before they proceeded further, to take a Standing Measure of their controversy. For how was it possible to be decided who writ the best plays, before we know what a Play should be? but this once agreed on by both parties, each might have recourse to it; either to prove his own advantages, or discover the failings of his adversary."

He had no sooner said this; but all desired the favour of him to give the definition of a Play: and they were the more importunate, because neither ARISTOTLE, nor HORACE, nor any other who writ of that subject, had ever done it.

LISIDEIUS, after some modest denials, at last, confessed he had a rude notion of it; indeed, rather a Description than a Definition; but which served to guide him in his private thoughts, when he was to make a judgment of what others writ. That he conceived a Play ought to be A JUST AND LIVELY IMAGE OF HUMAN NATURE, REPRESENTING ITS PASSIONS AND HUMOURS; AND THE CHANGES OF FORTUNE, TO WHICH IT IS SUBJECT: FOR THE DELIGHT AND INSTRUCTION OF MANKIND.

This Definition, though CRITES raised a logical objection against it (that "it was only *a genere et fine*," and so not altogether perfect), was yet well received by the rest.

And, after they had given order to the watermen to turn their barge, and row softly, that they might take the cool of the evening in their return: CRITES, being desired by the company to begin, spoke on behalf of the Ancients, in this manner.

"IF CONFIDENCE presage a victory; EUGENIUS, in his own opinion, has already triumphed over the Ancients. Nothing seems more easy to him, than to overcome those whom it is our greatest praise to have imitated well: for we do not only build upon their foundation, but by their models.

D

7

Dramatic Poesy had time enough, reckoning from THESPIS who first invented it, to ARISTOPHANES ; to be born, to grow up, and to flourish in maturity.

It has been observed of Arts and Sciences, that in one and the same century, they have arrived to a great perfection [p. 520]. And, no wonder ! since every Age has a kind of Universal Genius, which inclines those that live in it to some particular studies. The work then being pushed on by many hands, must, of necessity, go forward.

Is it not evident, in these last hundred years, when the study of Philosophy has been the business of all the *Virtuosi* in Christendom, that almost a new Nature has been revealed to us ? that more errors of the School have been detected, more useful experiments in Philosophy have been made, more noble secrets in Optics, Medicine, Anatomy, Astronomy, discovered ; than, in all those credulous and doting Ages, from ARISTOTLE to us [*p.* 520]? So true it is, that nothing spreads more fast than Science, when rightly and generally cultivated.

Add to this, *the more than common Emulation that was, in those times, of writing well* : which, though it be found in all Ages and all persons that pretend to the same reputation : yet *Poesy, being then in more esteem than now it is, had greater honours decreed to the Professors of it, and consequently the rivalship was more high between them.* They had Judges ordained to decide their merit, and prizes to reward it : and historians have been diligent to record of ÆSCHYLUS, EURIPIDES, SOPHOCLES, LYCOPHRON, and the rest of them, both who they were that vanquished in these Wars of the Theatre, and how often they were crowned : while the Asian Kings and Grecian Commonwealths scarce[ly] afforded them a nobler subject than the unmanly luxuries of a debauched Court, or giddy intrigues of a factious city. *Alit æmulatio ingenia,* says PATERCULUS, *et nunc invidia, nunc admiratio incitationem accendit* : 'Emulation is the spur of wit ; and sometimes envy, sometimes admiration quickens our endeavours.'

But now, since the rewards of honour are taken away : that Virtuous Emulation is turned into direct Malice ; yet so slothful, that it contents itself to condemn and cry down

others, without attempting to do better. 'Tis a reputation
too unprofitable, to take the necessary pains for it; yet
wishing they had it, is incitement enough to hinder others
from it. And this, in short, EUGENIUS, is the reason why
you have now so few good poets, and so many severe judges.
Certainly, to imitate the Ancients well, much labour and
long study is required: which pains, I have already shown,
our poets would want encouragement to take; if yet they had
ability to go through with it.

Those Ancients have been faithful Imitators and wise
Observers of that Nature, which is so torn and ill-repre-
sented in our Plays. They have handed down to us a perfect
Resemblance of Her, which we, like ill copyers, *neglecting to
look on*, have rendered monstrous and disfigured.

But that you may know, how much you are indebted to
your Masters! and be ashamed to have so ill-requited
them! I must remember you, that all the Rules by which
we practise the Drama at this day (either such as relate to
the Justness and Symmetry of the Plot; or the episodical
ornaments, such as Descriptions, Narrations, and other
beauties which are not essential to the play), were delivered
to us from the Observations that ARISTOTLE made of those
Poets, which either lived before him, or were his contemporaries. We have added nothing of our own, except we
have the confidence to say, 'Our wit is better!' which none
boast of in our Age, but such as understand not theirs.
Of that book, which ARISTOTLE has left us, $\pi\epsilon\rho\iota$ $\tau\hat{\eta}s$
$\Pi o\iota\eta\tau\iota\kappa\hat{\eta}s$; HORACE his *Art of Poetry* is an excellent *Comment*, and, I believe, restores to us, that Second Book of his
[*i.e.*, ARISTOTLE] concerning *Comedy*, which is wanting in
him.

Out of these two [Authors], have been extracted the
Famous Rules, which the French call, *Des trois Unités*,
or 'The Three Unities,' which ought to be observed in
every *regular* Play; namely, of TIME, PLACE, and
ACTION.

The UNITY OF TIME, they comprehend in Twenty-
four hours, *the compass of a natural Day*; or, as near it, as can
be contrived. And the reason of it is obvious to every one.
That *the Time* of the feigned Action or Fable of the Play

should be proportioned, as near as can be, *to the duration of that Time in which it is* REPRESENTED. Since therefore all plays are acted on the Theatre in a space of time *much within* the compass of Twenty-four hours; that Play is to be thought the *nearest Imitation* of Nature, whose Plot or Action is confined within that time.

And, by the same Rule which concludes this General Proportion of Time, it follows, *That all the parts of it are to be equally subdivided*. As, namely, that one Act take not up the supposed time of Half a day, which is out of proportion to the rest; since the other four are then to be straitened within the compass of the remaining half: for it is unnatural that one Act which, being spoken or written, is not longer than the rest; should be supposed longer by the audience. 'Tis therefore the Poet's duty to take care *that no Act* should be imagined to *exceed the Time in which it is Represented on the Stage*; and that the intervals and inequalities of time, be be supposed to fall out *between* the Acts.

This Rule of T I M E , how well it has been observed by the Ancients, most of their plays will witness. You see them, in their Tragedies (wherein to follow this Rule is certainly most difficult), from the very beginning of their Plays, falling close into that part of the Story, which they intend for the Action or principal Object of it: leaving the former part to be delivered by Narration. So that they set the audience, as it were, at the post where the race is to be concluded: and, saving them the tedious expectation of seeing the Poet set out and ride the beginning of the course; you behold him not, till he is in sight of the goal, and just upon you.

For the Second Unity, which is that of P L A C E; the Ancients meant by it, *That the scene* [locality] *ought to be continued*, through the Play, *in the same place, where it was laid in the beginning*. For *the Stage*, on which it is represented, *being but one, and the same place; it is unnatural to conceive it many, and those far distant from one another*. I will not deny but by the Variation of Painted scenes [*scenery was introduced about this time into the English theatres, by Sir WILLIAM D'AVENANT and BETTERTON the Actor: see Vol. II. p. 278*] the Fancy which, in these cases, will contribute to its own deceit, may sometimes imagine it several places, upon some appearance of probability : yet it still carries *the greater likelihood of truth*, if those places be supposed so near each other as in the same town or city, which may all be comprehended under the larger denomination of One Place ; for a greater distance will bear no proportion to the *shortness of time which is allotted in the acting*, to pass from one of them to another.

For the observation of this ; next to the Ancients, the French are most to be commended. They tie themselves so strictly to the Unity of Place, that you never see in any of their plays, a scene [*locality*] changed in the middle of an Act. If the Act begins in a garden, a street, or [a] chamber ; 'tis ended in the same place. And that you may know it to be the same, the Stage is so supplied with persons, that it is never empty all the time. He that enters the second has business with him, who was on before ; and before the second quits the stage, a third appears, who has business with him. This CORNEILLE calls *La Liaison des Scenes*, 'the Continuity or Joining of the Scenes' : and it is a good mark of a well contrived Play, when all the persons are known to each other, and every one of them has some affairs with all the rest.

As for the third Unity, which is that of A C T I O N, the Ancients meant no other by it, than what the Logicians do by their *Finis* ; the End or Scope of any Action, that which is the First in intention, and Last in execution.

Now the Poet is to aim at *one great and complete Action* ; to the carrying on of which, all things in the Play, even the very obstacles, are to be subservient. And the reason of this, is as evident as any of the former. For two Actions, equally laboured and driven on by the Writer, would destroy the Unity of the Poem. It would be no longer one Play, but two. Not but that there may be many actions in a Play (as BEN. JOHNSON has observed in his *Discoveries*), but they must be all subservient to the great one ; which our language happily expresses, in the name of Under Plots. Such as, in TERENCE's *Eunuch*, is the deference and reconcilement of *THAIS* and *PHÆDRIA* ; which is not the chief business of the Play, but promotes the marriage of *CHÆREA* and *CHREMES's sister*, principally intended by the Poet.

'There ought to be but one Action,' says CORNEILLE, 'that is, one complete Action, which leaves the mind of the audience in a full repose.' But this cannot be brought to pass, but by many other imperfect ones, which conduce to it, and hold the audience in a delightful suspense of what will be.

If by these Rules (to omit many others drawn from the Precepts and Practice of the Ancients), we should judge our modern plays, 'tis probable that few of them would endure the trial. That which should be the business of a Day, takes up, in some of them, an Age. Instead of One Action, they are the Epitome of a man's life. And for one spot of ground, which the Stage should represent; we are sometimes in more countries than the map can show us.

But if we will allow the Ancients to have *contrived* well; we must acknowledge them to have *writ* better. Questionless, we are deprived of a great stock of wit, in the loss of MENANDER among the Greek poets, and of CŒCILIUS, AFFRANIUS, and VARIUS among the Romans. We may guess of MENANDER's excellency by the Plays of TERENCE; who translated some of his, and yet wanted so much of him, that he was called by C. CÆSAR, the Half-MENANDER: and of VARIUS, by the testimonies of HORACE, MARTIAL, and VELLEIUS PATERCULUS. 'Tis probable that these, could they be recovered, would decide the controversy.

But so long as ARISTOPHANES in the Old Comedy, and PLAUTUS in the New are extant; while the Tragedies of EURIPIDES, SOPHOCLES, and SENECA are to be had: I can never see one of those Plays which are now written, but it increases my admiration of the Ancients. And yet I must acknowledge further, that to admire them as we ought, we should understand them better than we do. Doubtless, many things appear flat to us, whose wit depended upon some custom or story, which never came to our knowledge; or perhaps upon some criticism in their language, which, being so long dead, and only remaining in their books, it is not possible they should make us know it perfectly.

To read MACROBIUS explaining the propriety and elegancy of many words in VIRGIL, which I had before passed over without consideration as common things, is enough to assure me that I ought to think the same of TERENCE; and that, in the purity of his style, which TULLY so much valued that he ever carried his *Works* about him, there is yet left in him great room for admiration, if I knew but where to place it.

In the meantime, I must desire you to take notice that the greatest man of the last Age, BEN. JOHNSON, was willing to give place to them in all things. He was not only a professed imitator of HORACE, but a learned plagiary of all the others. You track him everywhere in their snow. If HORACE, LUCAN, PETRONIUS *Arbiter*, SENECA, and JUVENAL had their own from him; there are few serious thoughts that are new in him. You will pardon me, therefore, if I presume, he loved their fashion; when he wore their clothes.

But since I have otherwise a great veneration for him, and you, EUGENIUS! prefer him above all other poets: I will use no farther argument to you than his example. I will produce Father BEN. to you, dressed in all the ornaments and colours of the Ancients. You will need no other guide to our party, if you follow him: and whether you consider the bad plays of our Age, or regard the good ones of the last: both the best and worst of the Modern poets will equally instruct you to esteem the Ancients."

CRITES had no sooner left speaking; but EUGENIUS, who waited with some impatience for it, thus began:

 HAVE observed in your speech, that the former part of it is convincing, as to what the Moderns have profited by the Rules of the Ancients: but, in the latter, you are careful to conceal, how much they have excelled them.

We own all the helps we have from them; and want neither veneration nor gratitude, while we acknowledge that, to overcome them, we must make use of all the advantages we have received from them. But to these assistances, we have joined our own industry: for had we sate down with a dull imitation of them; we might then have lost somewhat of the old perfection, but never acquired any that was new. We draw not, therefore, after their lines; but those of Nature: and having the Life before us, besides the experience of all they knew, it is no wonder if we hit some airs and features, which they have missed.

I deny not what you urge of Arts and Sciences [*p*. 514]; that they have flourished in some ages more than others: but your instance in Philosophy [*p*. 514] makes for me.

For if Natural Causes be more known now, than in the time of ARISTOTLE, because more studied; it follows that Poesy and other Arts may, with the same pains, arrive still nearer to perfection. And that granted, it will rest for you to prove, that they wrought more perfect Images of Human Life than we.

Which, seeing, in your discourse, you have avoided to make good; it shall now be my task to show you some of their Defects, and some few Excellencies of the Moderns. And I think, there is none amongst us can imagine I do it enviously; or with purpose to detract from them: for what interest of Fame, or Profit, can the Living lose by the reputation of the Dead? On the other side, it is a great truth, which VELLEIUS PATERCULUS affirms, *Audita visis libentius laudamus; et praesentia invidia, praeterita admiratione prosequimur, et his nos obrui, illis instrui credimus,* ' That Praise or Censure is certainly the most sincere, which unbribed Posterity shall give us.'

Be pleased, then, in the first place, to take notice that the Greek Poesy, which CRITES has affirmed to have arrived to perfection in the reign of the Old Comedy [*p*. 514], was so far from it, that *the distinction of it into Acts was not known to them*; or if it were, it is yet so darkly delivered to us, that we cannot make it out.

All we know of it is, from the singing of their Chorus: and that too, is so uncertain, that in some of their Plays, we have reason to conjecture they sang more than five times.

ARISTOTLE, indeed, divides the integral parts of a Play into four.

Firstly. The *Protasis* or Entrance, which gives light only to the Characters of the persons; and proceeds very little into any part of the Action.

Secondly. The *Epitasis* or Working up of the Plot, where the Play grows warmer; the Design or Action of it is drawing on, and you see something promising, that it will come to pass.

Thirdly. The *Catastasis* or Counter-turn, which

destroys that expectation, embroils the action in new difficulties, and leaves you far distant from that hope in which it found you: as you may have observed in a violent stream, resisted by a narrow passage; it turns round to an eddy, and carries back the waters with more swiftness than it brought them on.

Lastly.   The *Catastrophe*, which the Grecians call δέσις; the French, *Le denoument*; and we, the Discovery or Unravelling of the Plot.   There, you see all things settling again upon the first foundations; and the obstacles, which hindered the Design or Action of the Play, once removed, it ends with that Resemblance of Truth or Nature, that the audience are satisfied with the conduct of it.

Thus this great man delivered to us the Image of a Play; and I must confess it is so lively, that, from thence, much light has been derived to the forming it more perfectly, into Acts and Scenes.   But what Poet first limited to Five, the number of the Acts, I know not: only we see it so firmly established in the time of HORACE, that he gives it for a rule in Comedy.

Neu brevior quinto, neu sit productior actu:

So that you see, the Grecians cannot be said to have consumated this Art: writing rather by Entrances than by Acts; and having rather a general indigested notion of a Play, than knowing how and where to bestow the particular graces of it.

But since the Spaniards, at this day, allow but three Acts, which they call *Jornadas*, to a Play; and the Italians, in many of theirs, follow them: when I condemn the Ancients, I declare it *is not altogether because they have not five Acts to every Play; but because they have not confined themselves to one certain number*. 'Tis building a house, without a model: and when they succeeded in such undertakings, they ought to have sacrificed to Fortune, not to the Muses.

Next, for the Plot, which ARISTOTLE called τό μῦθος, and often τῶν πραγμάτον σύνθεσις; and from him, the Romans, *Fabula*.   It has already been judiciously observed by a late Writer that 'in their *TRADGEDIES*, it was only some tale derived from Thebes or Troy; or, at least, something that happened in those two Ages: which was worn so threadbare by the pens of all the Epic Poets; and even, by tradition itself of the *talkative Greeklings*, as BEN. JOHNSON calls them, that before it came upon the Stage, it was already known to all the audience. And the people, as soon as ever they heard the name of Œ*DIPUS*, knew as well as the Poet, that he had killed his father by a mistake, and committed incest with his mother, before the Play; that they were now to hear of a great plague, an oracle, and the ghost of *LAIUS*: so that they sate, with a yawning kind of expectation, till he was to come, with his eyes pulled out, and speak a hundred or two of verses, in a tragic tone, in complaint of his misfortunes.'

But one Œ*DIPUS*, *HERCULES*, or *MEDEA* had been tolerable. Poor people! They scaped not so good cheap. They had still the *chapon bouillé* set before them, till their appetites were cloyed with the same dish; and the Novelty being gone, the Pleasure vanished. So that one main end of Dramatic Poesy, in its definition [*p.* 513] (which was, to cause *Delight*) was, of consequence, destroyed.

In their C O M E D I E S, the Romans generally borrowed their Plots from the Greek poets: and theirs were commonly a little girl stolen or wandered from her parents, brought back unknown to the same city, there got with child by some lewd young fellow, who (by the help of his servant) cheats his father. And when her time comes to cry *JUNO Lucina fer opem!* one or other sees a little box or cabinet, which was carried away with her, and so discovers her to her friends: if some god do not prevent [*anticipate*] it, by coming down in a machine [*i.e., supernaturally*], and take the thanks of it to himself.

By the Plot, you may guess much [*many*] of the characters of the Persons. An old Father that would willingly, before he dies, see his son well married. His debauched Son, kind in his nature to his wench, but miserably in want of money. A Servant or Slave, who has so much wit [as] to strike in with him, and help to dupe his father. A braggadochio Captain, a Parasite, and a Lady of Pleasure.

As for the poor honest maid, upon whom all the story is built, and who ought to be one of the principal Actors in the Play; she is commonly a Mute in it. She has the breeding

of the old ELIZABETH [*Elizabethan*] way, for " maids to be
seen, and not to be heard " : and it is enough, you know she
is willing to be married, when the Fifth Act requires it.

These are plots built after the Italian mode of houses.
You see through them all at once. The Characters, indeed,
are Imitations of Nature : but so narrow as if they had imitated only an eye or an hand, and did not dare to venture on
the lines of a face, or the proportion of a body.

But in how strait a compass sorever, they have bounded their
Plots and Characters, we will pass it by, if they have regularly pursued them, and perfectly observed those three Unities,
of T I M E, P L A C E, and A C T I O N ; the knowledge of which,
you say ! is derived to us from them.

But, in the first place, give me leave to tell you ! that the
Unity of P L A C E, however it might be practised by them,
was never any of their Rules. We neither find it in
ARISTOTLE, HORACE, or any who have written of it ; till, in
our Age, the French poets first made it a Precept of the Stage.

The Unity of T I M E, even TERENCE himself, who was
the best and most regular of them, has neglected. His
Heautontimoroumenos or " Self Punisher" takes up, visibly,
two days. " Therefore," says SCALIGER, " the two first Acts
concluding the first day, were acted overnight ; the last three
on the ensuing day."

And EURIPIDES, in tying himself to one day, has committed
an absurdity never to be forgiven him. For, in one of his
Tragedies, he has made THESEUS go from Athens to Thebes,
which was about forty English miles ; under the walls of it,
to give battle ; and appear victorious in the next Act : and yet,
from the time of his departure, to the return of the *Nuntius*,
who gives relation of his victory ; *ÆTHRA* and the *Chorus*
have but thirty-six verses, that is, not for every mile, a verse.

The like error is evident in TERENCE his *Eunuch ;* when
LACHES the old man, enters, in a mistake, the house of *THAIS* ;
where, between his *Exit* and the Entrance of *PYTHIAS* (who
comes to give an ample relation of the garboils he has raised
within), *PARMENO* who was left upon the stage, has not
above five lines to speak. *C'est bien employé, un temps si court !*
says the French poet, who furnished me with one of the[se]
observations.

And almost all their Tragedies will afford us examples of the like nature.

'Tis true, they have kept the Continuity, or as you called it, *Liaison des Scenes*, somewhat better. Two do not perpetually come in together, talk, and go out together; and other two succeeded them, and do the same, throughout the Act: which the English call by the name of "Single Scenes." But the reason is, because they have seldom above two or three Scenes, properly so called, in every Act. For it is to be accounted a *new* Scene, not every time the Stage is empty: but every person *who enters*, though to others, makes it so; because he introduces a new business.

Now the Plots of their Plays being narrow, and the persons few: one of their Acts was written in a less compass than one of our well-wrought Scenes; and yet they are often deficient even in this.

To go no further than TERENCE. You find in the *Eunuch*, ANTIPHO entering, single, in the midst of the Third Act, after CHREMES and PYTHIAS were gone off. In the same play, you have likewise DORIAS beginning the Fourth Act alone; and after she has made a relation of what was done at the soldier's entertainment (which, by the way, was very inartificial to do; because she was presumed to speak directly to the Audience, and to acquaint them with what was necessary to be known: but yet should have been so contrived by the Poet as to have been told by persons of the Drama to one another, and so by them, to have come to the knowledge of the people), she quits the Stage: and PHÆDRIA enters next, alone likewise. He also gives you an account of himself, and of his returning from the country, in monologue: to which unnatural way of Narration, TERENCE is subject in all his Plays.

In his *Adelphi* or "Brothers," SYRUS and DEMEA enter after the Scene was broken by the departure of SOSTRATA, GETA, and CANTHARA: and, indeed, you can scarce look into any of his Comedies, where you will not presently discover the same interruption.

And as they have failed both in [the] laying of the Plots, and managing of them, swerving from the Rules of their own Art, by misrepresenting Nature to us, in which they have ill satisfied one intention of a Play, which was Delight: so in the

Instructive part [*pp.* 513, 582-4], they have erred worse. Instead of punishing vice, and rewarding virtue; they have often shown a prosperous wickedness, and an unhappy piety. They have set before us a bloody Image of Revenge, in *MEDEA*; and given her dragons to convey her safe from punishment. A *PRIAM* and *ASTYANAX* murdered, and *CASSANDRA* ravished; and Lust and Murder ending in the victory of him that acted them. In short, there is no indecorum in any of our modern Plays; which, if I would excuse, I could not shadow with some Authority from the Ancients.

And one farther note of them, let me leave you! Tragedies and Comedies were not writ then, as they are now, promiscuously, by the same person: but he who found his genius bending to the one, never attempted the other way. This is so plain, that I need not instance to you, that ARISTOPHANES, PLAUTUS, TERENCE never, any of them, writ a Tragedy; ÆSCHYLUS, EURIPIDES, SOPHOCLES, and SENECA never meddled with Comedy. The Sock and Buskin were not worn by the same Poet. Having then so much care to excel in one kind; very little is to be pardoned them, if they miscarried in it.

And this would lead me to the consideration of their Wit, had not CRITES given me sufficient warning, not to be too bold in my judgement of it; because (the languages being dead, and many of the customs and little accidents on which it depended lost to us [*p.* 518]) we are not competent judges of it. But though I grant that, here and there, we may miss the application of a proverb or a custom; yet, a thing well said, will be Wit in all languages: and, though it may lose something in the translation; yet, to him who reads it in the original, 'tis still the same. He has an Idea of its excellency; though it cannot pass from his mind into any other expression or words than those in which he finds it.

When *PHÆDRIA*, in the *Eunuch*, had a command from his mistress to be absent two days; and encouraging himself to go through with it, said, *Tandem ego non illa caream, si opus sit, vel totum triduum?* *PARMENO*, to mock the softness of his master, lifting up his hands and eyes, cries out, as it were in admiration, *Hui! universum triduum!* The elegancy of which *universum*, though it cannot be rendered in our language; yet leaves an impression of the Wit on our souls.

But this happens seldom in him [*i.e.*, *TERENCE*]; in PLAUTUS oftner, who is infinitely too bold in his metaphors and coining words; out of which, many times, his Wit is nothing. Which, questionless, was one reason why HORACE falls upon him so severely in those verses.

> *Sed Proavi nostri Plautinos et numeros et*
> *Laudavere sales, nimium patienter utrumque*
> *Ne dicam stolidè.*

For HORACE himself was cautious to obtrude [*in obtruding*] a new word upon his readers : and makes custom and common use, the best measure of receiving it into our writings.

> *Multa renascentur quæ nunc cecidere, cadentque*
> *Quæ nunc sunt in honore vocabula, si volet usus*
> *Quem penes, arbitrium est, et jus, et norma loquendi.*

The not observing of this Rule, is that which the World has blamed in our satirist CLEVELAND. To express a thing hard and unnaturally is his New Way of Elocution. Tis true, no poet but may sometimes use a *catachresis*. VIRGIL does it,

> *Mistaque ridenti Colocasia fundet Acantho*—

in his Eclogue of *POLLIO*.
And in his Seventh *Æneid*—

> *Mirantur et unda,*
> *Miratur nemus, insuetam fulgentia longe,*
> *Scuta virum fluvio, pictaque innare carinas.*

And OVID once; so modestly, that he asks leave to do it.

> *Si verbo audacia detur*
> *Haud metuam summi dixisse Palatia cœli.*

calling the Court of JUPITER, by the name of AUGUSTUS his palace. Though, in another place, he is more bold ; where he says, *Et longas visent Capitolia pompas.*

But to do this always, and never be able to write a line without it, though it may be admired by some few pedants, will not pass upon those who know that *Wit is best conveyed to us in the most easy language: and is most to be admired, when a great thought comes dressed in words so commonly received, that it is understood by the meanest apprehensions; as the best meat is the most easily digested.* But we cannot read a verse of CLEVELAND's, without making a face at it; as if every word were a pill to swallow. He gives us, many times, a hard nut to break our teeth, without a kernel for our pains. So that there is this difference between his *Satires* and Doctor DONNE's: that the one [*DONNE*] gives us deep thoughts in common language, though rough cadence; the other [*CLEVELAND*] gives us common thoughts in abtruse words. 'Tis true, in some places, his wit is independent of his words, as in that of the *Rebel Scot*—

Had CAIN been Scot, GOD would have changed his doom,

Not forced him wander, but confined him home.

Si sic, omnia dixisset! This is Wit in all languages. 'Tis like MERCURY, never to be lost or killed. And so that other,

For beauty, like white powder, makes no noise,

And yet the silent hypocrite destroys.

You see the last line is highly metaphorical; but it is so soft and gentle, that it does not shock us as we read it.

But to return from whence I have digressed, to the consideration of the Ancients' Writing and Wit; of which, by this time, you will grant us, in some measure, to be fit judges.

Though I see many excellent thoughts in SENECA: yet he, of them, who had a genius most proper for the Stage, was OVID. He [*i.e., OVID*] had a way of writing so fit to stir up a pleasing admiration and concernment, which are the objects of a Tragedy; and to show the various movements of a soul combating betwixt different passions: that, had he lived in our Age, or (in his own) could have writ with our advantages, no man but must have yielded to him; and therefore, I am confident the *MEDEA* is none of his. For, though I esteem it, for the gravity and sentiousness of it (which he himself concludes to be suitable to a Tragedy, *Omne genus scripti gravitate Tragœdia vincit*; yet it moves not my soul enough, to judge that he, who, in the Epic way, wrote things so near the Drama (as the stories of *MYRRHA*, of *CAUNUS and BIBLIS*, and the rest) should stir up no more concernment, where he most endeavoured it.

The masterpiece of SENECA, I hold to be that Scene in the *Troades*, where *ULYSSES* is seeking for *ASTYANAX*, to kill him. There, you see the tenderness of a mother so represented in *ANDROMACHE*, that it raises compassion to a high degree in the reader; and bears the nearest resemblance, of anything in their Tragedies, to the excellent Scenes of Passion in SHAKESPEARE or in FLETCHER.

For Love Scenes, you will find but few among them. Their Tragic poets dealt not with that soft passion; but with Lust, Cruelty, Revenge, Ambition, and those bloody actions they produced, which were more capable of raising horror than compassion in an audience: leaving Love untouched, whose gentleness would have tempered them; which is the most frequent of all the passions, and which (being the private concernment of every person) is soothed by viewing its own Image [*p.* 549] in a public entertainment.

Among their Comedies, we find a Scene or two of tenderness: and that, where you would least expect it, in PLAUTUS. But to speak generally, their lovers say little, when they see each other, but *anima mea! vita mea!* ζωη και ψυχη! as the women, in JUVENAL's time, used to cry out, in the fury of their kindness.

Then indeed, to speak sense were an offence. Any sudden gust of passion, as an ecstasy of love in an unexpected meeting, cannot better be expressed than in a word and a sigh, breaking one another. Nature is dumb on such occasions; and to make her speak, would be to represent her unlike herself. But there are a thousand other concernments of lovers as jealousies, complaints, contrivances, and the like; where, not to open their minds at large to each other, were to be wanting to their own love, and to the expectation of the audience: who watch the Movements of their Minds, as much as the Changes of their Fortunes. For the Imaging of the first [*p.* 549], is properly the work of a Poet; the latter, he borrows of the Historian."

EUGENIUS was proceeding in that part of his discourse,
when CRITES interrupted him.

" SEE," said he, "EUGENIUS and I are never likely
to have this question decided betwixt us: for he
maintains the Moderns have acquired a *new perfection* in writing; I only grant, they have *altered the
mode* of it.

HOMER describes his heroes, [as] men of great appetites;
lovers of beef broiled upon the coals, and good fellows: contrary to the practice of the French romances, whose heroes
neither eat, nor drink, nor sleep for love.

VIRGIL makes ÆNEAS, a bold avower of his own virtues,

Sum pius ÆNEAS fama super æthera notus;

which, in the civility of our Poets, is the character of a
Fanfaron or Hector. For with us, the Knight takes occasion to
walk out, or sleep, to avoid the vanity of telling his own story;
which the trusty Squire is ever to perform for him [*p.* 535].

So, in their Love Scenes, of which EUGENIUS spoke last,
the Ancients were more hearty; we, the more talkative. They
writ love, as it was then the mode to make it.

And I will grant thus much to EUGENIUS, that, perhaps,
one of their Poets, had he lived in our Age,

Si foret hoc nostrum fato delupsus in ævum,

as HORACE says of LUCILIUS, he had altered many things:
not that they were not natural before; but that he might ac-
commodate himself to the Age he lived in. Yet, in the meantime, we are not to conclude anything rashly against those
great men; but preserve to them, the dignity of Masters: and
give that honour to their memories, *quos libitina sacravit*; part
of which, we expect may be paid to us in future times."

This moderation of CRITES, as it was pleasing to all the
company, so it put an end to that dispute: which EUGENIUS,
who seemed to have the better of the argument, would urge
no further.

But LISIDEIUS, after he had acknowledged himself of EUGE-
NIUS his opinion, concerning the Ancients; yet told him,

" He had forborne till his discourse was ended, to ask him, Why he preferred the English Plays above those of other nations? and whether we ought not to submit our Stage to the exactness of our next neighbours?"

"Though," said EUGENIUS, " I am, at all times, ready to defend the honour of my country against the French; and to maintain, we are as well able to vanquish them with our pens, as our ancestors have been with their swords: yet, if you please!" added he, looking upon NEANDER, " I will commit this cause to my friend's management. His opinion of our plays is the same with mine. And besides, there is no reason that CRITES and I, who have now left the Stage, should re-enter so suddenly upon it: which is against the laws of Comedy."

" IF THE question had been stated," replied LISIDEIUS, " Who had writ best, the French or English, forty years ago [*i.e., in* 1625]? I should have been of your opinion; and adjudged the honour to our own nation: but, since that time," said he, turning towards NEANDER, "we have been so long bad Englishmen, that we had not leisure to be good Poets. BEAUMONT [*d.* 1615], FLETCHER [*d.* 1625], and JOHNSON [*d.* 1637], who were only [*alone*] capable of bringing us to that degree of perfection which we have, were just then leaving the world; as if, in an Age of so much horror, Wit and those milder studies of humanity had no farther business among us. But the Muses, who ever follow peace, went to plant in another country. It was then, that the great Cardinal DE RICHELIEU began to take them into his protection; and that, by his encouragement, CORNEILLE and some other Frenchmen reformed their *Theatre*: which, before, was so much below ours, as it now surpasses it, and the rest of Europe. But because CRITES, in his discourse for the Ancients, has prevented [*anticipated*] me by touching on many Rules of the Stage, which the Moderns have borrowed from them; I shall only, in short, demand of you, ' Whether you are not convinced that, of all nations, the French have best observed them?'

In the Unity of T I M E, you find them so scrupulous, that it yet remains a dispute among their Poets, 'Whether the

artificial day, of twelve hours more or less, be not meant by
ARISTOTLE, rather that the natural one of twenty-four?' and
consequently, 'Whether all Plays ought not to be reduced into
that compass?'   This I can testify, that in all their dramas
writ within these last twenty years [1645–1665] and upwards,
I have not observed any, that have extended the time to thirty
hours.

In the Unity of P L A C E, they are full[y] as scrupulous.
For many of their critics limit it to that spot of ground, where
the Play is supposed to begin.   None of them exceed the
compass of the same town or city.

The Unity of A C T I O N in all their plays, is yet more
conspicuous.   For they do not burden them with Under Plots,
as the English do; which is the reason why many Scenes
of our Tragi-Comedies carry on a Design that is nothing
of kin to the main Plot: and that we see two distincts webs
in a Play, like those in ill-wrought stuffs; and two Actions
(that is, two Plays carried on together) to the confounding of
the audience: who, before they are warm in their concernments for one part, are diverted to another; and, by that
means, expouse the interest of neither.

From hence likewise, it arises that one half of our Actors
[*i.e., the Characters in a Play*] are not known to the other.
They keep their distances, as if they were MONTAGUES and
CAPULETS; and seldom begin an acquaintance till the last
Scene of the fifth Act, when they are all to meet on the Stage.

There is no *Theatre* in the world has anything so absurd
as the English Tragi-Comedy.   'Tis a Drama of our own
invention; and the fashion of it is enough to proclaim it so.
Here, a course of mirth; there, another of sadness and passion; a third of honour; and the fourth, a duel.   Thus, in
two hours and a half, we run through all the fits of Bedlam.

The French afford you as much variety, on the same
day; but they do it not so unseasonably, or *mal apropos*
as we.   Our Poets present you the Play and the Farce together; and our Stages still retain somewhat of the original
civility of the " Red Bull."

Atque ursum et pugiles media inter carmina poscunt.

'The end of Tragedies or serious Plays,' says ARISTOTLE, 'is
to beget Admiration [*wonderment*], Compassion, or Concern-

ment.' But are not mirth and compassion things incompatible?
and is it not evident, that the Poet must, of necessity, destroy
the former, by intermingling the latter? that is, he must ruin
the sole end and object of his Tragedy, to introduce somewhat
that is forced in, and is not of the body of it! Would you not
think that physician mad! who having prescribed a purge,
should immediately order you to take restringents upon it?

But to leave our Plays, and return to theirs. I have noted
one great advantage they have had in the Plotting of their
Tragedies, that is, they are always grounded upon some
known History, according to that of HORACE, *Ex noto fictum
carm n sequar*: and in that, they have so imitated the Ancients,
that they have surpassed them. For the Ancients, as was
observed before [*p.* 522], took for the foundation of their Plays
some poetical fiction; such as, under that consideration, could
move but little concernment in the audience, because they already knew the event of it. But the French[man] goes farther.

> *Atque ita mentitur, sic veris falso remiscet,*
> *Primo ne medium, medio ne discrepet imum.*

He so interweaves Truth with probable Fiction, that he
puts a pleasing fallacy upon us; mends the intrigues of Fate;
and dispenses with the severity of History, to reward that
virtue, which has been rendered to us, there, unfortunate.
Sometimes the Story has left the success so doubtful, that
the writer is free, by the privilege of a Poet, to take that
which, of two or more relations, will best suit his Design.
As, for example, the death of CYRUS; whom JUSTIN and
some others report to have perished in the Scythian War; but
XENOPHON affirms to have died in his bed of extreme old age.
Nay more, when the event is past dispute, even then, we
are willing to be deceived: and the Poet, if he contrives it
with appearance of truth, has all the audience of his party
[*on his side*], at least, during the time his Play is acting. So
na urally, we are kind to virtue (when our own interest is not
in question) that we take it up, as the general concernment
of mankind.

On the other side, if you consider the Historical Plays of
SHAKESPEARE; they are rather so many Chronicles of Kings,

or the business, many times, of thirty or forty years crampt
into a Representation of two hours and a half: which is not
to imitate or paint Nature, but rather to draw her in minia-
ture, to take her in little; to look upon her, through the
wrong of a perspective [*telescope*], and receive her Images [*pp.*
528, 549], not only much less, but infinitely more imperfect
than the Life. This, instead of making a Play delightful,
renders it ridiculous.

Quodcunque ostendis mihi sic, incredulus odi.

For the Spirit of Man cannot be satisfied but with Truth,
or, at least, Verisimilitude: and a Poem is to contain, if not
τα ἔτυμα, yet ἐτύμοισιν ὁμῖα; as one of the Greek poets has
expressed it. [*See p.* 589.]

Another thing, in which the French differ from us and
from the Spaniards, is that they do not embarrass or cumber
themselves with too much Plot. They only represent so
much of a Story as will constitute One whole and great
Action sufficient for a Play. We, who undertake more, do but
multiply *Adventures* [*pp.* 541, 552]; which (not being produced
from one another, as Effects from Causes, but, barely, following) constitute many Actions in the Drama, and consequently
make it many Plays.

But, by pursuing close[ly] one Argument, which is not
cloyed with many Turns; the French have gained more
liberty for Verse, in which they write. They have leisure to
dwell upon a subject which deserves it; and to represent the
passions [*p.* 542] (which we have acknowledged to be the Poet's
work) without being hurried from one thing to another, as
we are in the plays of CALDERON; which we have seen lately
upon our theatres, under the name of Spanish Plots.

I have taken notice but of one Tragedy of ours; whose
Plot has that uniformity and unity of Design in it, which I
have commended in the French; and that is, *ROLLO*, or
rather under the name of *ROLLO*, the story of *BASSANIUS
and GŒTA*, in HERODIAN. There, indeed, the plot is neither
large nor intricate; but just enough to fill the minds of the
audience, not to cloy them. Besides, you see it founded on
the truth of History; only the time of the Action is not
reduceable to the strictness of the Rules. And you see,

in some places, a little farce mingled, which is below the
dignity of the other parts. And in this, all our Poets are extremely peccant; even BEN. JOHNSON himself, in *SEJANUS*
and *CATILINE*, has given this Oleo [*hodge-podge*] of a Play,
this unnatural mixture of Comedy and Tragedy: which, to
me, sounds just as ridiculous as *The History of DAVID, with
the merry humours of GOLIAS*. In *SEJANUS*, you may take
notice of the Scene between *LIVIA* and the *Physician*; which
is a pleasant satire upon the artificial helps of beauty. In
CATILINE, you may see the Parliament of Women; the little
envies of them to one another; and all that passes betwixt
CURIO and *FULVIA*. Scenes, admirable in their kind, but
of an ill mingle with the rest.

But I return again to the French Writers: who, as I have
said, do not burden themselves too much with Plot; which
has been reproached to them by an Ingenious Person of our
nation, as a fault. For he says, 'They commonly make but
one person considerable in a Play. They dwell upon him
and his concernments; while the rest of the persons are
only subservient to set him off.' If he intends this by it, that
there is one person in the Play who is of greater dignity than
the rest; he must tax not only theirs, but those of the
Ancients, and (which he would be loath to do) the best of
ours. For it 'tis impossible but that one person must be
more conspicuous in it than any other; and consequently
the greatest share in the Action must devolve on him. We
see it so in the management of all affairs. Even in the most
equal aristocracy, the balance cannot be so justly poised,
but some one will be superior to the rest, either in parts,
fortune, interest, or the consideration of some glorious ex-
ploit; which will reduce [*lead*] the greatest part of business
into his hands.
But if he would have us to imagine, that in exalting of
one character, the rest of them are neglected; and that all of
them have not some share or other in the Action of the Play:
I desire him to produce any of CORNEILLE's Tragedies,
wherein every person, like so many servants in a well
governed family, has *not* some employment; and who is *not*
necessary to the carrying on of the Plot, or, at least, to your
understanding it.

There are, indeed, some protactic persons [*precursors*] in
the Ancients ; whom they make use of in their Plays, either
to hear or give the Relation : but the French avoid this with
great address ; making their Narrations only to, or by such,
who are some way interessed [*interested*] in the main Design.

And now I am speaking of R E L A T I O N S; I cannot
take a fitter opportunity to add this, in favour of the French,
that they often use them with better judgement, more *apropos*
than the English do.

Not that I commend N A R R A T I O N S in general; but
there are two sorts of them :

One, of those things which are antecedent to the Play, and
are related to make the Conduct of it more clear to us. But
'tis a fault to choose such subjects for the Stage, as will in-
force us upon that rock: because we see that they are seldom
listened to by the audience ; and that it is, many times, the
ruin of the play. For, being once let pass without attention,
the audience can never recover themselves to understand the
Plot; and, indeed, it is somewhat unreasonable that they
should be put to so much trouble, as that, to comprehend
what passes in their sight, they must have recourse to what
was done, perhaps ten or twenty years ago.

But there is another sort of R E L A T I O N S, that is, of things
happening in the Action of a Play, and supposed to be done
behind the scenes : and this is, many times, both convenient
and beautiful. For by it, the French avoid the tumult,
which we are subject to in England, by representing duels,
battles, and such like ; which renders our Stage too like the
theatres where they fight for prizes [*i.e., theatres used as
Fencing Schools, for Assaults of Arms, &c.*]. For what is more
ridiculous than to represent an army, with a drum and five
men behind it ? All which, the hero on the other side, is to
drive in before him. Or to see a duel fought, and one slain
with two or three thrusts of the foils ? which we know are
so blunted, that we might give a man an hour to kill another,
in good earnest, with them.

I have observed that in all our Tragedies, the audience
cannot forbear laughing, when the Actors are to die. 'Tis
the most comic part of the whole Play.

All Passions may be lively Represented on the Stage, if,

to the well writing of them, the Actor supplies a good
commanded voice, and limbs that move easily, and without
stiffness : but there are many Actions, which can never be
Imitated to a just height.

Dying, especially, is a thing, which none but a Roman gladi-
ator could naturally perform upon the Stage, when he did not
Imitate or Represent it, but naturally Do it. And, therefore,
it is better to omit the Representation of it. The words of a
good writer, which describe it lively, will make a deeper
impression of belief in us, than all the Actor can persuade us
to, when he seems to fall dead before us : as the Poet, in the
description of a beautiful garden, or meadow, will please our
Imagination more than the place itself will please our sight.
When we see death Represented, we are convinced it is but
fiction ; but when we hear it Related, our eyes (the strongest
witnesses) are wanting, which might have undeceived us :
and we are all willing to favour the sleight, when the Poet
does not too grossly impose upon us.

They, therefore, who imagine these Relations would make
no concernment in the audience, are deceived, by confounding them with the other ; which are of things antecedent to
the Play. Those are made often, in cold blood, as I may
say, to the audience ; but these are warmed with our concernments, which are, before, awakened in the Play.

What the philosophers say of Motion, that 'when it is once
begun, it continues of itself ; and will do so, to Eternity, without some stop be put to it,' is clearly true, on this occasion.
The Soul, being moved with the Characters and Fortunes of
those Imaginary Persons, continues going of its own accord ;
and we are no more weary to hear what becomes of them,
when they are not on the Stage, than we are to listen to the
news of an absent mistress.

But it is objected, 'That if one part of the Play may be
related ; then, why not all?'

I answer. Some parts of the Action are more fit to be
Represented ; some, to be Related. CORNEILLE says judiciously, 'That the Poet is not obliged to expose to view all
particular actions, which conduce to the principal. He
ought to select such of them to be Seen, which will appear
with the greatest beauty, either by the magnificence of the
shew, or the vehemence of the passions which they produce,

or some other charm which they have in them: and let the
rest arrive to the audience, by Narration.'

'Tis a great mistake in us, to believe the French present
no part of the Action upon the Stage. Every alteration, or
crossing of a Design; every new sprung passion, and turn of
it, is a part of the Action, and much the noblest: except we
conceive nothing to be Action, till they come to blows; as if
the painting of the Hero's Mind were not more properly the
Poet's work, than, the strength of his Body.

Nor does this anything contradict the opinion of HORACE,
where he tells us

> *Segnius irritant animos demissa per aurem*
> *Quam quæ sunt occulis subjecta fidelibus.*

For he says, immediately after,

> *Non tamen intus*
> *Digna geri promes in scenam, Multaque tolles*
> *Ex occulis, quæ mox narret facundia præsens.*

Among which "many," he recounts some,

> *Nec pueros coram populo MEDEA trucidet,*
> *Aut in avem PROGNE mutetur, CADMUS in anguem, &c.*

that is, 'Those actions, which, by reason of their cruelty, will
cause aversion in us; or (by reason of their impossibility) un-
belief [*pp.* 496, 545], ought either wholly to be avoided by
a Poet, or only delivered by Narration.' To which, we may
have leave to add, such as 'to avoid tumult,' as was before
hinted [*pp.* 535, 544]; or 'to reduce the Plot into a more
reasonable compass of time,' or 'for defect of beauty in them,'
are rather to be Related than presented to the eye.

Examples of all these kinds, are frequent; not only among
all the Ancients, but in the best received of our English poets.

We find BEN JOHNSON using them in his *Magnetic Lady*,
where one comes out from dinner, and Relates the quarrels
and disorders of it; to save the indecent appearing of them
on the Stage, and to abbreviate the story: and this, in express
imitation of TERENCE, who had done the same before him, in

his *Eunuch* ; where *PYTHIAS* makes the like Relation of what had happened within, at the soldiers' entertainment.

The Relations, likewise, of *SEƷANUS*'s death and the pro-digies before it, are remarkable.   The one of which, was hid from sight, to avoid the horror and tumult of the Representa-tion : the other, to shun the introducing of things impossible to be believed.

In that excellent Play, the *King and no King*, FLETCHER goes yet farther.   For the whole unravelling of the Plot is done by Narration in the Fifth Act, after the manner of the Ancients : and it moves great concernment in the audience; though it be only a Relation of what was done many years before the Play.

I could multiply other instances ; but these are sufficient to prove, that there is no error in chosing a subject which re-quires this sort of Narration.   In the ill managing of them, they may.

But I find, I have been too long in this discourse; since the French have many other excellencies, not common to us.

As that, *you never see any of their Plays end with a Con-version, or simple Change of Will* : which is the ordinary way our Poets use [*are accustomed*] to end theirs.

It shows little art in the conclusion of a Dramatic Poem, when they who have hindered the felicity during the Four Acts, desist from it in the Fifth, without some powerful cause to take them off : and though I deny not but such reasons may be found ; yet it is a path that is cautiously to be trod, and the Poet is to be sure he convinces the audience, that the motive is strong enough.

As, for example, the conversion of the *Usurer* in the *Scornful Lady*, seems to me, a little forced.   For, being a Usurer, which implies a Lover of Money in the highest degree of covetousness (and such, the Poet has represented him) ; the account he gives for the sudden change, is, that he has been duped by the wild young fellow : which, in reason, might render him more wary another time, and make him punish himself with harder fare and coarser clothes, to get it up again.   But that he should look upon it as a judgement, and so repent ; we may expect to hear of in a Sermon, but I should never endure it in a Play.

I pass by this.   Neither will I insist upon *the care they take, that no person, after his first entrance, shall ever appear; but the business which brings upon the Stage, shall be evident.*   Which, if observed, must needs render all the events of the Play more natural.   For there, you see the probability of every accident, in the cause that produced it; and that which appears chance in the Play, will seem so reasonable to you, that you will there find it almost necessary : so that in the Exits of their Actors, you have a clear account of their purpose and design in the next Entrance; though, if the Scene be well wrought, the event will commonly deceive you.   ' For there is nothing so absurd,' says CORNEILLE, ' as for an Actor to leave the Stage, only because he has no more to say ! '

I should now speak of *the beauty of their Rhyme,* and the just reason I have to prefer *that way of writing,* in Tragedies, *before ours, in Blank Verse.*   But, because it is partly received by us, and therefore, not altogether peculiar to them ; I will say no more of it, in relation to their Plays.   For our own; I doubt not but it will exceedingly beautify them : and I can see but one reason why it should not generally obtain ; that is, because our Poets write so ill in it [*pp.* 503, 578, 598]. This, indeed, may prove a more prevailing argument, than all others which are used to destroy it: and, therefore, I am only troubled when great and judicious Poets, and those who are acknowledged such, have writ or spoke against it.   As for others, they are to be answered by that one sentence of an ancient author.   *Sed ut primo ad consequendos eos quos priores ducimus accendimur, ita ubi aut præteriri, aut æquari eos posse desperavimus, studium cum spe senescit : quod, scilicet, assequi non potest, sequi desinit; præteritoque eo in quo eminere non possumus, aliquid in quo nitamur conquirimus.*"

LISIDEIUS concluded, in this manner; and NEANDER, after a little pause, thus answered him.

" I SHALL grant LISIDEIUS, without much dispute, a great part of what he has urged against us.

For I acknowledge *the French contrive their Plots more regularly; observe the laws of Comedy, and decorum of the Stage,* to speak generally, *with more exactness than the English.* Farther, I deny not but he has taxed us justly, in some irregularities of ours ; which he has mentioned. Yet, after all, I am of opinion, that neither our faults, nor their virtues are considerable enough to place them above us.

For *the lively Imitation of Nature* being the Definition of a Play [*p.* 513] ; those which best fulfil that law, ought to be esteemed superior to the others. 'Tis true those beauties of the French Poesy are such as will raise perfection higher where it is ; but are not sufficient to give it where it is not. They are, indeed, the beauties of a Statue, not of a Man ; because not animated with the Soul of Poesy, which is *Imitation of Humour and Passions.*

And this, LISIDEIUS himself, or any other, however biased to their party, cannot but acknowledge ; if he will either compare the Humours of our Comedies, or the Characters of our serious Plays with theirs.

He that will look upon theirs, which have been written till [within] these last ten years [*i.e.,* 1655, *when MOLIERE began to write*], or thereabouts, will find it a hard matter to pick out two or three passable Humours amongst them. CORNEILLE himself, their Arch Poet ; what has he produced, except the *Liar* ? and you know how it was cried up in France. But when it came upon the English Stage, though well translated, and that part of *DORANT* acted to so much advantage by Mr. HART, as, I am confident, it never received in its own country ; the most favourable to it, would not put it in competition with many of FLETCHER's or BEN. JOHNSON's. In the rest of CORNEILLE's Comedies you have little humour. He tells you, himself, his way is first to show two lovers in good intelligence with each other ; in the working up of the Play, to embroil them by some mistake ; and in the latter end, to clear it up.

But, of late years, DE MOLIERE, the younger CORNEILLE, QUINAULT, and some others, have been imitating, afar off, the quick turns and graces of the English Stage. They have mixed their serious Plays with mirth, like our Tragi-Comedies, since the death of Cardinal RICHELIEU [*in* 1642] : which LISIDEIUS and many others not observing, have commended that in them for a virtue [*p.* 531], which they themselves no longer practise.

Most of their new Plays are, like some of ours, derived from the Spanish novels. There is scarce one of them, without a veil ; and a trusty DIEGO, who drolls, much after the rate of the *Adventures* [*pp.* 533, 552]. But their humours, if I may grace them with that name, are so thin sown; that never above One of them comes up in a Play. I dare take upon me, to find more variety of them, in one play of BEN. JOHNSON's, than in all theirs together : as he who has seen the *Alchemist*, the *Silent Woman*, or *Bartholomew Fair*, cannot but acknowledge with me. I grant the French have performed what was possible on the ground work of the Spanish plays. What was pleasant before, they have made regular. But there is not above one good play to be writ upon all those Plots. They are too much alike, to please often ; which we need not [adduce] the experience of our own Stage to justify.

As for their New Way of mingling Mirth with serious Plot, I do not, with LISIDEIUS, condemn the thing ; though I cannot approve their manner of doing it. He tells us, we cannot so speedily re-collect ourselves, after a Scene of great Passion and Concernment, as to pass to another of Mirth and Humour, and to enjoy it with any relish. But why should he imagine the Soul of Man more heavy than his Senses? Does not the eye pass from an unpleasant object, to a pleasant, in a much shorter time than is required to this? and does not the unpleasantness of the first commend the beauty of the latter? The old rule of Logic might have convinced him, that 'Contraries when placed near, set off each other.' A continued gravity keeps the spirit too much bent. We must refresh it sometimes ; as we bait [*lunch*] upon a journey, that we may go on with greater ease. A Scene of Mirth mixed with Tragedy, has the same effect upon us, which our music has betwixt the Acts ; and that, we find a relief to us from the best Plots and Language of the Stage, if the discourses have been long.

I must, therefore, have stronger arguments, ere I am convinced that Compassion and Mirth, in the same subject, destroy each other : and, in the meantime, cannot but conclude to the honour of our Nation, that we have invented, increased, and perfected a more pleasant way of writing for the Stage than was ever known to the Ancients or Moderns of any nation ; which is, Tragi-Comedy.

And this leads me to wonder why LISIDEIUS [*p.* 533], and

many others, should cry up *the barrenness of the French Plots* above *the variety and copiousness of the English ?*

Their Plots are single. They carry on one Design, which is push forward by all the Actors ; every scene in the Play contributing and moving towards it. Ours, besides the main Design, have Under Plots or By-Concernments of less considerable persons and intrigues ; which are carried on, with the motion of the main Plot : just as they say the orb [*?orbits*] of the fixed stars, and those of the planets (though they have motions of their own), are whirled about, by the motion of the *Primum Mobile* in which they are contained. That similitude expresses much of the English Stage. For, if contrary motions may be found in Nature to agree, if a planet can go East and West at the same time ; one way, by virtue of his own motion, the other, by the force of the First Mover : it will not be difficult to imagine how the Under Plot, which is only different [from], not contrary to the great Design, may naturally be conducted along with it.

EUGENIUS [? *LISIDEIUS*] has already shown us [*p.* 534], from the confession of the French poets, that the Unity of Action is sufficiently preserved, if all the imperfect actions of the Play are conducing to the main Design : but when those petty intrigues of a Play are so ill ordered, that they have no coherence with the other ; I must grant, that LISIDEIUS has reason to tax that Want of due Connection. For Co-ordination in a Play is as dangerous and unnatural as in a State. In the meantime, he must acknowledge, our Variety (if well ordered) will afford a greater pleasure to the audience.

As for his other argument, that *by pursuing one single Theme, they gain an advantage to express, and work up the passions* [*p.* 533] ; I wish any example he could bring from them, would make it good. For I confess their verses are, to me, the coldest I have ever read.

Neither, indeed, is it possible for them, in the way they take, so to express Passion as that the effects of it should appear in the concernment of an audience ; their speeches being so many declamations, which tire us with the length : so that, instead of persuading us to grieve for their imaginary heroes, we are concerned for our own trouble, as we are, in the tedious visits of bad [*dull*] company ; we are in pain till they are gone.

When the French Stage came to be reformed by Cardinal RICHELIEU, those long harangues were introduced, to comply with the gravity of a Churchman. Look upon the *CINNA* and *POMPEY*! They are not so properly to be called Plays, as long Discourses of Reason[s] of State: and *POLIEUCTE*, in matters of Religion, is as solemn as the long stops upon our organs. Since that time, it has grown into a custom; and their Actors speak by the hour glass, as our Parsons do. Nay, they account it the grace of their parts! and think themselves disparaged by the Poet, if they may not twice or thrice in a Play, entertain the audience, with a speech of a hundred or two hundred lines.

I deny not but this may suit well enough with the French: for as we, who are a more sullen people, come to be diverted at our Plays; they, who are of an airy and gay temper, come thither to make themselves more serious. And this I conceive to be one reason why Comedy is more pleasing to us, and Tragedy to them.

But, to speak generally, it cannot be denied that *short* Speeches and Replies are more apt to move the passions, and beget concernment in us; than the other. For it is unnatural for any one in a gust of passion, to speak long together; or for another, in the same condition, to suffer him without interruption.

Grief and Passion are like floods raised in little brooks, by a sudden rain. They are quickly up; and if the Concernment be poured unexpectedly in upon us, it overflows us: but a long sober shower gives them leisure to run out as they came in, without troubling the ordinary current.

As for Comedy, Repartee is one of its chiefest graces. The greatest pleasure of the audience is a Chase of Wit, kept up on both sides, and swiftly managed. And this, our forefathers (if not we) have had, in FLETCHER's *Plays*, to a much higher degree of perfection, than the French Poets can arrive at.

There is another part of LISIDEIUS his discourse, in which he has rather excused our neighbours, than commended them; that is, *for aiming only* [simply] *to make one person considerable in their Plays.*

'Tis very true what he has urged, that one Character in all Plays, even without the Poet's care, will have the advantage of all the others; and that the Design of the whole Drama will chiefly depend on it. But this hinders not, that there may be more shining Characters in the Play; many persons of a second magnitude, nay, some so very near, so almost equal to the first, that greatness may be opposed to greatness: and all the persons be made considerable, not only by their Quality, but their Action.

'Tis evident that the more the persons are; the greater will be the variety of the Plot. If then, the parts are managed so regularly, that the beauty of the whole be kept entire; and that the variety become not a perplexed and confused mass of accidents: you will find it infinitely pleasing, to be led in a labyrinth of Design; where you see some of your way before you, yet discern not the end, till you arrive at it.

And that all this is practicable; I can produce, for examples, many of our English plays, as the *Maid's Tragedy*, the *Alchemist*, the *Silent Woman*.

I was going to have named the *Fox*; but that the Unity of Design seems not exactly observed in it. For there appear two Actions in the Play; the first naturally ending with the Fourth Act, the second forced from it, in the Fifth. Which yet, is the less to be condemned in him, because the disguise of *VOLPONE* (though it suited not with his character as a crafty or covetous person) agreed well enough with that of a voluptuary: and, by it, the Poet gained the end he aimed at, the punishment of vice, and reward of virtue; which that disguise produced. So that, to judge equally of it, it was an excellent Fifth Act; but not so naturally proceeding from the former.

But to leave this, and to pass to the latter part of LISIDEIUS his discourse; which concerns RELATIONS. I must acknowledge, with him, that the French have reason, *when they hide that part of the Action, which would occasion too much tumult on the Stage*; and choose rather to have it made known by Narration to the audience [*p.* 535]. Farther; I think it very convenient, for the reasons he has given, that *all incredible Actions were removed* [*p.* 537]: but, whether custom has so insinuated itself into our countrymen, or Nature has so formed them to fierceness, I know not; but they will scarcely suffer combats or other objects of horror to be taken from them. And indeed the *indecency* of tumults is all which can be objected against fighting. For why may not our imagination as well suffer itself to be deluded with the *probability* of it, as any other thing in the Play. For my part, I can, with as great ease, persuade myself that the blows, which are struck, are given in good earnest; as I can, that they who strike them, are Kings, or Princes, or those persons which they represent.

For *objects of incredibility* [*b.* 537], I would be satisfied from LISIDEIUS, whether we have any so removed from all appearance of truth, as are those in CORNEILLE's *ANDROMEDE* ? A Play that has been frequented [*repeated*] the most, of any he has writ. If the *PERSEUS* or the son of the heathen god, the *Pegasus*, and the Monster, were not capable to choke a strong belief? let him blame any representation of ours hereafter! Those, indeed, were objects of delight; yet the reason is the same as to the probability: for he makes it not a Ballette [*Ballet*] or Masque; but a Play, which is, *to resemble truth*.

As for *Death*, that *it ought not to be represented* [*p.* 536] : I have, besides the arguments alleged by LISIDEIUS, the authority of BEN. JOHNSON, who has foreborne it in his Tragedies : for both the death of *SEJANUS* and *CATILINE* are Related. Though, in the latter, I cannot but observe one irregularity of that great poet. He has removed the Scene in the same Act, from Rome to *CATILINE*'s army ; and from thence, again to Rome : and, besides, has allowed a very inconsiderable time after *CATILINE*'s speech, for the striking of the battle, and the return of *PETREIUS*, who is to relate the event of it to the Senate. Which I should not animadvert upon him, who was otherwise a painful observer of τὸ πρέπον or the Decorum of the Stage : if he had not used extreme severity in his judgement [*in his " Discoveries "*] upon the incomparable SHAKESPEARE, for the same fault.

To conclude on this subject of Relations, if we are to be blamed for showing too much of the Action ; the French are as faulty for discovering too little of it. A mean betwixt both, should be observed by every judicious writer, so as the audience may neither be left unsatisfied, by not seeing what is beautiful ; or shocked, by beholding what is either incredible or indecent.

I hope I have already proved in this discourse, that though

we are not altogether so punctual as the French, in observing the laws of Comedy : yet our errors are so few, and [so] little ; and those things wherein we excel them so considerable, that we ought, of right, to be preferred before them.

But what will LISIDEIUS say ? if they themselves acknowledge they are too strictly tied up by those laws : for the breaking which, he has blamed the English ? I will allege CORNEILLE's words, as I find them in the end of this *Discourse* of *The three Unities*. *Il est facile aux speculatifs d'être severe, &c.* ' 'Tis easy, for speculative people to judge severely : but if they would produce to public view, ten or twelve pieces of this nature ; they would, perhaps, give more latitude to the Rules, than I have done : when, by experience, they had known how much we are bound up, and constrained by them, and how many beauties of the Stage they banished from it.'

To illustrate, a little, what he has said. By their servile imitations of the UNITIES of TIME and PLACE, and INTEGRITY OF SCENES ; they have brought upon themselves the Dearth of Plot and Narrowness of Imagination which may be observed in all their Plays.

How many beautiful accidents might naturally happen in two or three days ; which cannot arrive, with any probability, in the compass of twenty-four hours ? There is time to be allowed, also, for maturity of design : which, amongst great and prudent persons, such as are often represented in Tragedy, cannot, with any likelihood of truth, be brought to pass at so short a warning.

Farther, by tying themselves strictly to the UNITY OF PLACE and UNBROKEN SCENES ; they are forced, many times, to omit some beauties which cannot be shown where the Act began : but might, if the Scene were interrupted, and the Stage cleared, for the persons to enter in another place. And therefore, the French Poets are often forced upon absurdities. For if the Act begins in a Chamber, all the persons in the Play must have some business or other to come thither ; or else they are not to be shown in that Act : and sometimes their characters are very unfitting to appear there. As, suppose it were the King's Bedchamber ; yet the meanest man in the Tragedy, must come and despatch his business there, rather than in the Lobby or Courtyard (which is [*were*] fitter for him), for fear the Stage should be cleared, and the Scenes broken.

Many times, they fall, by it, into a greater inconvenience: for they keep their Scenes Unbroken; and yet Change the Place. As, in one of their newest Plays [*i.e., before* 1665]. Where the Act begins in a Street: there, a gentleman is to meet his friend; he sees him, with his man, coming out from his father's house; they talk together, and the first goes out. The second, who is a lover, has made an appointment with his mistress: she appears at the Window; and then, we are to imagine the Scene lies under it. This gentleman is called away, and leaves his servant with his mistress. Presently, her father is heard from within. The young lady is afraid the servingman should be discovered; and thrusts him through a door. which is supposed to be her Closet [*Boudoir*]. After this, the father enters to the daughter; and now the Scene is in a House: for he is seeking, from one room to another, for his poor *PHILIPIN* or French *DIEGO*: who is heard from within, drolling, and breaking many a miserable conceit upon his sad condition. In this ridiculous manner, the Play goes on; the Stage being never empty all the while. So that the Street, the Window, the two Houses, and the Closet are made to walk about, and the Persons to stand still!

Now, what, I beseech you! is more easy than to write a regular French Play? or more difficult than to write an irregular English one, like those of FLETCHER, or of SHAKESPEARE?

If they content themselves, as CORNEILLE did, with some flat design, which (like an ill riddle) is found out ere it be half proposed; such Plots, we can make every way regular, as easily as they: but whene'er they endeavour to rise up to any quick Turns or Counter-turns of Plot, as some of them have attempted, since CORNEILLE's *Plays* have been less in vogue; you see they write as irregularly as we! though they cover it more speciously. Hence the reason is perspicuous, why no French plays, when translated, have, or ever can succeed upon the English Stage. For, if you consider the Plots, our own are fuller of variety; if the Writing, ours are more quick, and fuller of spirit: and therefore 'tis a strange mistake in those who decry the way of writing Plays in Verse; as if the English therein imitated the French.

We have borrowed nothing from them. Our Plots are weaved in English looms. We endeavour, therein, to follow the variety and greatness of Characters, which are derived to us from SHAKESPEARE and FLETCHER. The copiousness and well knitting of the Intrigues, we have from JOHNSON. And for the Verse itself, we have English precedents, of elder date than any of CORNEILLE's plays. Not to name our old Comedies before SHAKESPEARE, which are all writ in verse of six feet or Alexandrines, such as the French now use : I can show in SHAKESPEARE, many Scenes of Rhyme together ; and the like in BEN JOHNSON's tragedies. In *CATILINE* and *SEJANUS*, sometimes, thirty or forty lines. I mean, besides the Chorus or the Monologues ; which, by the way, showed BEN. no enemy to this way of writing: especially if you look upon his *Sad Shepherd*, which goes sometimes upon rhyme, sometimes upon blank verse ; like a horse, who eases himself upon trot and amble. You find him, likewise, commending FLETCHER's pastoral of the *Faithful Shepherdess*: which is, for the most part, [in] Rhyme; though not refined to that purity, to which it hath since been brought. And these examples are enough to clear us from a servile imitation of the French.

But to return, from whence I have digressed. I dare boldly affirm these two things of the English Drama.

First. That we have many Plays of ours as regular as any of theirs ; and which, besides, have more variety of Plot and Characters. And

Secondly. That in most of the irregular Plays of SHAKESPEARE or FLETCHER (for BEN. JOHNSON's are for the most part regular), there is a more masculine Fancy, and greater Spirit in all the Writing, than there is in any of the French.

I could produce, even in SHAKESPEARE's and FLETCHER's *Works*, some Plays which are almost exactly formed ; as the *Merry Wives of Windsor* and the *Scornful Lady*. But because, generally speaking, SHAKESPEARE, who writ first, did not perfectly observe the laws of Comedy; and FLETCHER, who came nearer to perfection [*in this respect*], yet, through carelessness, made many faults : I will take the pattern of a perfect Play from BEN JOHNSON, who was a careful and learned observer of the Dramatic Laws; and, from all his Comedies, I shall select the *Silent Woman* [*p.* 597], of which I will make a short examen [*examination*], according to those Rules which the French observe."

As NEANDER was beginning to examine the *Silent Woman*: EUGENIUS, looking earnestly upon him, "I beseech you, NEANDER!" said he, "gratify the company, and me in particular, so far, as, before you speak of the Play, to give us a Character of the Author: and tell us, frankly, your opinion! whether you do not think all writers, both French and English, ought to give place to him?"

 " FEAR," replied NEANDER, "that in obeying your commands, I shall draw a little envy upon myself. Besides, in performing them, it will be first necessary to speak somewhat of SHAKESPEARE and FLETCHER his Rivals in Poesy; and one of them, in my opinion, at least his Equal, perhaps his Superior.

To begin then with SHAKESPEARE. He was the man, who, of all Modern and perhaps Ancient poets, had the largest and most comprehensive Soul [*p.* 540]. All the Images of Nature [*pp.* 528, 533] were still present [*apparent*] to him [*p.* 489]: and he drew them not laboriously, but luckily [*felicitously*]. When he describes anything; you more than see it, you feel it too. Those who accuse him to have wanted learning; give him the greater commendation. He was naturally learned. He needed not the spectacles of books, to read Nature; he looked inwards, and found her there. I cannot say, he is everywhere alike. Were he so; I should do him injury to compare him [*even*] with the greatest of mankind. He is many times flat, insipid: his comic wit degenerating into clenches; his serious swelling, into bombast.

But he is always great, when some great occasion is presented to him. No man can say, he ever had a fit subject for his wit, and did not then raise himself as high above the rest of poets,

Quantum lenta solent, inter viberna cupressi.

The consideration of this, made Mr. HALES, of Eton, say, 'That there was no subject of which any poet ever writ; but he would produce it much better treated of in SHAKESPEARE.'

And however others are, now, generally preferred before him; yet the Age wherein he lived (which had contemporaries with him, FLETCHER and JOHNSON) never equalled them to him, in their esteem. And in the last King's [CHARLES I.] Court, when BEN.'s reputation was at [the] highest; Sir JOHN SUCKLING, and with him, the greater part of the Courtiers, set our SHAKESPEARE far above him.

BEAUMONT and FLETCHER (of whom I am next to speak), had, with the advantage of SHAKESPEARE's wit, which was their precedent, great natural gifts improved by study. BEAUMONT, especially, being so accurate a judge of plays, that BEN. JOHNSON, while he [i.e., BEAUMONT] lived, submitted all his writings to his censure; and, 'tis thought, used his judgement in correcting, if not contriving all his plots. What value he had for [i.e., attached to] him, appears by the verses he writ to him: and therefore I need speak no farther of it.

The first Play which brought FLETCHER and him in esteem, was their PHILASTER. For, before that, they had written two or three very unsuccessfully: as the like is reported of BEN. JOHNSON, before he writ Every Man in his Humour [acted in 1598]. Their Plots were generally more regular than SHAKESPEARE's, especially those which were made before BEAUMONT's death: and they understood, and imitated the conversation of gentlemen [in the conventional sense in which it was understood in DRYDEN's time], much better [i.e., than SHAKESPEARE]; whose wild debaucheries, and quickness of wit in repartees, no Poet can ever paint as they have done.

This Humour, which BEN. JOHNSON derived from particular persons; they made it not their business to describe. They represented all the passions very lively; but, above all, Love.

I am apt to believe the English language, in them, arrived to its highest perfection. What words have since been taken in, are rather superfluous than necessary.

Their Plays are now the most pleasant and frequent entertainments of the Stage; two of theirs being acted through the year, for one of SHAKESPEARE's or JOHNSON's. The reason is because there is a certain Gaiety in their Comedies, and Pathos in their more serious Plays, which suit generally with all men's humours. SHAKESPEARE's Language is likewise a little obsolete; and BEN. JOHNSON's Wit comes short of theirs.

As for JOHNSON, to whose character I am now arrived ; if
we look upon him, while he was himself (for his last Plays
were but his dotages) I think him the most learned and
judicious Writer which any *Theatre* ever had. He was a
most severe judge of himself, as well as others. One cannot
say he wanted Wit ; but rather, that he was frugal of it
[*p*. 572]. In his works, you find little to retrench or alter.

Wit and Language, and Humour also in some measure,
we had before him ; but something of Art was wanting to the
Drama, till he came. He managed his strength to more advantage than any who preceded him. You seldom find him making
love in any of his Scenes, or endeavouring to move the passions : his genius was too sullen and saturnine to do it grace-
fully ; especially when he knew, he came after those who had
performed both to such a height. Humour was his proper
sphere ; and in that, he delighted most to represent mechanic
[*uncultivated*] people.

He was deeply conversant in the Ancients, both Greek
and Latin ; and he borrowed boldly from them. There is
scarce a Poet or Historian, among the Roman authors of
those times, whom he has not translated in *SEJANUS*
and *CATILINE* : but he has done his robberies so openly,
that one may see he fears not to be taxed by any law.
He invades authors, like a Monarch ; and what would be
Theft in other Poets, is only Victory in him. With the spoils
of these Writers, he so represents old Rome to us, in its
rites, ceremonies, and customs ; that if one of their own poets
had written either of his Tragedies, we had seen less of it
than in him.

If there was any fault in his Language, 'twas that he
weaved it too closely and laboriously in his serious Plays.
Perhaps, too, he did a little too much Romanize our tongue ;
leaving the words which he translated, almost as much Latin
as he found them : wherein, though he learnedly followed the
idiom of their language, he did not enough comply with ours.

If I would compare him with SHAKESPEARE, I must acknowledge him, the more correct Poet ; but SHAKESPEARE, the
greater Wit. SHAKESPEARE was the HOMER, or Father of
our Dramatic Poets ; JOHNSON was the VIRGIL, the pattern
of elaborate writing. I admire him ; but I love SHAKESPEARE.

To conclude of him. As he has given us the most correct

Plays; so in the Precepts which he has laid down in his *Discoveries,* we have as many and profitable Rules as any wherewith the French can furnish us.

Having thus spoken of this author; I proceed to the examination of his Comedy, the *Silent Woman.*

Examen of the "Silent Woman."

TO begin, first, with the Length of the Action. It is so far from exceeding the compass of a natural day, that it takes not up an artificial one. 'Tis all included in the limits of three hours and a half; which is no more than is required for the presentment [*representation of it*] on the Stage. A beauty, perhaps, not much observed. If it had [been]; we should not have looked upon the Spanish Translation [*i.e., the adaptation from the Spanish*] of *Five Hours* [*pp.* 533, 541], with so much wonder.

The Scene of it is laid in London. The Latitude of Place is almost as little as you can imagine: for it lies all within the compass of two houses; and, after the First Act, in one.

The Continuity of Scenes is observed more than in any of our Plays, excepting his own *Fox* and *Alchemist.* They are not broken above twice, or thrice at the most, in the whole Comedy: and in the two best of CORNEILLE's Plays, the *CID* and *CINNA,* they are interrupted once a piece.

The Action of the Play is entirely One: the end or aim of which, is the settling *MOROSE*'s estate on *DAUPHINE.*

The Intrigue of it is the greatest and most noble of any pure unmixed Comedy in any language. You see in it, many persons of various Characters and Humours; and all delightful.

As first, *MOROSE,* an old man, to whom all noise, but his own talking, is offensive. Some, who would be thought critics, say, "This humour of his is forced." But, to remove that objection, we may consider him, first, to be naturally of a delicate hearing, as many are, to whom all sharp sounds are unpleasant: and, secondly, we may attribute much of it to the peevishness of his age, or the wayward authority of an old man in his own house, where he may make himself obeyed; and this the Poet seems to allude to, in his name MOROSE. Besides this, I am assured from divers persons, that BEN JOHNSON was actually acquainted with such a man, one altogether as ridiculous as he is here represented.

Others say, ' It is not enough, to find one man of such an humour. It must be common to more; and the more common, the more natural.' To prove this, they instance in the best of comical characters, *FALSTAFF*. There are many men resembling him; Old, Fat, Merry, Cowardly, Drunken, Amorous, Vain, and Lying. But to convince these people; I need but [to] tell them, that *Humour is the ridiculous extravagance of conversation, wherein one man differs from all others*. If then it be common, or communicated to any; how differs it from other men's? or what indeed causes it to be ridiculous, so much as the singularity of it. As for *FALSTAFF*, he is not properly one Humour; but a Miscellany of Humours or Images drawn from so many several men. That wherein he is singular is his Wit, or those things he says, *præter expectatum*, 'unexpected by the audience'; his quick evasions, when you imagine him surprised: which, as they are extremely diverting of themselves, so receive a great addition from his person; for the very sight of such an unwieldy old debauched fellow is a Comedy alone.

And here, having a place so proper for it, I cannot but enlarge somewhat upon this subject of Humour, into which I am fallen.

The Ancients had little of it in their Comedies: for the το γελοῖον [*facetious absurdities*] of the Old Comedy, of which ARISTOPHANES was chief, was not so much to imitate a man; as to make the people laugh at some odd conceit, which had commonly somewhat of unnatural or obscene in it. Thus, when you see *SOCRATES* brought upon the Stage, you are not to imagine him made ridiculous by the imitation of his actions: but rather, by making him perform something very unlike himself; something so childish and absurd, as, by comparing it with the gravity of the true SOCRATES, makes a ridiculous object for the spectators.

In the New Comedy which succeeded, the Poets sought, indeed, to express the ἦθος [*manners and habits*]; as in their

Tragedies, the πάθος [*sufferings*] of mankind. But this ἦθος contained only the general characters of men and manners; as [of] Old Men, Lovers, Servingmen, Courtizans, Parasites, and such other persons as we see in their Comedies. All which, they made alike: that is, one Old Man or Father, one Lover, one Courtizan so like another, as if the first of them had begot the rest of every [*each*] sort. *Ex homine hunc natum dicas.* The same custom they observed likewise in their Tragedies.

As for the French. Though they have the word *humeur* among them: yet they have small use of it in their Comedies or Farces: they being but ill imitations of the *ridiculum* or that which stirred up laughter in the Old Comedy. But among the English, 'tis otherwise. Where, by Humour is meant *some extravagant habit, passion, or affection, particular,* as I said before, *to some one person, by the oddness of which, he is immediately distinguished from the rest of men*: which, being lively and naturally represented, most frequently begets that malicious pleasure in the audience, which is testified by laughter: as all things which are deviations from common customs, are ever the aptest to produce it. Though, by the way, this Laughter is only accidental, as the person represented is fantastic or bizarre; but Pleasure is essential to it, as the Imitation of what is natural. This description of these Humours,* drawn from the knowledge and observation of particular persons, was the peculiar genius and talent of BEN. JOHNSON. To whose Play, I now return.

Besides *MOROSE*, there are, at least, nine or ten different Characters and Humours in the *Silent Woman*: all which persons have several concernments of their own; yet are all used by the Poet to the conducting of the main Design to perfection.

I shall not waste time in commending the Writing of this Play: but I will give you my opinion, that there is more Wit and Acuteness of Fancy in it, than in any of BEN.JOHNSON's. Besides that, he has here described the conversation of gentlemen, in the persons of *TRUE WIT* and his friends, with more gaiety, air, and freedom than in the rest of his Comedies.

For the Contrivance of the Plot: 'tis extreme[ly] elaborate;

* Compare DRYDEN's definition of Humour, with that of Lord MACAULAY, in his review of *Diary and Letters of Madame D'ARBLAY* (*Edinburgh Review*, Jan. 1843). E. A. 1880.

and yet, withal, easy.   For the δέσις, or Untying of it : 'tis so
admirable, that, when it is done, no one of the audience would
think the Poet could have missed it ; and yet, it was concealed so much before the last Scene, that any other way
would sooner have entered into your thoughts.

But I dare not take upon me, to commend the Fabric of
it ; because it is altogether so full of Art, that I must unravel
every Scene in it, to commend it as I ought.   And this
excellent contrivance is still the more to be admired ; because
'tis [a] Comedy where the persons are only of common rank ;
and their business, private ; not elevated by passions or high
concernments as in serious Plays.   Here, every one is a
proper judge of what he sees.   Nothing is represented but
that with which he daily converses : so that, by consequence,
all faults lie open to discovery ; and few are pardonable.
'Tis this, which HORACE has judiciously observed—

> *Creditur ex medio quia res arcessit habere*
> *Sudoris minimum, sed habet Comedia tanto*
> *Plus oneris, quanto veniæ minus.*

But our Poet, who was not ignorant of these difficulties, had
prevailed [? *availed*] himself of all advantages ; as he who
designs a large leap, takes his rise from the highest ground.

One of these Advantages is that, which CORNEILLE has
laid down as *the greatest which can arrive* [happen] *to any
Poem* ; and which he, himself, could never compass, above
thrice, in all his plays, viz., *the making choice of some signal
and long expected day ; whereon the action of the Play is to depend.*   This day was that designed by DAUPHINE, for the
settling of his uncle's estate upon him : which to compass,
he contrives to marry him.   That the marriage had been
plotted by him, long beforehand, is made evident, by what
he tells TRUE WIT, in the Second Act, that 'in one moment,
he [TRUE WIT] had destroyed what he had been raising
many months.'

There is another artifice of the Poet, which I cannot here
omit ; because, by the frequent practice of it in his Comedies,
he has left it to us, almost as a Rule : that is, *when he has
any Character or Humour, wherein he would show a* coup de
maître *or his highest skill ; he recommends it to your observation
by a pleasant description of it, before the person first appears.*

Thus, in *Bartholomew Fair*, he gives you the pictures of NUMPS and COKES; and in this, those of DAW, LAFOOLE, MOROSE, and the *Collegiate Ladies* : all which you hear described, before you, see them. So that, before they come upon the Stage, you have a longing expectation of them; which prepares you to receive them favourably : and when they are there, even from their first appearance, you are so far acquainted with them, that nothing of their humour is lost to you.

I will observe yet one thing further of this admirable Plot. The business of it rises in every Act. The Second is greater than the First; the Third, than the Second : and so forward, to the Fifth. There, too, you see, till the very last Scene, new difficulties arising to obstruct the Action of the Play : and when the audience is brought into despair that the business can naturally be effected ; then, and not before, the Discovery is made.

But that the Poet might entertain you with more variety, all this while ; he reserves some new Characters to show you, which he opens not till the Second and Third Acts. In the Second, MOROSE, DAW, *the Barber*, and OTTER ; in the Third, the *Collegiate Ladies*. All which, he moves, afterwards, in by-walks or under-plots, as diversions to the main Design, least it grow tedious : though they are still naturally joined with it ; and, somewhere or other, subservient to it. Thus, like a skilful chess player, by little and little, he draws out his men ; and makes his pawns of use to his greater persons.

If this Comedy and some others of his, were translated into French prose (which would now be no wonder to them, since MOLIERE has lately given them Plays out of Verse; which have not displeased them), I believe the controversy would soon be decided betwixt the two nations : even making them, the judges.

But we need not call our heroes to our aid. Be it spoken to the honour of the English ! our nation can never want, in any age, such, who are able to dispute the Empire of Wit with any people in the universe. And though the fury of a Civil War, and power (for twenty years together [1640–1660 A.D.]) abandoned to a barbarous race of men, enemies of all

good learning,* had buried the Muses under the ruins of
Monarchy : yet, with the Restoration of our happiness [1660],
we see revived Poesy lifting up its head, and already shaking
off the rubbish, which lay so heavy upon it.

We have seen, since His Majesty's return, many
Dramatic Poems which yield not to those of any foreign
nation, and which deserve all laurels but the English. I
will set aside flattery and envy. It cannot be denied but we
have had some little blemish, either in the Plot or Writing
of all those plays which have been made within these seven
years ; and, perhaps, there is no nation in the world so quick
to discern them, or so difficult to pardon them, as ours : yet,
if we can persuade ourselves to use the candour of that Poet
[*HORACE*], who, though the most severe of critics, has left us
this caution, by which to moderate our censures.

Ubi plura nitent in carmine non ego paucis offendar maculis.

If, in consideration of their many and great beauties, we can
wink at some slight and little imperfections ; if we, I say, can
be thus equal to ourselves : I ask no favour from the French.

And if I do not venture upon any particular judgement of
our late Plays : 'tis out of the consideration which an ancient
writer gives me. *Vivorum, ut magna admiratio ita censura
difficilis* ; ' betwixt the extremes of admiration and malice,
'tis hard to judge uprightly of the living.' Only, I think it
may be permitted me to say, that as it is no lessening to us,
to yield to some Plays (and those not many) of our nation,
in the last Age : so can it be no addition, to pronounce of
our present Poets, that *they have far surpassed all the Ancients,
and the Modern Writers of other countries.*"

This, my Lord ! [*i.e., the Dedicatee, the Lord* BUCKHURST,
p. 503] was the substance of what was then spoke, on that
occasion : and LISIDEIUS, I think, was going to reply ; when
he was prevented thus by CRITES.

 AM confident," said he, " the most material things
that can be said, have been already urged, on
either side. If they have not ; I must beg of
LISIDEIUS, that he will defer his answer till

another time.　For I confess I have a joint quarrel to you both: because you have concluded [*pp*. 539, 548], without any reason given for it, that *Rhyme is proper for the Stage*.

I will not dispute how ancient it hath been among us to write this way.　Perhaps our ancestors knew no better, till SHAKESPEARE's time.　I will grant, it was not altogether left by him; and that FLETCHER and BEN. JOHNSON used it frequently in their Pastorals, and sometimes in other Plays.

Farther; I will not argue, whether we received it originally from our own countrymen, or from the French.　For that is an inquiry of as little benefit as theirs, who, in the midst of the Great Plague [1665], were not so solicitous to provide against it; as to know whether we had it from the malignity of our own air, or by transportation from Holland.

I have therefore only to affirm that *it is not allowable in serious Plays*.　For Comedies. I find you are already concluding with me.

To prove this, I might satisfy myself to tell you, *how much in vain it is*, for you, *to strive against the stream of the People's inclination!* the greatest part of whom, are prepossessed so much with those excellent plays of SHAKESPEARE, FLETCHER, and BEN. JOHNSON, which have been written *out* of Rhyme, that (except you could bring them such as were written better *in* it; and those, too, by persons of equal reputation with them) it will be impossible for you to gain your cause with them: who will (still) be judges. This it is to which, in fine, all your reasons must submit. The unanimous consent of an audience is so powerful, that even JULIUS CÆSAR (as MACROBIUS reports of him), when he, was Perpetual Dictator, was not able to balance it, on the other side: but when LABERIUS, a Roman knight, at his request, contended in the *Mime* with another poet; he was forced to cry out, *Etiam favente me victus es Liberi*.

But I will not, on this occasion, take the advantage of the greater number; but only urge such reasons against Rhyme, as I find in the writings of those who have argued for the other way.

First, then, I am of opinion, that Rhyme is unnatural in a Play, because *Dialogue*, there, *is presented as the effect of sudden thought*.　For a Play is the Imitation of Nature: and

since no man, without premeditation, speaks in rhyme;
neither ought he to do it on the Stage.   This hinders not but
the Fancy may be, there, elevated to a higher pitch of
thought than it is in ordinary discourse; for there is a
probability that men of excellent and quick parts, may speak
noble things *ex tempore*: but those thoughts are never fettered
with the numbers and sound of Verse, without study; and
therefore it cannot be but unnatural, *to present the most free
way of speaking, in that which is the most constrained.*

'For this reason,' says ARISTOTLE, ''tis best, to write
Tragedy in that kind of Verse, which is the least such, or
which is nearest Prose': and this, among the Ancients, was
the *Iambic*; and with us, is *Blank Verse, or the Measure of
Verse kept exactly, without rhyme.*   These numbers, therefore,
are fittest for a Play: the others [*i.e., Rhymed Verse*] for a
paper of Verses, or a Poem [*p.* 566].   Blank Verse being as much
below them, as Rhyme is improper for the Drama: and, if
it be objected that neither are Blank Verses made *ex tempore*;
yet, as nearest Nature, they are still to be preferred.

But there are two particular exceptions [*objections*], which
many, beside myself, have had to Verse [*i.e., in rhyme*]; by
which it will appear yet more plainly, how improper it is
in Plays.   And the first of them is grounded upon that very
reason, for which some have commended Rhyme.   They
say, 'The quickness of Repartees in argumentative scenes,
receives an ornament from Verse [*pp.* 492, 498].'   Now,
*what is more unreasonable than to imagine that a man should not
only light upon the Wit, but the Rhyme too; upon the sudden?*
This nicking of him, who spoke before, both in Sound and
Measure, is so great a happiness [*felicity*], that you must, at
least, suppose the persons of your Play to be poets, *Arcades
omnes et cantare pares et respondere parati.*   They must have
arrived to the degree of *quicquid conabar dicere,* to make
verses, almost whether they will or not.

If they are anything below this, it will look rather like
the design of two, than the answer of one.   It will appear
that your Actors hold intelligence together; that they perform their tricks, like fortune tellers, by confederacy.   The
hand of Art will be too visible in it, against that maxim of
all professions, *Ars est celare artem;* 'that it is the greatest
perfection of Art, to keep itself undiscovered.'

Nor will it serve you to object, that however you manage it, 'tis still known to be a Play; and consequently the dialogue of two persons, understood to be the labour of one Poet. For a Play is still an Imitation of Nature. We know we are to be deceived, and we desire to be so: but no man ever was deceived, but with a *probability of Truth*; for who will suffer a gross lie to be fastened upon him? Thus, we sufficiently understand that the scenes [*i.e., the scenery which was just now coming into use on the English Stage*], which represent cities and countries to us, are not really such, but only painted on boards and canvas. But shall that excuse the ill painture [*painting*] or designment of them? Nay rather, ought they not to be laboured with so much the more diligence and exactness, to help the Imagination? since the Mind of Man doth naturally bend to, and seek after Truth; and therefore the nearer anything comes to the Imitation of it, the more it pleases.

Thus, you see! your Rhyme is incapable of expressing the greatest thoughts, naturally; and the lowest, it cannot, with any grace. For what is more unbefitting the majesty of Verse, than 'to call a servant,' or 'bid a door be shut' in Rhyme? And yet, this miserable necessity you are forced upon!

'But Verse,' you say, 'circumscribes a quick and luxuriant Fancy, which would extend itself too far, on every subject; did not the labour which is required to well-turned and polished Rhyme, set bounds to it [*pp*. 492–493].' Yet this argument, if granted, would only prove, that *we may write better in Verse*, but not *more naturally*.

Neither is it able to evince that. For he who *wants* judgement to confine his Fancy, in Blank Verse; may want it as well, in Rhyme: and he who has it, will avoid errors in both kinds [*pp*. 498, 571]. Latin Verse was as great a confinement to the imagination of those poets, as Rhyme to ours: and yet, you find OVID saying too much on every subject.

Nescivit, says SENECA, *quod bene cessit relinquere*: of which he [OVID] gives you one famous instance in his description of the Deluge.

Omnia pontus erat, deerant quoque litora ponto.

Now all was sea; nor had that sea a shore.

Thus OVID's Fancy was not limited by Verse; and VIRGIL needed not Verse to have bounded his.

In our own language, we see BEN. JOHNSON confining himself to what ought to be said, even in the liberty of Blank Verse; and yet CORNEILLE, the most judicious of the French poets, is still varying the same Sense a hundred ways, and dwelling eternally upon the same subject, though confined by Rhyme.

Some other exceptions, I have to Verse; but these I have named, being, for the most part, already public : I conceive it reasonable they should, first, be answered."

"IT concerns me less than any," said NEANDER, seeing he had ended, "to reply to this discourse, because when I should have proved that Verse may be *natural* in Plays; yet I should always be ready to confess that those which I [*i.e.*, DRYDEN, *see pp*. 503, 566] have written in this kind, come short of that perfection which is required. Yet since you are pleased I should undertake this province, I will do it : though, with all imaginable respect and deference both to that Person [*i.e.*, SIR ROBERT HOWARD, *see p*. 494] from whom you have borrowed your strongest arguments; and to whose judgement, when I have said all, I finally submit.

But before I proceed to answer your objections; I must first remember you, that I exclude all Comedy from my defence; and next, that I deny not but Blank Verse may be also used : and content myself only to assert that *in serious Plays*, where the Subject and Characters are great, and the Plot unmixed with mirth (which might allay or divert these concernments which are produced), *Rhyme is there, as natural, and more effectual than Blank Verse.*

And now having laid down this as a foundation : to begin with CRITES, I must crave leave to tell him, that some of his arguments against Rhyme, reach no farther that from *the faults or defects of ill Rhyme* to conclude against *the use of it in general* [*p.* 598]. May not I conclude against Blank Verse, by the same reason ? If the words of some Poets, who write in it, are either ill-chosen or ill-placed ; which makes not only Rhyme, but all kinds of Verse, in any language, unnatural: shall I, for their virtuous affectation, condemn those excellent lines of FLETCHER, which are written in that kind ? Is there anything in Rhyme more constrained, than this line in Blank Verse ?

> I, heaven invoke! and strong resistance make.

Where you see both the clauses are placed unnaturally ; that is, contrary to the common way of speaking, and that, without the excuse of a rhyme to cause it : yet you would think me very ridiculous, if I should accuse the stubbornness of Blank Verse for this ; and not rather, the stiffness of the Poet. Therefore, CRITES ! you must either prove that *words, though well chosen and duly placed, yet render not Rhyme natural in itself*; or that, *however natural and easy the Rhyme may be, yet it is not proper for a Play.*

If you insist on the former part; I would ask you what other conditions are required to make Rhyme natural in itself, besides an election of apt words, and a right disposing of them ? For the due *choice* of your words expresses your Sense naturally, and the due *placing* them adapts the Rhyme to it.

If you object that *one verse may be made for the sake of another, though both the words and rhyme be apt,* I answer it cannot possibly so fall out. For either there is a dependence of sense betwixt the first line and the second; or there is none. If there be that connection, then, in the natural position of the words, the latter line must, of necessity, flow from the former : if there be no dependence, yet, still, the due ordering of words makes the last line as natural in itself as the other. So that the necessity of a rhyme never forces any but bad or lazy writers, to say what they would not otherwise.

'Tis true, there is both care and art required to write in Verse. A good Poet never concludes upon the first line, till he has sought out such a rhyme as may fit the Sense already prepared, to heighten the second. Many times, the Close of the Sense falls into the middle of the next verse, or farther off : and he may often prevail [*avail*] himself of the same advantages in English, which VIRGIL had in Latin ; he may break off in the hemistich, and begin another line.

Indeed, the not observing these two last things, makes Plays that are writ in Verse so tedious : for though, most commonly, the Sense is to be confined to the Couplet ; yet, nothing that does *perpetuo tenore fluere*, ' run in the same channel,' can please always. 'Tis like the murmuring of a stream : which, not varying in the fall, causes at first attention ; at last, drowsiness. VARIETY OF CADENCES is the best Rule ; the greatest help to the Actors, and refreshment to the Audience.

If, then, Verse may be made *natural in itself; how becomes it improper to a Play* ? You say, ' The Stage is the Representation of Nature, and no man, in ordinary conversation, speaks in Rhyme ' : but you foresaw, when you said this, that it might be answered, ' Neither does any man speak in Blank Verse, or in measure without Rhyme !' therefore you concluded, ' That which is nearest Nature is still to be preferred.' But you took no notice that Rhyme might be made as natural as Blank Verse, by the well placing of the words, &c. All the difference between them, when they are both correct, is the sound in one, which the other wants : and if so, the sweetness of it, and all the advantages resulting from it which are handled in the *Preface* to the *Rival Ladies* [*pp*. 487-493], will yet stand good.

As for that place of ARISTOTLE, where he says, ' Plays should be writ in that kind of Verse which is nearest Prose' : it makes little for you, Blank Verse being, properly, but Measured Prose.

Now Measure, alone, in any modern language, does not constitute Verse. Those of the Ancients, in Greek and Latin, consisted in Quantity of Words, and a determinate number of Feet. But when, by the inundations of the Goths and Vandals, into Italy, new languages were brought in, and barbarously mingled with the Latin, of which, the Italian, Spanish, French, and ours (made out of them, and the Teutonic) are dialects : a New Way of Poesy was practised, new, I say, in those countries ; for, in all probability, it was that of the conquerors in their own nations. The New Way consisted of Measure or Number of Feet, *and* Rhyme.

The sweetness of Rhyme and observation of Accent, supplying the place of Quantity in Words: which could neither exactly be observed by those Barbarians who knew not the Rules of it; neither was it suitable to their tongues, as it had been to the Greek and Latin.

No man is tied in Modern Poesy, to observe any farther Rules in the Feet of his Verse, but that they be dissyllables (whether Spondee, Trochee, or Iambic, it matters not); only he is obliged to Rhyme. Neither do the Spanish, French, Italians, or Germans acknowledge at all, or very rarely, any such kind of Poesy as Blank Verse among them. Therefore, at most, 'tis but a Poetic Prose, *a sermo pedestris*; and, as such, most fit for Comedies: where I acknowledge Rhyme to be improper.

Farther, as to that quotation of ARISTOTLE, our Couplet Verses may be rendered *as near* Prose, as Blank Verse itself; by using those advantages I lately named, as Breaks in the Hemistich, or Running the Sense into another line: thereby, making Art and Order appear as loose and free as Nature. Or, not tying ourselves to Couplets strictly, we may use the benefit of the Pindaric way, practised in the *Siege of Rhodes*; where the numbers vary, and the rhyme is disposed carelessly, and far from often chiming.

Neither is that other advantage of the Ancients to be despised, of changing the Kind of Verse, when they please, with the change of the Scene, or some new Entrance. For they confine not themselves always to Iambics; but extend their liberty to all Lyric Numbers; and sometimes, even, to Hexameter.

But I need not go so far, to prove that Rhyme, as it succeeds to all other offices of Greek and Latin Verse, so especially to this of Plays; since the custom of all nations, at this day, confirms it. All the French, Italian, and Spanish Tragedies are generally writ in it; and, sure[ly], the Universal Consent of the most civilised parts of the world ought in this, as it doth in other customs, [to] include the rest.

But perhaps, you may tell me, I have proposed such a way to make Rhyme *natural*; and, consequently, proper to Plays, as is impracticable; and that I shall scarce find six or eight lines together in a Play, where the words are so placed and chosen, as is required to make it *natural*.

I answer, no Poet need constrain himself, at all times, to it. It is enough, he makes it his general rule. For I deny not but sometimes there may be a greatness in placing the words otherwise; and sometimes they may sound better. Sometimes also, the variety itself is excuse enough. But if, for the most part, the words be placed, as they are in the negligence of Prose; it is sufficient to denominate the way *practicable*: for we esteem that to be such, which, in the trial, oftener succeeds than misses. And thus far, you may find the practice made good in many Plays: where, you do not remember still! that if you cannot find six natural Rhymes together; it will be as hard for you to produce as many lines in Blank Verse, even among the greatest of our poets, against which I cannot make some reasonable exception.

And this, Sir, calls to my remembrance the beginning of your discourse, where you told us *we should never find the audience favourable to this kind of writing*, till we could produce as good plays *in* Rhyme, as BEN. JOHNSON, FLETCHER, and SHAKESPEARE had writ *out* of it [*p.* 558]. But it is to raise envy to the Living, to compare them with the Dead. They are honoured, and almost adored by us, as they deserve; neither do I know any so presumptuous of themselves, as to contend with them. Yet give me leave to say thus much, without injury to their ashes, that not only we shall never equal them; but they could never equal themselves, were they to rise, and write again. We acknowledge them our Fathers in Wit: but they have ruined their estates themselves before they came to their children's hands. There is scarce a Humour, a Character, or any kind of Plot; which they have not blown upon. All comes sullied or wasted to us: and were they to entertain this Age, they could not make so plenteous treatments out of such decayed fortunes. This, therefore, will be a good argument to us, either not to write at all; or to attempt some other way. There are no Bays to be expected in their walks, *Tentanda via est qua me quoque possum tollere humo.*

This way of Writing in Verse, they have only left free to us. Our Age is arrived to a perfection in it, which they never knew: and which (if we may guess by what of theirs we have seen in Verse, as the *Faithful Shepherdess* and *Sad*

Shepherd) 'tis probable they never could have reached. For the Genius of every Age is different : and though ours excel in this; I deny not but that to imitate Nature in that perfection which they did in Prose [*i.e., Blank Verse*] is a greater commendation than to write in Verse exactly.

As for what you have added, *that the people are not generally inclined to like this way* : if it were true, it would be no wonder but betwixt the shaking off of an old habit, and the introducing of a new, there should be difficulty. Do we not see them stick to HOPKINS and STERNHOLD's Psalms; and forsake those of DAVID, I mean SANDYS his Translation of them ? If, by the *people*, you understand the Multitude, the οἱ πολλοί; 'tis no matter, what they think ! They are sometimes in the right, sometimes in the wrong. Their judgement is a mere lottery. *Est ubi plebs recte putat, est ubi peccat.* HORACE says it of the Vulgar, judging Poesy. But if you mean, the mixed Audience of the Populace and the Noblesse : I dare confidently affirm, that a great part of the latter sort are already favourable to Verse; and that no serious Plays, written since the King's return [*May* 1660], have been more kindly received by them, than the *Siege of Rhodes*, the *MUSTAPHA*, the *Indian Queen* and *Indian Emperor*. [*See p.* 503.]

But I come now to the Inference of your first argument. You said, ' The dialogue of Plays is presented as the effect of sudden thought; but no one speaks suddenly or, *ex tempore*, in Rhyme ' [*p.* 498] : and your inferred from thence, *that Rhyme*, which you acknowledge to be proper to Epic Poesy [*p.* 559], *cannot equally be proper to Dramatic; unless we could suppose all men born so much more than poets, that verses should be made* in *them, not* by *them.*

It has been formerly urged by you [*p.* 499] and confessed by me [*p.* 563] that ' since no man spoke any kind of verse *ex tempore*; that which was *nearest* Nature was to be preferred.' I answer you, therefore, by distinguishing betwixt what is *nearest* to the nature of Comedy : which is the Imitation of common persons and Ordinary Speaking : and, what is *nearest* the nature of a serious Play. This last is, indeed, the Representation of Nature ; but 'tis Nature wrought up to an higher pitch. The Plot, the Characters, the Wit, the Passions, the Descriptions are all exalted above the level of

common converse [*conversation*], as high as the Imagination
of the Poet can carry them, with proportion to verisimility
[*verisimilitude*].

Tragedy, we know, is wont to Image to us the minds and
fortunes of noble persons: and to pourtray these exactly,
Heroic Rhyme is *nearest* Nature; as being the noblest kind
of Modern Verse.

> *Indignatur enim privatis, et prope socco,*
> *Dignis carminibus narrari cœna THYESTÆ.*

says HORACE. And in another place,

> *Effutire leveis indigna tragœdia versus.*

Blank Verse is acknowledged to be too low for a Poem,
nay more, for a paper of Verses [*pp.* 473, 498, 559]; but if
too low for an ordinary Sonnet, how much more for Tragedy!
which is, by ARISTOTLE, in the dispute between the Epic
Poesy and the Dramatic, (for many reasons he there alleges)
ranked above it.

But setting this defence aside, your argument is almost as
strong against the use of Rhyme in Poems, as in Plays. For
the Epic way is everywhere interlaced with Dialogue or Discoursive Scenes: and, therefore, you must either grant Rhyme
to be improper there, which is contrary to your assertion; or
admit it into Plays, by the same title which you have given
it to Poems.

For though Tragedy be justly preferred above the other,
yet there is a great affinity between them; as may easily be
discovered in that Definition of a Play, which LISIDEIUS gave
us [*p.* 513]. The genus of them is the same, A JUST AND
LIVELY IMAGE OF HUMAN NATURE, IN ITS
ACTIONS, PASSIONS, AND TRAVERSES OF
FORTUNE: so is the End, namely, FOR THE DE-
LIGHT AND BENEFIT OF MANKIND. The
Characters and Persons are still the same, viz., the greatest
of both sorts: only the *manner of acquainting us* with those
actions, passions, and fortunes is different. Tragedy performs
it, *viva voce*, or by Action in Dialogue: wherein it excels the
Epic Poem; which does it, chiefly, by Narration, and there-
fore is not so lively an Image of Human Nature. However,

the agreement betwixt them is such, that if Rhyme be proper for one, it must be for the other.

Verse, 'tis true, is not 'the effect of Sudden Thought.' But this hinders not, that Sudden Thought may be represented in Verse: since those thoughts are such, as must be higher than Nature can raise them without premeditation, especially, to a continuance of them, even out of Verse: and, consequently, you cannot imagine them, to have been sudden, either in the Poet or the Actors.

A Play, as I have said, to be like Nature, is to be set above it; as statues which are placed on high, are made greater than the life, that they may descend to the sight, in their just proportion.

Perhaps, I have insisted too long upon this objection; but the clearing of it, will make my stay shorter on the rest.

You tell us, CRITES! that 'Rhyme is most unnatural in Repartees or Short Replies: when he who answers, it being presumed he knew not what the other would say, yet makes up that part of the Verse which was left incomplete; and supplies both the sound and the measure of it. This,' you say, 'looks rather like the Confederacy of two, than the Answer of one.'

This, I confess, is an objection which is in every one's mouth, who loves not Rhyme; but suppose, I beseech you! the Repartee were made only in Blank Verse; might not part of the same argument be turned against you? For the measure is as often supplied there, as it is in Rhyme: the latter half of the hemistich as commonly made up, or a second line subjoined as a reply to the former; which any one leaf in JOHNSON's Plays will sufficiently make clear to you.

You will often find in the Greek Tragedians, and in SENECA; that when a Scene grows up into the warmth of Repartees, which is the close fighting of it, the latter part of the trimeter is supplied by him who answers: and yet it was never observed as a fault in them, by any of the Ancient or Modern critics. The case is the same in our verse, as it was in theirs: Rhyme to us, being in lieu of Quantity to them.

But if no latitude is to be allowed a Poet; you take from him, not only his license of *quidlibet audendi*: but you tie him up in a straighter compass than you would a Philosopher.

This is, indeed, *Musas colere severiores*. You would have him follow Nature, but he must follow her on foot. You have dismounted him from his *Pegasus*!

But you tell us 'this supplying the last half of a verse, or adjoining a whole second to the former, looks more like the Design of two, than the Answer of one [*pp.*498, 559].' Suppose we acknowledge it. How comes this Confederacy to be more displeasing to you, than a dance which is well contrived? You see there, the united Design of many persons to make up one Figure. After they have separated themselves in many petty divisions; they rejoin, one by one, into the gross. The Confederacy is plain amongst them; for Chance could never produce anything so beautiful, and yet there is nothing in it that shocks your sight.

I acknowledge that the hand of Art appears in Repartee, as, of necessity, it must in all kind[s] of Verse. But there is, also, the quick and poignant brevity of it (which is a high Imitation of Nature, in those sudden gusts of passion) to mingle with it: and this joined with the cadency and sweetness of the Rhyme, leaves nothing in the Soul of the Hearer to desire. 'Tis an Art which *appears*; but it *appears* only like the shadowings of painture [*painting*], which, being to cause the rounding of it, cannot be absent: but while that is considered, they are lost. So while we attend to the other beauties of the Matter, the care and labour of the Rhyme is carried from us; or, at least, drowned in its own sweetness, as bees are some times buried in their honey.

When a Poet has found the Repartee; the last perfection he can add to it, is to put it into Verse. However good the Thought may be, however apt the Words in which 'tis couched; yet he finds himself at a little unrest, while Rhyme is wanting. He cannot leave it, till that comes naturally; and then is at ease, and sits down contented.

From Replies, which are the most *elevated* thoughts of Verse, you pass to the most *mean* ones, those which are common with the lowest of household conversation. In these you say, the majesty of the Verse suffers. You instance in "the calling of a servant" or "commanding a door to be shut" in Rhyme. This, CRITES! is a good observation of yours; but no argument. For it proves no more, but that such thoughts should be waved, as often as may be, by the address of the Poet.   But suppose they *are* necessary in the places where he uses them ; yet there is no need to put them into rhyme.   He may place them in the beginning of a verse and break it off, as unfit (when so debased) for any other use: or granting the worst, that they require more room than the hemistich will allow ; yet still, there is a choice to be made of best words and least vulgar (provided they be apt) to express such thoughts.

Many have blamed Rhyme in general for this fault, when the Poet, with a little care, might have redressed it : but they do it, with no more justice, than if English Poesy should be made ridiculous, for the sake of [JOHN TAYLOR] the Water Poet's rhymes.

Our language is noble, full, and significant ; and I know not why he who is master of it, may not clothe ordinary things in it, as decently as the Latin ; if he use the same diligence in his choice of words.

Delectus verborum origo est eloquentiæ was the saying of JULIUS CÆSAR ; one so curious in his, that none of them can be changed but for the worse.

One would think "Unlock the door !" was a thing as vulgar as could be spoken ; and yet SENECA could make it sound high and lofty, in his Latin—

Reserate clusos regii postes Laris.

But I turn from this exception, both because it happens not above twice or thrice in any Play, that those vulgar thoughts are used : and then too, were there no other apology to be made, yet the necessity of them (which is, alike, in all kind[s] of writing) may excuse them.   Besides that, the great eagerness and precipitation with which they are spoken, makes us rather mind the substance than the dress ; that for which they are spoken, rather than what is spoke[n].   For they are always the effect of some hasty concernment ; and something of consequence depends upon them.

Thus, CRITES ! I have endeavoured to answer your objections.   It remains only that I should vindicate an argument for Verse, which you have gone about to overthrow.

It had formerly been said [*p. 492*] that, 'The easiness of

Blank Verse renders the Poet too luxuriant; but that the labour of Rhyme bounds and circumscribes an over fruitful fancy: the Sense there being commonly confined to the Couplet; and the words so ordered that the Rhyme naturally follows them, not they, the Rhyme.'

To this, you answered, that 'It was no argument to the question in hand: for the dispute was not which way *a man may write best*; but which is *most proper for the subject on which he writes.*'

First. Give me leave, Sir, to remember you! that the argument on which you raised this objection was only secondary. It was built upon the hypothesis, that to write in Verse was proper for serious Plays. Which supposition being granted (as it was briefly made out in that discourse, by shewing how Verse might be made *natural*): it asserted that this way of writing was a help to the Poet's judgement, by putting bounds to a wild, overflowing Fancy. I think therefore it will not be hard for me to make good what it was to prove.

But you add, that, 'Were this let pass; yet he who wants judgement in the liberty of the Fancy, may as well shew the defect of it, when he is confined to Verse: for he who has judgement, will avoid errors; and he who has it not will commit them in all kinds of writing.'

This argument, as you have taken it from a most acute person, so I confess it carries much weight in it. But by using the word Judgement here indefinitely, you seem to have put a fallacy upon us. I grant he who has judgement, that is, so profound, so strong, so infallible a judgement that he needs no helps to keep it always poised and upright, will commit no faults; either in Rhyme, or out of it: and, on the other extreme, he who has a judgement so weak and crazed, that no helps can correct or amend it, shall write scurvily out of Rhyme; and worse in it. But the first of these Judgements, is nowhere to be found; and the latter is not fit to write at all.

To speak, therefore, of Judgement as it is in the best Poets; they who have the greatest proportion of it, want other helps than from it within: as, for example, you would be loath to say that he who was endued with a sound judgement, had no need of history, geography, or moral philosophy, to write correctly.

Judgement is, indeed, the Master Workman in a Play; but he requires many subordinate hands, many tools to his assistance. And Verse, I affirm to be one of these. 'Tis a ' Rule and Line' by which he keeps his building compact and even; which, otherwise, lawless Imagination would raise, either irregularly or loosely. At least, if the Poet commits errors with this help; he would make greater and more without it. 'Tis, in short, a slow and painful, but the surest kind of working.

OVID, whom you accuse [p. 561] for luxuriancy in Verse, had, perhaps, been farther guilty of it, had he writ in Prose. And for your instance of BEN. JOHNSON [p. 561]; who, you say, writ exactly, without the help of Rhyme: you are to remember, 'tis only an aid to a *luxuriant* Fancy; which his was not [p. 551]. As he did not want Imagination; so, none ever said he had much to spare. Neither was Verse then refined so much, to be a help to that Age as it is to ours.

Thus then, the second thoughts being usually the best, as receiving the maturest digestion from judgement; and the last and most mature product of those thoughts, being artfull and laboured Verse: it may well be inferred, that Verse is a great help to a luxuriant Fancy. And this is what that argument, which you opposed, was to evince.

NEANDER was pursuing this discourse so eagerly that EUGENIUS had called to him twice or thrice, ere he took notice that the barge stood still; and that they were at the foot of Somerset Stairs, where they had appointed it to land.

The company were all sorry to separate so soon, though a great part of the evening was already spent: and stood a while, looking back upon the water; which the moonbeams played upon, and made it appear like floating quicksilver.

At last, they went up, through a crowd of French people, who were merrily dancing in the open air, and nothing concerned for the noise of the guns, which had alarmed the Town that afternoon.

Walking thence together to the Piazza, they parted there, EUGENIUS and LISIDEIUS, to some pleasant appointment they had made; and CRITES and NEANDER to their several lodgings.

FINIS.

The Honourable Sir ROBERT HOWARD, Auditor of the Exchequer.

Preface to *The great Favourite, or the Duke of LERMA.*

[Published in 1668.]

TO THE READER.

CANNOT plead the usual excuse for publishing this trifle, which is commonly the subject of most Prefaces, by charging it upon the importunity of friends; for I confess I was myself willing, at the first desire of Mr. HERRINGMAN [*the Publisher*], to print it: not for any great opinion that I had entertained; but for the opinion that others were pleased to express. Which, being told me by some friends, I was concerned to let the World judge what subject matter of offence was contained in it. Some were pleased to believe little of it mine; but they are both obliging to me, though perhaps not intentionally: the last, by thinking there was anything in it that was worth so ill designed an envy, as to place it to another author; the others, perhaps the best bred Informers, by continuing their displeasure towards me, since I most gratefully acknowledge to have received some advantage in the opinion of the sober part of the World, by the loss of theirs.

For the subject, I came accidentally to write upon it. For a gentleman brought a Play to the King's Company, called, *The Duke of LERMA*; and, by them, I was desired to peruse it, and return my opinion, "Whether I thought it fit for the Stage!" After I had read it, I acquainted them that, "In my judgement, it would not be of much use for such a design, since the Contrivance scarce would merit the name of a Plot; and some of that, assisted by a disguise : and it ended abruptly. And on the person of PHILIP III., there was fixed such a mean Character ; and on the daughter of the Duke of LERMA, such a vicious one : that I could not but judge it unfit to be presented by any that had a respect, not only to Princes, but indeed, to either Man or Woman."

And, about that time, being to go in the country, I was persuaded by Mr. HART to make it my diversion there, that so great a hint might not be lost, as the Duke of LERMA saving himself, in his last extremity, by his unexpected disguise : which is as well in the true Story [*history*], as the old Play. And besides that and the Names ; my altering the most part of the Characters, and the whole Design, made me uncapable to use much more, though, perhaps, written with higher Style and Thoughts than I could attain to.

I intend not to trouble myself nor the World any more in such subjects ; but take my leave of these my too long acquaintances : since that little Fancy and Liberty I once enjoyed, is now fettered in business of more unpleasant natures. Yet, were I free to apply my thoughts, as my own choice directed them ; I should hardly again venture into the Civil Wars of Censures.

Ubi . . . Nullos habitura triumphos.

In the next place. I must ingeniously confess that the manner of Plays, which now are in most esteem, is beyond my power to perform [*p.* 587]; nor do I condemn, in the least, anything, of what nature soever, that pleases ; since nothing could appear to me a ruder folly, than to censure the satisfaction of others. I rather blame the unnecessary understanding of some, that have laboured to give strict Rules to things that are not mathematical ; and, with such eagerness, pursuing their own seeming reasons, that, at last, we are to apprehend such Argumentative Poets will grow as strict as SANCHO PANZA's Doctor was, to our very appetites : for in the difference of Tragedy and Comedy, and of Fars [*farce*] itself, there can be no determination, but by the taste ; nor in the manner of their composure. And, who-

ever would endeavour to like or dislike, by the Rules of
others; he will be as unsuccessful, as if he should try to be
persuaded into a power of believing, not what he must, but
what others direct him to believe.

But I confess, 'tis not necessary for Poets to study strict
Reason: since they are so used to a greater latitude [*pp*. 568,
588], than is allowed by that severe Inquisition, that they
must infringe their own Jurisdiction, to profess themselves
obliged to argue well. I will not, therefore, pretend to say,
why I writ this Play, some Scenes in Blank Verse, others in
Rhyme; since I have no better a reason to give than Chance,
which waited upon my present Fancy: and I expect no
better reason from any Ingenious Person, than his Fancy,
for which he best relishes.

I cannot, therefore, but beg leave of the Reader, to take a
little notice of the great pains the author of an *Essay of Dramatic Poesy* has taken, to prove " Rhyme as *natural* in a serious
Play, and more *effectual* than Blank Verse" [*pp*.561, 581]. Thus
he states the question, but pursues that which he calls *natural*,
in a wrong application: for 'tis not the question, whether
Rhyme or not Rhyme be best or most natural for a grave or
serious Subject: but what is *nearest the nature* of that which
it presents.

Now, after all the endeavours of that Ingenious Person, a
Play will still be supposed to be a Composition of several persons speaking *ex tempore* and 'tis as certain, that good verses
are the hardest things that can be imagined, to be so spoken
[*p*. 582]. So that if any will be pleased to impose the rule of
measuring things to be the best, by *being nearest* Nature;
it is granted, by consequence, that which is most remote from
the thing supposed, must needs be most improper: and, therefore, I may justly say, that both I and the question were
equally mistaken. For I do own I had rather read good verses,
than either Blank Verse or Prose; and therefore the author
did himself injury, if he like Verse so well in Plays, to lay down
Rules to raise arguments, only unanswerable against himself.

But the same author, being filled with the precedents of
the Ancients writing their Plays in Verse, commends the
thing; and assures us that "our language is noble, full, and
significant," charging all defects upon the ill placing of words;

and proves it, by quoting SENECA loftily expressing such an ordinary thing, as "shutting a door."

Reserate clusos regii postes Laris.

I suppose he was himself highly affected with the sound of these words. But to have completed his Dictates [*injunctions*]; together with his arguments, he should have obliged us by charming our ears with such an art of placing words, as, in an English verse, to express so loftily "the shutting of a door" : that we might have been as much affected with the sound of his words.

This, instead of being an argument upon the question, rightly stated, is an attempt to prove, that Nothing may seem Something by the help of a verse ; which I easily grant to be the ill fortune of it : and therefore, the question being so much mistaken, I wonder to see that author trouble himself twice about it, with such an absolute Triumph declared by his own imagination. But I have heard that a gentleman in Parliament, going to speak twice, and being interrupted by another member, as against the Orders of the House : he was excused, by a third [member] assuring the House he had not yet spoken to the question.

But, if we examine the General Rules laid down for Plays by strict Reason ; we shall find the errors equally gross: for the great Foundation that is laid to build upon, is Nothing, as it is generally stated ; which will appear on the examination of the particulars.

First. We are told the Plot should not be so ridiculously contrived, as to crowd several Countries into one Stage. Secondly, to cramp the accidents of many years or days, into the Representation of two hours and a half. And, lastly, a conclusion drawn that the only remaining dispute, is concerning Time ; whether it should be contained in twelve or four and twenty hours ; and the Place to be limited to the spot of ground, either in town or city, where the Play is supposed to begin [*p.* 531]. And this is called *nearest* to Nature. For that is concluded most natural, which is most *probable*, and *nearest* to that which it presents.

I am so well pleased with any ingenious offers, as all these

are, that I should not examine this strictly, did not the confidence of others force me to it: there being not anything
more unreasonable to my judgement, than the attempts to infringe the Liberty of Opinion by Rules so little demonstrative.

To shew, therefore, upon what ill grounds, they dictate Laws
for Dramatic Poesy; I shall endeavour to make it evident that
there's no such thing, as what they All pretend [*p.* 592]. For, if
strictly and duly weighed, 'tis as impossible for one Stage to
represent two houses or two rooms truly, as two countries or
kingdoms; and as impossible that five hours or four and
twenty hours should be two hours and a half, as that a
thousand hours or years should be less than what they are,
or the greatest part of time to be comprehended in the less.
For *all* being impossible; they are none of them nearest the
Truth, or nature of what they present. For impossibilities
are all equal, and admit no degrees. And, then, if all those
Poets that have so fervently laboured to give Rules as
Maxims, would but be pleased to abbreviate; or endure to
hear their Reasons reduced into one strict Definition; it must
be, That there are *degrees* in impossibilities, and that many
things, which are not possible, may yet be more or less impossible; and from this, proceed to give Rules to observe the
least absurdity in things, which are not at all.

I suppose, I need not trouble the Reader, with so impertinent a delay, to attempt a further confutation of such ill
grounded Reasons, than, thus, by opening the true state of
the case. Nor do I design to make any further use of it, than
from hence, to draw this modest conclusion:

That I would have all attempts of this nature, be submitted
to the Fancy of others; and bear the name of Propositions [*p.*
590], not of confident Laws, or Rules made by demonstration.

And, then, I shall not discommend any Poet that dresses
his Play in such a fashion as his Fancy best approves: and
fairly leave it for others to follow, if it appears to them most
convenient and fullest of ornament.

But, writing this *Epistle*, in much haste; I had almost
forgot one argument or observation, which that author has
most good fortune in. It is in his *Epistle Dedicatory*, before
his *Essay of Dramatic Poesy*, where, speaking of Rhymes in
Plays, he desires it may be observed, "That none are

H   7

violent against it ; but such as have not attempted it; or who have succeeded ill in the attempt [*pp.* 503, 539, 598]," which, as to myself and him, I easily acknowledge : for I confess none has written, in that way, better than himself; nor few worse than I. Yet, I hope he is so ingenious, that he would not wish this argument should extend further than to him and me. For if it should be received as a good one : all Divines and Philosophers would find a readier way of confutation than they yet have done, of any that should oppose the least Thesis or Definition, by saying, " They were denied by none but such as never attempted to write, or succeeded ill in the attempt."

Thus, as I am one, that am extremely well pleased with most of the *Propositions*, which are ingeniously laid down in that *Essay*, for regulating the Stage : so I am also always concerned for the true honour of Reason, and would have no spurious issue fathered upon her Fancy, may be allowed her wantonness.

But Reason is always pure and chaste : and, as it resembles the sun, in making all things clear ; it also resembles it, in its several positions. When it shines in full height, and directly ascendant over any subject, it leaves but little shadow : but, when descended and grown low, its oblique shining renders the shadow larger than the substance ; and gives the deceived person [*i.e.*, DRYDEN] a wrong measure of his own proportion.

Thus, begging the Reader's excuse, for this seeming impertinency ; I submit what I have written to the liberty of his unconfined opinion : which is all the favour I ask of others, to afford me.

JOHN DRYDEN.

A Defence of An Essay of Dramatic Poesy.

Being an Answer to the Preface of *The great Favourite or the Duke of* LERMA.

[Prefaced to the Second Edition of *The Indian Emperor.* 1668.]

HE former Edition of the *Indian Emperor*, being full of faults, which had escaped the printer; I have been willing to overlook this Second with more care : and, though I could not allow myself so much time as was necessary, yet, by that little I have done, the press is freed from some gross errors which it had to answer for before.

As for the more material faults of writing, which are properly mine; though I see many of them, I want leisure to amend them. 'Tis enough for those, who make one Poem the business of their lives, to leave that correct; yet, excepting VIRGIL, I never met with any which was so, in any language.

But while I was thus employed about this impression, there came to my hands, a new printed Play, called, *The great Favourite, or the Duke of* LERMA. The author of which, a noble and most ingenious Person, has done me the favour to make some observations and animadversions upon my *Dramatic Essay.*

I must confess he might have better consulted his reputation, than by matching himself with so weak an adversary. But if his honour be diminished in the choice of his antagonist, it is sufficiently recompensed in the election of his

cause : which being the weaker, in all appearance (as combating the received opinions of the best Ancient and Modern
authors), will add to his glory, if he overcome ; and to the
opinion of his generosity, if he be vanquished, since he
engages at so great odds, and so (like a Cavalier) undertakes
the protection of the weaker party.

I have only to fear, on my own behalf, that so good a
cause as mine, may not suffer by my ill management or weak
defence ; yet I cannot, in honour, but take the glove, when
'tis offered me : though I am only a Champion, by succession;
and, no more able to defend the right of ARISTOTLE and
HORACE, than an infant DYMOCK, to maintain the title of
a King.

For my own concernment in the controversy, it is so
small, that I can easily be contented to be driven from a few
Notions of Dramatic Poesy, especially by one who has the
reputation of understanding all things [!] : and I might justly
make that excuse for my yielding to him, which the Philosopher made to the Emperor, "Why should I offer to contend
with him, who is Master of more than twenty Legions of
Arts and Sciences ! " But I am forced to fight, and therefore it will be no shame to be overcome.

Yet, I am so much his servant as not to meddle with
anything which does not concern *me* in his Preface. Therefore, I leave the good sense, and other excellencies of the
first twenty lines [*i.e., of the Preface, see p.* 573] to be considered by the critics.

As for the Play of *The Duke of* LERMA; having so much
al ered and beautified it, as he has done, it can be justly
belong to none but him. Indeed, they must be extreme[ly]
ignorant as well as envious, who would rob him of that
honour : for you see him putting in his claim to it, even in
the first two lines.

> *Repulse upon repulse, like waves thrown back,*
> *That slide to hang upon obdurate rocks.*

After this, let Detraction do its worst ! for if this be not his, it deserves to be. For my part, I declare for Distributive Justice! and from this, and what follows, he certainly deserves *those advantages*, which he acknowledges, to *have received from the opinion of sober men.*

In the next place, I must beg leave to observe his great address in courting the Reader to his party. For, intending to assault all Poets both Ancient and Modern, he discovers not his whole Design at once; but seems only to aim at me, and attack me on my weakest side, my Defence of Verse.

To begin with me. He gives me the compellation of "The Author of a *Dramatic Essay*"; which is a little Discourse in dialogue, for the most part borrowed from the observations of others. Therefore, that I may not be wanting to him in civility, I return his compliment, by calling him, "The Author of *The Duke of LERMA.*"

But, that I may pass over his salute, he takes notice [*p.* 575] of my great pains to prove "Rhyme as *natural* in a serious Play; and more *effectual* that Blank Verse" [*p.* 561]. Thus, indeed, I did state the question, but he tells me, *I pursue that which I call* natural, *in a wrong application; for 'tis not the question whether* Rhyme *or* not Rhyme *be best or most natural for a serious Subject; but what is nearest the nature of that it represents.*

If I have formerly mistaken the question; I must confess my ignorance so far, as to say I continue still in my mistake. But he ought to have proved that I mistook it; for 'tis yet but *gratis dictum.* I still shall think I have gained my point, if I can prove that "Rhyme is best or most *natural* for a serious Subject."

As for the question, as he states it, "Whether Rhyme be nearest the nature of what it represents"; I wonder he should think me so ridiculous as to dispute whether Prose or Verse be nearest to ordinary conversation?

It still remains for him, to prove his Inference, that, Since Verse is granted to be more remote than Prose from ordinary conversation; therefore no serious Plays ought to be writ in Verse: and when he clearly makes that good, I will acknowledge his victory as absolute as he can desire it.

The question now is, which of us two has mistaken it?

And if it appear I have not, the World will suspect *what gentle-man that was, who was allowed to speak twice in Parliament, because he had not yet spoken to the question* [*p.* 576]: and, per-haps, conclude it to be the same, who (as 'tis reported) maintained a contradiction *in terminis*, in the face of three hundred persons.

But to return to Verse. Whether it be natural or not in Plays, is a problem which is not demonstrable, of either side. 'Tis enough for me, that he acknowledges that he had rather read good Verse than Prose [*p.* 575]: for if all the enemies of Verse will confess as much, I shall not need to prove that it is *natural*. I am satisfied, if it cause Delight; for Delight is the chief, if not the only end of Poesy. Instruction can be admitted but in the second place; for Poesy only instructs as it delights.

'Tis true, that to Imitate Well is a Poet's work: but to affect the soul, and excite the passions, and, above all, to move Admiration [*wondering astonishment*] (which is the Delight of serious Plays), a bare Imitation will not serve. The converse [*conversation*] therefore, which a Poet is to *imitate*, must be *heightened* with all the arts and ornaments of Poesy; and must be such as, *strictly considered*, could never be supposed [to be] spoken by any, without premeditation.

As for what he urges, that, *A Play will still be supposed to be a composition of several persons speaking* ex tempore ; *and that good verses are the hardest things, which can be imagined, to be so spoken* [*p.*575]: I must crave leave to dissent from his opinion, as to the former part of it. For, if I am not deceived, A Play is supposed to be the work of the Poet, *imitating* or *representing* the conversation of several persons: and this I think to be as clear, as he thinks the contrary.

But I will be bolder, and do not doubt to make it good, though a paradox, that, One great reason why Prose is not to be used in serious Plays is because it is too near the nature of converse [*conversation*]. There may be too great a likeness. As the most skilful painters affirm there may be too near a resemblance in a picture. To take every lineament and feature is not to make an excellent piece, but to take so much only as will make a beautiful resemblance of the whole; and,

with an ingenious flattery of Nature, to heighten the beauties
of some parts, and hide the deformities of the rest. For so,
says HORACE—

> *Ut pictura Poesis erit*
> *Hæc amat obscurum; vult hæc sub luce videri,*
> *Judicis argutum quæ non formidat acumen.*
> > *Et quæ*
> *Desperat, tractata nitescere posse, relinquit.*

In *Bartholomew Fair*, or the lowest kind of Comedy, that
degree of heightening is used which is proper to set off that
subject. 'Tis true, the author was not there to go out of
Prose, as he does in his higher arguments of Comedy, the
Fox and *Alchemist*; yet he does so raise his matter in that
Prose, as to render it delightful: which he could never have
performed had he only said or done those very things that
are daily spoken or practised in the Fair. For then, the Fair
itself would be as full of pleasure to an Ingenious Person, as
the Play; which we manifestly see it is not: but he hath
made an excellent Lazar of it. The copy is of price, though
the origin be vile.

You see in *CATILINE* and *SEJANUS*; where the argument
is great, he sometimes ascends to Verse, which shews he
thought it not unnatural in serious Plays: and had his genius
been as proper for Rhyme as it was for Humour, or had the
Age in which he lived, attained to as much knowledge in
Verse, as ours; 'tis probable he would have adorned those
Subjects with that kind of writing.

Thus PROSE, though the rightful Prince, yet is, by
common consent, deposed; as too weak for the Government
of serious Plays: and he failing, there now start up two
competitors! one, the nearer in blood, which is BLANK
VERSE; the other, more fit for the ends of Government,
which is RHYME. BLANK VERSE is, indeed, the
nearer PROSE; but he is blemished with the weakness of
his predecessor. RHYME (for I will deal clearly!) has
somewhat of the Usurper in him; but he is brave and
generous, and his dominion pleasing. For this reason of
Delight, the Ancients (whom I will still believe as wise as
those who so confidently correct them) wrote all their

Tragedies in Verse: though they knew it most remote from conversation.

But I perceive I am falling into the danger of another rebuke from my opponent : for when I plead that " the Ancients used Verse," I prove not that, They would have admitted Rhyme, had it then been written.

All I can say, is, That it seems to have succeeded Verse, by the general consent of Poets in all modern languages. For almost all their serious Plays are written in it : which, though it be no Demonstration that therefore it ought to be so ; yet, at least, the Practice first, and then the Continuation of it shews that it attained the end, which was, to Please. And if that cannot be compassed here, I will be the first who shall lay it down.

For I confess my chief endeavours are *to delight the Age in which I live* [*p.* 582]. If the Humour of this, be for Low Comedy, small Accidents [*Incidents*], and Raillery ; I will force my genius to obey it : though, with more reputation, I could write in Verse. I know, I am not so fitted, by nature, to write Comedy. I want that gaiety of Humour which is required to it. My conversation is dull and slow. My Humour is saturnine and reserved. In short, I am none of those, who endeavour to break jests in company, or make repartees. So that those who decry my Comedies, do me no injury, except it be in point of profit. Reputation in *them* is the last thing to which I shall pretend.

I beg pardon for entertaining the reader with so ill a subject : but before I quit that argument, which was the cause of this digression ; I cannot but take notice how I am corrected for my quotation of SENECA, in my defence of Plays in Verse.

My words were these [*p.* 570]: "Our language is noble, full, and significant ; and I know not why he, who is master of it, may not clothe ordinary things in it, as decently as the Latin ; if he use the same diligence in his *choice of words*."

One would think, " Unlock the door," was a thing as vulgar as could be spoken : yet SENECA could make it sound high and lofty in his Latin.

Reserate clusos regii postes Laris

But he says of me, *That being filled with the precedents of the Ancients who Writ their Plays in Verse, I commend the thing; declaring our language to be full, noble, and significant, and charging all the defects upon the* ill placing of words; *which I prove by quoting* SENECA's *loftily expressing such an ordinary thing as* shutting the door.

Here he manifestly mistakes. For I spoke not of the Placing, but the Choice of words: for which I quoted that aphorism of JULIUS CÆSAR, *Delectus verborum est origo eloquentiæ.* But *delectus verborum* is no more Latin for the "Placing of words;" than *Reserate* is Latin for "*Shut* the the door!" as he interprets it; which I, ignorantly, construed "*Unlock* or *open* it!"

He supposes I was highly affected with the Sound of these words; and I suppose I may more justly imagine it of him: for if he had not been extremely satisfied with the Sound, he would have minded the Sense a little better.

But these are, now, to be no faults. For, ten days after his book was published, and that his mistakes are grown so famous that they are come back to him, he sends his *Errata* to be printed, and annexed to his Play; and desires that instead of *Shutting*, you should read *Opening*, which, it seems, was the printer's fault. I wonder at his modesty! that he did not rather say it was SENECA's or mine: and that in some authors, *Reserate* was to *Shut* as well as to *Open*; as the word *Barach*, say the learned, is [*in Hebrew*] both to *Bless* and *Curse*.

Well, since it was the printer['s fault]; he was a naughty man, to commit the same mistake twice in six lines.

I warrant you! *Delectus verborum* for *Placing* of words, was his mistake too; though the author forgot to tell him of it. If it were my book, I assure you it should [be]. For those rascals ought to be the proxies of every Gentleman-Author; and to be chastised fòr him, when he is not pleased to own an error.

Yet, since he has given the *Errata*, I wish he would have enlarged them only a few sheets more; and then he would have spared me the labour of an answer. For this cursed printer is so given to mistakes, that there is scarce a sentence in the Preface without some false grammar, or hard sense [*i.e., difficulty in gathering the meaning*] in it; which will all be

charged upon the Poet: because he is so good natured as
to lay but three errors to the Printer's account, and to take
the rest upon himself; who is better able to support them.
But he needs not [to] apprehend that I should strictly
examine those little faults; except I am called upon to do it.
I shall return, therefore, to that quotation of SENECA; and
answer not to what he *writes*, but to what he *means*.

I never intended it as an Argument, but only as an Illustration of what I had said before [*p.* 570] concerning the
Election of words. And all he can charge me with, is only this,
That if SENECA could make an ordinary thing sound well in
Latin by the choice of words; the same, with like care, might
be performed in English. If it cannot, I have committed
an error on the right hand, by commending too much, the
copiousness and well sounding of our language: which I hope
my countrymen will pardon me. At least, the words which
follow in my *Dramatic Essay* will plead somewhat in my behalf. For I say there [*p.* 570], That this objection happens
but seldom in a Play; and then too, either the meanness of
the expression may be avoided, or shut out from the verse by
breaking it in the midst.

But I have said too much in the Defence of Verse. For,
after all, 'tis a very indifferent thing to me, whether it obtain
or not. I am content, hereafter to be ordered by his rule,
that is, "to write it, sometimes, because it pleases me"
[*p.* 575]; and so much the rather, because "he has declared
that it pleases him."

But, he has taken his last farewell of the Muses; and he
has done it civilly, by honouring them with the name of *his
long acquaintances* [*p.* 574]: which is a compliment they have
scarce deserved from him.

For my own part, I bear a share in the public loss; and
how emulous soever I may be, of his Fame and Reputation,
I cannot but give this testimony of his Style, that it is extreme[ly] poetical, even in Oratory; his Thoughts elevated,
sometimes above common apprehension; his Notions politic
and grave, and tending to the instruction of Princes and reformation of State: that they are abundantly interlaced with
variety of fancies, tropes, and figures, which the Critics have

enviously branded with the name of Obscurity and False Grammar.

Well, *he is now fettered in business of more unpleasant nature* [*p.* 574]. The Muses have lost him, but the Commonwealth gains by it. The corruption of a Poet is the generation of a Statesman.

He will not venture again into the Civil Wars of Censure [Criticism].

> *Ubi . . . . nullos habitura triumphos.*

If he had not told us, he had left the Muses; we might have half suspected it by that word, *ubi*, which does not any way belong to *them*, in that place. The rest of the verse is indeed LUCAN's: but that *ubi*, I will answer for it, is his own.

Yet he has another reason for this disgust of Poesy. For he says, immediately after, that *the manner of Plays which are now in most esteem, is beyond his power to perform* [*p.* 574]. To *perform* the *manner* of a thing, is new English to me.

However he condemns not the satisfaction of others, but rather their unnecessary understanding; who, like SANCHO PANZA's Doctor, prescribe too strictly to our appetites. For, says he, *in the difference of Tragedy and Comedy and of Farce itself; there can be no determination but by the taste; nor in the manner of their composure.*

We shall see him, now, as great a Critic as he was a Poet: and the reason why he excelled so much in Poetry will be evident; for it will have proceeded from the exactness of his Judgement.

In the difference of Tragedy, Comedy, and Farce itself; there can be no determination but by the taste. I will not quarrel with the obscurity of this phrase, though I justly might: but beg his pardon, if I do not rightly understand him. If he means that there is no essential difference betwixt Comedy, Tragedy, and Farce; but only what is made by people's taste, which distinguishes one of them from the other: that is so manifest an error, that I need lose no time to contradict it.

Were there neither Judge, Taste, or Opinion in the world; yet they would differ in their natures. For the Action,

Character, and Language of Tragedy would still be great and high : that of Comedy, lower and more familiar. Admiration would be the Delight of the one : Satire, of the other.

I have but briefly touched upon these things ; because, whatever his words are, I can scarce[ly] imagine that *he who is always concerned for the true honour of Reason, and would have no spurious issue fathered upon her* [*p.* 578], should mean anything so absurd, as to affirm *that there is no difference between Comedy and Tragedy, but what is made by taste only* : unless he would have us understand the Comedies of my Lord L. [?] ; where the First Act should be *Potages*, the Second, *Fricasses, &c.*, and the Fifth, a *chère entière* of women.

I rather guess, he means that betwixt one Comedy or Tragedy and another ; there is no other difference but what is made by the liking or disliking of the audience. This is, indeed, a less error than the former ; but yet it is a great one.

The liking or disliking of the people gives the Play the *denomination* of " good " or " bad " ; but does not really make or constitute it such. To please the people ought to be the Poet's aim [*pp.* 513, 582, 584] ; because Plays are made for their delight : but it does not follow, that they are always pleased with good plays ; or that the plays which please them, are always good.

The Humour of the people is now for Comedy ; therefore, in hope to please them, I write Comedies rather than serious Plays ; and, so far, their taste prescribes to me. But it does not follow from that reason, that Comedy is to be preferred before Tragedy, in its own nature. For that which is so, in its own nature, cannot be otherwise ; as a man cannot but be a rational creature : but the opinion of the people may alter ; and in another Age, or perhaps in this, serious Plays may be set up above Comedies.

This I think a sufficient answer. If it be not, he has provided me of [*with*] an excuse. It seems, in his wisdom, he foresaw my weakness ; and has found out this expedient for me, *That it is not necessary for Poets to study strict Reason : since they are so used to a greater latitude than is allowed by that severe inquisition ; that they must infringe their own jurisdiction to profess themselves obliged to argue well.*

I am obliged to him, for discovering to me this back door ;

but I am not yet resolved on my retreat. For I am of opinion, that they cannot be good Poets, who are not accustomed to argue well. False Reasonings and Colours of Speech are the certain marks of one who does not understand the Stage. For Moral Truth is the Mistress of the Poet as much as of the Philosopher. Poesy must *resemble* Natural Truth; but it must *be* Ethical. Indeed the Poet dresses Truth, and adorns Nature; but does not alter them.

Ficta voluptatis causa sint proxima veris.

Therefore that is not the best Poesy which resembles notions of *things, which are not,* to *things which are*: though the Fancy may be great, and the Words flowing; yet the Soul is but half satisfied, when there is not Truth in the foundation [*p.* 560].

This is that which makes VIRGIL [to] be preferred before the rest of poets. In Variety of Fancy, and Sweetness of Expression, you see OVID far above him; for VIRGIL rejected many of those things which OVID wrote. "A great Wit's great work, is to refuse," as my worthy friend, Sir JOHN BIRKENHEAD has ingeniously expressed it. You rarely meet with anything in VIRGIL but Truth; which therefore leaves the strongest impression of Pleasure in the Soul. This I thought myself obliged to say in behalf of Poesy: and to declare (though it be against myself) that when poets do not argue well, the defect is in the Workmen, not in the Art.

And, now, I come to the boldest part of his Discourse, wherein he attacks not me, but all the Ancient and Moderns; and undermines, as he thinks, the very foundations on which Dramatic Poesy is built. I could wish he would have declined that envy, which must, of necessity, follow such an undertaking: and contented himself with triumphing over me, in my opinions of Verse; which I will never, hereafter, dispute with him. But he must pardon me, if I have that veneration for ARISTOTLE, HORACE, BEN. JOHNSON, and CORNEILLE, that I dare not serve him in such a cause, and against such heroes: but rather fight under their protection; as HOMER reports of little TEUCER, who shot the Trojans from under the large buckler of AJAX Telamon—

Στῆ δ'ἄρ' ἀπ' Αιαντος σακέϊ Τελαμωνιάδαω, &c.

He stood beneath his brother's ample shield ;
And, covered there, shot death through all the field.

The words of my noble adversary are these—
*But if we examine the general Rules laid down for Plays, by
strict Reason, we shall find the errors equally gross ; for the great
Foundation which is laid to build upon, is Nothing, as it is generally stated : as will appear upon the examination of the particulars.*

These particulars, in due time, shall be examined. In the
meanwhile, let us consider, what this great Foundation is;
which, he says, is " Nothing, as it is generally stated."

I never heard of any other Foundation of Dramatic Poesy,
than the Imitation of Nature : neither was there ever pretended any other, by the Ancients or Moderns, or me who
endeavoured to follow them in that Rule. This I have
plainly said, in my Definition of a Play, that I T IS A J UST
AND LIVELY IMAGE OF HUMAN NATURE, &c.

Thus 'the Foundation, as it is generally stated," will stand
sure, if this Definition of a Play be true. If it be not, he
ought to have made his exception against it ; by proving that
a Play is *not* an Imitation of Nature, but somewhat else,
which he is pleased to think it.

But 'tis very plain, that he has mistaken the Foundation, for
that which is built upon it ; though not immediately. For
the direct and immediate consequence is this. If Nature be
to be imitated, then there is a Rule for imitating Nature
rightly ; otherwise, there may be an End, and no Means conducing to it.

Hitherto, I have proceeded by demonstration. But as our
Divines, when they have proved a Deity (because there is
Order), and have inferred that this Deity ought to be worshipped, differ, afterwards, in the Manner of the Worship :
so, having laid down, that "Nature is to be imitated ;" and
that Proposition [*p.* 577] proving the next, that, then, "there
are means, which conduce to the imitating of Nature"; I
dare proceed no farther, positively, but have only laid down
some opinions of the Ancients and Moderns, and of my own, as

Means which they used, and which I thought probable, for the attaining of that End.

Those Means are the same, which my antagonist calls the Foundations : how properly the World may judge! And to prove that this is his meaning, he clears it immediately to you, by enumerating those Rules or Propositions, against which he makes his particular exceptions, as namely, those of T I M E and P L A C E, in these words.

First, we are told the Plot should not be so ridiculously contrived, as to crowd several Countries into one Stage. Secondly, to cramp the accidents of many years or days, into the Representation of two hours and a half. And, lastly, a conclusion drawn that the only remaining dispute, is concerning Time ; whether it should be contained in Twelve or Four and twenty hours ; and the Place to be limited to the spot of ground, [either in town or city] where the Play is supposed to begin. And this is called nearest to Nature. For that is concluded most natural; which is most probable and nearest to that which it presents.

Thus he has, only, made a small Mistake of the Means conducing to the end, for the End itself ; and of the Superstructure for the Foundation. But he proceeds,

To shew, therefore, upon what ill grounds, they dictate Laws for Dramatic Poesy &c.

He is, here, pleased to charge me with being Magisterial ; as he has done in many other places of his Preface.

Therefore, in vindication of myself, I must crave leave to say, that my whole Discourse was sceptical, according to that way of reasoning which was used by Socrates, Plato, and all the Academics of old ; which Tully and the best of the Ancients followed, and which is imitated by the modest Inquisitions of the Royal Society.

That it is so, not only the name will show, which is *An Essay*; but the frame and composition of the work. You see it is a dialogue sustained by persons of several opinions, all of them left doubtful, to be determined by the readers in general; and more particularly deferred to the accurate judgement of my Lord Buckhurst, to whom I made a dedication of my book. These are my words, in my *Epistle*, speaking of the persons, whom I introduced in my dialogue, " 'Tis true, they differed in their opinions, as 'tis probable they would ;

neither do I take upon me to reconcile, but to relate them: leaving your Lordship to decide it, in favour of that part, which you shall judge most reasonable."

And, after that, in my *Advertisements to the Reader;* I said this, "The drift of the ensuing Discourse was chiefly to vindicate the honour of our English Writers, from the censure of those who injustly prefer the French before them. This I intimate, lest any should think me so exceeding vain, as to teach others an Art, which they understand much better than myself."

But this is more than [is] necessary to clear my modesty in that point : and I am very confident that there is scarce any man, who has lost so much time as to read that trifle, but will be my compurgator as to that arrogance whereof I am accused. The truth is, if I had been naturally guilty of so much vanity, as to dictate my opinions; yet I do not find that the Character of a Positive or Self Conceited Person is of such advantage to any in this Age, that I should labour to be Publicly Admitted of that Order.

But I am not, now, to defend my own cause, when that of all the Ancients and Moderns is in question. For this gentleman, who accuses me of arrogance, has taken a course not to be taxed with the other extreme of modesty. Those Propositions which are laid down in my Discourse, as Helps to the better Imitation of Nature, are *not* mine, as I have said; nor were ever pretended so to be : but were derived from the authority of ARISTOTLE and HORACE, and from the rules and examples of BEN. JOHNSON and CORNEILLE. These are the men, with whom be properly he contends : and against *whom he will endeavour to make it evident, that there is no such thing as what they All pretend.*

His argument against the Unities of P L A C E and T I M E is this.

That 'tis as impossible for one Stage to present two Rooms or Houses truly, as two Countries or Kingdoms ; and as impossible that Five hours or Twenty-four hours should be Two hours as that a Thousand years or hours should be less than what they are, or the greatest part of time to be comprehended in the less : for all of them being impossible they are none of them nearest the Truth or

Nature of what they present, for impossibilities are all equal, and admit of no degrees.

This argument is so scattered into parts, that it can scarce be united into a Syllogism: yet, in obedience to him, *I will abbreviate*, and comprehend as much of it, as I can, in few words; that my Answer to it, may be more perspicuous.

I conceive his meaning to be what follows, as to the Unity of P L A C E. If I mistake, I beg his pardon! professing it is not out of any design to play the *argumentative Poet.* "If one Stage cannot properly present two Rooms or Houses, much less two Countries or Kingdoms; then there can be no Unity of Place: but one Stage cannot properly perform this; therefore, there can be no Unity of Place."

I plainly deny his Minor Proposition: the force of which if I mistake not, depends on this; that "the Stage being one place, cannot be two." This, indeed, is as great a secret as that, "we are all mortal." But, to requite it with another, I must crave leave to tell him, that "though the Stage cannot be two places, yet it may properly Represent them, successively or at several times."

His argument is, indeed, no more than a mere fallacy: which will evidently appear, when we distinguished Place as it relates to Plays, into Real and Imaginary. The Real place is that theatre or piece of ground, on which the Play is acted. The Imaginary, that house, town, or country, where the action of the Drama is supposed to be; or, more plainly, where the Scene of the Play is laid.

Let us now apply this to that Herculean argument, *which if strictly and duly weighed, is to make it evident, that there is no such thing as what they All pretend.* 'Tis impossible, he says, *for one Stage to present two Rooms or Houses.* I answer, "Tis neither impossible, nor improper, for one *real* place to represent two or more *imaginary* places: so it be done successively," which, in other words, is no more than this, "That the Imagination of the Audience, aided by the words of the Poet, and painted scenes [*scenery*], nay *suppose* the Stage to be sometimes one place, sometimes another; now a garden or wood, and immediately a camp;" which I appeal to every man's imagination, if it be not true!

Neither the Ancients nor Moderns (as much fools as he is

I   7 pleased to think them) ever asserted that they could make one place, two: but they might hope, by the good leave of this author! that the change of a Scene might lead the Imagination to suppose the place altered. So that he cannot fasten those absurdities upon this Scene of a Play or Imaginary Place of Action; that it is one place, and yet two.

And this being so clearly proved, that 'tis past any shew of a reasonable denial; it will not be hard to destroy that other part of his argument, which depends upon it: that *'tis as impossible for a Stage to represent two Rooms or Houses, as two Countries or Kingdoms*: for his reason is already overthrown, which was, *because both were alike impossible*. This is manifestly otherwise: for 'tis proved that a stage may properly Represent two Rooms or Houses. For the Imagination, being judge of what is represented, will, in reason, be less chocqued [*shocked*] with the appearance of two rooms in the same house, or two houses in the same city; than with two distant cities in the same country, or two remote countries in the same universe.

Imagination in a man or reasonable creature is supposed to participate of Reason; and, when that governs (as it does in the belief of fiction) reason is not destroyed, but misled or blinded. That can prescribe to the Reason, during the time of the representation, somewhat like a weak belief of what it sees and hears; and Reason suffers itself to be so hoodwinked, that it may better enjoy the pleasures of the fiction: but it is never so wholly made a captive as to be drawn headlong into a persuasion of those things which are most remote from probability. 'Tis, in that case, a free born subject, not a slave. It will contribute willingly its assent, as far as it sees convenient: but will not be forced.

Now, there is a greater Vicinity, in Nature, betwixt two rooms than betwixt two houses; betwixt two houses, than betwixt two cities: and so, of the rest. Reason, therefore, can sooner be led by Imagination, to step from one room to another, than to walk to two distant houses: and yet, rather to go thither, than to fly like a witch through the air, and be hurried from one region to another. Fancy and Reason go hand in hand. The first cannot leave the last behind: and though Fancy, when it sees the wide gulf, would venture over, as the nimbler; yet, it is withheld by Reason, which will refuse to take the leap, when the distance, over it, appears

too large. If BEN. JOHNSON himself, will remove the scene
from Rome into Tuscany, in the same Act; and from thence,
return to Rome, in the Scene which immediate follows; Reason
will consider there is no proportionable allowance of time to
perform the journey; and therefore, will choose to stay at home.

So then, the less change of place there is, the less time is
taken up in transporting the persons of the Drama, with
Analogy to Reason: and in that Analogy or Resemblance of
Fiction to Truth consists the excellency of the Play.

For what else concerns the Unity of PLACE; I have already
given my opinion of it in my *Essay*, that "there is a latitude
to be allowed to it, as several places in the same town or
city; or places adjacent to each other, in the same country;
which may all be comprehended under the larger denomination
of One Place; yet, with this restriction, the nearer and fewer
those imaginary places are, the greater resemblance they will
have to Truth: and Reason which cannot *make* them One,
will be more easily led to *suppose* them so."

What has been said of the Unity of P L A C E , may easily
be applied to that of TIME. I grant it to be impossible that
the greater part of time should be comprehended in the less, that
Twenty-four hours should be crowded into three. But there is no
necessity of that supposition.

For as Place, so T I M E relating to a Play, is either Imaginary or Real. The Real is comprehended in those three
hours, more or less, in the space of which the Play is Represented. The Imaginary is that which is Supposed to be
taken up in the representation; as twenty-four hours, more or
less. Now, no man ever could suppose that twenty-four *real*
hours could be included in the space of three: but where is
the absurdity of affirming, that the feigned business of twenty-
four *imagined* hours, may not more naturally be represented
in the compass of three *real* hours, than the like feigned
business of twenty-four years in the same proportion of real
time? For the *proportions* are always real; and much nearer,
by his permission! of twenty-four to three, than of 4000 to it.

I am almost fearful of illustrating *anything* by Similitude;
lest he should confute it for an Argument: yet, I think the
comparison of a Glass will discover, very aptly, the fallacy of
his argument, both concerning Time and Place. The strength

of his Reason depends on this, "That the less cannot comprehend the greater." I have already answered that we need not suppose it does. I say not, that the less can *comprehend* the greater; but only that it may *represent* it; as in a mirror, of half a yard [in] diameter, a whole room, and many persons in it, may be seen at once: not that it can *comprehend* that room or those persons, but that it *represents them to the sight.*

But the Author of *The Duke of LERMA* is to be excused for his declaring against the Unity of TIME. For, if I be not much mistaken, he is an interessed [*interested*] person; the time of that Play taking up so many years as the favour of the Duke of LERMA continued: nay, the Second and Third Acts including all the time of his prosperity, which was a great part of the reign of PHILIP III.; for in the beginning of the Second Act, he was not yet a favourite, and before the end of the Third, was in disgrace.

I say not this, with the least design of limiting the Stage too servilely to twenty-four hours: however he be pleased to tax me with dogmatizing in that point. In my Dialogue, as I before hinted, several persons maintained their several opinions. One of them, indeed, who supported the cause of the French Poesy, said, how strict they were in that particular [*p.* 531]: but he who answered in behalf of our nation, was willing to give more latitude to the Rule; and cites the words of CORNEILLE himself, complaining against the severity of it, and observing what beauties it banished from the Stage, page 44, of my *Essay.*

In few words, my own opinion is this; and I willingly submit it to my adversary, when he will please impartially to consider it. That the Imaginary Time of every Play ought to be contrived into as narrow a compass, as the nature of the Plot, the quality of the Persons, and variety of Accidents will allow. In Comedy, I would not exceed twenty-four or thirty hours; for the Plot, Accidents, and Persons of Comedy are small, and may be naturally turned in a little compass. But in Tragedy, the Design is weighty, and the Persons great; therefore there will, naturally, be required a greater space of time, in which to move them.

And this, though BEN. JOHNSON has not told us, yet 'tis, manifestly, his opinion. For you see, that, to his Comedies, he allows generally but twenty-four hours: to his two Tragedies *SEJANUS* and *CATILINE*, a much larger time; though he draws both of them into as narrow a compass as he can. For he shows you only the latter end of *SEJANUS* his favour; and the conspiracy of *CATILINE* already ripe, and just breaking out into action.

But as it is an error on the one side, to make too great a disproportion betwixt the *imaginary* time of the Play, and the *real* time of its representation: so, on the other side, 'tis an oversight to compress the Accidents of a Play into a narrower compass than that in which they could naturally be produced.

Of this last error, the French are seldom guilty, because the thinness of their Plots prevents them from it: but few Englishmen, except BEN. JOHNSON, have ever made a Plot, with variety of Design in it, included in twenty-four hours; which was altogether natural. For this reason, I prefer the *Silent Woman* before all other plays; I think, justly: as I do its author, in judgement, above all other poets. Yet of the two, I think that error the most pardonable, which, in too straight a compass, crowds together many accidents: since it produces more variety, and consequently more pleasure to the audience; and because the nearness of proportion betwixt the imaginary and real time does speciously cover the compression of the Accidents.

Thus I have endeavoured to answer the *meaning* of his argument. For, as he drew it, I humbly conceive, it was none. As will appear by his Proposition, and the proof of it. His Proposition was this, *If strictly and duly weighed, 'tis as impossible for one Stage to present two Rooms or Houses, as two countries or kingdoms, &c.* And his Proof this, *For all being impossible, they are none of them, nearest the Truth or Nature of what they present.*

Here you see, instead of a Proof or Reason, there is only a *petitio principii*. For, in plain words, his sense is this, "Two things are as impossible as one another: because they are both equally impossible." But he takes those two things to be *granted* as impossible; which he ought to have *proved* such, before he had proceeded to prove them equally impossible. He should have made out, first, that it was impossible for one Stage to represent two Houses; and then have gone forward, to prove that it was as equally impossible for a Stage to present two Houses, as two Countries.

After all this, the very absurdity to which he would reduce me, is none at all. For his only drives at this. That if his argument be true, I must then acknowledge that there are degrees in impossibilities. Which I easily grant him, without dispute. And if I mistake not, ARISTOTLE and the School are of my opinion. For there are some things which are absolutely impossible, and others which are only so, *ex parte.* As, 'tis absolutely impossible for a thing *to be* and *not to be*, at the same time : but, for a stone to move naturally upward, is only impossible *ex parte materiæ;* but it is not impossible for the First Mover to alter the nature of it.

His last assault, like that of a Frenchman, is most feeble. For where I have observed that " None have been violent against Verse; but such only as have not attempted it, or have succeeded ill in their attempt " [*pp.* 503, 539, 561, 578], he will needs, according to his usual custom, improve my Observation into an Argument, that he might have the glory to confute it.

But I lay my observation at his feet: as I do my pen, which I have often employed, willingly, in his deserved commendations; and, now, most unwillingly, against his judgement. For his person and parts, I honour them, as much as any man living: and have had so many particular obligations to him, that I should be very ungrateful, if I did not acknowledge them to the World.

But I gave not the first occasion of this Difference in Opinions. In my *Epistle Dedicatory*, before my *Rival Ladies* [*pp.* 487–493], I said somewhat in behalf of Verse: which he was pleased to answer in his *Preface* to his *Plays* [*pp.* 494–500]. That occasioned my reply in my *Essay* [*pp.* 501–572]: and that reply begot his rejoinder in his *Preface* to *The Duke of LERMA* [*pp.* 573–578]. But, as I was the last who took up arms; I will be the first to lay them down. For what I have here written, I submit it wholly to him [*p.* 561]; and, if I do not hereafter answer what may be objected to this paper, I hope the World will not impute it to any other reason, than only the due respect which I have for so noble an opponent.

THOMAS ELLWOOD.

Relations with JOHN MILTON.

 MENTIONED, before, that, when I was a boy, I made some good progress in learning; and lost it all again before I came to be a man: nor was I rightly sensible of my loss therein, until I came amongst the Quakers. But then, I both saw my loss, and lamented it; and applied myself with the utmost diligence, at all leisure times, to recover it: so false I found that charge to be, which, in those times, was cast as a reproach upon the Quakers, that "they despised and decried all human learning" because they denied it to be *essentially necessary* to a Gospel Ministry; which was one of the controversies of those times.

But though I toiled hard, and spared no pains, to regain what once I had been master of; yet I found it a matter of so great difficulty, that I was ready to say as the noble eunuch to PHILIP, in another case, "How can I! unless I had some man to guide me?"

This, I had formerly complained of to my especial friend ISAAC PENINGTON, but now more earnestly; which put him upon considering and contriving a means for my assistance.

He had an intimate acquaintance with Dr. PAGET, a physician of note in London; and he, with JOHN MILTON, a gentleman of great note in learning, throughout the learned world, for the accurate pieces he had written on various subjects and occasions.

This person, having filled a public station in the former times, lived now a private and retired life in London : and, having wholly lost his sight, kept a man to read to him; which, usually, was the son of some gentleman of his acquaintance, whom, in kindness, he took to improve in his learning.

Thus, by the mediation of my friend ISAAC PENINGTON, with Dr. PAGET; and of Dr. PAGET with JOHN MILTON, was I admitted to come to him : not as a servant to him (which, at that time, he needed not), nor to be in the house with him; but only to have the liberty of coming to his house, at certain hours, when I would, and to read to him, what books he should appoint me, which was all the favour I desired.

But this being a matter which would require some time to bring it about, I, in the meanwhile, returned to my father's house [at Crowell] in Oxfordshire.

I had, before, received direction by letters from my eldest sister, written by my father's command, to put off [*dispose of*] what cattle he had left about his house, and to discharge his servants; which I had done at the time called Michaelmas [1661] before.

So that, all that winter when I was at home, I lived like a hermit, all alone; having a pretty large house, and nobody in it but myself, at nights especially. But an elderly woman, whose father had been an old servant to the family, came every morning, and made my bed; and did what else I had occasion for her to do : till I fell ill of the small-pox, and then I had her with me, and the nurse.

But now, understanding by letter from my sister, that my father did not intend to return and settle there; I made off [*sold*] those provisions which were in the house, that they might not be spoiled when I was gone : and because they were what I should have spent, if I had tarried there, I took the money made of them, to myself, for my support at London; if the project succeeded for my going thither. This done, I committed the care of the house to a tenant of my father's, who lived in the town; and taking my leave of Crowell, went up to my sure friend ISAAC PENINGTON again. Where, understanding that the mediation used for my admittance to

JOHN MILTON had succeeded so well, that I might come when I would : I hastened to London [*in the Spring of* 1662], and, in the first place, went to wait upon him.

He received me courteously, as well for the sake of Dr. PAGET, who introduced me; as of ISAAC PENINGTON, who recommended me : to both of whom, he bore a good respect. And having inquired divers things of me, with respect to my former progression in learning, he dismissed me, to provide myself of such accommodation as might be most suitable to my future studies.

I went, therefore, and took myself a lodging as near to his house, which was then in Jewin Street, as conveniently as I could ; and from thenceforward, went every day in the afternoon, except on the First Days of the week ; and, sitting by him in his dining-room, read to him, in such books in the Latin tongue as he pleased to hear me read.

At my first sitting to read to him, observing that I used the English pronounciation ; he told me, " If I would have the benefit of the Latin tongue, not only to read and understand Latin authors, but to converse with foreigners, either abroad or at home ; I must learn the foreign pronounciation."

To this, I consenting, he instructed me how to sound the vowels so different[ly] from the common pronounciation used by the English, who speak *Anglice* their Latin, that (with some few other variations, in sounding some consonants : in particular case[s], as *c* before *e* or *i*, like *ch* ; *sc* before *i*, like *sh*, &c.) the Latin, thus spoken, seemed as different from that which was delivered as the English generally speak it, as if it were another language.

I had, before, during my retired life at my father's, by unwearied diligence and industry, so far recovered the Rules of Grammar (in which, I had, once, been very ready) that I could both read a Latin author ; and, after a sort, hammer out his meaning. But this change of pronounciation proved a new difficulty to me. It was now harder for me to read ; than it was, before, to understand, when read. But

Labor omnia vincit
Improbus.

Incessant pains,
The end obtains.

And so, did I : which made my reading the more acceptable to my Master. He, on the other hand, perceiving with what earnest desire, I pursued learning, gave me not only all the encouragement, but all the help he could. For, having a curious ear, he understood by my tone, when I understood what I read, and when I did not ; and, accordingly, would stop me, examine me, and open the most difficult passages.

Thus I went on, for about six weeks' time, reading to him in the afternoons; and exercising myself with my own books, in my chamber, in the forenoons. I was sensible of an improvement.

But, alas, I had fixed my studies in a wrong place. London and I could never agree, for health. My lungs, as I suppose, were too tender, to bear the sulphurous air of that city : so that, I soon began to droop, and in less than two months' time, I was fain to leave both my studies and the city ; and return into the country to preserve life, and much ado I had to get thither.

I chose to go down to Wiccombe, and to JOHN RANCE's house there : both as he was a physician, and his wife a honest, hearty, discreet, and grave matron, whom I had a very good esteem of ; and who, I knew, had a good regard for me.

There, I lay ill a considerable time ; and to that degree of weakness, that scarcely any who saw me, expected my life [that I should live] : but the LORD was both gracious to me, in my illness; and was pleased to raise me up again, that I might serve Him in my generation.

As soon as I had recovered so much strength, as to be fit to travel ; I obtained of my father (who was then at his house in Crowell, to dispose of some things he had there ; and who, in my illness, had come to see me) so much money as would clear all charges in the house, for physic, food, and attendance : and having fully discharged all, I took leave of my friends in that family, and town ; and returned [? in October 1662] to my studies at London.

I was very kindly received by my Master, who had conceived so good an opinion of me, that my conversation, I found, was acceptable to him ; and he seemed heartily glad of my recovery and return : and into our old method of study, we fell again ; I reading to him, and he explaining to me as occasion required.

But as if learning had been a forbidden fruit to me; scarce was I well settled in my work; before I met with another diversion [*hindrance*], which turned me quite out of my work.

For a sudden storm arising (from, I know not what surmise of a plot; and thereby danger to the Government); the meetings of Dissenters, such, I mean, as could be found (which, perhaps, were not many besides the Quakers) were broken up throughout the City: and the prisons mostly filled with our Friends.

I was, that morning, which was the 26th day of the 8th month [*which, according to the reckoning of the Society of Friends, was October. Their First month down to* 1752, *was March*], 1662, at the Meeting, at the *Bull and Mouth*, by Alders Gate: when, on a sudden, a party of soldiers, of the Trained Bands of the City, rushed in with noise and clamour: being led by one, who was called Major Rosewell: an apothecary if I misremember not; and, at that time, under the ill name of a Papist.

[So the Friends there, with Ellwood, are taken; and sent to Bridewell till the 19th December following: when they were taken to Newgate, expecting to be called at the Old Bailey sessions: but, not being called, were sent back to Bridewell again. On the 29th December, they were brought up at the Sessions, and, refusing to swear, were all committed to the "Common Side" of Newgate; but that prison being so full, they were sent back to Bridewell again. Then we have the following extraordinary circumstance.]

Having made up our packs, and taken our leave of our Friends, whom we were to leave behind; we took our bundles on our shoulders, and walked, two and two a breast, through the Old Bailey into Fleet Street, and so to Old Bridewell. And it being about the middle of the afternoon, and the streets pretty full of people; both the shopkeepers at their doors, and passengers in the way would stop us, and ask us, "What we were? and whither we were going?"

And when we had told them, "We were prisoners, going from one prison to another (from Newgate to Bridewell)."

"What," said they, "without a keeper?"

"No," said we, "for our Word, which we have given, is our keeper."

Some thereupon would advise us, not to go to prison; but to go home. But we told them, "We could not do so. We could suffer for our testimony; but could not fly from it."

I do not remember we had any abuse offered us; but were generally pitied by the people.

When we were come to Bridewell, we were not put up into the great room in which we had been before : but into a low room, in another fair court, which had a pump in the middle of it. And, here, we were not shut up as before : but had the liberty of the court, to walk in ; and of the pump, to wash and drink at. And, indeed, we might easily have gone quite away, if we would ; there was a passage through the court into the street: but we were true and steady prisoners, and looked upon this liberty arising from their confidence in us, to be a kind of *parole* upon us ; so that both Conscience and Honour stood now engaged for our true imprisonment.

*   *   *   *   *

And this privilege we enjoyed by the indulgence of our Keeper, whose heart GOD disposed to favour us : so that both the Master and his porter were very civil and kind to us, and had been so, indeed, all along. For when we were shut up before ; the porter would readily let some of us go home in an evening, and stay at home till next morning, which was a great conveniency to men of trade and business : which I, being free from, forbore asking for myself, that I might not hinder others.

*   *   •   •   •

Under this easy restraint, we lay till the Court sate at the Old Bailey again ; and, then (whether it was that the heat of the storm was somewhat abated, or by what other means Providence wrought it, I know not), we were called to the bar; and without further question, discharged.

Whereupon we returned to Bridewell again ; and having raised some monies among us, and therewith gratified both the Master and his porter, for their kindness to us : we spent some time in a solemn meeting, to return our thankful acknowledgment to the LORD; both for His preservation of us in prison, and deliverance of us out of it. And then, taking a solemn farewell of each other ; we departed with bag and baggage [*at the end of January* 1663].

[Thus, by such magnificent patience under arbitrary injustice, these invincible Quakers shamed the reckless Crime which, in those days, went by the name of The Law : and such stories as ELLWOOD's *Life* and GEORGE FOX's *Journal* abound with like splendid victories of patience, by men who were incapable of telling a lie or of intentionally breaking their word.

JOHN BUNYAN's imprisonment at this time was much of the same kind as ELLWOOD's, as soon as the Keeper of Bedford gaol found he could trust him.]

Being now at liberty, I visited more generally my friends, that were still in prison : and, more particularly, my friend and benefactor, WILLIAM PENINGTON, at his house; and then, went to wait upon my Master, MILTON. With whom, yet, I could not propose to enter upon my intermitted studies, until I had been in Buckinghamshire, to visit my worthy friends, ISAAC PENINGTON and his virtuous wife, with other friends in that country [*district or county*].

Thither, therefore, I betook myself; and the weather being frosty, and the ways by that means clean and good; I walked it through in a day : and was received by my friends there, with such demonstration of hearty kindness, as made my journey very easy to me.

I intended only a visit hither, not a continuance; and therefore purposed, after I had stayed a few days, to return to my lodging and former course [*i.e., of reading to MILTON*] in London. But Providence ordered otherwise.

ISAAC PENINGTON had, at that time, two sons and one daughter, all then very young : of whom, the eldest son, JOHN PENINGTON, and the daughter, MARY (the wife of DANIEL WHARLEY), are yet living at the writing of this [? 1713]. And being himself both skilful and curious in pronounciation; he was very desirous to have them well grounded in the rudiments of the English tongue. To which end, he had sent for a man, out of Lancashire, whom, upon inquiry, he had heard of; who was, undoubtedly, the most accurate English teacher, that ever I met with or have heard of. His name was RICHARD BRADLEY. But as he pretended no higher than the English tongue, and had led them, by grammar rules, to the highest improvement they were capable of, in that; he had then taken his leave, and was gone up to London, to teach an English school of Friends' children there.

This put my friend to a fresh strait. He had sought for a new teacher to instruct his children in the Latin tongue, as the old had done in the English : but had not yet found one. Wherefore, one evening, as we sate together by the fire, in his bedchamber, which, for want of health, he kept : he asked me, his wife being by, " If I would be so kind to him, as to stay a while with him ; till he could hear of such a man as he aimed at: and, in the meantime, enter his children in the rudiments of the Latin tongue ? "

This question was not more unexpected, than surprising to me ; and the more, because it seemed directly to thwart my former purpose and undertaking, of endeavouring to improve myself, by following my studies with my Master, MILTON : which this would give, at least, a present diversion from ; and, for how long, I could not foresee.

But the sense I had, of the manifold obligations I lay under to these worthy friends of mine, shut out all reasonings ; and disposed my mind to an absolute resignation to their desire, that I might testify my gratitude by a willingness to do them any friendly service, that I could be capable of.

And though I questioned my ability to carry on that work to its due height and proportion ; yet, as that was not proposed, but an initiation only by Accidence into Grammar, I consented to the proposal, as a present expedient, till a more qualified person should be found : without further treaty or mention of terms between us, than that of mutual friendship.

And to render this digression from my own studies, the less uneasy to my mind ; I recollected, and often thought of, that Rule of LILLY—

> Qui docet indoctos, licet indoctissimus esset,
> Ipse brevi reliquis, doctior esse queat.

He that th'unlearned doth teach, may quickly be
More learned than they, though most unlearned he.

With this consideration, I undertook this province ; and left it not until I married : which was not till [the 28th October in] the year 1669, near[ly] seven years from the time I came thither.

In which time, having the use of my friend's books, as well as of my own, I spent my leisure hours much in reading; not without some improvement to myself in my private studies : which (with the good success of my labours bestowed on the children, and the agreeableness of con-

versation which I found in the family) rendered my undertaking more satisfactory; and my stay there more easy to
me.

*   *   *   *   *

Although the storm raised by the *Act for Banishment* [16
Car. II. c. 4. 1664], fell with the greatest weight and force
upon some other parts, as at London, Hertford, &c.: yet were
we, in Buckinghamshire, not wholly exempted therefrom.
For a part of that shower reached us also.

For a Friend, of Amersham, whose name was EDWARD
PEROT or PARRET, departing this life; and notice being given,
that his body would be buried there on such a day (which
was the First Day of the Fifth Month [*July*], 1665): the
Friends of the adjacent parts of the country, resorted pretty
generally to the burial. So that there was a fair appearance
of Friends and neighbours; the deceased having been well
beloved by both.

After we had spent some time together, in the house
(MORGAN WATKINS, who, at that time, happened to be at
ISAAC PENINGTON's, being with us); the body was taken
up, and borne on Friends' shoulders, along the street, in
order to be carried to the burying-ground: which was at the
town's end; being part of an orchard belonging to the
deceased, which he, in his lifetime, had appointed for that
service.

It so happened, that one AMBROSE BENNET, a Barrister at
Law, and a Justice of the Peace for that county, was riding
through the town [of Amersham] that morning, in his way
to Aylesbury: and was, by some ill-disposed person or other,
informed that there was a Quaker to be buried there that
day; and that most of the Quakers in the country [*county*]
were come thither to the burial.

Upon this, he set up his horses, and stayed. And when
we, not knowing anything of his design against us, went
innocently forward to perform our Christian duty, for the
interment of our Friend; he rushed out of his Inn upon us,
with the Constables and a rabble of rude fellows whom he
had gathered together: and, having his drawn sword in his
hand, struck one of the foremost of the bearers, with it;
commanding them "To set down the coffin!" But the Friend,
who was so stricken, whose name was THOMAS DELL (being

more concerned for the safety of the dead body than his own, lest it should fall from his shoulder, and any indecency thereupon follow) held the coffin fast. Which the Justice observing, and being enraged that his word (how unjust soever) was not forthwith obeyed, set his hand to the coffin; and, with a forcible thrust, threw it off the bearers' shoulders, so that it fell to the ground, in the midst of the street : and there, we were forced to leave it.

For, immediately thereupon, the Justice giving command for the apprehending us ; the Constables with the rabble fell on us, and drew some, and drove others in the Inn : giving thereby an opportunity to the rest, to walk away.

Of those that were thus taken, I was one. And being, with many more, put into a room, under a guard ; we were kept there, till another Justice, called Sir Thomas Clayton, whom Justice Bennet had sent for, to join with him in committing us, was come.

And then, being called forth severally before them, they picked out ten of us ; and committed us to Aylesbury gaol : for what, neither we, nor *they* knew. For we were not convicted of having either done or said anything, which the law could take hold of.

For they took us up in the open street, the King's highway, not doing any unlawful act; but peaceably carrying and accompanying the corpse of our deceased Friend, to bury it. Which they would not suffer us to do ; but caused the body to lie in the open street, and in the cartway : so that all the travellers that passed by (whether horsemen, coaches, carts, or waggons) were fain to break out of the way, to go by it, that they might not drive over it; until it was almost night. And then, having caused a grave to be made in the unconsecrated part, as it is accounted, of that which is called the Church Yard : they forcibly took the body from the widow (whose right and property it was), and buried it there.

When the Justices had delivered us prisoners to the Constable, it being then late in the day, which was the seventh day of the week : he (not willing to go so far as Aylesbury, nine long miles, with us, that night; nor to put the town [of Amersham] to the charge of keeping us, there, that night and the First day and night following) dismissed us, upon our *parole*, to come to him again at a set hour, on the Second day morning.

Whereupon, we all went home to our respective habitations; and coming to him punctually [*on Monday, 3rd July, 1665*] according to promise, were by him, without guard, conducted to the Prison.

The Gaoler, whose name was NATHANIEL BIRCH, had, not long before, behaved himself very wickedly, with great rudeness and cruelty, to some of our Friends of the lower side of the country [*i.e., Buckinghamshire*]; whom he, combining with the Clerk of the Peace, whose name was HENRY WELLS, had contrived to get into his gaol: and after they were legally discharged in Court, detained them in prison, using great violence, and shutting them up close in the Common Gaol among the felons; because they would not give him his unrighteous demand of Fees, which they were the more straitened in, from his treacherous dealing with them. And they having, through suffering, maintained their freedom, and obtained their liberty: we were the more concerned to keep what they had so hardly gained; and therefore resolved not to make any contract or terms for either Chamber Rent or Fees, but to demand a Free Prison. Which we did.

When we came in, the gaoler was ridden out to wait on the Judges, who came in, that day [*3rd July*, 1665], to begin the Assize; and his wife was somewhat at a loss, how to deal with us. But being a cunning woman, she treated us with a great appearance of courtesy, offering us the choice of all her rooms; and when we asked, " Upon what terms ? " she still referred us to her husband; telling us, she " did not doubt, but that he would be very reasonable and civil to us." Thus, she endeavoured to have drawn us to take possession of some of her chambers, at a venture; and trust to her husband's kind usage : but, we, who, at the cost of our Friends, had a proof of his kindness, were too wary to be drawn in by the fair words of a woman : and therefore told her, " We would not settle anywhere till her husband came home; and then would have a Free Prison, wheresoever he put us."

Accordingly, walking all together into the court of the

K   7 prison, in which was a well of very good water; and having, beforehand, sent to a Friend in the town, a widow woman, whose name was SARAH LAMBARN, to bring us some bread and cheese: we sate down upon the ground round about the well; and when we had eaten, we drank of the water out of the well.

Our great concern was for our Friend, ISAAC PENINGTON, because of the tenderness of his constitution: but he was so lively in his spirit, and so cheerfully given up to suffer; that he rather encouraged us, than needed any encouragement from us.

In this posture, the gaoler, when he came home, found us. And having, before he came to us, consulted his wife; and by her, understood on what terms we stood: when he came to us, he hid his teeth, and putting on a shew of kindness, seemed much troubled that we should sit there abroad [*in the open air*], especially his old friend, Mr. PENINGTON; and thereupon, invited us to come in, and take what rooms in his house we pleased. We asked, "Upon what terms?" letting him know, withal, that we were determined to have a Free Prison.

He (like the Sun and the Wind, in the fable, that strove which of them should take from the traveller, his cloak) having, like the wind, tried rough, boisterous, violent means to our Friends before, but in vain; resolved now to imitate the Sun, and shine as pleasantly as he could upon us. Wherefore, he told us, "We should make the terms ourselves; and be as free as we desired. If we thought fit, when we were released, to give him anything; he would thank us for it: and if not, he would demand nothing."

Upon these terms, we went in: and dispose ourselves, some in the dwelling-house, others in the malt-house: where they chose to be.

During the Assize, we were brought before Judge MORTON [*Sir WILLIAM MORTON, Recorder of Gloucester*], a sour angry man, who [*being an old Cavalier Officer, naturally,*] very rudely reviled us, but would not hear either us or the cause; referring the matter to the two Justices, who had committed us.

They, when the Assize was ended, sent for us, to be

brought before them, at their Inn [at Aylesbury]; and fined us, as I remember, 6s. 8d. a piece : which we not consenting to pay, they committed us to prison again, for one month from that time; on the *Act for Banishment*.

When we had lain there that month [*i.e., not later than the middle of August*, 1665], I, with another, went to the gaoler, to demand our liberty : which he readily granted, telling us, " The door should be opened, when we pleased to go."

This answer of his, I reported to the rest of my Friends there ; and, thereupon, we raised among us a small sum of money, which they put into my hand, for the gaoler. Whereupon, I, taking another with me, went to the gaoler, with the money in my hand; and reminding him of the terms, upon which we accepted the use of his rooms, I told him, " That though we could not pay Chamber Rent nor Fees, yet inasmuch as he had now been civil to us, we were willing to acknowledge it by a small token " : and thereupon, gave him the money. He, putting it into his pocket, said, " I thank you, and your Friends for it! and to let you see that I take it as a gift, not a debt; I will not look on it, to see how much it is."

The prison door being then set open for us ; we went out, and departed to our respective homes.

     •   *   •   *   •

Some little time before I went to Aylesbury prison [*on 3rd July*, 1665], I was desired by my quondam Master, MILTON, to take a house for him in the neighbourhood where I dwelt ; that he might get out of the City, for the safety of himself and his family : the Pestilence then growing hot in London.

I took a pretty box for him [*i.e., in June*, 1665] in Giles-Chalfont [*Chalfont St. Giles*], a mile from me [*ELLWOOD was then living in* ISAAC PENINGTON'S *house, called The Grange, at Chalfont St. Peter ; or Peter's Chalfont, as he calls it*], of which, I gave him notice : and intended to have waited on him, and seen him well settled in it ; but was prevented by that imprisonment. [*Therefore* MILTON *did not come into Buckinghamshire at this time, till after the 3rd July*, 1665.]

But, now [*i.e., not later than the middle of August*, 1665], being released, and returned home ; I soon made a visit to him, to welcome him into the country [*county*].

After some common discourses had passed between us [*evidently at ELLWOOD's first visit*], he called for a manuscript of his: which being brought, he delivered to me; bidding me, "Take it home with me, and read it at my leisure; and, when I had so done, return it to him, with my judgement thereupon!"

When I came home [*i.e., The Grange; from which ISAAC PENINGTON, with his family (including THOMAS ELLWOOD) was,* by military force, *expelled about a month after their first return from Aylesbury gaol (i.e., about the middle of September); and he again sent to the same prison*], and had set myself to read it; I found it was that excellent poem, which he entitled, *Paradise Lost.*

After I had, with the best attention, read it through: I made him another visit, and returned him his book; with due acknowledgment of the favour he had done me, in communicating it to me.

He asked me, "How I liked it? And what I thought of it?" Which I, modestly but freely, told him.

And, after some further discourse about it, I pleasantly said to him, "Thou hast said much, here, of *Paradise lost*: but what hast thou to say of *Paradise found*?

He made me no answer; but sate some time in a muse: then brake off that discourse, and fell upon another subject.

After the sickness [*Plague*] was over; and the City well cleansed, and become safely habitable again: he returned thither.

And when, afterwards [*probably in* 1668 *or* 1669], I went to wait on him there (which I seldom failed of doing, whenever my occasions drew me to London), he showed me his second poem, called *Paradise Regained*: and, in a pleasant tone, said to me, "This is owing to you! For you put it into my head, by the question you put to me at Chalfont! which, before, I had not thought of."

[*Paradise Regained* was licensed for publication on 2nd July, 1670.]

ADVICE

TO A

YOUNG REVIEWER,

WITH A

SPECIMEN OF THE ART.

OXFORD:

SOLD BY J. PARKER AND J. COOKE;
AND BY

F. C. AND J. RIVINGTON, ST. PAUL'S
CHURCHYARD, LONDON.

1807.

ADVICE

TO A

YOUNG REVIEWER, &c.

OU are now about to enter on a Profession which has the means of doing much good to society, and scarcely any temptation to do harm. You may encourage Genius, you may chastise superficial Arrogance, expose False-hood, correct Error, and guide the Taste and Opinions of the Age in no small degree by the books you praise and recommend. And this too may be done without running the risk of making any enemies; or sub-jecting yourself to be called to account for your criticism, however severe. While your name is unknown, your person is invulnerable: at the same time your aim is sure, for you may take it at your leisure; and your blows fall heavier than those of any Writer whose name is given, or who is simply anonymous. There is a mysterious authority in the plural, *We*, which no single name, whatever may be its reputation, can acquire; and, under the sanction of this imposing style, your strictures, your praises, and your dogmas, will command universal attention; and be received as the fruit of united talents, acting on one common principle—as the judgments of a tribunal who decide only on mature deliberation, and who protect the interests of Literature with unceasing vigilance.

Such being the high importance of that Office, and such its opportunities; I cannot bestow a few hours of leisure better than in furnishing you with some hints for the more

easy and effectual discharge of it : hints which are, I
confess, loosely thrown together ; but which are the result
of long experience, and of frequent reflection and comparison.   And if anything should strike you, at first sight, as
rather equivocal in point of morality, or deficient in liberality
and feeling ; I beg you will suppress all such scruples,
and consider them as the offspring of a contracted education and narrow way of thinking, which a little inter-
course with the World and sober reasoning will speedily
overcome.

Now as in the conduct of life nothing is more to be
desired than some Governing Principle of action, to which
all other principles and motives must be made subservient ;
so in the Art of Reviewing I would lay down as a funda-
mental position, which you must never lose sight of, and
which must be the mainspring of all your criticisms—
Write what will sell! To this Golden Rule every minor
canon must be subordinate ; and must be either immediately
deducible from it, or at least be made consistent with
it.
Be not staggered at the sound of a precept which, upon
examination, will be found as honest and virtuous as it
is discreet. I have already sketched out the great services
which it is in your power to render mankind ; but all
your efforts will be unavailing if men did not read what
you write. Your utility therefore, it is plain, depends upon
your popularity ; and popularity cannot be attained without
humouring the taste and inclinations of men.
Be assured that, by a similar train of sound and judicious
reasoning, the consciences of thousands in public life are
daily quieted. It is better for the State that their Party
should govern than any other. The good which they can
effect by the exercise of power is infinitely greater than
any which could arise from a rigid adherence to certain
subordinate moral precepts ; which therefore should be
violated without scruple whenever they stand in the way of
their leading purpose. He who sticks at these can never
act a great part in the World, and is not fit to act it if he
could.   Such maxims may be very useful in ordinary
affairs, and for the guidance of ordinary men : but when

we mount into the sphere of public utility, we must adopt more enlarged principles ; and not suffer ourselves to be cramped and fettered by petty notions of Right and Moral Duty.

When you have reconciled yourself to this liberal way of thinking ; you will find many inferior advantages resulting from it, which at first did not enter into your consideration. In particular, it will greatly lighten your labours, to *follow* the public taste, instead of taking upon you to *direct* it. The task of Pleasing is at all times easier than that of Instructing : at least it does not stand in need of painful research and preparation ; and may be effected in general by a little vivacity of manner, and a dexterous morigeration [*compliance, or obsequiousness*], as Lord BACON calls it, to the humours and frailties of men. Your responsibility too is thereby much lessened. Justice and Candour can only be required of you so far as they coincide with this Main Principle : and a little experience will convince you that these are not the happiest means of accomplishing your purpose.

It has been idly said, That a Reviewer acts in a judicial capacity, and that his conduct should be regulated by the same rules by which the Judge of a Civil Court is governed : that he should rid himself of every bias ; be patient, cautious, sedate, and rigidly impartial ; that he should not seek to shew off himself, and should check every disposition to enter into the case as a partizan.

Such is the language of superficial thinkers ; but in reality there is no analogy between the two cases. A Judge is promoted to that office by the authority of the State ; a Reviewer by his own. The former is independent of control, and may therefore freely follow the dictates of his own conscience : the latter depends for his very bread upon the breath of public opinion ; the great law of self-preservation therefore points out to him a different line of action. Besides, as we have already observed, if he ceases to please, he is no longer read ; and consequently is no longer useful. In a Court of Justice, too, the part of amusing the bystanders rests with the Counsel : in the case of criticism, if the Reviewer himself does not undertake it, who will ?

Instead of vainly aspiring to the gravity of a Magistrate; I would advise him, when he sits down to write, to place himself in the imaginary situation of a cross-examining Pleader. He may comment, in a vain of agreeable irony, upon the profession, the manner of life, the look, dress, or even the name, of the witness he is examining: when he has raised a contemptuous opinion of him in the minds of the Court, he may proceed to draw answers from him capable of a ludicrous turn; and he may carve and garble these to his own liking.

This mode of proceeding you will find most practicable in Poetry, where the boldness of the image or the delicacy of thought (for which the Reader's mind was prepared in the original) will easily be made to appear extravagant, or affected, if judiciously singled out, and detached from the group to which it belongs. Again, since much depends upon the rhythm and the terseness of expression (both of which are sometimes destroyed by dropping a single word, or transposing a phrase), I have known much advantage arise from *not* quoting in the form of a literal extract: but giving a brief summary in prose, of the contents of a poetical passage; and interlarding your own language, with occasional phrases of the Poem marked with inverted commas.

These, and a thousand other little expedients, by which the arts of Quizzing and Banter flourish, practice will soon teach you. If it should be necessary to transcribe a dull passage, not very fertile in topics of humour and raillery; you may introduce it as a "favourable specimen of the Author's manner."

Few people are aware of the powerful effects of what is philosophically termed Association. Without any positive violation of truth, the whole dignity of a passage may be undermined by contriving to raise some vulgar and ridiculous notions in the mind of the reader: and language teems with examples of words by which the same idea is expressed, with the difference only that one excites a feeling of respect, the other of contempt. Thus you may call a fit of melancholy, "the sulks"; resentment, "a pet"; a steed, "a nag"; a feast, "a junketing"; sorrow and affliction, "whining and blubbering". By transferring the terms peculiar to one state of society, to analogous situations and characters in another, the same object is attained. "A Drill Serjeant" or "a Cat and Nine Tails" in the Trojan War, "a Lesbos smack putting into the Piræus," "the Penny Post of Jerusalem," and other combinations of the like nature which, when you have a little indulged in that vein of thought, will readily suggest themselves, never fail to raise a smile, if not immediately at the expense of the Author, yet entirely destructive of that frame of mind which his Poem requires in order to be relished.

I have dwelt the longer on this branch of Literature, because you are chiefly to look here for materials of fun and irony.

Voyages and Travels indeed are no barren ground; and you must seldom let a Number of your *Review* go abroad without an Article of this description. The charm of this species of writing, so universally felt, arises chiefly from its uniting Narrative with Information. The interest we take in the story can only be kept alive by minute incident and occasional detail; which puts us in possession of the traveller's feelings, his hopes, his fears, his disappointments, and his pleasures. At the same time the thirst for knowledge and love of novelty is gratified by continual information respecting the people and countries he visits.

If you wish therefore to run down the book, you have only to play off these two parts against each other. When the Writer's object is to satisfy the first inclination, you are to thank him for communicating to the World such valuable facts as, whether he lost his way in the night, or sprained his ankle, or had no appetite for his dinner. If he is busied about describing the Mineralogy, Natural History, Agriculture, Trade, etc. of a country: you may mention a hundred books from whence the same information may be obtained; and deprecate the practice of emptying old musty Folios into new Quartos, to gratify that sickly taste for a smattering about everything which distinguishes the present Age.

In Works of Science and recondite Learning, the task

you have undertaken will not be so difficult as you may imagine. Tables of Contents and Indexes are blessed helps in the hands of a Reviewer; but, more than all, the Preface is the field from which his richest harvest is to be gathered.

In the Preface, the Author usually gives a summary of what has been written on the same subject before; he acknowledges the assistance he has received from different sources, and the reasons of his dissent from former Writers; he confesses that certain parts have been less attentively considered than others, and that information has come to his hands too late to be made use of; he points out many things in the composition of his Work which he thinks may provoke animadversion, and endeavours to defend or palliate his own practice.

Here then is a fund of wealth for the Reviewer, lying upon the very surface. If he knows anything of his business, he will turn all these materials against the Author: carefully suppressing the source of his information; and as if drawing from the stores of his own mind long ago laid up for this very purpose. If the Author's references are correct, a great point is gained; for by consulting a few passages of the original Works, it will be easy to discuss the subject with the air of having a previous knowledge of the whole.

Your chief vantage ground is, That you may fasten upon any position in the book you are reviewing, and treat it as principal and essential; when perhaps it is of little weight in the main argument: but, by allotting a large share of your criticism to it, the reader will naturally be led to give it a proportionate importance, and to consider the merit of the Treatise at issue upon that single question.

If anybody complains that the greater and more valuable parts remain unnoticed; your answer is, That it is impossible to pay attention to all; and that your duty is rather to prevent the propagation of error, than to lavish praises upon that which, if really excellent, will work its way in the World without your help.

Indeed, if the plan of your *Review* admits of selection, you had better not meddle with Works of deep research and original speculation; such as have already attracted much notice, and cannot be treated superficially without fear of being found out. The time required for making yourself thoroughly master of the subject is so great, that you may depend upon it they will never pay for the reviewing. They are generally the fruit of long study, and of talents concentrated in the steady pursuit of one object : it is not likely therefore that you can throw much new light on a question of this nature, or even plausibly combat the Author's propositions ; in the course of a few hours, which is all you can well afford to devote to them. And without accomplishing one or the other of these points; your *Review* will gain no celebrity, and of course no good will be done.

Enough has been said to give you some insight into the facilities with which your new employment abounds. I will only mention one more, because of its extensive and almost universal application to all Branches of Literature ; the topic, I mean, which by the old Rhetoricians was called ἐξ ἐναντίων, That is, when a Work excels in one quality ; you may blame it for not having the opposite.

For instance, if the biographical sketch of a Literary Character is minute and full of anecdote ; you may enlarge on the advantages of philosophical reflection, and the superior mind required to give a judicious analysis of the Opinions and Works of deceased Authors. On the contrary, if the latter method is pursued by the Biographer ; you can, with equal ease, extol the lively colouring, and truth, and interest, of exact delineation and detail.

This topic, you will perceive, enters into Style as well as Matter ; where many virtues might be named *which are incompatible* : and whichever the Author has preferred, it will be the signal for you to launch forth on the praises of its opposite ; and continually to hold up that to your Reader as the model of excellence in this species of Writing.

You will perhaps wonder why all my instructions are pointed towards the Censure, and not the Praise, of Books ; but many reasons might be given why it should be so. The chief are, that this part is both easier, and will sell better.

Let us hear the words of Mr BURKE on a subject not very dissimilar :

"In such cases," says he, " the Writer has a certain fire and alacrity inspired into him by a consciousness that (let it fare how it will with the subject) his ingenuity will be sure of applause : and this alacrity becomes much greater, if he acts upon the offensive ; by the impetuosity that always accompanies an attack, and the unfortunate propensity which mankind have to finding and exaggerating faults." Pref., *Vindic. Nat. Soc.*, p. 6.

You will perceive that I have on no occasion sanctioned the baser motives of private pique, envy, revenge, and love of detraction. At least I have not recommended harsh treatment upon any of these grounds. I have argued simply on the abstract moral principle which a Reviewer should ever have present to his mind : but if any of these motives insinuate themselves as secondary springs of action, I would not condemn them. They may come in aid of the grand Leading Principle, and powerfully second its operation.

But it is time to close these tedious precepts, and to furnish you with, what speaks plainer than any precept, a Specimen of the Art itself, in which several of them are embodied. It is hastily done : but it exemplifies well enough what I have said of the Poetical department ; and exhibits most of those qualities which disappointed Authors are fond of railing at, under the names of Flippancy, Arrogance, Conceit, Misrepresentation, and Malevolence : reproaches which you will only regard as so many acknowledgments of success in your undertaking ; and infallible tests of an established fame, and [a] rapidly increasing circulation.

L'Allegro. A Poem.

By John Milton.

No Printer's name.

IT has become a practice of late with a certain description of people, who have no visible means of subsistence, to string together a few trite images of rural scenery, interspersed with vulgarisms in dialect, and traits of vulgar manners ; to dress up these materials in a Sing-Song jingle ; and to offer them for sale as a Poem.   According to the most approved recipes, something about the heathen gods and goddesses ; and the schoolboy topics of Styx and Cerberus, and Elysium ; are occasionally thrown in, and the composition is complete. The stock in trade of these Adventurers is in general scanty enough ; and their Art therefore consists in disposing it to the best advantage. But if such be the aim of the Writer, it is the Critic's business to detect and defeat the imposture ; to warn the public against the purchase of shop-worn goods and tinsel wares ; to protect the fair trader, by exposing the tricks of needy Quacks and Mountebanks ; and to chastise that forward and noisy importunity with which they present themselves to the public notice.

How far Mr. MILTON is amenable to this discipline, will best appear from a brief analysis of the Poem before us.

In the very opening he assumes a tone of authority which might better suit some veteran Bard than a raw candidate for the Delphic bays : for, before he proceeds to the regular process of Invocation, he clears the way, by driving from his presence (with sundry hard names ; and bitter reproaches on her father, mother, and all the family) a venerable Personage, whose age at least and staid matron-like appearance, might have entitled her to more civil language.

Hence, loathèd Melancholy !
Of CERBERUS and blackest Midnight born,
In Stygian cave forlorn, &c.

There is no giving rules, however, in these matters, without a knowledge of the case. Perhaps the old lady had been frequently warned off before ; and provoked this violence by continuing still to lurk about the Poet's dwelling. And, to say the truth, the Reader will have but too good reason to remark, before he gets through the Poem, that it is one thing to tell the Spirit of Dulness to depart ; and another to get rid of her in reality. Like GLENDOWER's Spirits, any one may order them away ; "but will they go, when you do order them ? "

But let us suppose for a moment that the Parnassian decree is obeyed ; and, according to the letter of the *Order* (which is as precise and wordy as if Justice SHALLOW himself had drawn it) that the obnoxious female is sent back to the place of her birth,

'Mongst horrid shapes, shrieks, sights, *&c.*

At which we beg our fair readers not to be alarmed ; for we can assure them they are only words of course in all poetical Instruments of this nature, and mean no more than the "force and arms" and "instigation of the Devil" in a common Indictment.

This nuisance then being abated ; we are left at liberty to contemplate a character of a different complexion, "buxom, blithe, and debonair" : one who, although evidently a great favourite of the Poet's and therefore to be received with all due courtesy, is notwithstanding introduced under the suspicious description of an *alias.*

In heaven, ycleped EUPHROSYNE ;
And by men, heart-easing Mirth.

Judging indeed from the light and easy deportment of this gay Nymph ; one might guess there were good reasons for a change of name as she changed her residence.

But of all vices there is none we abhor more than that of slanderous insinuation. We shall therefore confine our moral strictures to the Nymph's mother ; in whose defence the Poet has little to say himself. Here too, as in the case of the *name,* there is some doubt. For the uncertainty of descent on the Father's side having become trite to a proverb ; the Author, scorning that beaten track, has

left us to choose between two mothers for his favourite :
and without much to guide our choice ; for, whichever
we fix upon, it is plain she was no better than she
should be.   As he seems however himself inclined to
the latter of the two, we will even suppose it so to be.

> Or whether (as some sager say)
> The frolic *wind that breathes the Spring*,
> ZEPHYR with AURORA playing,
> *As he met her once a Maying ;*
> There on beds of violets blue,
> And fresh-blown roses washed in dew, *&c.*

Some dull people might imagine that *the wind* was more
like *the breath of Spring* ; than *Spring, the breath of the
wind* : but we are more disposed to question the Author's
Ethics than his Physics ; and accordingly cannot dismiss
these May gambols without some observations.

In the first place, Mr. M. seems to have higher notions
of the antiquity of the May Pole than we have been
accustomed to attach to it.   Or perhaps he sought to
shelter the equivocal nature of this affair under that
sanction.   To us, however, who can hardly subscribe to
the doctrine that "Vice loses half its evil by losing all
its grossness" ; neither the remoteness of time, nor the
gaiety of the season, furnishes a sufficient palliation.
"Violets blue" and "fresh-blown roses" are, to be sure,
more agreeable objects of the Imagination than a gin shop
in Wapping or a booth in Bartholomew Fair ; but, in point
of morality, these are distinctions without a difference :
or it may be the cultivation of mind (which teaches us to
reject and nauseate these latter objects) aggravates the case,
if our improvement in taste be not accompanied by a proportionate improvement of morals.

If the Reader can reconcile himself to this latitude of
principle, the anachronism will not long stand in his way.
Much indeed may be said in favour of this union of ancient
Mythology with modern notions and manners.   It is a
sort of chronological metaphor—an artificial analogy, by
which ideas, widely remote and heterogeneous, are brought
into contact ; and the mind is delighted by this unexpected
assemblage, as it is by the combinations of figurative
language.

L   7

Thus in that elegant Interlude, which the pen of BEN JONSON has transmitted to us, of the loves of HERO and LEANDER :

> Gentles, that no longer your expectations may wander,
> Behold our chief actor, amorous LEANDER !
> With a great deal of cloth, lapped about him like a scarf:
> For he yet serves his father, a Dyer in Puddle Wharf :
> Which place we'll make bold with, to call it our Abydus ;
> As the Bankside is our Sestos, and *let it not be denied us.*

And far be it from us to deny the use of so reasonable a liberty ; especially if the request be backed (as it is in the case of Mr. M.) by the craving and imperious necessities of rhyme. What man who has ever bestrode Pegasus for an hour, will be insensible to such a claim ?

> *Haud ignara mali miseris succurrere disco.*

We are next favoured with an enumeration of the Attendants of this " debonair " Nymph, in all the minuteness of a German *Dramatis Personæ,* or a Ropedancer's Handbill.

> Haste thee, Nymph ; and bring with thee
> Jest and youthful Jollity,
> Quips and cranks and wanton wiles,
> Nods and becks and wreathèd smiles,
> Such as hang on HEBE's cheek
> And love to live in dimple sleek ;
> Sport that wrinkled Care derides,
> And Laughter holding both his sides.

The Author, to prove himself worthy of being admitted of the crew, skips and capers about upon " the light fantastic toe," that there is no following him. He scampers through all the Categories, in search of his imaginary beings, from Substance to Quality, and back again ; from thence to Action, Passion, Habit, &c. with incredible celerity. Who, for instance, would have expected *cranks, nods, becks,* and *wreathèd smiles* as part of a group in which Jest, Jollity, Sport, and Laughter figure away as full-formed entire Personages? The family likeness is certainly very strong in the two last ; and if we had not been told, we should perhaps have thought the act of *deriding* as appropriate to Laughter as to Sport.

But how are we to understand the stage directions?

> *Come*, and trip it as you *go*.

Are the words used synonymously? Or is it meant that this airy gentry shall come in a Minuet step, and go off in a Jig? The phenomenon of a *tripping crank* is indeed novel, and would doubtless attract numerous spectators.

But it is difficult to guess to whom, among this jolly company, the Poet addresses himself: for immediately after the Plural appellative *you*, he proceeds,

> And in *thy* right hand lead with *thee*
> The mountain Nymph, sweet Liberty.

No sooner is this fair damsel introduced; but Mr M., with most unbecoming levity, falls in love with her: and makes a request of her companion which is rather greedy, that he may live with both of them.

> To live with her, and live with thee.

Even the gay libertine who sang "How happy could I be with either!" did not go so far as this. But we have already had occasion to remark on the laxity of Mr M.'s amatory notions.

The Poet, intoxicated with the charms of his Mistress, now rapidly runs over the pleasures which he proposes to himself in the enjoyment of her society. But though he has the advantage of being his own caterer, either his palate is of a peculiar structure, or he has not made the most judicious selection.

To begin the day well, he will have the *sky-lark*

> to come *in spite of sorrow*
> And at his window bid "Good Morrow!"

The sky-lark, if we know anything of the nature of that bird, must come "in spite" of something else as well as "of sorrow," to the performance of this office.

In the next image, the Natural History is better preserved; and, as the thoughts are appropriate to the time of day, we will venture to transcribe the passage, as a favourable specimen of the Author's manner:

> While the Cock, with lively din,
> Scatters the rear of darkness thin,
> And to the stack, or the barn door,
> Stoutly struts his dames before;

> Oft listening how the hounds and horns
> Cheerly rouse the slumbering morn,
> From the side of some hoar hill,
> Through the high wood echoing still.

Is it not lamentable that, after all, whether it is the Cock, or the Poet, that listens, should be left entirely to the Reader's conjectures? Perhaps also his embarrassment may be increased by a slight resemblance of character in these two illustrious Personages, at least as far as relates to the extent and numbers of their seraglio.

After a *flaming* description of sunrise, on which the clouds attend in their very best liveries ; the Bill of Fare for the day proceeds in the usual manner. Whistling Ploughmen, singing Milkmaids, and sentimental Shepherds are always to be had at a moment's notice ; and, if well grouped, serve to fill up the landscape agreeably enough.

On this part of the Poem we have only to remark, that if Mr JOHN MILTON proposeth to make himself merry with

> Russet lawns, and fallows grey
> Where the nibbling flocks *do* stray ;
> Mountains on whose barren breast
> The labouring clouds *do* often rest,
> Meadows trim with daisies pied,
> Shallow brooks, and rivers wide,
> Towers and battlements, &c. &c. &c.

he will either find himself egregiously disappointed ; or he must possess a disposition to merriment which even DEMOCRITUS himself might envy. To such a pitch indeed does this solemn indication of joy sometimes rise, that we are inclined to give him credit for a literal adherence to the Apostolic precept, " Is any merry, let him sing Psalms ! "

At length, however, he hies away at the sound of bell-ringing, and seems for some time to enjoy the tippling and fiddling and dancing of a village wake : but his fancy is soon haunted again by spectres and goblins, a set of beings not, in general, esteemed the companions or inspirers of mirth.

> With stories told of many a feat,
> How fairy MAB the junkets eat.
> She was pinched, and pulled, she **said** :

And he, by friar's lanthern led,
Tells how the drudging Goblin sweat
To earn his cream-bowl duly set ;
When, in one night, ere glimpse of morn,
His shadowy Flail hath threshed the corn
That ten day-labourers could not end.
Then lies him down the lubbar Fiend ;
And, stretched out all the chimney's length,
Basks at the fire his hairy strength :
And, crop-full, out of door he flings
Ere the first cock his Matins rings.

Mr. M. seems indeed to have a turn for this species of Nursery Tales and prattling Lullabies ; and, if he will studiously cultivate his talent, he need not despair of figuring in a conspicuous corner of Mr NEWBERY's shop window : unless indeed Mrs. TRIMMER should think fit to proscribe those empty levities and idle superstitions, by which the World has been too long abused.

From these rustic fictions, we are transported to another species of *hum*.

Towered cities please us then,
And the busy hum of men ;
Where throngs of Knights and Barons bold,
In weeds of peace, high triumphs hold :
With *store of Ladies*, whose bright eyes
Rain influence, and judge the Prize
Of Wit or Arms ; while both contend
To win her grace, whom all commend.

To talk of the bright eyes of Ladies judging the Prize of Wit is indeed with the Poets a legitimate species of humming : but would not, we may ask, the *rain* from these Ladies' bright eyes rather tend to dim their lustre ? Or is there any quality in a shower of *influence* ; which, instead of deadening, serves only to brighten and exhilarate ?

Whatever the case may be, we would advise Mr. M. by all means to keep out of the way of these " Knights and Barons bold " : for, if he has nothing but his Wit to trust to, we will venture to predict that, without a large share of most undue influence, he must be content to see the Prize adjudged to his competitors.

Of the latter part of the Poem little need be said.

The Author does seem somewhat more at home when he gets among the Actors and Musicians : though his head is still running upon ORPHEUS and EURYDICE and PLUTO, and other sombre personages ; who are ever thrusting themselves in where we least expect them, and who chill every rising emotion of mirth and gaiety.

He appears however to be so ravished with this sketch of festive pleasures, or perhaps with himself for having sketched them so well, that he closes with a couplet which would not have disgraced a STERNHOLD.

> These delights if thou canst give,
> Mirth, with thee I *mean* to live.

Of Mr. M.'s good *intentions* there can be no doubt ; but we beg leave to remind him that there are two opinions to be consulted. He presumes perhaps upon the poetical powers he has displayed, and considers them as irresistible : for every one must observe in how different a strain he avows his attachment now, and at the opening of the Poem. Then it was

> If I give thee honour due,
> Mirth, admit me of thy crew !

But having, it should seem, established his pretensions ; he now thinks it sufficient to give notice that he means to live with her, because he likes her.

Upon the whole, Mr. MILTON seems to be possessed of some fancy and talent for rhyming ; two most dangerous endowments which often unfit men for acting a useful part in life without qualifying them for that which is great and brilliant. If it be true, as we have heard, that he has declined advantageous prospects in business, for the sake of indulging his poetical humour ; we hope it is not yet too late to prevail upon him to retract his resolution. With the help of COCKER and common industry, he may become a respectable Scrivener : but it is not all the ZEPHYRS, and AURORAS, and CORYDONS, and THYRSIS's ; aye, nor his " junketing Queen MAB " and " drudging Goblins," that will ever make him a Poet.

PREDICTIONS

FOR THE

YEAR 1708.

Wherein the Month and Day of
the Month are set down, the
Persons named, and the great
Actions and Events of next Year
particularly related, as they will
come to pass.

---

*Written to prevent the People of England
from being further imposed on by vulgar
Almanack Makers.*

By ISAAC BICKERSTAFF, Esq.

Sold by JOHN MORPHEW, near Stationers' Hall.
MDCCVIII.

PREDICTIONS

for the Year 1708, &c.

 HAVE long considered the gross abuse of Astrology in this Kingdom; and upon debating the matter with myself, I could not possibly lay the fault upon the Art, but upon those gross Impostors who set up to be the Artists.

I know several Learned Men have contended that the whole is a cheat; that it is absurd and ridiculous to imagine the stars can have any influence at all on human actions, thoughts, or inclinations: and whoever has not bent his studies that way, may be excused for thinking so, when he sees in how wretched a manner this noble Art is treated by a few mean illiterate traders between us and the stars; who import a yearly stock of nonsense, lies, folly, and impertinence, which they offer to the world as genuine from the planets, although they descend from no greater height than their own brains.

I intend, in a short time, to publish a large and rational Defence of this Art; and therefore shall say no more in its justification at present than that it hath been, in all Ages, defended by many Learned Men; and, among the rest, by SOCRATES himself, whom I look upon as undoubtedly the wisest of uninspired mortals. To which if we add, that those who have condemned this Art, although otherwise learned, having been such as either did not apply their studies this way, or at least did not succeed in their applications; their testimonies will not be of much weight to its disadvantage, since they are liable to the common objection of condemning what they did not understand.

Nor am I at all offended, or think it an injury to the Art, when I see the common dealers in it, the *Students in*

Astronomy, the *Philomaths*, and the rest of that tribe, treated by wise men with the utmost scorn and contempt : but I rather wonder, when I observe Gentlemen in the country, rich enough to serve the nation in Parliament, poring in *PARTRIDGE's Almanack* to find out the events of the year, at home and abroad; not daring to propose a hunting match, unless GADBURY or he have fixed the weather.

I will allow either of the two I have mentioned, or any others of the fraternity, to be not only Astrologers, but Conjurers too, if I do not produce a hundred instances in all their *Almanacks*, to convince any reasonable man that they do not so much as understand Grammar and Syntax; that they are not able to spell any word out of the usual road, nor even, in their *Prefaces*, to write common sense, or intelligible English.

Then as their Observations or Predictions, they are such as will suit any Age or country in the world.

This month, a certain great Person will be threatened with death or sickness. This the News Paper will tell them. For there we find at the end of the year, that no month passeth without the death of some Person of Note : and it would be hard if it should be otherwise, where there are at least two thousand Persons of Note in this kingdom, many of them old; and the *Almanack* maker has the liberty of choosing the sickliest season of the year, where he may fix his prediction.

Again, *This month, an eminent Clergyman will be preferred.* Of which, there may be some hundreds, half of them with one foot in the grave.

Then, *Such a Planet in such a House shews great machinations, plots, and conspiracies, that may, in time, be brought to light.* After which, if we hear of any discovery, the Astrologer gets the honour : if not, his prediction still stands good.

And, at last, *God preserve King WILLIAM from all his open and secret enemies, Amen.* When, if the King should happen to have died, the Astrologer plainly foretold it! otherwise it passeth but for the pious ejaculation of a loyal subject: although it unluckily happened in some of their *Almanacks*, that poor King WILLIAM was prayed for, many months after he was dead; because it fell out, that he died about the beginning of the year.

To mention no more of their impertinent Predictions, What have we to do with their advertisements about pills, or their

mutual quarrels in verse and prose of Whig and Tory ? wherewith the stars have little to do.

Having long observed and lamented these, and a hundred
other abuses of this Art too tedious to repeat ; I resolved to
proceed in a New Way ; which, I doubt not, will be to the
general satisfaction of the Kingdom. I can, this year, produce but a specimen of what I design for the future : having
employed the most part of my time in adjusting and correcting the calculations I made for some years past ; because
I would offer nothing to the World, of which I am not as fully
satisfied as that I am now alive.

For these last two years, I have not failed in above one or two
particulars, and those of no very great moment. I exactly
foretold the miscarriage at Toulon [*fruitlessly besieged by Prince
EUGENE, between 26th July, and 21st August, 1707*] with all its
particulars : and the loss of Admiral [Sir CLOUDESLY] SHOVEL
[*at the Scilly isles, on 22nd October, 1707*] ; although I was
mistaken as to the day, placing that accident about thirty-six
hours sooner than it happened ; but upon reviewing my
Schemes, I quickly found the cause of that error. I likewise
foretold the battle of Almanza [*25th April, 1707*] to the very
day and hour, with the loss on both sides, and the consequences
thereof. All which I shewed to some friends many months
before they happened : that is, I gave them papers sealed up,
to open in such a time, after which they were at liberty to
read them ; and there they found my Predictions true in every
Article, except one or two very minute.

As for the few following Predictions I now offer the World,
I forbore to publish them until I had perused the several
Almanacks for the year we are now entered upon. I found
them all in the usual strain ; and I beg the reader will compare their manner with mine.

And here I make bold to tell the World that I lay the whole
credit of my Art upon the truth of these Predictions ; and I will
be content that PARTRIDGE and the rest of his clan may hoot
me for a cheat and impostor, if I fail in any single particular of
moment. I believe any man who reads this Paper [*pamphlet*],
will look upon me to be at least a person of as much honesty
and understanding as the common maker of *Almanacks*. I do
not lurk in the dark. I am not wholly unknown to the World.

I have set my name at length, to be a mark of infamy to mankind, if they shall find I deceive them.

In one thing, I must desire to be forgiven : that I talk more sparingly of home affairs. As it would be imprudence to discover Secrets of State, so it would be dangerous to my person : but in smaller matters, and that as are not of public consequence, I shall be very free : and the truth of my conjectures will as much appear from these, as the other.

As for the most signal events abroad, in France, Flanders, Italy, and Spain : I shall make no scruple to predict them in plain terms. Some of them are of importance ; and I hope I shall seldom mistake the day they will happen. Therefore I think good to inform the reader, that I, all along, make use of the Old Style observed in England ; which I desire he will compare with that of the News Papers at the time they relate the actions I mention.

I must add one word more. I know it hath been the opinion of several Learned [Persons], who think well enough of the true Art of Astrology, that the stars do only *incline* and not *force* the actions or wills of men : and therefore, however I may proceed by right rules ; yet I cannot, in prudence, so confidently assure that the events will follow exactly as I predict them.

I hope I have maturely considered this objection, which, in some cases, is of no little weight. For example, a man may, by the influence of an overruling planet, be disposed or inclined to lust, rage, or avarice ; and yet, by the force of reason, overcome that evil influence. And this was the case of SOCRATES. But the great events of the World usually depending upon numbers of men ; it cannot be expected they should *all* unite to cross their inclinations, from pursuing a general design wherein they unanimously agree. Besides, the influence of the stars reacheth to many actions and events which are not, in any way, in the power of Reason, as sickness, death, and what we commonly call accidents ; with many more, needless to repeat.

But now it is time to proceed to my Predictions : which I have begun to calculate from the time that the sun entereth into *Aries* [*April*] ; and this I take to be properly the beginning of the natural year. I pursue them to the time that he entereth *Libra* [*September*] or somewhat more; which is the busy period of the year. The remainder I have not yet adjusted, upon account of several impediments needless here to mention. Besides, I must remind the reader again, that this is but a specimen of what I design, in succeeding years, to treat more at large; if I may have liberty and encouragement.

My first Prediction is but a trifle; yet I will mention it to shew how ignorant those sottish pretenders to Astrology are in their own concerns. It relateth to Partridge the *Almanack* maker. I have consulted the star of his nativity by my own rules; and find he will infallibly die upon the 29th of March [1708] next, about eleven at night, of a raging fever. Therefore I advise him to consider of it, and settle his affairs in time.

The month of A P R I L will be observable for the death of many Great Persons.

On the 4th will die the Cardinal de Noailles, Archbishop of Paris.

On the 11th, the young Prince of the Asturias, son to the Duke of Anjou.

On the 14th, a great Peer of this realm will die at his country house.

On the 19th, an old Layman of great fame and learning; and on the 23rd, an eminent goldsmith in Lombard street.

I could mention others, both at home and abroad, if I did not consider it is of very little use or instruction to the Reader, or to the World.

As to Public Affairs. On the 7th of this month, there will be an insurrection in Dauphiny, occasioned by the oppressions of the people; which will not be quieted in some months.

On the 15th, there will be a violent storm on the south-east coast of France; which will destroy many of their ships, and some in the very harbours.

The 19th will be famous for the revolt of a whole Province or Kingdom, excepting one city: by which the affairs of a certain Prince in the Alliance will take a better face.

M A Y, against common conjectures, will be no very busy month in Europe; but very signal for the death of the Dauphin [*Note, how SWIFT is killing off all the Great Men on the French side, one after another: because that would jump with the inclination of the nation just at the moment*]; which will happen on the 7th, after a short fit of sickness, and grievous torments with the stranguary. He dies less lamented by the Court than the Kingdom.

On the 9th, a Marshal of France will break his leg by a fall from his horse. I have not been able to discover whether he will then die or not.

On the 11th, will begin a most important siege, which the eyes of all Europe will be upon. I cannot be more particular; for in relating affairs that so nearly concern the Confederates, and consequently this Kingdom; I am forced to confine myself, for several reasons very obvious to the reader.

On the 15th, news will arrive of a *very surprising* event; than which, nothing could be more unexpected.

On the 19th, three noble Ladies of this Kingdom, will, against all expectation, prove with child; to the great joy of their husbands.

On the 23rd, a famous buffoon of the Play House will die a ridiculous death, suitable to his vocation.

J U N E. This month will be distinguished at home by the utter dispersing of those ridiculous deluded enthusiasts, commonly called Prophets [*Scotch and English Jesuits affecting inspiration, under the name of the French Prophets*], occasioned chiefly by seeing the time come when many of their prophecies were to be fulfilled; and then finding themselves deceived by the contrary events. It is indeed to be admired [*astonished at*] how any deceiver can be so weak to foretell things near at hand; when a very few months must, of necessity, discover the imposture to all the world: in this point, less prudent than common *Almanack* makers, who are so wise [as] to wander in generals, talk dubiously, and leave to the reader the business of interpreting.

On the 1st of this month, a French General will be killed by a random shot of a cannon ball.

On the 6th, a fire will break out in all the suburbs of Paris, which will destroy above a thousand houses; and seems to be the foreboding of what will happen, to the surprise of all Europe, about the end of the following month.

On the 10th, a great battle will be fought, which will begin at four of the clock in the afternoon, and last until nine at night, with great obstinacy, but no very decisive event. I shall not name the place, for the reasons aforesaid; but the

Commanders of each left wing will be killed. . . . I see bonfires, and hear the noise of guns for a victory.

On the 14th, there will be a false report of the French King's death.

On the 20th, Cardinal PORTOCARRERO will die of a dysentery, with great suspicion of poison: but the report of his intentions to revolt to King CHARLES will prove false.

J U L Y. The 6th of this month, a certain General will, by a glorious action, recover the reputation he lost by former misfortunes.

On the 12th, a great Commander will die a prisoner in the hands of his enemies.

On the 14th, a shameful discovery will be made of a French Jesuit giving poison to a great foreign General; and, when he is put to the torture, [he] will make wonderful discoveries.

In short, this will prove a month of great action, if I might have liberty to relate the particulars.

At home, the death of an old famous Senator will happen on the 15th, at his country house, worn [out] with age and diseases.

But that which will make this month memorable to all posterity, is the death of the French King LEWIS XIV., after a week's sickness at Marli; which will happen on the 29th, about six o'clock in the evening. It seemeth to be an effect of the gout in his stomach followed by a flux. And in three days after, Monsieur CHAMILLARD will follow his master; dying suddenly of an apoplexy.

In this month likewise, an Ambassador will die in London; but I cannot assign the day.

A U G U S T. The affairs of France will seem to suffer no change for a while, under the Duke of BURGUNDY's administration. But the Genius that animated the whole machine being gone, will be the cause of mighty turns and revolutions in the following year. The new King maketh yet little change, either in the army or the Ministry; but the libels against his [grand]father that fly about his very Court, give him uneasiness.

I see an Express in mighty haste, with joy and wonder in his looks, arriving by the break of day on the 26th of this month, having travelled, in three days, a prodigious journey by land and sea. In the evening, I hear bells and guns, and see the blazing of a thousand bonfires.

A young Admiral, of noble birth, doth likewise, this month, gain immortal honour by a great achievement.

The affairs of Poland are, this month, entirely settled. AUGUSTUS resigns his pretensions, which he had again taken up for some time. STANISLAUS is peaceably possessed of the throne: and the King of SWEDEN declares for the Emperor.

I cannot omit one particular accident here at home: that, near the end of this month, much mischief will be done at Bartholomew Fair [*held on August 24th*], by the fall of a booth.

SEPTEMBER. This month begins with a very surprising fit of frosty weather, which will last near [ly] twelve days.

The Pope having long languished last month, the swellings in his legs breaking, and the flesh mortifying; he will die on the 11th instant. And, in three weeks' time, after a mighty contest, he will be succeeded by a Cardinal of the Imperial faction, but a native of Tuscany, who is now about 61 years old.

The French army acts now wholly on the defensive, strongly fortified in their trenches: and the young French King sendeth overtures for a treaty of peace, by the Duke of MANTUA; which, because it is a matter of State that concerneth us here at home, I shall speak no further of.

I shall add but one Prediction more, and that in mystical terms, which shall be included in a verse out of VIRGIL.

> *Alter erit jam* TETHYS, *et altera quæ vehat* ARGO
> *Dilectos Heroas.*

Upon the 25th day of this month, the fulfilling of this Prediction will be manifest to everybody.

This is the furthest I have proceeded in my calculations for the present year. I do not pretend that these are all the great events which will happen in this period; but that those I have set down will infallibly come to pass.

It may perhaps, still be objected, why I have not spoken more particularly of affairs at home, or of the success of our armies abroad; which I might, and could very largely have done. But those in Power have wisely discouraged men from meddling in public concerns: and I was resolved, by no means, to give the least offence. This I *will* venture to say, that it will be a glorious campaign for the Allies, wherein the English forces, both by sea and land, will have their full share of honour; that Her Majesty Queen ANNE will continue in health and prosperity; and that no ill accident will arrive to any in the chief Ministry.

As to the particular events I have mentioned, the readers may judge by the fulfilling of them, whether I am of the level with common Astrologers, who, with an old paltry cant, and a few Pothooks for Planets to amuse the vulgar, have, in my opinion, too long been suffered to abuse the World. But an honest Physician ought not to be despised because there are such things as mountebanks.

I hope I have some share of reputation; which I would not willingly forfeit for a frolic, or humour: and I believe no Gentleman, who reads this Paper, will look upon it to be of the same last and mould with the common scribbles that are every day hawked about. My fortune hath placed me above the little regard of writing for a few pence, which I neither value nor want. Therefore, let not any wise man too hastily condemn this Essay, intended for a good design, to cultivate and improve an ancient Art, long in disgrace by having fallen into mean unskilful hands. A little time will determine whether I have deceived others, or myself: and I think it is no very unreasonable request, that men would please to suspend their judgements till then.

I was once of the opinion with those who despise all Predictions from the stars, till, in the year 1686, a Man of Quality shewed me written in his album, that the most learned astronomer, Captain H[ALLEY], assured him he would never believe anything of the stars' influence, if there were not a great Revolution in England in the year 1688. Since that time, I began to have other thoughts [*SWIFT does not say on what subject*]; and, after eighteen years' [1690–1708] diligent study and application [*in what ?*], I think I have no reason to repent of my pains.

I shall detain the reader no longer than to let him know, that the account I design to give of next year's events shall take in the principal affairs that happen in Europe. And if I be denied the liberty of offering it to my own country; I shall appeal to the Learned World, by publishing it in Latin, and giving order to have it printed in Holland.

FINIS.

A Revenue Officer

[*JONATHAN SWIFT.*]

A Letter to a Lord.

[30 March 1708.]

MY LORD,

N OBEDIENCE to your Lordship's commands, as well as to satisfy my own curiosity; I have, for some days past, inquired constantly after PARTRIGE the *Almanack* maker: of whom, it was foretold in Mr. BICKERSTAFF's *Predictions*, published about a month ago, that he should die, the 29th instant, about eleven at night, of a raging fever.

I had some sort of knowledge of him, when I was employed in the Revenue; because he used, every year, to present me with his *Almanack*, as he did other Gentlemen, upon the score of some little gratuity we gave him.

I saw him accidentally once or twice, about ten days before he died: and observed he began very much to droop and languish; although I hear his friends did not seem to apprehend him in any danger.

About two or three days ago, he grew ill; was confined first to his chamber, and in a few hours after, to his bed: where Dr. CASE and Mrs. KIRLEUS [*two London quacks*] were sent for, to visit, and to prescribe to him.

Upon this intelligence, I sent thrice every day a servant or other, to inquire after his health: and yesterday, about four in the afternoon, word was brought me, that he was past hopes.

Upon which, I prevailed with myself to go and see him: partly, out of commiseration: and, I confess, partly out of curiosity. He knew me very well, seemed surprised at my condescension, and made me compliments upon it, as well as he could in the condition he was. The people about him, said he had been delirious : but, when I saw him, he had his understanding as well as ever I knew, and spoke strong and hearty, without any seeming uneasiness or constraint.

After I had told him, I was sorry to see him in those melancholy circumstances, and said some other civilities suitable to the occasion ; I desired him to tell me freely and ingenuously, whether the *Predictions*, Mr. BICKERSTAFF had published relating to his death, had not too much affected and worked on his imagination ?

He confessed he often had it in his head, but never with much apprehension till about a fortnight before : since which time, it had the perpetual possession of his mind and thoughts, and he did verily believe was the true natural cause of his present distemper. " For," said he, " I am thoroughly persuaded, and I think I have very good reasons, that Mr. BICKERSTAFF spoke altogether by guess, and knew no more what will happen this year than I did myself."

I told him, " His discourse surprised me, and I would be glad he were in a state of health to be able to tell me, what reason he had, to be convinced of Mr. BICKERSTAFF's ignorance."

He replied, " I am a poor ignorant fellow, bred to a mean trade ; yet I have sense enough to know that all pretences of foretelling by Astrology are deceits : for this manifest reason, because the wise and learned (who can only judge whether there be any truth in this science), do all unanimously agree to laugh at and despise it ; and none but the poor ignorant vulgar give it any credit, and that only upon the word of such silly wretches as I and my fellows, who can hardly write or read." I then asked him, " Why he had not calculated his own nativity, to see whether it agreed with BICKERSTAFF's Predictions ? "

At which, he shook his head, and said, " O, Sir ! this is no time for jesting, but for repenting those fooleries, as I do now from the very bottom of my heart."

" By what I can gather from you," said I, " the Observations and Predictions you printed with your *Almanacks*, were mere impositions upon the people."

He replied, " If it were otherwise, I should have the less to answer for. We have a common form for all those things.

As to foretelling the weather, we never meddle with that!
but leave it to the printer, who taketh it out of any old
Almanack, as he thinketh fit. The rest was my own invention, to make my *Almanack* sell; having a wife to maintain,
and no other way to get my bread: for mending old shoes is
a poor livelihood! And," added he, sighing, "I wish I may
not have done more mischief by my physic than by astrology! although I had some good receipts from my grand-
mother, and my own compositions were such as I thought
could, at least, do no hurt."

I had some other discourse with him, which now I cannot call
to mind: and I fear I have already tired your Lordship. I
shall only add one circumstance. That on his deathbed, he
declared himself a Nonconformist, and had a Fanatic [*the
political designation of Dissenters*] preacher to be his spiritual
guide.

After half an hour's conversation, I took my leave; being
almost stifled by the closeness of the room.

I imagined he could not hold out long; and therefore
withdrew to a little coffee-house hard by, leaving a servant
at the house, with orders to come immediately, and tell me
as near as he could the minute when PARTRIGE should
expire: which was not above two hours after, when, looking
upon my watch, I found it to be above Five minutes after
Seven. By which it is clear that Mr. BICKERSTAFF was
mistaken almost four hours in his calculation [*see p. 173*].
In the other circumstances he was exact enough.

But whether he hath not been the cause of this poor man's
death as well as the Predictor may be very reasonably disputed. However, it must be confessed the matter is odd
enough, whether we should endeavour to account for it by
chance or the effect of imagination.

For my own part, although I believe no man has less faith
in these matters, yet I shall wait with some impatience, and
not without expectation, the fulfilling of Mr. BICKERSTAFF's
second prediction, that the Cardinal DE NOAILLES is to die
upon the 4th of April [1708]; and if that should be verified
as exactly as this of poor PARTRIGE, I must own I shall be
wholly surprised, and at a loss, and infallibly expect the
accomplishment of all the rest.

[In the original broadside, there are Deaths with darts, winged hour-glasses, crossed marrow-bones, &c.]

[JONATHAN SWIFT.]

An Elegy on Mr. PATRIGE, the Almanack *maker, who died on the* 29th *of this instant March,* 1708.

[Original broadside in the British Museum, C. 39. k./74.]

 ELL, 'tis as BICKERSTAFF has guest ;
Though we all took it for a jest ;
PATRIGE is dead ! nay more, he died
Ere he could prove the good Squire lied !
Strange, an Astrologer should die
Without one wonder in the sky
Not one of all his crony stars
To pay their duty at his hearse !
No meteor, no eclipse appeared,
No comet with a flaming beard !
The sun has rose and gone to bed
Just as if PATRIGE were not dead;
Nor hid himself behind the moon
To make a dreadful night at noon.
He at fit periods walks through *Aries,*
Howe'er our earthly motion varies;
And twice a year he'll cut th'Equator,
As if there had been no such matter.
   Some Wits have wondered what analogy
There is 'twixt* Cobbling and Astrology?   * PATRIDGE was a cobbler
How PATRIGE made his optics rise
From a shoe-sole, to reach the skies ?
A list, the cobblers' temples ties,

To keep the hair out of their eyes;
From whence, 'tis plain, the diadem
That Princes wear, derives from them:
And therefore crowns are now-a-days
Adorned with golden stars and rays;
Which plainly shews the near alliance
'Twixt Cobbling and the Planet science.

Besides, that slow-paced sign *Bo-otes*
As 'tis miscalled; we know not who 'tis?
But PATRIGE ended all disputes;
He knew his trade! and called it *Boots*! *
The Horned Moon which heretofore
Upon their shoes, the Romans wore,
Whose wideness kept their toes from corns,
And whence we claim our Shoeing Horns,
Shews how the art of Cobbling bears
A near resemblance to the Spheres.

* See his *Almanack.*

A scrap of parchment hung by Geometry,
A great refinement in Barometry,
Can, like the stars, foretell the weather:
And what is parchment else, but leather?
Which an Astrologer might use
Either for *Almanacks* or shoes.

Thus PATRIGE, by his Wit and parts,
At once, did practise both these Arts;
And as the boding owl (or rather
The bat, because her wings are leather)
Steals from her private cell by night,
And flies about the candle light:
So learned PATRIGE could as well
Creep in the dark, from leathern cell;
And in his fancy, fly as far,
To peep upon a twinkling star!
Besides, he could confound the Spheres
And set the Planets by the ears.
To shew his skill, he, Mars would join

To Venus, in *aspect malign*,
Then call in Mercury for aid,
And cure the wounds that Venus made.

Great scholars have in LUCIAN read
When PHILIP, King of Greece was dead,
His soul and spirit did divide,
And each part took a different side:
One rose a Star; the other fell
Beneath, and mended shoes in hell.

Thus PATRIGE still shines in each Art,
The Cobbling, and Star-gazing Part;
And is installed as good a star
As any of the CÆSARS are.

Thou, high exalted in thy sphere,
May'st follow still thy calling there!
To thee, the *Bull* will lend his hide,
By *Phœbus* newly tanned and dried!
For thee, they *Argo*'s hulk will tax,
And scrape her pitchy sides for wax!
Then *Ariadne* kindly lends
Her braided hair, to make thee ends!
The point of *Sagittarius*' dart
Turns to an awl, by heavenly art!
And *Vulcan*, wheedled by his wife,
Will forge for thee, a paring-knife!

Triumphant Star! some pity shew
On Cobblers militant below!
* But do not shed thy influence down
Upon St. James's end o' the Town!
Consider where the moon and stars
Have their devoutest worshippers!
Astrologers and lunatics
Have in Moorfields their stations fixt:
Hither, thy gentle aspect bend,
† Nor look asquint on an old friend!

* *Sed nec in
Arctoo sede,
tibi legeris
Orbe, &c.*

† *Neve tuam
videas obliquo
idere Romam.*

⌈ J. Swift.
⌊30 Mar. 1708.

THE EPITAPH.

ERE five foot deep, lies on his back,
A Cobbler, Starmonger, and Quack ;
Who to the stars, in pure good will,
Does to his best, look upward still.
Weep all you customers, that use
His Pills, his Almanacks, *or Shoes !*
And you that did your fortunes seek,
Step to this grave, but once a week !
This earth which bears his body's print
You'll find has so much virtue in it ;
That I durst pawn my ears, 'twill tell
Whate'er concerns you, full as well
(In physic, stolen goods, or love)
As he himself could, when above !

L O N D O N : Printed in the Year 1708.

Squire BICKERSTAFF detected;

OR THE

Astrological Impostor convicted.

BY

JOHN PARTRIDGE,

Student in Physic and Astrology.

[This was written for PARTRIDGE, either by NICHOLAS ROWE or Dr. YALDEN, and put forth by him, in good faith, in proof of his continued existence.]

IT IS hard, my dear countrymen of these United Nations! it is very hard, that a Britain born, a Protestant Astrologer, a man of Revolution Principles, an assertor of the Liberty and Property of the people, should cry out in vain, for justice against a Frenchman, a Papist, and an illiterate pretender to Science, that would blast my reputation, most inhumanly bury me alive, and defraud my native country of those services which, in my double capacity [*Physician and Astrologer*], I daily offer the public.

What great provocations I have received, let the impartial reader judge! and how unwillingly, even in my own defence, I now enter the lists against Falsehood, Ignorance, and Envy! But I am exasperated at length, to drag out this CACUS from the den of obscurity, where he lurketh, to detect him by the light of those stars he hath so impudently traduced, and to shew there is not a Monster in the skies so pernicious and malevolent to mankind as an ignorant pretender to Physic and Astrology.

I shall not directly fall on the many gross errors, nor expose the notorious absurdities of this prostituted libeller, until I have let the Learned World fairly into the controversy depending; and then leave the unprejudiced to judge of the merits and justice of my cause.

It was towards the conclusion of the year 1707 [*according to the old way of reckoning the year from March 25th. The precise date is February, 1708, see p. 469*], when an impudent Pamphlet crept into the world, intituled *Predictions &c. by ISAAC BICKERSTAFF, Esquire.* Among the many arrogant assertions laid down by that lying Spirit of Divination; he was pleased to pitch on the Cardinal DE NOAILLES and myself, among many other eminent and illustrious persons that were to die within the confines of the ensuing year, and peremptorily fixed the month, day, and hours of our deaths.

This, I think, is sporting with Great Men, and Public Spirits, to the scandal of Religion, and reproach of Power: and if Sovereign Princes and Astrologers must make diversion for the vulgar, why then, Farewell, say I, to all Governments, Ecclesiastical and Civil! But, I thank my better stars! I am alive to confront this false and audacious Predictor, and to make him rue the hour he ever affronted a Man of Science and Resentment.

The Cardinal may take what measures he pleases, with him: as His Excellency is a foreigner and a Papist, he hath no reason to rely on me for his justification. I shall only assure the World that he is alive! but as he was bred to Letters, and is master of a pen, let him use it in his own defence!

In the meantime, I shall present the Public with a faithful Narrative of the ungenerous treatment and hard usage I have received from the virulent Papers and malicious practices of this pretended Astrologer.

A true and impartial

ACCOUNT

OF THE

PROCEEDINGS

OF

ISAAC BICKERSTAFF, Esq.,

against Me.

HE 29th of March, *Anno Dom.*, 1708, being the night this Sham Prophet had so impudently fixed for my last; which made little impression on myself, but I cannot answer for my whole family.   For my wife, with a concern more than usual, prevailed on me to take somewhat to sweat for a cold; and between the hours of 8 and 9, to go to bed.

The maid as she was warming my bed, with the curiosity natural to young women, runs to the window, and asks of one passing the street, " Who the bell tolled for ? "

" Dr. PARTRIDGE," says he, " the famous *Almanack* maker, who died suddenly this evening."

The poor girl provoked, told him, " He lied like a rascal ! "

The other very sedately replied, " The sexton had so informed him; and if false, he was to blame for imposing on a stranger."

She asked a second, and a third as they passed ; and every one was in the same tone.

Now I don't say these were accomplices to a certain astrological Squire, and that one BICKERSTAFF might be sauntering thereabouts; because I will assert nothing here but what I dare attest, and plain matter of fact.

My wife, at this, fell into a violent disorder; and I must own I was a little discomposed at the oddness of the accident.

In the meantime, one knocks at the door. BETTY runneth down and opening, finds a sober grave person, who modestly inquires "If this was Dr. PARTRIDGE's?"

She, taking him for some cautious City patient, that came at that time for privacy, shews him into the dining-room.

As soon as I could compose myself, I went to him; and was surprised to find my gentleman mounted on a table with a two-foot rule in his hand, measuring my walls, and taking the dimensions of the room.

"Pray, Sir," says I, "not to interrupt you, have you any business with me?"

"Only, Sir," replies he, "to order the girl to bring me a better light: for this is but a dim one."

"Sir," sayeth I, "my name is PARTRIDGE!"

"Oh! the Doctor's brother, belike," cries he. "The staircase, I believe, and these two apartments hung in close mourning will be sufficient; and only a strip of Bays [cloth] round the other rooms. The Doctor must needs die rich. He had great dealings in his way, for many years. If he had no family Coat [of arms], you had as good use the scutcheons of the Company. They are as showish and will look as magnificent as if he were descended from the Blood-Royal."

With that, I assumed a greater air of authority, and demanded, "Who employed him? and how he came there?"

"Why, I was sent, Sir, by the Company of Undertakers," saith he, "and they were employed by the honest gentleman who is the executor to the good Doctor departed: and our rascally porter, I believe is fallen fast asleep with the black cloth and sconces or he had been here; and we might have been tacking up by this time."

"Sir," says I, "pray be advised by a friend, and make the best of your speed out of my doors; for I hear my wife's voice," which, by the way, is pretty distinguishable! "and in that corner of the room stands a good cudgel which somebody [i.e., himself] has felt ere now. If that light in her hands, and she knew the business you came about; without consulting the stars, I can assure you it will be employed very much to the detriment of your person."

"Sir," cries he, bowing with great civility, "I perceive

extreme grief for the loss of the Doctor disorders you a little at present: but early in the morning, I'll wait on you, with all necessary materials."

Now I mention no Mr. BICKERSTAFF, nor do I say that a certain star-gazing Squire has been a playing my executor before his time: but I leave the World to judge, and if it puts things to things fairly together, it won't be much wide of the mark.

Well, once more I get my doors closed, and prepare for bed, in hopes of a little repose, after so many ruffling adventures. Just as I was putting out my light in order to it, another bounceth as hard as he can knock.

I open the window and ask, "Who is there, and what he wants?"

"I am NED the Sexton," replies he, "and come to know whether the Doctor left any orders for a Funeral Sermon? and where he is to be laid? and whether his grave is to be plain or bricked?"

"Why, Sirrah!" says I, "you know me well enough. You know I am not dead; and how dare you affront me after this manner!"

"Alack a day, Sir," replies the fellow, "why it is in print, and the whole Town knows you are dead. Why, there's Mr. WHITE the joiner is but fitting screws to your coffin! He'll be here with it in an instant. He was afraid you would have wanted it before this time."

"Sirrah! sirrah!" saith I, "you shall know to-morrow to your cost that I am alive! and alive like to be!"

"Why, 'tis strange, Sir," says he, "you should make such a secret of your death to us that are your neighbours. It looks as if you had a design to defraud the Church of its dues: and let me tell you, for one who has lived so long by the heavens, that is unhandsomely done!"

"Hist! hist!" says another rogue that stood by him, "away, Doctor! into your flannel gear as fast as you can! for here is a whole pack of dismals coming to you with their black equipage; how indecent will it look for you to stand frightening folks at your window, when you should have been in your coffin this three hours!"

In short, what with Undertakers, Embalmers, Joiners, Sextons, and your *Elegy* hawkers *upon a late practitioner in Physic and Astrology*; I got not one wink of sleep that night, nor scarce a moment's rest ever since.

Now, I doubt not but this villanous Squire has the impudence to assert that these are entirely strangers to him; he,
good man! knoweth nothing of the matter! and honest
ISAAC BICKERSTAFF, I warrant you! is more a man of honour
than to be an accomplice with a pack of rascals that walk the
streets on nights, and disturb good people in their beds.   But
he is out, if he thinks the whole World is blind! for there is
one JOHN PARTRIDGE can smell a knave as far as Grub street,
although he lies in the most exalted garret, and writeth
himself "Squire"! But I will keep my temper! and proceed
in the Narration.

I could not stir out of doors for the space of three months
after this; but presently one comes up to me in the street:
"Mr. PARTRIDGE, that coffin you were last buried in, I have
not yet been paid for."

"Doctor!" cries another dog, "How do you think people
can live by making graves for nothing?   Next time you die,
you may even toll out the bell yourself, for NED!"

A third rogue tips me by the elbow, and wonders "how I
have the conscience to sneak abroad, without paying my
funeral expenses."

"Lord!" says one, "I durst have sworn that was honest
Dr. PARTRIDGE, my old friend; but, poor man, he is gone!"

"I beg your pardon," says another, "you look so like my
old acquaintance that I used to consult on some private
occasions: but, alack, he is gone the way of all flesh."

"Look, look!" cries a third, after a competent space of star-
ing at me; "would not one think our neighbour the *Almanack*
maker was crept out of his grave, to take another peep at
the stars in this world, and shew how much he is improved
in fortune telling by having taken a journey to the other."

Nay, the very Reader of our parish (a good sober discreet
person) has sent two or three times for me to come and be
buried decently, or send him sufficient reasons to the contrary: or if I have been interred in any other parish, to
produce my certificate as the *Act* requires.

My poor wife is almost run distracted with being called
Widow PARTRIDGE, when she knows it's false: and once a
Term, she is cited into the Court, to take out Letters of
Administration.

But the greatest grievance is a paltry Quack that takes up my calling just under my nose; and in his printed directions with a, *N. B.*☞, says : *He lives in the house of the late ingenious Mr. JOHN PARTRIDGE, an eminent Practitioner in Leather, Physic, and Astrology.*

But to shew how far the wicked spirit of envy, malice, and resentment can hurry some men, my nameless old persecutor had provided a monument at the stone-cutter's, and would have it erected in the parish church: and this piece of notorious and expensive villany had actually succeeded, if I had not used my utmost interest with the Vestry; where it was carried at last but by two voices, that I am alive.

That stratagem failing, out cometh a long sable *Elegy* bedecked with hour-glasses, mattocks, skulls, spades, and skeletons, with an *Epitaph* [*see p.* 486] as confidently written to abuse me and my profession, as if I had been under ground these twenty years.

And, after such barbarous treatment as this, can the World blame me, when I ask, What is become of the freedom of an Englishman? and, Where is the Liberty and Property that my old glorious Friend [*WILLIAM III.*] came over to assert? We have driven Popery out of the nation! and sent Slavery to foreign climes! The Arts only remain in bondage, when a Man of Science and Character shall be openly insulted! in the midst of the many useful services he is daily paying the public. Was it ever heard, even in Turkey or Algiers, that a State Astrologer was bantered out of his life, by an ignorant impostor? or bawled out of the world, by a pack of villanous deep-mouthed hawkers?

Though I print *Almanacks*, and publish *Advertisements*; although I produce certificates under the Minister's and Churchwardens' hands, that I am alive: and attest the same, on oath, at Quarter Sessions: out comes *A full and true Relation of the death and interment of JOHN PARTRIDGE.* Truth is borne down; Attestations, neglected; the testimony of sober persons, despised: and a man is looked upon by his neighbours as if he had been seven years dead, and is buried alive in the midst of his friends and acquaintance.

Now can any man of common sense think it consistent with the honour of my profession, and not much beneath the dignity of a philosopher, to stand bawling, before his own door, "Alive! Alive! Ho! the famous Doctor PARTRIDGE! no counterfeit, but all alive!" as if I had the twelve celestial Monsters of the *Zodiac* to shew within, or was forced for a livelihood, to turn retailer to May and Bartholomew Fairs.

Therefore, if Her Majesty would but graciously be pleased to think a hardship of this nature worthy her royal consideration; and the next Parl[ia]m[en]t, in their great wisdom, cast but an eye towards the deplorable case of their old *Philomath* that annually bestoweth his poetical good wishes on them: I am sure there is one ISAAC BICKERSTAFF, Esquire, would soon be trussed up! for his bloody persecution, and putting good subjects in terror of their lives. And that henceforward, to murder a man by way of Prophecy, and bury him in a printed *Letter,* either *to a Lord* or Commoner, shall as legally entitle him to the present possession of Tyburn, as if he robbed on the highway, or cut your throat in bed.

Advertisement.

N.B.☞ *There is now in the Press, my Appeal to the Learned; Or my general Invitation to all Astrologers, Divines, Physicians, Lawyers, Mathematicians, Philologers, and to the* Literati *of the whole World, to come and take their Places in the Common Court of Knowledge, and receive the Charge given in by me, against* ISAAC BICKERSTAFF, Esq., *that most notorious Impostor in Science and illiterate Pretender to the Stars; where I shall openly convict him of ignorance in his profession, impudence and falsehood in every assertion, to the great detriment and scandal of Astrology. I shall further demonstrate to the Judicious, that France and Rome are at the bottom of this horrid conspiracy against me; and that the Culprit aforesaid is a Popish emissary, has paid his visits to St. Germains, and is now in the Measures of* LEWIS XIV.; *that in attempting my reputation, there is a general Massacre of Learning designed in these realms; and, through my sides, there is a wound given to all the Protestant* Almanack *makers in the universe.*

Vivat Regina!

Not satisfied with this *Impartial Account*, when next Almanack time came (in the following November, 1708), PARTRIDGE's *Almanack* for 1709 P.P. 2465/8] contained the following :

You may remember that there was a Paper published predicting my death upon the 29th March at night, 1708, and after the day was past, the same villain told the World I was dead, and how I died, and that he was with me at the time of my death.

I thank GOD, by whose mercy I have my Being, that I am still alive, and (excepting my age) as well as ever I was in my life : as I was also at that 29th of March. And that Paper was said to be done by one BICKERSTAFF, Esq. But that was a sham name, it was done by an impudent lying fellow.

But his Prediction did not prove true! What will he say to that? For the fool had considered the "Star of my Nativity" as he said. Why the truth is, he will be hard put to it to find a *salvo* for his Honour. It was a bold touch! and he did not know but it might prove true.

One hardly knows whether to wonder most at the self-delusion or credulity of this last paragraph by the old quack.

This called forth from SWIFT :

A
VINDICATION
OF
ISAAC BICKERSTAFF, Esq, *&c.*

R. PARTRIDGE hath been lately pleased to treat me after a very rough manner, in that which is called his *Almanack* for the present year. Such usage is very undecent from one Gentleman to another, and does not at all contribute to the discovery of Truth, which ought to be the great End in all disputes of the Learned. To call a man, *fool*, and *villain*, and *impudent fellow*, only for differing from him in a point merely speculative, is, in my humble opinion, a very improper style for a person of his Education.

I appeal to the Learned World, whether, in my last year's

Predictions, I gave him the least provocation for such unworthy treatment. Philosophers have differed in all Ages; but the discreetest among them, have always differed as became Philosophers. Scurrility and Passion in a Controversy among Scholars, is just so much of nothing to the purpose; and, at best, a tacit confession of a weak cause.

My concern is not so much for my own reputation, as that of the Republic of Letters; which Mr. PARTRIDGE hath endeavoured to wound through my sides. If men of public spirit must be superciliously treated for their ingenious attempts; how will true useful knowledge be ever advanced? I wish Mr. PARTRIDGE knew the thoughts which foreign Universities have conceived of his ungenerous proceeding with me: but I am too tender of his reputation to publish them to the World. That spirit of envy and pride, which blasts so many rising Geniuses in our nation, is yet unknown among Professors abroad. The necessity of justifying myself will excuse my vanity, when I tell the reader that I have received nearly a hundred Honorary Letters from several part of Europe, some as far as Muscovey, in praise of my performance: besides several others, which (as I have been credibly informed) were opened in the P[ost] Office, and never sent me.

It is true, the Inquisition in P[ortuga]l was pleased to burn my *Predictions* [*A fact, as Sir PAUL METHUEN, the English Ambassador there, informed SWIFT*], and condemned the Author and the readers of them: but, I hope at the same time, it will be considered in how deplorable a state Learning lieth at present in that Kingdom. And, with the profoundest reverence for crowned heads, I will presume to add, that it a little concerned His Majesty of Portugal to interpose his authority in behalf of a Scholar and a Gentleman, the subject of a nation with which he is now in so strict an alliance.

But the other Kingdoms and States of Europe have treated me with more candour and generosity. If I had leave to print the Latin letters transmitted to me from foreign parts, they would fill a Volume! and be a full defence against all that Mr. PARTRIDGE, or his accomplices of the P[ortuga]l Inquisition, will be ever able to object: who, by the way, are the only enemies my *Predictions* have ever met with, at home or abroad. But I hope I know better what is due to the honour of a Learned Correspondence in so tender a point.

Yet some of those illustrious Persons will, perhaps, excuse me for transcribing a passage or two, in my own vindication.

* The most learned Monsieur LEIBNITZ thus addresseth to me his third Letter, *Illustrissimo BICKERSTAFFIO Astrologico Instauratori, &c.* Monsieur LE CLERC, quoting my *Predictions* in a treatise he published last year, is pleased to say, *Ita nuperrime BICKERSTAFFIUS, magnum illud Angliæ sidus.* Another great Professor writing of me, has these words, *BICKERSTAFFIUS nobilis Anglus, Astrologarum hujusce seculi facile Princeps.* Signior MAGLIABECCHI, the Great Duke's famous Library Keeper, spendeth almost his whole Letter in compliments and praises. It is true the renowned Professor of Astronomy at Utrecht seemeth to differ from me in one article; but it is after the modest manner that becometh a Philosopher, as *Pace tanti viri dixerim*: and, page 55, he seemeth to lay the error upon the printer, as, indeed it ought, and sayeth, *vel forsan error typographi, cum alioquin BICKER-STAFFIUS vir doctissimus, &c.*

If Mr. PARTRIDGE had followed these examples in the controversy between us, he might have spared me the trouble of justifying myself in so public a manner. I believe few men are readier to own their error than I, or more thankful to those who will please to inform him of them. But it seems this Gentleman, instead of encouraging the progress of his own Art, is pleased to look upon all Attempts of this kind as an invasion of his Province.

He has been indeed so wise, as to make no objection against the truth of my *Predictions*, except in one single point, relating to himself. And to demonstrate how much men are blinded by their own partiality, I do solemnly assure the reader, that he is the *only* person from whom I ever heard that objection offered! which consideration alone, I think, will take off its weight.

With my utmost endeavours, I have not been able to trace above two Objections ever made against the truth of my last year's *Prophecies*.

The first was of a Frenchman, who was pleased to publish to the World, that *the Cardinal DE NOAILLES was still alive, notwithstanding the pretended Prophecy of Monsieur BIQUER-*

* The quotations here, are said to be a parody of those of BENTLEY in his controversy with BOYLE.

STAFFE. But how far a Frenchman, a Papist, and an enemy is to be believed, in his own cause, against an English Protestant, who is *true to the Government*, I shall leave to the candid and impartial reader!

The other objection is the unhappy occasion of this Discourse, and relateth to an article in my *Predictions*, which foretold the death of Mr. PARTRIDGE to happen on March 29, 1708. *This*, he is pleased to contradict absolutely, in the *Almanack* he has published for the present year; and in that ungentlemanly manner (pardon the expression!) as I have above related.

In that Work, he very roundly asserts that *he is not only now alive, but was likewise alive upon that very 29th of March, when I had foretold he should die.*

This is the subject of the present Controversy between us, which I design to handle with all brevity, perspicuity, and calmness. In this dispute, I am sensible the eyes, not only of England, but of all Europe will be upon us: and the Learned in every country will, I doubt not, take part on that side where they find most appearance of Reason and Truth.

Without entering into criticisms of Chronology about the hour of his death, I shall only prove that *Mr. PARTRIDGE is not alive.*

And my first argument is thus. Above a thousand Gentlemen having bought his *Almanack* for this year, merely to find what he said against me: at every line they read, they would lift up their eyes, and cry out, between rage and laughter, *They were sure, no man alive ever wrote such stuff as this!* Neither did I ever hear that opinion disputed. So that Mr. PARTRIDGE lieth under a dilemma, either of disowning his *Almanack*, or allowing himself to be *no man alive*.

Death is defined by all Philosophers [as] a separation of the soul and body. Now it is certain that the poor woman [*Mrs. PARTRIDGE*] who has best reason to know, has gone about, for some time, to every alley in the neighbourhood, and swore to her gossips that *her husband had neither life nor soul in him*. Therefore, if an *uninformed* Carcass walks still about, and is pleased to call itself PARTRIDGE; Mr. BICKERSTAFF doth not think himself any way answerable for that! Neither had the said Carcass any right to beat the poor boy, who happened to pass by it in the street, crying *A full and true Account of Dr. PARTRIDGE's death, &c.*

SECONDLY. Mr. PARTRIDGE pretendeth to tell fortunes and recover stolen goods, which all the parish says, he must do by conversing with the Devil and other evil spirits : and no wise man will ever allow, he could converse personally with either, until after he was dead.

THIRDLY. I will plainly prove him to be dead out of his own *Almanack* for this year; and from the very passage which he produceth to make us think him alive. He there sayeth, *He is not only now alive, but was also alive upon that very 29th of March, which I foretold he should die on*. By this, he declareth his opinion that a man may be alive *now*, who was not alive a twelve month ago. And, indeed, here lies the sophistry of his argument. He dareth not assert he was alive *ever since the 29th of March!* but that he is *now alive*, and *was so on that day*. I grant the latter, for he did not die until night, as appeareth in a printed account of his death, in a *Letter to a Lord;* and whether he be since revived, I leave the World to judge! This indeed is perfect cavilling ; and I am ashamed to dwell any longer upon it.

FOURTHLY. I will appeal to Mr. PARTRIDGE himself, whether it be probable I could have been so indiscreet as to begin my *Predictions* with the *only* falsehood that ever was pretended to be in them! and this in an affair at home, where I had so many opportunities to be exact, and must have given such advantages against me, to a person of Mr. PARTRIDGE's Wit and Learning: who, if he could possibly have raised one single objection more against the truth of my Prophecies, would hardly have spared me!

And here I must take occasion to reprove the above-mentioned Writer [*i.e.*, SWIFT *himself, see p.* 482] of the Relation of Mr. PARTRIDGE's death, in a *Letter to a Lord*, who was pleased to tax me with a mistake of *four whole hours* in my calculation of that event. I must confess, this censure, pronounced with an air of certainty, in a matter that so nearly concerned me, and by a grave *judicious* author, moved me not a little. But though I was at that time out of Town, yet several of my friends, whose curiosity had led them to be exactly informed (as for my own part ; having no doubt at all of the matter, I never once thought of it!) assured me, I computed to something under half an hour: which (I speak my private opinion!) is an error of no very great magnitude, that men should raise clamour about it!

I shall only say, it would not be amiss, if that Author would henceforth be more tender of other men's reputation, as well as of his own! It is well there were no more mistakes of that kind: if there had been, I presume he would have told me of them, with as little ceremony.

There is one objection against Mr. PARTRIDGE's death, which I have sometimes met with, although indeed very slightly offered, That he still continueth to write *Almanacks*. But this is no more than what is common to all of that Profession. *GADBURY*, *Poor Robin*, *DOVE*, *WING*, and several others, do yearly publish their *Almanacks*, though several of them have been dead since before the Revolution. Now the natural reason of this I take to be, that whereas it is the privilege of other Authors, *to live* after their deaths; *Almanack* makers are only excluded, because their Dissertations, treating only upon the Minutes as they pass, become useless as those go off: in consideration of which, Time, whose Registers they are, gives them a lease in reversion, to continue their Works after their death. Or, perhaps, a *Name* can *make* an *Almanack* as well as *sell* one. And to strengthen this conjecture, I have heard the booksellers affirm, that they have desired Mr. PARTRIDGE to spare himself further trouble, and only to lend his Name; which could make *Almanacks* much better than himself.

I should not have given the Public or myself, the trouble of this *Vindication*, if my name had not been made use of by several persons, to whom I never lent it: one of which, a few days ago, was pleased to father on me, a new set of *Predictions*. But I think these are things too serious to be trifled with. It grieved me to the heart, when I saw my Labours, which had cost me so much thought and watching, bawled about by the common hawkers of Grub street; which I only intended for the weighty consideration of the gravest persons. This prejudiced the World so much at first, that several of my friends had the assurance to ask me, " Whether I were in jest ? " To which I only answered coldly, that " the event will shew! " But it is the talent of our Age and nation to turn things of the greatest importance into ridicule. When the end of the year had *verified all* my *Predictions*; out cometh Mr. PARTRIDGE's *Almanack!* disputing the point of his death. So that I am employed, like the General who

was forced to kill his enemies twice over, whom a
necromancer had raised to life. If Mr. PARTRIDGE has
practised the same experiment upon himself, and be again
alive; long may he continue so! But that doth not, in the
least, contradict my veracity! For I think I have clearly
proved, *by invincible demonstration*, that he died, at farthest,
within half an hour of the time I foretold [; and not four
hours sooner, as the above-mentioned Author, in his *Letter
to a Lord* hath maliciously suggested, with a design to blast
my credit, by charging me with so gross a mistake].

F I N I S.

Under the combined assault of the Wits, PARTRIDGE ceased to publish
his *Almanack* for a while; but afterwards took heart again, publishing
his "*Merlinus Redivivus*, being an Almanack for the year 1714, by JOHN
PARTRIDGE, a Lover of Truth [P.P. 2465/6];" at *p.* 2 of which is the
following epistle.

To ISAAC BICKERSTAFF, Esq.

SIR,
There seems to be a kind of fantastical propriety in
a dead man's addressing himself to a person not in Being.
ISAAC BICKERSTAFF [*i.e., RICHARD STEELE*] is no more [*the*
Tatler *having come to an end*], and I have now nothing to
dispute with on the subject of his fictions concerning me, *sed
magni nominis umbra*, "a shadow only, and a mighty name."
I have indeed been for some years silent, or, in the language of Mr. BICKERSTAFF, "dead"; yet like many an old
man that is reported so by his heirs, I have lived long enough
to bury my successor [*the* Tatler *having been discontinued*]. In
short, I am returned to Being after you have left it; and since
you were once pleased to call yourself my brother-astrologer,
the world may be apt to compare our story to that of the twin-
stars CASTOR and POLLUX, and say it was our destiny, not to appear together, but according to the fable, to live and die by turns.
Now, Sir, my intention in this Epistle is to let you know
that I shall behave myself in my new Being with as much
moderation as possible, and that I have no longer any
quarrel with you [*i.e., STEELE*], for the accounts you inserted
in your writings [*the joke was continued in the* Tatler] concerning my death, being sensible that you were no less
abused in that particular than myself.

The person from whom you took up that report, I know, was your namesake, the author of BICKERSTAFF's *Predictions*, * *Vide* Dr. a notorious cheat.* And if you had been indeed as S[WI]FT. much an Astrologer as you pretended, you might have known that his word was no more to be taken than that of an Irish evidence [*SWIFT was now Dean of St. Patrick's*] : that not being the only *Tale of a Tub* he had vented. The only satisfaction therefore, I expect is, that your bookseller in the next edition of your Works [*The Tatler*], do strike out my name and insert his in the room of it. I have some thoughts of obliging the World with his nativity, but shall defer that till another opportunity.

I have nothing to add further, but only that when you think fit to return to life again in whatever shape, of Censor [*the designation of the supposed Writer of the* Tatler], a *Guardian*, an *Englishman*, or any other figure, I shall hope you will do justice to   Your revived friend and servant,

JOHN PARTRIDGE.

On the last leaf of this *Almanack* is the following notice :—

This is to give notice to all people, that all those *Prophecies*, *Predictions*, *Almanacks*, and other pamphlets, that had my name either true, or shammed with the want of a Letter [*i.e., spelling his name* PARTRIGE *instead of* PARTRIDGE] : I say, they are all impudent forgeries, by a breed of villains, and wholly without my knowledge or consent. And I doubt not but those beggarly villains that have scarce bread to eat without being rogues, two or three poor printers and a book-binder, with honest BEN, will be at their old Trade again of Prophesying in my name. This is therefore to give notice, that if there is anything in print in my name beside this *Almanack*, you may depend on it that it is a lie, and he is a villain that writes and prints it.

In his *Almanack* for 1715 [P.P. 2465/7], PARTRIDGE says—

It is very probable, that the beggarly knavish Crew will be this year also printing *Prophecies* and *Predictions* in my name, to cheat the country as they used to do. This is therefore to give notice, that if there is anything of that kind done in my name besides this *Almanack* printed by the Company of Stationers, you may be certain it is not mine, but a cheat, and therefore refuse it,

THE

𝔓𝔯𝔢𝔰𝔢𝔫𝔱 𝔖𝔱𝔞𝔱𝔢

OF

WIT,

IN A

LETTER

TO A

Friend in the Country.

LONDON:
Printed in the Year, M D C C X I.
(Price 3*d*.)

THE
𝕻𝖗𝖊𝖘𝖊𝖓𝖙 𝕾𝖙𝖆𝖙𝖊
OF
WIT, &c.

SIR,

Ou acquaint me in your last, that you are still so busy building at ——, that your friends must not hope to see you in Town this year: at the same time, you desire me, that you may not be quite at a loss in conversation among the *beau monde* next winter, to send you an account of the present State of Wit in Town: which, without further preface, I shall endeavour to perform; and give you the histories and characters of all our Periodical Papers, whether monthly, weekly, or diurnal, with the same freedom I used to send you our other Town news.

I shall only premise, that, as you know, I never cared one farthing, either for Whig or Tory: so I shall consider our Writers purely as they are such, without any respect to which Party they belong.

Dr. KING has, for some time, lain down his monthly *Philosophical Transactions*, which the title-page informed us at first, were only to be continued as they sold; and though that gentleman has a world of Wit, yet as it lies in one particular way of raillery, the Town soon grew weary of his Writings: though I cannot but think that their author deserves a much better fate than to languish out the small remainder of his life in the Fleet prison.

About the same time that the Doctor left off writing, one Mr. OZELL put out his *Monthly Amusement*; which is still continued : and as it is generally some French novel or play indifferently translated, it is more or less taken notice of, as the original piece is more or less agreeable.

As to our Weekly Papers, the poor *Review* [*by* DANIEL DEFOE] is quite exhausted, and grown so very contemptible, that though he has provoked all his Brothers of the Quill round, none of them will enter into a controversy with him. This fellow, who had excellent natural parts, but wanted a small foundation of learning, is a lively instance of those Wits who, as an ingenious author says, " will endure but one skimming " [!].

The *Observator* was almost in the same condition ; but since our party struggles have run so high, he is much mended for the better : which is imputed to the charitable assistance of some outlying friends.

These two authors might however have flourished some time longer, had not the controversy been taken up by abler hands.

The *Examiner* is a paper which all men, who speak without prejudice, allow to be well written. Though his subject will admit of no great variety ; he is continually placing it in so many different lights, and endeavouring to inculcate the same thing by so many beautiful changes of expression, that men who are concerned in no Party, may read him with pleasure. His way of assuming the Question in debate is extremely artful ; and his *Letter to Crassus* is, I think, a masterpiece. As these Papers are supposed to have been written by several hands, the critics will tell you that they can discern a difference in their styles and beauties ; and pretend to observe that the first *Examiners* abound chiefly in Wit, the last in Humour.

Soon after their first appearance, came out a Paper from the other side, called the *Whig Examiner*, written with so much fire, and in so excellent a style, as put the Tories in no small pain for their favourite hero. Every one cried, " *BICKERSTAFF* must be the author ! " and people were the more confirmed in this opinion, upon its being so soon laid down : which seemed to shew that it was only written to bind the *Examiners* to their good behaviour, and was never designed to be a Weekly Paper.

The *Examiners*, therefore, have no one to combat with, at present, but their friend the *Medley*: the author of which Paper, though he seems to be a man of good sense, and expresses it luckily now and then, is, I think, for the most part, perfectly a stranger to fine writing.

I presume I need not tell you that the *Examiner* carries much the more sail, as it is supposed to be written by the direction, and under the eye of some Great Persons who sit at the helm of affairs, and is consequently looked on as a sort of Public Notice which way they are steering us.

The reputed author is Dr. S[WIF]T, with the assistance, sometimes, of Dr. ATT[ERBUR]Y and Mr. P[RIO]R.

The *Medley* is said to be written by Mr. OLD[MIXO]N ; and supervised by Mr. MAYN[WARIN]G, who perhaps might entirely write those few Papers which are so much better than the rest.

Before I proceed further in the account of our Weekly Papers, it will be necessary to inform you that at the beginning of the winter [*on Jan.* 2, *1711*], to the infinite surprise of all men, Mr. STEELE flang up his *Tatler*; and instead of *ISAAC BICKERSTAFF, Esquire,* subscribed himself RICHARD STEELE to the last of those Papers, after a handsome compliment to the Town for their kind acceptance of his endeavours to divert them.

The chief reason he thought fit to give for his leaving off writing was, that having been so long looked on in all public places and companies as the Author of those papers, he found that his most intimate friends and acquaintance were in pain to speak or act before him.

The Town was very far from being satisfied with this reason, and most people judged the true cause to be, either

That he was quite spent, and wanted matter to continue his undertaking any longer ; or

That he laid it down as a sort of submission to, and composition with, the Government, for some past offences; or, lastly,

That he had a mind to vary his Shape, and appear again in some new light.

However that were, his disappearance seemed to be bewailed as some general calamity. Every one wanted so agreeable an amusement, and the Coffee-houses began to be sensible that the *Esquire*'s *Lucubrations* alone had brought them more customers, than all their other News Papers put together.

It must indeed be confessed that never man threw up his pen, under stronger temptations to have employed it longer. His reputation was at a greater height, than I believe ever any living author's was before him. It is reasonable to suppose that his gains were proportionably considerable. Every one read him with pleasure and good-will; and the Tories, in respect to his other good qualities, had almost forgiven his unaccountable imprudence in declaring against them.

Lastly, it was highly improbable that, if he threw off a Character the ideas of which were so strongly impressed in every one's mind, however finely he might write in any new form, that he should meet with the same reception.

To give you my own thoughts of this Gentleman's Writings, I shall, in the first place, observe, that there is a noble difference between him and all the rest of our Polite and Gallant Authors. The latter have endeavoured to please the Age by falling in with them, and encouraging them in their fashionable vices and false notions of things. It would have been a jest, some time since, for a man to have asserted that anything witty could be said in praise of a married state, or that Devotion and Virtue were any way necessary to the character of a Fine Gentleman. *BICKERSTAFF* ventured to tell the Town that they were a parcel of fops, fools, and coquettes; but in such a manner as even pleased them, and made them more than half inclined to believe that he spoke truth.

Instead of complying with the false sentiments or vicious tastes of the Age—either in morality, criticism, or good breeding—he has boldly assured them, that they were altogether in the wrong; and commanded them, with an authority which perfectly well became him, to surrender themselves to his arguments for Virtue and Good Sense.

It is incredible to conceive the effect his writings have had on the Town; how many thousand follies they have either

quite banished or given a very great check to! how much
countenance, they have added to Virtue and Religion! how
many people they have rendered happy, by shewing them it
was their own fault if they were not so! and, lastly, how
entirely they have convinced our young fops and young
fellows of the value and advantages of Learning!

He has indeed rescued it out of the hands of pedants and
fools, and discovered the true method of making it amiable
and lovely to all mankind. In the dress he gives it, it is a
most welcome guest at tea-tables and assemblies, and is
relished and caressed by the merchants on the Change.
Accordingly there is not a Lady at Court, nor a Banker in
Lombard Street, who is not verily persuaded that Captain
STEELE is the greatest Scholar and best Casuist of any man
in England.

Lastly, his writings have set all our Wits and Men of Letters
on a new way of Thinking, of which they had little or no
notion before: and, although we cannot say that any of them
have come up to the beauties of the original, I think we may
venture to affirm, that every one of them writes and thinks
much more justly than they did some time since.

The vast variety of subjects which Mr. STEELE has treated
of, in so different manners, and yet ALL so perfectly well,
made the World believe that it was impossible they should
all come from the same hand. This set every one upon
guessing who was the *Esquire*'s friend? and most people at
first fancied it must be Doctor SWIFT; but it is now no
longer a secret, that his only great and constant assistant
was Mr. ADDISON.

This is that excellent friend to whom Mr. STEELE owes so
much; and who refuses to have his name set before those
Pieces which the greatest pens in England would be proud
to own. Indeed, they could hardly add to this Gentleman's
reputation: whose works in Latin and English Poetry long
since convinced the World, that he was the greatest Master
in Europe of those two languages.

I am assured, from good hands, that all the visions, and
other tracts of that way of writing, with a very great
number of the most exquisite pieces of wit and raillery
throughout the *Lucubrations* are entirely of this Gentleman's
composing: which may, in some measure, account for that

different Genius, which appears in the winter papers, from those of the summer; at which time, as the *Examiner* often hinted, this friend of Mr. STEELE was in Ireland.

Mr. STEELE confesses in his last Volume of the *Tatlers* that he is obliged to Dr. SWIFT for his *Town Shower*, and the *Description of the Morn*, with some other hints received from him in private conversation.

I have also heard that several of those *Letters*, which came as from unknown hands, were written by Mr. HENLEY: which is an answer to your query, " Who those friends are, whom Mr. STEELE speaks of in his last *Tatler*?"

But to proceed with my account of our other papers. The expiration of *BICKERSTAFF*'s *Lucubrations* was attended with much the same consequences as the death of *MELIBŒUS*'s *Ox* in VIRGIL: as the latter engendered swarms of bees, the former immediately produced whole swarms of little satirical scribblers.

One of these authors called himself the *Growler*, and assured us that, to make amends for Mr. STEELE's silence, he was resolved to *growl* at us weekly, as long as we should think fit to give him any encouragement. Another Gentleman, with more modesty, called his paper, the *Whisperer*; and a third, to please the Ladies, christened his, the *Tell tale*.

At the same time came out several *Tatlers*; each of which, with equal truth and wit, assured us that he was the genuine *ISAAC BICKERSTAFF*.

It may be observed that when the *Esquire* laid down his pen; though he could not but foresee that several scribblers would soon snatch it up, which he might (one would think) easily have prevented: he scorned to take any further care about it, but left the field fairly open to any worthy successor. Immediately, some of our Wits were for forming themselves into a Club, headed by one Mr. HARRISON, and trying how they could shoot in this Bow of ULYSSES; but soon found that this sort of writing requires so fine and particular a manner of Thinking, with so exact a Knowledge of the World, as must make them utterly despair of success.

They seemed indeed at first to think, that what was only the garnish of the former *Tatlers*, was that which recom-

mended them; and not those Substantial Entertainments
which they everywhere abound in. According they were
continually talking of their *Maid, Night Cap, Spectacles,* and
CHARLES LILLIE. However there were, now and then, some
faint endeavours at Humour and sparks of Wit: which the
Town, for want of better entertainment, was content to hunt
after, through a heap of impertinences; but even those are,
at present, become wholly invisible and quite swallowed up
in the blaze of the *Spectator*.

You may remember, I told you before, that one cause
assigned for the laying down the *Tatler* was, Want of
Matter; and, indeed, this was the prevailing opinion in
Town: when we were surprised all at once by a paper
called the *Spectator*, which was promised to be continued
every day; and was written in so excellent a style, with so
nice a judgment, and such a noble profusion of Wit and
Humour, that it was not difficult to determine it could
come from no other hands but those which had penned the
Lucubrations.

This immediately alarmed these gentlemen, who, as it is
said Mr. STEELE phrases it, had "the Censorship in Commission." They found the new *Spectator* came on like a
torrent, and swept away all before him. They despaired
ever to equal him in Wit, Humour, or Learning; which had
been their true and certain way of opposing him: and therefore rather chose to fall on the Author; and to call out for
help to all good Christians, by assuring them again and
again that they were the First, Original, True, and Undis-
puted *ISAAC BICKERSTAFF*.

Meanwhile, the *Spectator*, whom we regard as our Shelter
from that flood of false wit and impertinence which was breaking in upon us, is in every one's hands; and a constant topic
for our morning conversation at tea-tables and coffee-houses.
We had at first, indeed, no manner of notion how a diurnal
paper could be continued in the spirit and style of our present
Spectators: but, to our no small surprise, we find them still
rising upon us, and can only wonder from whence so prodigious a run of Wit and Learning can proceed; since some
of our best judges seem to think that they have hitherto, in
general, outshone even the *Esquire*'s first *Tatlers*.

Most people fancy, from their frequency, that they must be

composed by a Society : I withal assign the first places to Mr. STEELE and his Friend.

I have often thought that the conjunction of those two great Geniuses, who seem to stand in a class by themselves, so high above all our other Wits, resembled that of two statesmen in a late reign, whose characters are very well expressed in their two mottoes, viz., *Prodesse quam conspici* [LORD SOMERS], and *Otium cum dignitate* [CHARLES MONTAGU, Earl of HALIFAX]. Accordingly the first [*ADDISON*] was continually at work behind the curtain, drew up and prepared all those schemes, which the latter still drove on, and stood out exposed to the World, to receive its praises or censures.

Meantime, all our unbiassed well-wishers to Learning are in hopes that the known Temper and prudence of one of these Gentlemen will hinder the other from ever lashing out into Party, and rendering that Wit, which is at present a common good, odious and ungrateful to the better part of the Nation [*by which, of course, GAY meant the Tories*].

If this piece of imprudence does not spoil so excellent a Paper, I propose to myself the highest satisfaction in reading it with you, over a dish of tea, every morning next winter.

As we have yet had nothing new since the *Spectator*, it only remains for me to assure you, that I am

Yours, *&c.*,

J[O H N]. G[A Y].

Westminster, May 3, 1711.

POSTCRIPT.

Upon a review of my letter, I find I have quite forgotten the *British Apollo*; which might possibly have happened, from its having, of late, retreated out of this end of the Town into the country : where, I am informed however, that it still recommends itself by deciding wagers at cards, and giving good advice to shopkeepers and their apprentices.

FINIS.

THOMAS TICKELL.

Life of JOSEPH ADDISON.

[*Preface* to first edition of ADDISON's *Works* 1721.]

JOSEPH ADDISON, the son of LANCELOT ADDISON, D.D., and of JANE, the daughter of NATHANIEL GULSTON, D.D., and sister of Dr. WILLIAM GULSTON, Bishop of BRISTOL, was born at Milston, near Ambrosebury, in the county of Wilts, in the year 1671.

His father, who was of the county of Westmoreland, and educated at Queen's College in Oxford, passed many years in his travels through Europe and Africa; where he joined to the uncommon and excellent talents of Nature, a great knowledge of Letters and Things: of which, several books published by him, are ample testimonies. He was Rector of Milston, above mentioned, when Mr. ADDISON, his eldest son, was born: and afterwards became Archdeacon of Coventry, and Dean of Lichfield.

Mr. ADDISON received his first education at the *Chartreuse* [*Charterhouse School in London*]; from whence he was removed very early to Queen's College, in Oxford. He had been there about two years, when the accidental sight of a Paper of his verses, in the hands of Dr. LANCASTER, then Dean of that House, occasioned his being elected into Magdalen College.

He employed his first years in the study of the old Greek and Roman Writers; whose language and manner he caught, at that time of life, as strongly as other young people gain a French accent, or a genteel air.

An early acquaintance with the Classics is what may be called the Good Breeding of Poetry, as it gives a certain gracefulness which never forsakes a mind that contracted it in youth; but is seldom, or never, hit by those who would learn it too late.

He first distinguished himself by his Latin compositions, published in the *Musæ Anglicanæ*: and was admired as one of the best Authors since the Augustan Age, in the two universities and the greatest part of Europe, before he was talked of as a Poet in Town.

There is not, perhaps, any harder task than to tame the natural wildness of Wit, and to civilize the Fancy. The generality of our old English Poets abound in forced conceits and affected phrases; and even those who are said to come the nearest to exactness, are but too often fond of unnatural beauties, and aim at something better than perfection. If Mr. ADDISON's example and precepts be the occasion that there now begins to be a great demand for Correctness, we may justly attribute it to his being first fashioned by the ancient Models, and familiarized to Propriety of Thought and Chastity of Style.

Our country owes it to him, that the famous Monsieur BOILEAU first conceived an opinion of the English Genius for Poetry, by perusing the present he made him of the *Musæ Anglicanæ*. It has been currently reported, that this famous French poet, among the civilities he shewed Mr. ADDISON on that occasion, affirmed that he would not have written against PERRAULT, had he before seen such excellent Pieces by a modern hand. Such a saying would have been impertinent, and unworthy [of] BOILEAU! whose dispute with PERRAULT turned chiefly upon some passages in the Ancients, which he rescued from the misinterpretations of his adversary. The true and natural compliment made by him, was that those books had given him a very new Idea of the English Politeness, and that he did not question but there were excellent compositions in the native language of a country, that professed the Roman Genius in so eminent a degree.

The first English performance made public by him, is a short copy of verses *To Mr. DRYDEN*, with a view particularly to his Translations.

This was soon followed by a Version of the fourth *Georgic* of VIRGIL; of which Mr. DRYDEN makes very honourable mention in the *Postscript* to his own Translation of VIRGIL's *Works*: wherein, I have often wondered that he did not, at the same time, acknowledge his obligation to Mr. ADDISON, for giving the *Essay upon the Georgics*, prefixed to Mr. DRYDEN's

Translation. Lest the honour of so exquisite a piece of criticism should hereafter be transferred to a wrong Author, I have taken care to insert it in this Collection of his *Works*.

Of some other copies of Verses, printed in the *Miscellanies* while he was young, the largest is *An Account of the greatest English Poets*; in the close of which, he insinuates a design he then had of going into Holy Orders, to which he was strongly importuned by his father. His remarkable seriousness and modesty, which might have been urged as powerful reasons for his choosing that life, proved the chief obstacles to it. These qualities, by which the Priesthood is so much adorned, represented the duties of it as too weighty for him, and rendered him still the more worthy of that honour, which they made him decline. It is happy that this very circumstance has since turned so much to the advantage of Virtue and Religion; in the cause of which, he has bestowed his labours the more successfully, as they were his voluntary, not his necessary employment. The World became insensibly reconciled to Wisdom and Goodness, when they saw them recommended by him, with at least as much Spirit and Elegance as they had been ridiculed [with] for half a century.

He was in his twenty-eighth year [1699], when his inclination to see France and Italy was encouraged by the great Lord Chancellor SOMERS, one of that kind of patriots who think it no waste of the Public Treasure, to purchase Politeness to their country. His Poem upon one of King WILLIAM's Campaigns, addressed to his Lordship, was received with great humanity; and occasioned a message from him to the Author, to desire his acquaintance.

He soon after obtained, by his Interest, a yearly pension of three hundred pounds from the Crown, to support him in his travels. If the uncommonness of a favour, and the distinction of the person who confers it, enhance its value; nothing could be more honourable to a young Man of Learning, than such a bounty from so eminent a Patron.

How well Mr. ADDISON answered the expectations of my Lord SOMERS, cannot appear better than from the book of *Travels*, he dedicated to his Lordship at his return. It is not hard to conceive why that performance was at first but indifferently relished by the bulk of readers; who expected an

Account, in a common way, of the customs and policies of the several Governments in Italy, reflections upon the Genius of the people, a Map [*description*] of the Provinces, or a measure of their buildings. How were they disappointed! when, instead of such particulars, they were presented only with a Journal of Poetical Travels, with Remarks on the present picture of the country compared with the landskips [*landscapes*] drawn by Classic Authors, and others the like unconcerning parts of knowledge! One may easily imagine a reader of plain sense but without a fine taste, turning over these parts of the Volume which make more than half of it, and wondering how an Author who seems to have so solid an understanding when he treats of more weighty subjects in the other pages, should dwell upon such trifles, and give up so much room to matters of mere amusement. There are indeed but few men so fond of the Ancients, as to be transported with every little accident which introduces to their intimate acquaintance. Persons of that cast may here have the satisfaction of seeing Annotations upon an old Roman Poem, gathered from the hills and valleys where it was written. The Tiber and the Po serve to explain the verses which were made upon their banks; and the Alps and Apennines are made Commentators on those Authors, to whom they were subjects, so many centuries ago.

Next to personal conversation with the Writers themselves, this is the surest way of coming at their sense; a compendious and engaging kind of Criticism which convinces at first sight, and shews the vanity of conjectures made by Antiquaries at a distance. If the knowledge of Polite Literature has its use, there is certainly a merit in illustrating the Perfect Models of it; and the Learned World will think some years of a man's life not misspent in so elegant an employment. I shall conclude what I had to say on this Performance, by observing that the fame of it increased from year to year; and the demand for copies was so urgent, that their price rose to four or five times the original value, before it came out in a second edition.

The *Letter from Italy* to my Lord HALIFAX may be considered as the Text, upon which the book of *Travels* is a large Comment; and has been esteemed by those who have a relish for Antiquity, as the most exquisite of his poetical per-

formances. A Translation of it, by Signor SALVINI, Professor
of the Greek tongue, at Florence, is inserted in this edition;
not only on account of its merit, but because it is the
language of the country, which is the subject of the Poem.

The materials for the *Dialogues upon Medals*, now first
printed from a manuscript of the Author, were collected in
the native country of those coins. The book itself was
begun to be cast in form, at Vienna; as appears from a letter
to Mr. STEPNEY, then Minister at that Court, dated in
November, 1702.

Some time before the date of this letter, Mr. ADDISON had
designed to return to England; when he received advice from
his friends that he was pitched upon to attend the army
under Prince EUGENE, who had just begun the war in Italy,
as Secretary from His Majesty. But an account of the death
of King WILLIAM, which he met with at Geneva, put an end
to that thought : and, as his hopes of advancement in his own
country, were fallen with the credit of his friends, who were
out of power at the beginning of her late Majesty's reign,
he had leisure to make the tour of Germany, in his way home.

He remained, for some time after his return to England,
without any public employment: which he did not obtain till
the year 1704, when the Duke of MARLBOROUGH arrived at
the highest pitch of glory, by delivering all Europe from
slavery ; and furnished Mr. ADDISON with a subject worthy
of that Genius which appears in his Poem, called *The Campaign*.

The Lord Treasurer GODOLPHIN, who was a fine judge of
poetry, had a sight of this Work when it was only carried on
as far as the applauded simile of the Angel ; and approved of
the Poem, by bestowing on the Author, in a few days after,
the place of Commissioner of Appeals, vacant by the removal
of the famous Mr. [JOHN] LOCKE to the Council of Trade.

His next advancement was to the place of Under Secretary, which he held under Sir CHARLES HEDGES, and the
present Earl of SUNDERLAND. The opera of *Rosamond* was
written while he possessed that employment. What doubts
soever have been raised about the merit of the Music, which,
as the Italian taste at that time began wholly to prevail, was
thought sufficient inexcusable, because it was the composition of an Englishman; the Poetry of this Piece has given

as much pleasure in the closet, as others have afforded from the Stage, with all the assistance of voices and instruments.

The Comedy called *The Tender Husband* appeared much about the same time ; to which Mr. ADDISON wrote the *Prologue.* Sir RICHARD STEELE surprised him with a very handsome *Dedication* of his Play ; and has since acquainted the Public, that he owed some of the most taking scenes of it, to Mr. ADDISON.

His next step in his fortune, was to the post of Secretary under the late Marquis of WHARTON, who was appointed Lord Lieutenant of Ireland, in the year 1709. As I have proposed to touch but very lightly on those parts of his life, which do not regard him as an Author ; I shall not enlarge upon the great reputation he acquired, by his turn for business, and his unblemished integrity, in this and other employments.

It must not be omitted here, that the salary of Keeper of the Records in Ireland was considerably raised, and that post bestowed upon him at this time, as a mark of the Queen's favour.

He was in that Kingdom, when he first discovered Sir. RICHARD STEELE to be the Author of the *Tatler*, by an observation upon VIRGIL, which had been by him communicated to his friend. The assistance he occasionally gave him afterwards, in the course of the Paper, did not a little contribute to advance its reputation ; and, upon the Change of the Ministry, he found leisure to engage more constantly in that Work : which, however, was dropped at last, as it had been taken up, without his participation.

In the last Paper, which closed those celebrated Performances, and in the *Preface* to the last Volume, Sir RICHARD STEELE has given to Mr. ADDISON, the honour of the most applauded Pieces in that Collection. But as that acknowledgement was delivered only in general terms, without directing the Public to the several Papers ; Mr. ADDISON (who was content with the praise arising from his own Works, and too delicate to take any part of that which belonged to others), afterwards, thought fit to distinguish his Writings in the *Spectators* and *Guardians,* by such marks as might remove the least possibility of mistake in the most undiscerning readers.

It was necessary that his share in the *Tatlers* should be adjusted in a complete Collection of his *Works*: for which reason, Sir RICHARD STEELE, in compliance with the request of his deceased friend, delivered to him by the Editor, was pleased to mark with his own hand, those *Tatlers*, which are inserted in this edition; and even to point out several, in the writing of which, they were both concerned.

The Plan of the *Spectator*, as far as regards the feigned Person of the Author, and of the several Characters that compose his Club, was projected in concert with Sir RICHARD STEELE. And because many passages in the course of the Work would otherwise be obscure, I have taken leave to insert one single Paper written by Sir RICHARD STEELE, wherein those Characters are drawn; which may serve as a *Dramatis Personæ*, or as so many pictures for an ornament and explication of the whole.

As for the distinct Papers, they were never or seldom shewn to each other, by their respective Authors; who fully answered the Promise they had made, and far outwent the Expectation they had raised, of pursuing their Labour in the same Spirit and Strength with which it was begun.

It would have been impossible for Mr. ADDISON (who made little or no use of letters sent in, by the numerous correspondents of the *Spectator*) to have executed his large share of his task in so exquisite a manner; if he had not engrafted into it many Pieces that had lain by him, in little hints and minutes, which he from time to time collected and ranged in order, and moulded into the form in which they now appear. Such are the Essays upon *Wit*, the *Pleasures of the Imagination*, the *Critique upon MILTON*, and some others: which I thought to have connected in a continued Series in this Edition, though they were at first published with the interruption of writings on different subjects. But as such a scheme would have obliged me to cut off several graceful introductions and circumstances peculiarly adapted to the time and occasion of printing then; I durst not pursue that attempt.

The Tragedy of *CATO* appeared in public in the year 1713; when the greatest part of the last *Act* was added by the Author, to the foregoing which he had kept by him for many years. He took up a design of writing a play upon this subject, when he was very young at the University; and even attempted something in it there, though not a line as it now stands. The work was performed by him in his travels, and retouched in England, without any formed resolution of bringing it upon the Stage, until his friends of the first Quality and Distinction prevailed on him, to put the last finishing to it, at a time when they thought the Doctrine of Liberty very seasonable.

It is in everybody's memory, with what applause it was received by the Public; that the first run of it lasted for a month, and then stopped only because one of the performers became incapable of acting a principal part.

The Author received a message that the Queen would be pleased to have it dedicated to her: but as he had designed that compliment elsewhere, he found himself obliged, by his duty on the one side, and his honour on the other, to send it into the World without any *Dedication*.

The fame of this tragedy soon spread through Europe; and it has not only been translated, but acted in most of the languages of Christendom. The Translation of it into Italian by Signor SALVINI is very well known: but I have not been able to learn, whether that of Signor VALETTA, a young Neapolitan Nobleman, has ever been made public.

If he had found time for the writing of another tragedy, the Death of SOCRATES would have been the story. And, however unpromising that subject may appear; it would be presumptuous to censure his choice, who was so famous for raising the noblest plants from the most barren soil. It serves to shew that he thought the whole labour of such a Performance unworthy to be thrown away upon those Intrigues and Adventures, to which the romantic taste has confined Modern Tragedy: and, after the example of his predecessors in Greece, would have employed the Drama *to wear out of our minds everything that is mean or little, to cherish and cultivate that Humanity which is the ornament of our nature, to soften Insolence, to soothe Affliction, and to subdue our minds to the dispensations of Providence.* (*Spectator.* No. 39.)

Upon the death of the late Queen, the Lords Justices, in whom the Administration was lodged, appointed him their Secretary.

Soon after His Majesty's arrival in Great Britain, the

Earl of SUNDERLAND, being constituted Lord Lieutenant of
Ireland; Mr. ADDISON became, a second time, Secretary for
the Affairs of that Kingdom : and was made one of the Lords
Commissioners of Trade, a little after his Lordship resigned
the post of Lord Lieutenant.

The Paper called the *Freeholder*, was undertaken at the time
when the Rebellion broke out in Scotland.

The only Works he left behind for the Public, are the *Dialogues upon medals*, and the Treatise upon the *Christian Religion*.
Some account has been already given of the former : to which
nothing is now to be added, except that a great part of the
Latin quotations were rendered into English in a very hasty
manner by the Editor and one of his friends who had the good
nature to assist him, during his avocations of business. It
was thought better to add these translations, such as they
are; than to let the Work come out unintelligible to those
who do not possess the learned languages.

The Scheme for the Treatise upon the *Christian Religion*
was formed by the Author, about the end of the late Queen's
reign; at which time, he carefully perused the ancient
Writings, which furnish the materials for it. His continual
employment in business prevented him from executing it, until
he resigned his office of Secretary of State; and his death put
a period to it, when he had imperfectly performed only one
half of the design : he having proposed, as appears from the
Introduction, to add the Jewish to the Heathen testimonies
for the truth of the Christian History. He was more as-
siduous than his health would well allow, in the pursuit of
this Work : and had long determined to dedicate his Poetry
also, for the future, wholly to religious subjects.

Soon after, he was, from being one of the Lords Commissioners of Trade, advanced to the post of Secretary of State;
he found his health impaired by the return of that asthmatic
indisposition; which continued often, to afflict him during his
exercise of that employment : and, at last, obliged him to beg
His Majesty's leave to resign.

His freedom from the anxiety of business so far re-estab-
lished his health, that his friends began to hope he might
last for many years : but (whether it were from a life too

sedentary; or from his natural constitution, in which was one circumstance very remarkable, that, from his cradle, he never had a regular pulse) a long and painful relapse into an asthma and dropsy deprived the World of this great man, on the 17th of June, 1719.

He left behind him only one daughter, by the Countess of WARWICK; to whom he was married in the year 1716.

Not many days before his death, he gave me directions to collect his Writings, and at the same time committed to my care the *Letter* addressed *to Mr.* CRAGGS, his successor as Secretary of State, wherein he bequeaths them to him, as a token of friendship.

Such a testimony, from the First Man of our Age, in such a point of time, will be perhaps as great and lasting an honour to that Gentleman as any even he could acquire to himself; and yet it is no more than was due from an affection that justly increased towards him, through the intimacy of several years. I cannot, save with the utmost tenderness, reflect on the kind concern with which Mr. ADDISON left Me as a sort of incumbrance upon this valuable legacy. Nor must I deny myself the honour to acknowlege that the goodness of that Great Man to me, like many other of his amiable qualities, seemed not so much to be renewed, as continued in his successor; who made me an example, that nothing could be indifferent to him which came recommended to Mr. ADDISON.

Could any circumstance be more severe to me, while I was executing these Last Commands of the Author, than to see the Person to whom his Works were presented, cut off in the flower of his age, and carried from the high Office wherein he had succeeded Mr. ADDISON, to be laid next him, in the same grave? I might dwell upon such thoughts as naturally rise from these minute resemblances in the fortune of two persons, whose names probably will be seldom mentioned asunder while either our Language or Story subsist; were I not afraid of making this *Preface* too tedious : especially since I shall want all the patience of the reader, for having enlarged it with the following verses.

To the EARL OF WARWICK

On the Death of MR. ADDISON.

IF dumb too long, the drooping muse hath stay'd
And left her debt to Addison unpaid,
Blame not her silence, Warwick, but bemoan,
And judge, oh judge, my bosom by your own.
What mourner ever felt poetic fires!
Slow comes the verse that real woe inspires:
Grief unaffected suits but ill with art,
Or flowing numbers with a bleeding heart.
  Can I forget the dismal night that gave
My soul's best part for ever to the grave!
How silent did his old companions tread
By midnight lamps, the mansions of the dead
Through breathing statues, then unheeded things,
Through rows of warriors, and through walks of kings!
What awe did the slow solemn knell inspire;
The pealing organ, and the pausing choir;
The duties by the lawn-rob'd prelate paid;
And the last words, that dust to dust convey'd!

While speechless o'er thy closing grave we bend,
Accept these tears, thou dear departed friend.
Oh gone for ever! take this long adieu;
And sleep in peace, next thy lov'd Montague.
To strew fresh laurels, let the task be mine,
A frequent pilgrim, at thy sacred shrine;
Mine with true sighs thy absence to bemoan,
And grave with faithful epitaphs thy stone.
If e'er from me thy lov'd memorial part,
May shame afflict this alienated heart;
Of thee forgetful if I form a song,
My lyre be broken, and untun'd my tongue,
My grief be doubled from thy image free,
And mirth a torment, unchastis'd by thee.

Oft let me range the gloomy aisles alone,
Sad luxury! to vulgar minds unknown,
Along the walls, where speaking marbles show
What worthies form the hallow'd mould below;
Proud names who once the reins of empire held;
In arms who triumphed; or in arts excelled;
Chiefs graced with scars and prodigal of blood;
Stern patriots who for sacred freedom stood;
Just men, by whom impartial laws were given;
And saints who taught and led the way to heaven;
Ne'er to these chambers, where the mighty rest
Since their foundation came a nobler guest;
Nor e'er was to the bowers of bliss convey'd
A fairer spirit or more welcome shade.

In what new region to the just assigned,
What new employments please th' unbody'd mind;
A wingèd virtue, through th' ethereal sky
From world to world unweary'd does he fly?
Or curious trace the long laborious maze
Of heaven's decrees where wondering angels gaze;
Does he delight to hear bold seraphs tell
How Michael battl'd and the dragon fell,
Or mixed with milder cherubim to glow
In hymns of love not ill-essay'd below?
Or dost thou warn poor mortals left behind
A task well suited to thy gentle mind?
Oh! if sometimes thy spotless form descend
To me thy aid, thou guardian genius lend
When rage misguides me or when fear alarms,
When pain distresses or when pleasure charms,
In silent whisperings purer thoughts impart,
And turn from ill a frail and feeble heart;
Lead through the paths thy virtue trod before,
Till bliss shall join nor death can part us more.

That awful form, which, so the heavens decree,
Must still be loved and still deplor'd by me
In nightly visions seldom fails to rise,
Or rous'd by fancy, meets my waking eyes.
If business calls, or crowded courts invite;
Th' unblemish'd statesman seems to strike my sight;
If in the stage I seek to soothe my care
I meet his soul which breathes in Cato there;

If pensive to the rural shades I rove,
His shape o'ertakes me in the lonely grove;
'Twas there of just and good he reason'd strong,
Clear'd some great truth, or rais'd some serious song:
There patient show'd us the wise course to steer,
A candid censor, and a friend severe;
There taught us how to live; and (oh! too high
The price for knowledge) taught us how to die.

．　　．　　．　　．　　．　　．　　．

Sir RICHARD STEELE.

Dedicatory Epistle to WILLIAM CONGREVE.

[This Dedication is prefixed to the Second
Edition of ADDISON's *Drummer*, 1722.]

To Mr. CONGREVE:
occasioned by Mr. TICKELL's *Preface* to the four
volumes of Mr. ADDISON's *Works.*

SIR,

 HIS is the second time that I have, without your leave, taken the liberty to make a public address to you.

However uneasy you may be, for your own sake, in receiving compliments of this nature, I depend upon your known humanity for pardon; when I acknowledge that you have this present trouble, for mine. When I take myself to be ill treated with regard to my behaviour to the merit of other men; my conduct towards you is an argument of my candour that way, as well as that your name and authority will be my protection in it. You will give me leave therefore, in a matter that concerns us in the Poetical World, to make you my judge whether I am not injured in the highest manner! for with men of your taste and delicacy, it is a high crime and misdemeanour to be guilty of anything that is disingenuous. But I will go into my matter.

Upon my return from Scotland, I visited Mr. TONSON's shop, and thanked him for his care in sending to my house, the Volumes of my dear and honoured friend Mr. ADDISON; which are, at last, published by his Secretary, Mr. TICKELL: but took occasion to observe, that I had not seen the Work before it came out; which he did not think fit to excuse any otherwise than by a recrimination, that I had put into his hands, at a high price, a Comedy called *The*

Drummer; which, by my zeal for it, he took to be written by Mr. ADDISON, and of which, after his [*ADDISON's*] death, he said, I directly acknowleged he was the author.

To urge this hardship still more home, he produced a receipt under my hand, in these words—

March 12, 1715[–16].

Received then, the sum of Fifty Guineas for the Copy [copy-right] *of the Comedy called,* The Drummer or the Haunted House. *I say, received by order of the Author of the said Comedy,*   R I C H A R D   S T E E L E .

and added, at the same time, that since Mr. TICKELL had not thought fit to make that play a part of Mr. ADDISON's *Works;* he would sell the Copy to any bookseller that would give most for it [*i.e.,* TONSON *threw the onus of the authenticity of the* Drummer *on* STEELE].

This is represented thus circumstantially, to shew how incumbent it is upon me, as well in justice to the bookseller, as for many other considerations, to produce this Comedy a second time [*It was first printed in* 1716] ; and take this occasion to vindicate myself against certain insinuations thrown out by the Publisher [*THOMAS TICKELL*] of Mr. ADDISON's Writings, concerning my behaviour in the nicest circumstance—that of doing justice to the Merit of my Friend.

I shall take the liberty, before I have ended this Letter, to say why I believe the *Drummer* a performance of Mr. ADDISON : and after I have declared this, any surviving writer may be at ease ; if there be any one who has hitherto been vain enough to hope, or silly enough to fear, it may be given to himself.

Before I go any further, I must make my Public Appeal to you and all the Learned World, and humbly demand, Whether it was a decent and reasonable thing, that Works written, as a great part of Mr. ADDISON's were, in correspondence [*coadjutorship*] with me, ought to have been published without my review of the Catalogue of them ; or if there were any exception to be made against any circumstance in my conduct, Whether an opportunity to explain myself should not have been allowed me, before any Reflections were made on me in print.

When I had perused Mr. TICKELL's *Preface,* I had soon

so many objections, besides his omission to say anything of
the *Drummer*, against his long-expected performance : the
chief intention of which (and which it concerns me first to
examine) seems to aim at doing the deceased Author justice,
against me! whom he insinuates to have assumed to myself,
part of the merit of my friend.

He is pleased, Sir, to express himself concerning the
present Writer, in the following manner—

The Comedy called The Tender Husband, *appeared much
about the same time; to which Mr.* ADDISON *wrote the* Prologue:
Sir RICHARD STEELE *surprised him with a very handsome*
Dedication *of this Play; and has since acquainted the Public,
that he owed some of the most taking scenes of it, to Mr.* ADDISON.
Mr. TICKELL'S *Preface.* Pag. 11.

He was in that Kingdom [Ireland], *when he first discovered
Sir* RICHARD STEELE *to be the Author of the* Tatler, *by an
observation upon* VIRGIL, *which had been by him communicated
to his friend. The assistance he occasionally gave him afterwards,
in the course of the Paper, did not a little contribute to advance its
reputation; and, upon the Change of the Ministry* [in the autumn
of 1710], *he found leisure to engage more constantly in that
Work : which, however, was dropped at last, as it had been taken
up, without his participation.*

*In the last Paper which closed those celebrated Performances,
and in the* Preface *to the last Volume, Sir* RICHARD STEELE
has given to Mr. ADDISON, *the honour of the most applauded
Pieces in that Collection. But as that acknowledgement was
delivered only in general terms, without directing the Public to
the several Papers; Mr.* ADDISON (*who was content with the
praise arising from his own Works, and too delicate to take any
part of that which belonged to others*), *afterwards thought fit to
distinguish his Writings in the* Spectators *and* Guardians *by
such marks as might remove the least possibility of mistake in the
most undiscerning readers. It was necessary that his share in the*
Tatlers *should be adjusted in a complete Collection of his* Works :
for which reason, Sir RICHARD STEELE, *in compliance with the
request of his deceased friend, delivered to him by the Editor, was
pleased to mark with his own hand, those* Tatlers *which are
inserted in this edition; and even to point out several, in the
writing of which, they both were concerned.* Pag. 12.

The Plan of the Spectator, *as far as it related to the feigned Person of the Author, and of the several Characters that compose his Club, was projected in concert with Sir* RICHARD STEELE : *and because many passages in the course of the Work would otherwise be obscure, I have taken leave to insert one Paper written by Sir* RICHARD STEELE, *wherein those Characters are drawn ; which may serve as a* Dramatis Personæ, *or as so many pictures for an ornament and explication of the whole. As for the distinct Papers, they were never or seldom shewn to each other, by their respective Authors ; who fully answered the Promise they made, and far outwent the Expectation they had raised, of pursuing their Labour in the same Spirit and Strength with which it was begun.* Page 13.

It need not be explained that it is here intimated, that I had not sufficiently acknowledged what was due to Mr. ADDISON in these Writings. I shall make a full Answer to what seems intended by the words, *He was too delicate to take any part of that which belonged to others* ; if I can recite out of my own Papers, anything that may make it appear groundless.

The subsequent [*following*] encomiums bestowed by me on Mr. ADDISON will, I hope, be of service to me in this particular.

But I have only one Gentleman, who will be nameless, to thank for any frequent assistance to me : which indeed it would have been barbarous in him, to have denied to one with whom he has lived in an intimacy from childhood ; considering the great Ease with which he is able to despatch the most entertaining Pieces of this nature. This good office he performed with such force of Genius, Humour, Wit, and Learning, that I fared like a distressed Prince who calls in a powerful neighbour to his aid ; I was undone by my auxiliary ! When I had once called him in, I could not subsist without dependence on him.

The same Hand wrote the distinguishing Characters of Men and Women under the names of Musical Instruments, *the* Distress of the News-Writers, *the* Inventory of the Play House, *and the* Description of the Thermometer; *which I cannot but look upon, as the greatest embellishments of this Work.* Pref. *to the* 4th Vol. *of the* Tatlers.

As to the Work itself, the acceptance it has met with is the best proof of its value : but I should err against that candour which an honest man should always carry about him, if I did not own that the most approved Pieces in it were written by others; and those, which have been most excepted against by myself. The Hand that has assisted me in those noble Discourses upon the Immortality of the Soul, the Glorious Prospects of another Life, and the most sublime ideas of Religion and Virtue, is a person, who is too fondly my friend ever to own them: but I should little deserve to be his, if I usurped the glory of them. I must acknowledge, at the same time, that I think the finest strokes of Wit and Humour in all Mr. BICKERSTAFF's Lucubrations, are those for which he is also beholden to him. Tatler, No. 271.

I hope the Apology I have made as to the license allowable to a feigned Character may excuse anything which has been said in these Discourses of the Spectator and his Works. But the imputation of the grossest vanity would still dwell upon me, if I did not give some account by what means I was enabled to keep up the Spirit of so long and approved a performance. All the Papers marked with a C, L, I, or O—that is to say, all the Papers which I have distinguished by any letter in the name of the Muse C L I O— were given me by the Gentleman, of whose assistance I formerly boasted in the Preface and concluding Leaf of the Tatler. I am indeed much more proud of his long-continued friendship, than I should be of the fame of being thought the Author of any Writings which he himself is capable of producing.

I remember, when I finished the Tender Husband; I told him, there was nothing I so ardently wished as that we might, some time or other, publish a Work written by us both; which should bear the name of the Monument, in memory of our friendship. I heartily wish what I have done here, were as honorary to that sacred name, as Learning, Wit, and Humanity render those Pieces, which I have taught the reader how to distinguish for his.

When the Play above mentioned was last acted, there were so many applauded strokes in it which I had from the same hand, that I thought very meanly of myself that I had never publicly acknowledged them.

After I have put other friends upon importuning him to publish Dramatic as well as other Writings, he has by him; I shall end what I think I am obliged to say on this head, by giving the reader this hint for the better judgement of my productions: that the best Comment upon them would be, an Account when the Patron [i.e., ADDISON] *to the Tender Husband was in England or abroad* [i.e., Ireland]. Spectator, No 555

My purpose in this Application is only to shew the esteem I have for you, and that I look upon my intimacy with you as one of the most valuable enjoyments of my life. Dedication before the *Tender Husband.*

I am sure, you have read my quotations with indignation against the little [*petty*] zeal which prompted the Editor (who by the way, has himself done nothing in applause of the Works which he prefaces) to the mean endeavour of adding to Mr. ADDISON, by disparaging a man who had (for the greatest part of his life) been his known bosom friend, and shielded him from all the resentments which many of his own Works would have brought upon him, at the time they were written. It is really a good office to Society, to expose the indiscretion of Intermedlers int he friendship and correspondence [*coadjutorship*] of men, whose sentiments, passions, and resentments are too great for their proportion of soul!

Could the Editor's indiscretion provoke me, even so far as (within the rules of strictest honour) I could go; and I were not restrained by supererogatory affection to dear Mr. ADDISON, I would ask this unskilful Creature, What he means, when he speaks in an air of a reproach, *that the* Tatler *was laid down as it was taken up, without his participation?* Let him speak out and say, why *without his knowledge* would not serve his purpose as well!

If, as he says, he restrains himself to "Mr. ADDISON's character as a Writer;" while he attempts to lessen me, he exalts me! for he has declared to all the World what I never have so explicitly done, that I am, to all intents and purposes, *the Author of the* Tatler! He very justly says, the occasional assistance Mr. ADDISON gave me. in the course of that Paper, "did not a little contribute to advance its reputation, especially when, upon the Change of Ministry [*August*, 1710], he found leisure to engage more constantly in it." It was advanced indeed! for it was raised to a greater thing than I intended it! For the elegance, purity, and correctness which appeared in his Writings were not so much my purpose; as (in any intelligible manner, as I could) to rally all those Singularities of human life, through the different Professions and Characters in it, which obstruct anything that was truly good and great.

After this Acknowledgement, you will see; that is, such
a man as you will see, that I rejoiced in being excelled!
and made those little talents (whatever they are) which I
have, give way and be subservient to the superior qualities of
a Friend, whom I loved! and whose modesty would never
have admitted them to come into daylight, but under such a
shelter.

So that all which the Editor has said (either out of design,
or incapacity), Mr. Congreve! must end in this: that
Steele has been so candid and upright, that he owes
nothing to Mr. Addison as a Writer; but whether he do, or
does not, whatever Steele owes to Mr. Addison, the Public
owe Addison to Steele!

But the Editor has such a fantastical and ignorant zeal
for his Patron, that he will not allow his correspondents
[coadjutors] to conceal anything of his; though in obedience
to his commands!

What I never did declare was Mr. Addison's, I had his
direct injunctions to hide; against the natural warmth and
passion of my own temper towards my friends.

Many of the Writings now published as his, I have been
very patiently traduced and culminated for; as they were
pleasantries and oblique strokes upon certain of the wittiest
men of the Age: who will now restore me to their goodwill,
in proportion to the abatement of [the] Wit which they
thought I employed against them.

But I was saying, that the Editor won't allow us to obey
his Patron's commands in anything which he thinks would
redound to his credit, if discovered. And because I would
shew a little Wit in my anger, I shall have the discretion to
shew you that he has been guilty, in this particular, towards
a much greater man than your humble servant, and one
whom you are much more obliged to vindicate.

Mr. Dryden, in his VIRGIL, after having acknowledged
that a "certain excellent young man" [i.e., W. Congreve
himself] had shewed him many faults in his translation of
VIRGIL, which he had endeavoured to correct, goes on to
say, "Two other worthy friends of mine, who desire to have
their names concealed, seeing me straightened in my time,
took pity on me, and gave me the Life of VIRGIL, the two Prefaces to the Pastorals and the Georgics, and all the Arguments

in prose to the whole Translation." If Mr. ADDISON is one of the two friends, and the *Preface* to the *Georgics* be what the Editor calls the *Essay upon the Georgics* as one may adventure to say they are, from their being word for word the same, he has cast an inhuman reflection upon Mr. DRYDEN : who, though tied down not to name Mr. ADDISON, pointed at him so as all Mankind conservant in these matters knew him, with an eulogium equal to the highest merit, considering who it was that bestowed it. I could not avoid remarking upon this circumstance, out of justice to Mr. DRYDEN : but confess, at the same time, I took a great pleasure in doing it ; because I knew, in exposing this outrage, I made my court to Mr. CONGREVE.

I have observed that the Editor will not let me or any one else obey Mr. ADDISON's commands, in hiding anything he desired to be concealed.

I cannot but take further notice, that the circumstance of marking his *Spectators* [*with the letters C, L, I, O,*], which I did not know till I had done with the Work ; I made my own act ! because I thought it too great a sensibility in my friend ; and thought it (since it was done) better to be supposed marked by me than the Author himself. The real state of which, this zealot rashly and injudiciously exposes ! I ask the reader, Whether anything but an earnestness to disparage me could provoke the Editor, in behalf of Mr. ADDISON, to say that he marked it out of caution against me : when I had taken upon me to say, it was I that did it ! out of tenderness to him.

As the imputation of any the Least Attempt of arrogating to myself, or detracting from Mr. ADDISON, is without any Colour of Truth : you will give me leave to go on in the same ardour towards him, and resent the cold, unaffectionate, dry, and barren manner, in which this Gentleman gives an Account of as great a Benefactor as any one Learned Man ever had of another. Would any man, who had been produced from a College life, and pushed into one of the most considerable Employments of the Kingdom as to its weight and trust, and greatly lucrative with respect to a Fellowship [*i.e., of a College*] : and who had been daily and hourly with one of the greatest men of the Age, be satisfied with himself, in saying *nothing* of such a Person besides what all the World knew !

except a particularity (and that to his disadvantage !) which
I, his friend from a boy, don't know to be true, to wit, that
" he never had a regular pulse " !

As for the facts, and considerable periods of his life, he
either knew nothing of them, or injudiciously places them in
a worse light than that in which they really stood.

When he speaks of Mr. ADDISON'S declining to go into
Orders, his way of doing it is to lament *his seriousness and
modesty*, which might have recommended him, *proved the
chief obstacles to it, it seems these qualities, by which the Priesthood
is so much adorned, represented the duties of it as too weighty for him,
and rendered him still more worthy of that honour which they
made him decline.* These, you know very well ! were not the
Reasons which made Mr. ADDISON turn his thoughts to the
civil World ; and, as you were the instrument of his becoming acquainted with my Lord HALIFAX, I doubt not but you
remember the warm instances that noble Lord made to the
Head of the College, not to insist upon Mr. ADDISON'S going
into Orders. His arguments were founded on the general
pravity [*depravity*] and corruption of men of business [*public
men*] who wanted liberal education. And I remember, as if
I read the letter yesterday, that my Lord ended with a
compliment, that "however he might be represented as no
friend to the Church, he would never do it any other injury
than keeping Mr. ADDISON out of it ! "

The contention for this man in his early youth, among the
people of greatest power ; Mr. Secretary TICKELL, the
Executor for his Fame, is pleased to ascribe to " a serious
visage and modesty of behaviour."

When a Writer is grossly and essentially faulty, it were a
jest to take notice of a false expression or a phrase, otherwise
Priesthood in that place, might be observed upon ; as a term
not used by the real well-wishers to Clergymen, except when
they would express some solemn act, and not when that
Order is spoken of as a Profession among Gentlemen. I will
not therefore busy myself about the " unconcerning parts of
knowledge, but be content like a reader of plain sense without
politeness." And since Mr. Secretary will give us no account
of this Gentleman, I admit "the Alps and Apennines" instead
of the Editor, to be " Commentators of his Works," which,
as the Editor says, " have raised a demand for correctness."

This " demand," by the way, ought to be more strong upon those who were most about him, and had the greatest advantage of his example. But as our Editor says, "that those who come nearest to exactness are but too often fond of unnatural beauties, and aim at something better than perfection."

Believe me, Sir, Mr. ADDISON's example will carry no man further than that height for which Nature capacitated him : and the affectation of following great men in works above the genius of their imitators, will never rise farther than the production of uncommon and unsuitable ornaments in a barren discourse, like flowers upon a heath, such as the Author's phrase of " something better than perfection."

But in his *Preface*, if ever anything was, is that " something better : " for it is so extraordinary, that we cannot say, it is too long or too short, or deny but that it is both. I think I abstract myself from all manner of prejudice when I aver that no man, though without any obligation to Mr. ADDISON, would have represented him in his family and in his friendships, or his personal character, so disadvantageously as his Secretary (in preference of whom, he incurred the warmest resentments of other Gentlemen) has been pleased to describe him in those particulars.

Mr. Dean ADDISON, father of this memorable Man, left behind him four children, each of whom, for excellent talents and singular preferments, was as much above the ordinary World as their brother JOSEPH was above them. Were things of this nature to be exposed to public view, I could shew under the Dean's own hand, in the warmest terms, his blessing on the friendship between his son and me ; nor had he a child who did not prefer me in the first place of kindness and esteem, as their father loved me like one of them : and I can with pleasure say, I never omitted any opportunity of shewing that zeal for their persons and Interests as became a Gentleman and a Friend.

Were I now to indulge myself, I could talk a great deal to you, which I am sure would be entertaining : but as I am speaking at the same time to all the World, I consider it would be impertinent.

Let me then confine myself awhile to the following Play [*The Drummer*], which I at first recommended to the Stage, and carried to the Press.

No one who reads the *Preface* which I published with it, will imagine I could be induced to say so much, as I then did, had I not known the man I best loved had had a part in it; or had I believed that any other concerned had much more to do than as an amanuensis.

But, indeed, had I not known at the time of the transaction concerning the acting on the Stage and the sale of the Copy; I should, I think, have seen Mr. ADDISON in every page of it! For he was above all men in that talent we call Humour; and enjoyed it in such perfection, that I have often reflected, after a night spent with him apart from the World, that I had had the pleasure of conversing with an intimate acquaintance of TERENCE and CATULLUS, who had all their Wit and Nature heightened with Humour more exquisite and delightful than any other man ever possessed.

They who shall read this Play, after being let into the secret that it was written by Mr. ADDISON or under his direction, will probably be attentive to those excellencies which they before overlooked, and wonder they did not till now observe that there is not an expression in the whole Piece which has not in it the most nice propriety and aptitude to the Character which utters it. Here is that smiling Mirth, that delicate Satire and genteel Raillery, which appeared in Mr. ADDISON when he was free among intimates; I say, when he was free from his *remarkable* bashfulness, which is a cloak that hides and muffles merit: and his abilities were covered only by modesty, which doubles the beauties which are seen, and gives credit and esteem to all that are concealed.

The *Drummer* made no great figure on the Stage, though exquisitely well acted: but when I observe this, I say a much harder thing of the Stage, than of the Comedy.

When I say the Stage in this place, I am understood to mean, in general, the present Taste of theatrical representations: where nothing that is not violent, and as I may say, grossly delightful, can come on, without hazard of being condemned or slighted.

It is here republished, and recommended as a closet piece [*i.e., for private reading*], to recreate an intelligent mind in a vacant hour: for vacant the reader must be, from every strong prepossession, in order to relish an entertainment, *quod nequeo monstrare et sentio tantum*, which cannot be enjoyed to the degree it deserves, but by those of the most polite Taste among Scholars, the best Breeding among Gentlemen, and the least acquainted with sensual Pleasure among the Ladies.

The Editor [*THOMAS TICKELL*] is pleased to relate concerning *CATO*, that a Play under that design was projected by the Author very early, and wholly laid aside; in advanced years, he reassumed the same design ; and many years after Four acts were finished, he wrote the Fifth; and brought it upon the Stage.

All the Town knows, how officious I was in bringing it on, and you (that know the Town, the Theatre, and Mankind very well) can judge how necessary it was, to take measures for making a performance of that sort, excellent as it is, run into popular applause.

I promised before it was acted (and performed my duty accordingly to the Author), that I would bring together so just an audience on the First Days of it, it should be impossible for the vulgar to put its success or due applause at any hazard : but I don't mention this, only to shew how good an Aide-de-Camp I was to Mr. ADDISON; but to shew also that the Editor does as much to cloud the merit of this Work, as I did to set it forth.

Mr. TICKELL's account of its being taken up, laid down, and at last perfected, after such long intervals and pauses, would make any one believe, who did not know Mr. ADDISON, that it was accomplished with the greatest pain and labour; and the issue rather of Learning and Industry than Capacity and Genius : but I do assure you, that never Play which could bring the author any reputation for Wit and Conduct, notwithstanding it was so long before it was finished, employed the Author so little a time in writing.

If I remember right, the Fifth Act was written in less than a week's time ! For this was particular in this Writer, that when he had taken his resolution, or made his Plan for what he designed to write ; he would walk about the room and dictate it into Language, with as much freedom and ease as

any one could write it down : and attend to the Coherence
and Grammar of what he dictated.

I have been often thus employed by him; and never took
it into my head, though he only spoke it and I took all the
pains of throwing it upon paper, that I ought to call myself
the Writer of it.

I will put all my credit among men of Wit for the truth of
my averment, when I presume to say that no one but Mr.
ADDISON was, in any other way, the Writer of the *Drummer*.

At the same time, I will allow, that he sent for me (which
he could always do, from his natural power over me, as much
as he could send for any of his clerks when he was Secretary
of State), and told me that a Gentleman then in the room
had written a play that he was sure I would like ; but it was
to be a secret : and he knew I would take as much pains,
since he recommended it, as I would for him.

I hope nobody will be wronged or think himself aggrieved,
that I give this rejected Work [*the Comedy of* The Drummer *not
included by* TICKELL *in his collected edition of* ADDISON's *Works*]
where I do : and if a certain Gentleman [TICKELL] is injured
by it, I will allow I have wronged him upon this issue; that
if the reputed translator [TICKELL] of the *First Book of
HOMER* shall please to give us another *Book*, there shall
appear another good Judge in poetry, besides Mr. ALEXANDER
POPE, who shall like it !

But I detain you too long upon things that are too personal
to myself, and will defer giving the World a true Notion of
the Character and Talents of Mr. ADDISON, till I can speak
of that amiable Gentlemen on an occasion void of controversy.

I shall then perhaps say many things of him which will be
new even to you, with regard to him in all parts of his
Character : for which I was so zealous, that I could not
be contented with praising and adorning him as much as lay
in my own power ; but was ever soliciting and putting my
friends upon the same office.

And since the Editor [TICKELL] has adorned his heavy

Discourse with Prose in rhyme at the end of it, upon Mr. ADDISON's death: give me leave to atone for this long and tedious *Epistle*, by giving after it, what I dare say you will esteem, an excellent Poem on his marriage [*by Mr. WELSTED*].

I must conclude without satisfying as strong a desire, as every man had, of saying something remarkably handsome to the Person to whom I am writing: for you are so good a judge, that you would find out the Endeavourer to be witty! and therefore, as I have tired you and myself, I will be contented with assuring you, which I do very honestly, I would rather have you satisfied with me on this subject, than any other man living.

You will please pardon me, that I have, thus, laid this nice affair before a person who has the acknowledged superiority to all others; not only in the most excellent talents; but possessing them with an equanimity, candour, and benevolence which render those advantages a pleasure as great to the rest of the World as they can be to the owner of them. And since Fame consists in the Opinion of wise and good men: you must not blame me for taking the readiest way to baffle any Attempt upon my Reputation, by an Address to one, whom every wise and good man looks upon, with the greatest affection and veneration.

I am, Sir,
Your most obliged,
most obedient, and
most humble servant,
RICHARD STEELE.

EDWARD CHAMBERLAYNE.

The social position of the English Established Clergy, in 1669, A.D.

[*Angliæ Notitia*, or the Present State of England. 1st *Ed.* 1669.]

T PRESENT, the revenues of the English Clergy are generally very small and insufficient: above a third of the best benefices of England, having been anciently, by the Pope's grant, appropriated to monasteries, were on their dissolution, made *Lay fees*; besides what hath been taken by secret and indirect means, through corrupt compositions and compacts and customs in many other parishes. And also many estates being wholly exempt from paying tithes, as the lands that belonged to the Cistercian Monks, and to the Knights Templars and Hospitallers.

And those benefices that are free from these things are yet (besides First Fruits and Tenths to the King, and Procurations to the Bishop) taxed towards the charges of their respective parishes, and towards the public charges of the nation, above and beyond the proportion of the Laity.

The Bishoprics of England have been also since the latter of HENRY VIII.'s reign, to the coming in of King JAMES, most miserably robbed and spoiled of the greatest part of their lands and revenues. So that, at this day [1669], a mean gentleman of £200 from land yearly, will not change his worldly estate and condition with divers Bishops: and an Attorney, a shopkeeper, a common artisan will hardly change theirs, with the ordinary Pastors of the Church.

Some few Bishoprics do yet retain a competency. Amongst which, the Bishopric of Durham is accounted one of the chief: the yearly revenues whereof, before the late troubles [*i.e., the Civil Wars*] were above £6,000 [=£25,000 *now*]: of which by the late *Act for abolishing Tenures in capite* [1660], was lost about £2,000 yearly.

Out of this revenue, a yearly pension of £800 is paid to the Crown, ever since the reign of Queen ELIZABETH; who promised, in lieu thereof, so much in Impropriations: which was never performed.

Above £340 yearly is paid to several officers of the County Palatine of Durham.

The Assizes and Sessions, also, are duly kept in the Bishop's House, at the sole charges of the Bishop.

Also the several expenses for keeping in repair certain banks of rivers in that Bishopric, and of several Houses belonging to the Bishopric.

Moreover, the yearly Tenths, public taxes, the charges of going to and waiting at Parliament, being deducted; there will remain, in ordinary years, to the Bishop to keep hospitality, which must be great, and to provide for those of his family, but about £1,500 [=£4,500 *now*] yearly.

The like might be said of some other principal Bishoprics.

The great diminution of the revenues of the Clergy, and the little care of augmenting and defending the patrimony of the Church, is the great reproach and shame of the English Reformation; and will, one day, prove the ruin of Church and State.

" It is the last trick," saith St. GREGORY, " that the Devil hath in this world. When he cannot bring the Word and Sacraments into disgrace by errors and heresies; he invents this project, to bring the Clergy into contempt and low esteem."

As it is now in England, where they are accounted by many, the Dross and Refuse of the nation. Men think it a stain to their blood to place their sons in that function; and women are ashamed to marry with any of them.

It hath been observed, even by strangers, that the iniquity of the present Times in England is such, that the English Clergy are not only hated by the Romanists on the one side, and maligned by the Presbyterians on the other . . . ; but also that, of all the Christian Clergy of Europe, whether Romish, Lutheran, or Calvinistic, none are so little *respected*, *beloved*, *obeyed*, or *rewarded*, as the present pious, learned, loyal Clergy of England; even by those who have always professed themselves of that Communion.

THE
GROUNDS & OCCASIONS
OF THE
CONTEMPT
OF THE
CLERGY
AND
RELIGION
Enquired into.

In a LETTER *written to* R. L.

LONDON,

Printed by W. GODBID for N. BROOKE at the
Angel in Cornhill. 1670.

This work is dated August 8, 1670. ANTHONY À WOOD in his *Life* (*Ath. Oxon.* I. lxx. Ed. 1813), gives the following account of our Author.

February 9 [1672] A. W. went to London, and the next day he was kindly receiv'd by Sir LIOLIN JENKYNS, in his apartment in Exeter house in the Strand, within the city of Westminster.

Sunday 11 [Feb. 1672], Sir LIOLIN JENKYNS took with him, in the morning, over the water to Lambeth, A. WOOD, and after prayers, he conducted him up to the dining rome, where archb. SHELDON received him, and gave him his blessing. There then dined among the company, JOHN ECHARD, the author of *The Contempt of the Clergy*, who sate at the lower end of the table between the archbishop's two chaplayns SAMUEL PARKER and THOMAS THOMKINS, being the first time that the said ECHARD was introduced into the said archbishop's company. After dinner, the archbishop went into his withdrawing roome, and ECHARD with the chaplaynes and RALPH SNOW to their lodgings to drink and smoak.

JOHN EACHARD, S.T.P., was appointed Master of Catherine Hall, Cambridge, in 1675.]

243

THE PREFACE TO THE READER.

CAN very easily fancy that many, upon the very first sight of the title, will presently imagine that the Author does either want the Great Tithes, lying under the pressure of some pitiful vicarage; or that he is much out of humour, and dissatisfied with the present condition of affairs; or, lastly, that he writes to no purpose at all, there having been an abundance of unprofitable advisers in this kind.

As to my being under some low Church dispensation; you may know, I write not out of a pinching necessity, or out of any rising design. You may please to believe that, although I have a most solemn reverence for the Clergy in general, and especially for that of England; yet, for my own part, I must confess to you, I am not of that holy employment; and have as little thought of being Dean or Bishop, as they that think so, have hopes of being all Lord Keepers.

Nor less mistaken will they be, that shall judge me in the least discontented, or any ways disposed to disturb the peace of the present settled Church: for, in good truth, I have neither lost King's, nor Bishop's lands, that should incline me to a surly and quarrelsome complaining; as many be, who would have been glad enough to see His Majesty restored, and would have endured Bishops daintily well, had they lost no money by their coming in.

I am not, I will assure you, any of those Occasional Writers, that, missing preferment in the University, can presently write you their new ways of Education; or being a little tormented with *an ill-chosen wife, set forth the doctrine of Divorce to be truly evangelical.*

The cause of these few sheets was honest and innocent, and as free from all passion as any design.

As for the last thing which I supposed objected, viz., that this book is altogether needless, there having been an infinite number of Church- and Clergy-menders, that have made many tedious and unsuccessful offers: I must needs confess, that it were very unreasonable for me to expect a better reward.

Only thus much, I think, with modesty may be said: that I cannot at present call to mind anything that is propounded but what is very hopeful, and easily accomplished. For, indeed, should I go about to tell you, that a child can never prove a profitable Instructor of the people, unless born when the sun is in Aries; *or brought up in a school that stands full South: that he can never be able to govern a parish, unless he can ride the great horse; or that he can never go through the great work of the Ministry, unless for three hundred years backward it can be proved that none of his family ever had cough, ague, or grey hair: then I should very patiently endure to be reckoned among the vainest that ever made attempt.*

But believe me, Reader! I am not, as you will easily see, any contriver of an incorruptible and pure crystaline Church, or any expecter of a reign of nothing but Saints and Worthies: but only an honest and hearty Wisher that the best of our Clergy might, for ever, continue as they are, rich and learned! and that the rest might be very useful and well esteemed in their Profession!

THE
GROUNDS AND OCCASIONS
OF THE
CONTEMPT
OF THE
CLERGY AND RELIGION
Enquired into.

SIR,

HAT short discourse which we lately had concerning the Clergy, continues so fresh in your mind, that, I perceive by your last, you are more than a little troubled to observe that Disesteem that lies upon several of those holy men. Your good wishes for the Church, I know, are very strong and unfeigned; and your hopes of the World receiving much more advantage and better advice from some of the Clergy, than usually it is found by experience to do, are neither needless nor impossible.

And as I have always been a devout admirer as well as strict observer of your actions; so I have constantly taken a great delight to concur with you in your very thoughts. Whereupon it is, Sir, that I have spent some few hours upon that which was the occasion of your last letter, and the subject of our late discourse.

And before, Sir, I enter upon telling you what are my apprehensions; I must most heartily profess that, for my own part, I did never think, since at all I understood the excellency and perfection of a Church, but that Ours, now lately Restored, as formerly Established, does far outgo, as to all Christian ends and purposes, either the pomp and bravery of Rome herself, or the best of Free Spiritual States [*Nonconformists*].

But if so be, it be allowable (where we have so undoubtedly learned and honourable a Clergy) to suppose that some of that sacred profession might possibly have attained to a greater degree of esteem and usefulness to the World : then I hope what has thus long hindered so great and desirable a blessing to the nation, may be modestly guessed at! either without giving any wilful offence to the present Church ; or any great trouble, dear Sir, to yourself. And, if I be not very much mistaken, whatever has heretofore, or does at present, lessen the value of our Clergy, or render it in any degree less serviceable to the World than might be reasonably hoped ; may be easily referred to two very plain things—the IGNORANCE of some, and the POVERTY of others of the Clergy.

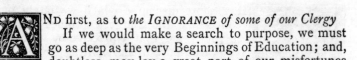

ND first, as to *the IGNORANCE of some of our Clergy* If we would make a search to purpose, we must go as deep as the very Beginnings of Education; and, doubtless, may lay a great part of our misfortunes to the old-fashioned methods and discipline of Schooling itself: upon the well ordering of which, although much of the improvement of our Clergy cannot be denied mainly to depend: yet by reason this is so well known to yourself, as also that there have been many of undoubted learning and experience, that have set out their several models for this purpose ; I shall therefore only mention such Loss of Time and Abuse of Youth as is most remarkable and mischievous, and as could not be conveniently omitted in a Discourse of this nature, though ever so short.

And first of all, it were certainly worth the considering. Whether it be unavoidably necessary to keep lads to 16 or 17 years of age, *in pure slavery to a few Latin or Greek words*? or Whether it may not be more convenient, especially if we call to mind their natural inclinations to ease and idleness, and how hardly they are persuaded of the excellency of the liberal Arts and Sciences (any further than the smart of the

last piece of discipline is fresh in their memories), Whether,
I say, it be not more proper and beneficial to mix with those
unpleasant tasks and drudgeries, something that, in probability, might not only take much better with them, but
might also be much easier obtained?

As, suppose some part of time was allotted them, for the
reading of some innocent English Authors! where they need
not go, every line, so unwillingly to a tormenting Dictionary,
and whereby they might come in a short time, to apprehend
common sense, and to begin to judge what is true. For you
shall have lads that are arch knaves at the Nominative Case,
and that have a notable quick eye at spying out of the Verb;
who, for want of reading such common and familiar books,
shall understand no more of what is very plain and easy, than
a well educated dog or horse.

Or suppose they were taught, as they might much easier
be than what is commonly offered to them, the principles of
Arithmetic, Geometry, and such alluring parts of Learning.
As these things undoubtedly would be much more useful, so
much more delightful to them, than to be tormented with a
tedious story how PHÆTON broke his neck, or how many
nuts and apples TITYRUS had for his supper.

For, most certainly, youths, if handsomely dealt with, are
much inclinable to emulation, and to a very useful esteem of
glory; and more especially, if it be the reward of knowledge:
and therefore, if such things were carefully and discreetly
propounded to them, wherein they might not only earnestly
contend amongst themselves, but might also see how far
they outskill the rest of the World, a lad hereby would think
himself high and mighty; and would certainly take great
delight in contemning the next unlearned mortal he meets
withal.

But if, instead hereof, you diet him with nothing but with
Rules and Exceptions, with tiresome repetitions of *Amo* and
Τύπτω, setting a day also apart also to recite *verbatim* all the
burdensome task of the foregoing week (which I am confident
is usually as dreadful as an old Parliament Fast) we must
needs believe that such a one, thus managed, will scarce
think to prove immortal, by such performances and accomplishments as these.

You know very well, Sir, that lads in general have but a

kind of ugly and odd conception of Learning; and look upon it as such a starving thing, and unnecessary perfection, especially as it is usually dispensed out unto them, that Nine-pins or Span-counter are judged much more heavenly employments! And therefore what pleasure, do we think, can such a one take in being bound to get against breakfast, two or three hundred Rumblers out of Homer, in commendation of Achilles's toes, or the Grecians' boots; or to have measured out to him, very early in the morning, fifteen or twenty well laid on lashes, for letting a syllable slip too soon, or hanging too long on it? Doubtless instant execution upon such grand miscarriages as these, will eternally engage him to a most admirable opinion of the Muses!

Lads, certainly, ought to be won by all possible arts and devices : and though many have invented fine pictures and games, to cheat them into the undertaking of unreasonable burdens; yet this, by no means, is such a lasting temptation as the propounding of that which in itself is pleasant and alluring. For we shall find very many, though of no excelling quickness, will soon perceive the design of the landscape; and so, looking through the veil, will then begin to take as little delight in those pretty contrivances, as in getting by heart three or four leaves of ungayed nonsense.

Neither seems the stratagem of Money to be so prevailing and catching, as a right down offer of such books which are ingenious and convenient : there being but very few so intolerably careful of their bellies, as to look upon the hopes of a cake or a few apples, to be a sufficient recompense, for cracking their pates with a heap of independent words.

I am not sensible that I have said anything in disparagement of those two famous tongues, the Greek and Latin; there being much reason to value them beyond others, because the best of Human Learning has been delivered unto us in those languages. But he that worships them, purely out of honour to Rome and Athens, having little or no respect to the usefulness and excellency of the books themselves, as many do : it is a sign he has a great esteem and reverence of antiquity; but I think him, by no means comparable, for happiness, to him who catches frogs or hunts butterflies.

That some languages therefore ought to be studied is in a manner absolutely necessary: unless all were brought to one;

which would be the happiest thing that the World could wish for!

But whether the beginning of them might not be more insensibly instilled, and more advantageously obtained by reading philosophical as well as other ingenious Authors, than *Janua linguarum*, crabbed poems, and cross-grained prose, as it has been heretofore by others: so it ought to be afresh considered by all well-wishers, either to the Clergy or Learning.

I know where it is the fashion of some schools, to prescribe to a lad, for his evening refreshment, out of COMMENIUS, all the Terms of Art [*technical terms*] belonging to Anatomy, Mathematics, or some such piece of Learning. Now, is it not a very likely thing, that a lad should take most absolute delight in conquering such a pleasant task; where, perhaps, he has two or three hundred words to keep in mind, with a very small proportion of sense thereunto belonging: whereas the use and full meaning of all those difficult terms would have been most insensibly obtained, by leisurely reading in particular, this or the other science?

Is it not also likely to be very savoury, and of comfortable use to one that can scarce distinguish between Virtue and Vice, to be tasked with high and moral poems? It is usually said by those that are intimately acquainted with him, that HOMER's *Iliad* and *Odyssey* contain, mystically, all the Moral Law for certain, if not a great part of the Gospel (I suppose much after that rate that RABELAIS said his *Gargantua* contained all the Ten Commandments!); but perceivable only to those that have a poetical discerning spirit: with which gift, I suppose, few at school are so early qualified.

Those admirable verses, Sir, of yours, both English and others, which you have sometimes favoured me with a sight of, will not suffer me to be so sottish as to slight and undervalue so great and noble an accomplishment. But the committing of such high and brave sensed poems to a school-boy (whose main business is to search out cunningly the Antecedent and the Relative; to lie at catch for a spruce Phrase, a Proverb, or a quaint and pithy Sentence) is not only to very little purpose, but that having gargled only those elegant books at school, this serves them instead of reading them afterwards; and does, in a manner, prevent their being further looked into. So that all improvement, whatsoever it be, that may be reaped out of the best and choicest poets, is for the most part utterly lost, in that a time is usually chosen of reading them, when discretion is much wanting to gain thence any true advantage. Thus that admirable and highly useful morality, TULLY's *Offices,* because it is a book commonly construed at school, is generally afterwards so contemned by Academics, that it is a long hour's work to convince them that it is worthy of being looked into again; because they reckon it as a book read over at school, and, no question! notably digested.

If, therefore the ill methods of schooling do not only occasion a great loss of time there, but also do beget in lads a very odd opinion and apprehension of Learning, and much disposes them to be idle when they are got a little free from the usual severities; and that the hopes of more or less improvement in the Universities very much depend hereupon: it is, without all doubt, the great concernment of all that wish to the Church, that such care and regard be had to the management of schools, that the Clergy be not so much obstructed in their first attempts and preparations to Learning.

I cannot, Sir, possibly be so ignorant as not to consider that what has been now offered upon this argument, has not only been largely insisted on by others; but also refers not particularly to the Clergy (whose welfare and esteem, I seem at present in a special manner solicitous about), but in general to all learned professions, and therefore might reasonably have been omitted: which certainly I had done, had not I called to mind that of those many that propound to themselves Learning for a profession, there is scarce one in ten but that his lot, choice, or necessity determines him to the study of Divinity.

Thus, Sir, I have given you my thoughts concerning the orders and customs of common schools. A consideration, in my apprehension, not slightly to be weighed: being that upon which to me seems very much to depend the learning and wisdom of the Clergy, and the prosperity of the Church.

The next unhappiness that seems to have hindered some of our Clergy from arriving to that degree of understanding that becomes such a holy office, whereby their company and discourses might be much more, than they commonly are, valued and desired, is the inconsiderate sending of all kinds of lads to the Universities; let their parts be ever so low and pitiful, the instructions they have lain under ever so mean and contemptible, and the purses of their friends ever so short to maintain them there. If they have but the commendation of some lamentable and pitiful Construing Master, it passes for sufficient evidence that they will prove persons very eminent in the Church. That is to say, if a lad has but a lusty and well bearing memory, this being the usual and almost only thing whereby they judge of their abilities; if he can sing over very tunably three or four stanzas of LILLY's Poetry; be very quick and ready to tell what is Latin for all the instruments belonging to his father's shop; if presently [*at sight*], upon the first scanning, he knows a Spondee from a Dactyl, and can fit a few of those same, without any sense, to his fingers' ends; if, lastly, he can say perfectly by heart his Academic Catechism, in pure and passing Latin, *i.e.*, "What is his Name?" "Where went he to School?" and "What author is he best and chiefly skilled in?" "A forward boy!" cries the Schoolmaster: "a very pregnant child! Ten thousand pities, but he should be a Scholar; he proves a brave Clergyman, I'll warrant you!"

Away to the University he must needs go! Then for a little Logic, a little Ethics, and, GOD knows! a very little of everything else! And the next time you meet him, he is in the pulpit!

Neither ought the mischief which arises from small country schools to pass unconsidered. The little mighty Governors whereof, having, for the most part, not sucked in above six or seven mouthsful of University air, must yet, by all means, suppose themselves so notably furnished with all sorts of instructions, and are so ambitious of the glory of being counted able to send forth, now and then, to Oxford or Cambridge, from the little house by the Churchyard's side, one of their ill-educated disciples, that to such as these ofttimes is committed the guidance and instruction of a whole parish: whose parts and improvements duly considered, will scarce render them fit Governors of a small Grammar Castle.

Not that it is necessary to believe, that there never was

a learned or useful person in the Church, but such whose education had been at Westminster or St. Paul's. But, whereas most of the small schools, being by their first founders designed only for the advantage of poor parish children, and also that the stipend is usually so small and discouraging that very few who can do much more than teach to write and read, will accept of such preferment : for these to pretend to rig out their small ones for a University life, proves ofttimes a very great inconvenience and damage to the Church.

And as many such Dismal Things are sent forth thus, with very small tackling; so not a few are predestinated thither by their friends, from the foresight of a good benefice. If there be rich pasture, profitable customs, and that HENRY VIII. has taken out no toll, the Holy Land is a very good land, and affords abundance of milk and honey! Far be it from their consciences, the considering whether the lad is likely to be serviceable to the Church, or to make wiser and better any of his parishioners!

All this may seem, at first sight, to be easily avoided by a strict examination at the Universities ; and so returning by the next carrier, all that was sent up not fit for their purpose. But because many of their relations are ofttimes persons of an inferior condition; and who (either by imprudent counsellors, or else out of a tickling conceit of their sons being, forsooth, a University Scholar) have purposely omitted all other opportunities of a livelihood; to return such, would seem a very sharp and severe disappointment.

Possibly, it might be much better, if parents themselves or their friends, would be much more wary of determining their children to the trade of Learning. And if some of undoubted knowledge and judgement, would offer their advice; and speak their hopes of a lad, about 13 or 14 years of age (which, I will assure you, Sir, may be done without conjuring!) ; and never omit to inquire, Whether his relations are able and willing to maintain him seven years at the University, or see some certain way of being continued there so long, by the help of friends or others, as also upon no such conditions as shall, in likelihood, deprive him of the greatest parts of his studies ?

For it is a common fashion of a great many to compliment and invite inferior people's children to the University, and there pretend to make such an all bountiful provision for them, as they shall not fail of coming to a very eminent degree of Learning; but when they come there, they shall save a servant's wages. They took therefore, heretofore, a very good method to prevent Sizars overheating their brains. Bed-making, chamber-sweeping, and water-fetching were doubt-less great preservatives against too much vain philosophy. Now certainly such pretended favours and kindnesses as these, are the most right down discourtesies in the World. For it is ten times more happy, both for the lad and the Church, to be a corn-cutter or tooth-drawer, to make or mend shoes, or to be of any inferior profession; than to be invited to, and promised the conveniences of, a learned education; and to have his name only stand airing upon the College Tables [Notice-boards], and his chief business shall be, to buy eggs and butter.

Neither ought lads' parts, before they be determined to the University, be only considered, and the likelihood of being disappointed in their studies; but also abilities or hopes of being maintained until they be Masters of Arts. For whereas 200, for the most part, yearly Commence [Matriculate], scarce the fifth part of these continue after their taking the First Degree [B.A.]. As for the rest, having exactly learned, Quid est Logica? and Quot sunt Virtutes Morales? down they go, by the first carrier, on the top of the pack, into the West, or North, or elsewhere, according as their estates lie; with BURGESDICIUS, EUSTACHIUS, and such great helps of Divinity; and then, for propagation of the Gospel! By that time they can say the Predicaments and Creed; they have their choice of preaching or starving! Now what a Champion of Truth is such a thing likely to be! What a huge blaze he makes in the Church! What a Raiser of Doctrines! What a Confounder of Heresies! What an able Interpreter of hard Places! What a Resolver of Cases of Conscience! and what a prudent guide must he needs be to all his parish!

You may possibly think, Sir, that this so early preaching might be easily avoided, by withholding Holy Orders; the Church having very prudently constituted in her Canons, that none under twenty-three years of age, which is the usual age after seven years being at the University, should be admitted to that great employment.

This indeed might seem to do some service, were it carefully observed; and were there not a thing to be got, called a *Dispensation*, which will presently [*at once*] make you as old as you please.

But if you will, Sir, we will suppose that Orders were strictly denied to all, unless qualified according to *Canon*. I cannot foresee any other remedy but that most of those University youngsters must fall to the parish, and become a town charge until they be of spiritual age. For Philosophy is a very idle thing, when one is cold! and a small *System of Divinity*, though it be WOLLEBIUS himself, is not sufficient when one is hungry!

What then shall we do with them? and where shall we dispose of them, until they come to a holy ripeness?

May we venture them into the Desk to read *Service*? That cannot be, because not capable! Besides, the tempting Pulpit usually stands too near. Or shall we trust them in some good Gentleman's house, there to perform holy things? With all my heart! so that they may not be called down from their studies to say Grace to every Health; that they may have a little better wages than the Cook or Butler; as also that there be a Groom in the house, besides the Chaplain (for sometimes to the £10 a year, they crowd [in] the looking after couple of geldings): and that he may not be sent from table, picking his teeth, and sighing with his hat under his arm; whilst the Knight and my Lady eat up the tarts and chickens!

It may be also convenient, if he were suffered to speak now and then in the Parlour, besides at Grace and Prayer time; and that my cousin ABIGAIL and he sit not too near one another at meals, nor be presented together to the little vicarage!

All this, Sir, must be thought on! For, in good earnest, a person at all thoughtful of himself and conscience, had much better choose to live with nothing but beans and pease pottage, so that he might have the command of his thoughts and time; than to have his Second and Third Courses, and to obey the unreasonable humours of some families.

And as some think two or three years' continuance in the University, to be time sufficient for being very great Instruments in the Church: so others we have, so moderate as to count that a solemn admission and a formal paying of College Detriments, without the trouble of Philosophical discourses, disputations, and the like, are virtues that will influence as far as Newcastle, and improve though at ever such a distance.

So strangely possessed are people in general, with the easiness and small preparation that are requisite to the undertaking of the Ministry, that whereas in other professions, they plainly see, what considerable time is spent before they have any hopes of arriving to skill enough to practise with any confidence what they have designed; yet to preach to ordinary people, and govern a country parish, is usually judged such an easy performance, that anybody counts himself fit for the employment. We find very few so unreasonably confident of their parts, as to profess either Law or Physic, without either a considerable continuance in some of the Inns of Courts, or an industrious search in herbs, Anatomy, Chemistry, and the like, unless it be only to make a bond [*bandage*] or give a glyster [*an injection*]. But as for "the knack of Preaching" as they call it, that is such a very easy attainment, that he is counted dull to purpose, that is not able, at a very small warning, to fasten upon any text of Scripture, and to tear and tumble it, till the glass [*the hour-glass on the pulpit*] be out.

Many, I know very well, are forced to discontinue [*at College*], having neither stock [*capital*] of their own, nor friends to maintain them in the University. But whereas a man's profession and employment in this world is very much in his own, or in the choice of such who are most nearly concerned for him; he therefore, that foresees that he is not likely to have the advantage of a continued education, he had much better commit himself to an approved-of cobbler or tinker, wherein he may be duly respected according to his office and condition of life; than to be only a disesteemed pettifogger or empiric in Divinity.

By this time, Sir, I hope you begin to consider what a great disadvantage it has been to the Church and Religion, the mere venturous and inconsiderate determining of Youths to the profession of Learning.

There is still one thing, by very few, at all minded, that ought also not to be overlooked: and that is, a good constitution and health of body. And therefore discreet and wise physicians ought also to be consulted, before an absolute resolve be made to live the Life of the Learned. For he that has strength enough to buy and bargain, may be of a very unfit habit of body to sit still so much, as, in general, is requisite to a competent degree of Learning. For although reading and thinking break neither legs nor arms ; yet, certainly, there is nothing that flags the spirits, disorders the blood, and enfeebles the whole body of Man, as intense studies.

As for him that rives blocks or carries packs, there is no great expense of parts, no anxiety of mind, no great intellectual pensiveness. Let him but wipe his forehead, and he is perfectly recovered ! But he that has many languages to remember, the nature of almost the whole world to consult, many histories, Fathers, and Councils to search into ; if the fabric of his body be not strong and healthful, you will soon find him as thin as a piece of metaphysics, and look as piercing as a School subtilty.

This, Sir, could not be conveniently omitted ; not only because many are very careless in this point, and, at a venture, determine their young relations to Learning : but because, for the most part, if, amongst many, there be but one of all the family that is weak and sickly, that is languishing and consumptive ; this, of all the rest, as counted not fit for any coarse employment, shall be picked out as a Choice Vessel for the Church ! Whereas, most evidently, he is much more able to dig daily in the mines, than to set cross-legged, musing upon his book.

I am very sensible, how obvious it might be, here, to hint that this so curious and severe Inquiry would much hinder the practice, and abate the flourishing of the Universities : as also, there have been several, and are still, many Living Creatures in the world, who, whilst young, being of a very slow and meek apprehension, have yet afterward cheered up into a great briskness, and become masters of much reason. And others there have been, who, although forced to a short continuance in the University, and that ofttimes interrupted by unavoidable services, have yet, by singular care and industry, proved very famous in their generation. And lastly, some also, of very feeble and crazy constitutions in their childhood, have out-studied their distempers, and have become very healthful and serviceable in the Church.

As for the flourishing, Sir, of the Universities—what has

been before said, aims not in the least at Gentlemen, whose
coming thither is chiefly for the hopes of single [*personal*] improvement; and whose estates do free them from the necessity
of making a gain of Arts and Sciences : but only at such as
intend to make Learning their profession, as well as [their]
accomplishment. So that our Schools may be still as full of
flourishings, of fine clothes, rich gowns, and future benefactors,
as ever.

And suppose we do imagine, as it is necessary we should,
that the number should be a little lessened; this surely will
not abate the true splendour of a University in any man's
opinion, but his who reckons the flourishing thereof, rather
from the multitude of mere gowns than from the Ingenuity
and Learning of those that wear them : no more than we
have reason to count the flourishing of the Church from that
vast number of people that crowd into Holy Orders, rather
than from those learned and useful persons that defend her
Truths, and manifest her Ways.

But I say, I do not see any perfect necessity that our
Schools should hereupon be thinned and less frequented :
having said nothing against the Multitude, but the *indiscreet
choice*. If therefore, instead of such, either of inferior
parts or a feeble constitution, or of unable friends; there
were picked out those that were of a tolerable ingenuity
[*natural capacity*], of a study-bearing body, and had good
hopes of being continued; as hence there is nothing to
hinder our Universities from being full, so likewise from
being of great credit and learning.

Not to deny, then, but that, now and then, there has been
a lad of very submissive parts, and perhaps no great share
of time allowed him for his studies, who has proved, beyond
all expectation, brave and glorious : yet, surely, we are not
to over-reckon this so rare a hit, as to think that one such
proving lad should make recompense and satisfaction for
those many "weak ones," as the common people love to
phrase them, that are in the Church. And that no care
ought to be taken, no choice made, no maintenance provided
or considered ; because (now and then in an Age) one,
miraculously, beyond all hopes, proves learned and useful ;
is a practice, whereby never greater mischiefs and disesteem
have been brought upon the Clergy.

I have, in short, Sir, run over what seemed to me, the First Occasions of that Small Learning that is to be found amongst some of the Clergy. I shall now pass from Schooling to the Universities.

I am not so unmindful of that devotion which I owe to those places, nor of that great esteem I profess to have of the Guides and Governors thereof, as to go about to prescribe new Forms and Schemes of Education ; where Wisdom has laid her top-stone. Neither shall I here examine which Philosophy, the Old or New, makes the best sermons. It is hard to say, that exhortations can be to *no* purpose, if the preacher believes that the earth turns round ! or that his reproofs can take *no* effect, unless he will suppose a vacuum ! There have been good sermons, no question ! made in the days of *Materia Prima* and Occult Qualities : and there are, doubtless, still good discourses now, under the reign of Atoms.

There are but two things, wherein I count the Clergy chiefly concerned, as to University Improvements, that, at present, I shall make Inquiry into.

And the first is this : Whether or not it were not highly useful, especially for the Clergy who are supposed to speak English to the people, that *English Exercises were imposed upon lads,* if not in Public Schools, yet at least privately. Not but that I am abundantly satisfied that Latin (O Latin ! it is the all in all ! and the very cream of the jest !) ; as also, that Oratory is the same in all languages, the same rules being observed, the same method, the same arguments and arts of persuasion : but yet, it seems somewhat beyond the reach of ordinary youth so to apprehend those general Laws as to make a just and allowable use of them in all languages, unless exercised particularly in them.

Now we know the language that the very learned part of this nation must trust to live by, unless it be to make a bond [*bandage*] or prescribe a purge (which possibly may not oblige or work so well in any other language as Latin) is the English : and after a lad has taken his leave of Madame University, GOD bless him ! he is not likely to deal afterwards with much Latin ; unless it be to checker [*variegate*]

a sermon, or to say *Salveto!* to some travelling *Dominatio
vestra*. Neither is it enough to say, that the English is the
language with which we are swaddled and rocked asleep; and
therefore there needs none of this artificial and superadded
care. For there be those that speak very well, plainly, and
to the purpose; and yet write most pernicious and fantastical
stuff: thinking that whatsoever is written must be more than
ordinary, must be beyond the guise [*manner*] of common
speech, must savour of reading and Learning, though it be
altogether needless, and perfectly ridiculous.

Neither ought we to suppose it sufficient that English books
be frequently read, because there be of all sorts, good and bad;
and the worst are likely to be admired by Youth more than
the best : unless Exercises be required of lads; whereby it
may be guessed what their judgement is, where they be
mistaken, and what authors they propound to themselves for
imitation. For by this means, they may be corrected and
advised early, according as occasion shall require : which, if
not done, their ill style will be so confirmed, their impro-
prieties of speech will become so natural, that it will be a
very hard matter to stir or alter their fashion of writing.

It is very curious to observe what delicate letters, your
young students write! after they have got a little smack of
University learning. In what elaborate heights, and tossing
nonsense, will they greet a right down English father, or
country friend! If there be a plain word in it, and such as
is used at home, this "tastes not," say they, " of education
among philosophers!" and is counted damnable duncery and
want of fancy. Because "Your loving friend" or "humble
servant" is a common phrase in country letters; therefore
the young Epistler is "Yours, to the Antipodes!" or at least
"to the Centre of the earth!": and because ordinary folks
"love" and "respect" you; therefore you are to him, "a
Pole Star!" "a Jacob's Staff!" "a Loadstone!" and "a
damask Rose!"

And the misery of it is, that this pernicious accustomed
way of expression does not only, ofttimes, go along with them
to their benefice, but accompanies them to the very grave.

And, for the most part, an ordinary cheesemonger or plum-
seller, that scarce[ly] ever heard of a University, shall write
much better sense, and more to the purpose than these young

philosophers, who injudiciously hunting only for great words, make themselves learnedly ridiculous.

Neither can it be easily apprehended, how the use of English Exercises should any ways hinder the improvement in the Latin tongue; but rather be much to its advantage: and this may be easily believed, considering what dainty stuff is usually produced for a Latin entertainment! Chicken broth is not thinner than that which is commonly offered for a Piece of most pleading and convincing Sense!

For, I will but suppose an Academic youngster to be put upon a Latin Oration. Away he goes presently to his magazine of collected phrases! He picks out all the Glitterings he can find. He hauls in all Proverbs, " Flowers," Poetical snaps [*snatches*], Tales out of the *Dictionary*, or else ready Latined to his hand, out of LYCOSTHENES.

This done, he comes to the end of the table, and having made a submissive leg [*made a submissive bow*] and a little admired [*gazed at*] the number, and understanding countenances of his auditors : let the subject be what it will, he falls presently into a most lamentable complaint of his insufficiency and tenuity [*slenderness*] that he, poor thing! " hath no acquaintance with above a Muse and a half!" and "that he never drank above six quarts of Helicon!" and you "have put him here upon such a task" (perhaps the business is only, Which is the nobler creature, a Flea or a Louse?) "that would much better fit some old soaker at Parnassus, than his sipping unexperienced bibbership." Alas, poor child! he is " sorry, at the very soul! that he has no better speech! and wonders in his heart, that you will lose so much time as to hear him! for he has neither squibs nor fireworks, stars nor glories! The cursed carrier lost his best Book of Phrases ; and the malicious mice and rats eat up all his *Pearls* and *Golden Sentences*."

Then he tickles over, a little, the skirts of the business. By and by, for similitude from the Sun and Moon, or if they be not at leisure, from " the grey-eyed Morn," or "a shady grove," or "a purling stream."

This done, he tells you that " *Barnaby Bright* would be much too short, for him to tell you all that he could say ": and so, "fearing he should break the thread of your patience," he concludes.

Now it seems, Sir, very probable, that if lads did but first of all, determine in English what they intended to say in Latin ; they would, of themselves, soon discern the trifling-ness of such Apologies, the pitifulness of their Matter, and the impertinency of their Tales and Fancies : and would (according to their subject, age, and parts) offer that which would be much more manly, and towards tolerable sense.

And if I may tell you, Sir, what I really think, most of that ridiculousness, of those phantastical phrases, harsh and sometimes blasphemous metaphors, abundantly foppish similitudes, childish and empty transitions, and the like, so commonly uttered out of pulpits, and so fatally redounding to the discredit of the Clergy, may, in a great measure, be charged upon the want of that, which we have here so much contended for.

The second Inquiry that may be made is this : *Whether or not Punning, Quibbling, and that which they call Joquing* [joking], *and such delicacies of Wit, highly admired in some Academic Exercises, might not be very conveniently omitted* ?

For one may desire but to know this one thing : In what Profession shall that sort of Wit prove of advantage ? As for Law, where nothing but the most reaching subtility and the closest arguing is allowed of ; it is not to be imagined that blending now and then a piece of a dry verse, and wreathing here and there an odd Latin Saying into a dismal jingle, should give Title to an estate, or clear out an obscure evidence ! And as little serviceable can it be to Physic, which is made up of severe Reason and well tried Experiments !

And as for Divinity, in this place I shall say no more, but that those usually that have been Rope Dancers in the Schools, ofttimes prove Jack Puddings in the Pulpit.

For he that in his youth has allowed himself this liberty of Academic Wit ; by this means he has usually so thinned his judgement, becomes so prejudiced against sober sense, and so altogether disposed to trifling and jingling ; that, so soon as he gets hold of a text, he presently thinks he has catched one of his old School Questions ; and so falls a flinging it out of one hand into another ! tossing it this way, and that ! lets it run a little upon the line, then " *tanutus* ! high jingo ! come again !" here catching at a word ! there lie nibbling and sucking at an *and*, a *by*, a *quis* or a *quid*, a *sic* or a *sicut* ! and

thus minces the Text so small that his parishioners, until he
rendezvous [*reassemble*] it again, can scarce tell, what is become
of it.

But "Shall we debar Youth of such an innocent and
harmless recreation, of such a great quickener of Parts and
promoter of sagacity?"

As for the first, its innocency of being allowed of for a
time; I am so far from that persuasion that, from what has
been before hinted, I count it perfectly contagious! and as
a thing that, for the most part, infects the whole life, and
influences most actions! For he that finds himself to have
the right knack of letting off a joque, and of pleasing the
Humsters; he is not only very hardly brought off from
admiring those goodly applauses, and heavenly shouts; but
it is ten to one! if he directs not the whole bent of his studies
to such idle and contemptible books as shall only furnish
him with materials for a laugh; and so neglects all that
should inform his Judgement and Reason, and make him a
man of sense and reputation in this world.

And as for the pretence of making people sagacious, and
pestilently witty; I shall only desire that the nature of that
kind of Wit may be considered! which will be found to
depend upon some such fooleries as these—

As, first of all, the lucky ambiguity of some word or
sentence. O, what a happiness is it! and how much does
a youngster count himself beholden to the stars! that
should help him to such a taking jest! And whereas
there be so many thousand words in the World, and that
he should luck upon the right one! that was so very
much to his purpose, and that at the explosion, made
such a goodly report!

Or else they rake Lilly's *Grammar*; and if they can
but find two or three letters of any name in any of the
Rules or *Examples* of that good man's Works; it is as
very a piece of Wit as any has passed in the Town since
the King came in [1660]!

O, how the Freshmen will skip, to hear one of those
lines well laughed at, that they have been so often yerked
[*chided*] for!

It is true, such things as these go for Wit so long as they
continue in Latin; but what dismally shrimped things would

they appear, if turned into English! And if we search into what was, or might be pretended; we shall find the advantages of Latin-Wit to be very small and slender, when it comes into the World. I mean not only among strict Philosophers and Men of mere Notions, or amongst all-damning and illiterate HECTORS; but amongst those that are truly ingenious and judicious Masters of Fancy. We shall find that a quotation out of *Qui mihi*, an Axiom out of Logic, a Saying of a Philosopher, or the like, though managed with some quickness and applied with some seeming ingenuity, will not, in our days, pass, or be accepted, for Wit.

For we must know that, as we are now in an Age of great Philosophers and Men of Reason, so of great quickness and fancy! and that Greek and Latin, which heretofore (though never so impertinently fetched in) was counted admirable, because it had a learned twang; yet, now, such stuff, being out of fashion, is esteemed but very bad company!

For the World is now, especially in discourse, for One Language! and he that has somewhat in his mind of Greek and Latin, is requested, now-a-days, "to be civil, and translate it into English, for the benefit of the company!" And he that has made it his whole business to accomplish himself for the applause of boys, schoolmasters, and the easiest of Country Divines; and has been shouldered out of the Cockpit for his Wit: when he comes into the World, is the most likely person to be kicked out of the company, for his pedantry and overweening opinion of himself.

And, were it necessary, it is an easy matter to appeal to Wits, both ancient and modern, that (beyond all controversy) have been sufficiently approved of, that never, I am confident! received their improvements by employing their time in Puns and Quibbles. There is the prodigious LUCIAN, the great Don [QUIXOTE] of Mancha; and there are many now living, Wits of our own, who never, certainly, were at all inspired from a *Tripus*'s, *Terræ-filius*'s, or *Prævarecator*'s speech.

I have ventured, Sir, thus far, not to find fault with; but only to inquire into an ancient custom or two of the Universities; wherein the Clergy seem to be a little concerned, as to their education there.

I shall now look on them as beneficed, and consider their

preaching. Wherein I pretend to give no rules, having neither any gift at it, nor authority to do it : but only shall make some conjectures at those useless and ridiculous things commonly uttered in pulpits, that are generally disgusted [*disliked*], and are very apt to bring contempt upon the preacher, and that religion which he professes.

Amongst the first things that seem to be useless, may be reckoned *the high tossing and swaggering preaching*, either mountingly eloquent, or profoundly learned. For there be a sort of Divines, who, if they but happen of an unlucky hard word all the week, they think themselves not careful of their flock, if they lay it not up till Sunday, and bestow it amongst them, in their next preachment. Or if they light upon some difficult and obscure notion, which their curiosity inclines them to be better acquainted with, how useless soever! nothing so frequent as for them, for a month or two months together, to tear and tumble this doctrine! and the poor people, once a week, shall come and gaze upon them by the hour, until they preach themselves, as they think, into a right understanding.

Those that are inclinable to make these useless speeches to the people; they do it, for the most part, upon one of these two considerations. Either out of simple phantastic glory, and a great studiousness of being wondered at: as if getting into the pulpit were a kind of Staging [*acting*]; where nothing was to be considered but how much the sermon takes! and how much stared at! Or else, they do this to gain a respect and reverence from their people: "who," say they, "are to be puzzled now and then, and carried into the clouds! For if the Minister's words be such as the Constable uses; his matter plain and practical, such as comes to the common market : he may pass possibly for an honest and well-meaning man, but by no means for any scholar! Whereas if he springs forth, now and then, in high raptures towards the uppermost heavens; dashing, here and there, an all-confounding word! if he soars aloft in unintelligible huffs! preaches points deep and mystical, and delivers them as darkly and phantastically! this is the way," say they, " of being accounted a most able and learned Instructor."

Others there be, whose parts stand not so much towards Tall Words and Lofty Notions, but consist in scattering up and down and besprinkling all their sermons with plenty of Greek and Latin. And because St. PAUL, once or so, was pleased to make use of a little heathen Greek; and that only, when he had occasion to discourse with some of the learned ones that well understood him: therefore must they needs bring in twenty Poets and Philosophers, if they can catch them, into an hour's talk [*evidently the ordinary length of a sermon at this time, see pp.* 259, 313]; spreading themselves in abundance of Greek and Latin, to a company, perhaps, of farmers and shepherds.

Neither will they rest there, but have at the Hebrew also! not contenting themselves to tell the people in general, that they "have skill in the Text, and the exposition they offer, agrees with the Original"; but must swagger also over the poor parishioners, with the dreadful Hebrew itself! with their BEN-ISRAELS! BEN-MANASSES! and many more BENS that they are intimately acquainted with! whereas there is nothing in the church, or near it by a mile, that understands them, but GOD Almighty! whom, it is supposed, they go not about to inform or satisfy.

This learned way of talking, though, for the most part, it is done merely out of ostentation: yet, sometimes (which makes not the case much better), it is done in compliment and civility to the all-wise Patron, or all-understanding Justice of the Peace in the parish; who, by the common farmers of the town, must be thought to understand the most intricate notions, and the most difficult languages.

Now, what an admirable thing this is! Suppose there should be one or so, in the whole church, that understands somewhat besides English: shall I not think that he understands that better? Must I (out of courtship to his Worship and Understanding; and because, perhaps, I am to dine with him) prate abundance of such stuff, which, I must needs know, nobody understands, or that will be the better for it but himself, and perhaps scarcely he?

This, I say, because I certainly know several of that disposition: who, if they chance to have a man of any learning or understanding more than the rest in the parish, preach wholly at him! and level most of their discourses at his supposed capacity; and the rest of the good people shall have only a handsome gaze or view of the parson! As if plain words, useful and intelligible instructions were not as good for an Esquire, or one that is in Commission from the King, as for him that holds the plough or mends hedges.

Certainly he that considers the design of his Office, and has a conscience answerable to that holy undertaking, must needs conceive himself engaged, not only to mind this or that accomplished or well-dressed person, but must have a universal care and regard of all his parish. And as he must think himself bound, not only to visit down beds and silken curtains, but also flocks and straw [*mattresses*], if there be need: so ought his care to be as large to instruct the poor, the weak, and despicable part of his parish, as those that sit in the best pews. He that does otherwise, thinks not at all of a man's soul: but only accommodates himself to fine clothes, an abundance of ribbons, and the highest seat in the church; not thinking that it will be as much to his reward in the next world, by sober advice, care, and instruction, to have saved one that takes collection [*alms*] as him that is able to relieve half the town. It is very plain that neither our Saviour, when he was upon earth and taught the World, made any such distinction in his discourses. What is more intelligible to all mankind than his *Sermon upon the Mount*! Neither did the Apostles think of any such way. I wonder, whom they take for a pattern!

I will suppose once again, that the design of these persons is to gain glory: and I shall ask them, Can there be any greater in the world, than doing general good? To omit future reward, Was it not always esteemed of old, that correcting evil practices, reducing people that lived amiss, was much better than making a high rant about a shuttlecock, and talking *tara-tantara* about a feather? Or if they would be only admired, then would I gladly have them consider, What a thin and delicate kind of admiration is likely to be produced, by that which is not at all understood? Certainly, that man has a design of building up to himself real fame in good earnest, by things well laid and spoken: his way to effect it is not by talking staringly, and casting a mist before the people's eyes; but by offering such things by which he may be esteemed, with knowledge and understanding.

Thus far concerning Hard Words, High Notions, and Unprofitable Quotations out of learned languages.

I shall now consider such things *as are ridiculous*, that serve for chimney and market talk, after the sermon be done; and that do cause, more immediately, the preacher to be scorned and undervalued.

I have no reason, Sir, to go about to determine what style or method is best for the improvement and advantage of *all* people. For, I question not but there have been as many several sorts of Preachers as Orators; and though very different, yet useful and commendable in their kind. TULLY takes very deservedly with many, SENECA with others, and CATO, no question! said things wisely and well. So, doubtless, the same place of Scripture may by several, be variously considered: and although their method and style be altogether different, yet they may all speak things very convenient for the people to know and be advised of. But yet, certainly, what is most undoubtedly useless and empty, or what is judged absolutely ridiculous, not by this or that curious or squeamish auditor, but by every man in the Corporation that understands but plain English and common sense, ought to be avoided. For all people are naturally born with such a judgement of true and allowable Rhetoric, that is, of what is decorous and convenient to be spoken, that whatever is grossly otherwise is usually ungrateful, not only to the wise and skilful part of the congregation, but shall seem also ridiculous to the very unlearned tradesmen [*mechanics*] and their young apprentices. Amongst which, may be chiefly reckoned these following, *harsh Metaphors, childish Similitudes*, and *ill-applied Tales*.

The first main thing, I say, that makes many sermons so ridiculous, and the preachers of them so much disparaged and undervalued, is *an inconsiderate use of frightful Metaphors*: which making such a remarkable impression upon the ears, and leaving such a jarring twang behind them, are oftentimes remembered to the discredit of the Minister as long as he continues in the parish.

I have heard the very children in the streets, and the little boys close about the fire, refresh themselves strangely but with the repetition of a few of such far-fetched and odd sounding expressions. TULLY, therefore, and CÆSAR, the

two greatest masters of Roman eloquence, were very wary
and sparing of that sort of Rhetoric. We may read many a
page in their works before we meet with any of those bears ;
and if you do light upon one or so, it shall not make your
hair stand right up ! or put you into a fit of convulsions ! but
it shall be so soft, significant, and familiar, as if it were made
for the very purpose.

But as for the common sort of people that are addicted to
this sort of expression in their discourses ; away presently to
both the Indies ! rake heaven and earth ! down to the bottom
of the sea ! then tumble over all Arts and Sciences ! ransack
all shops and warehouses ! spare neither camp nor city, but
that they will have them ! So fond are such deceived ones
of these same gay words, that they count all discourses
empty, dull, and cloudy; unless bespangled with these
glitterings. Nay, so injudicious and impudent together will
they sometimes be, that the Almighty Himself is often in
danger of being dishonoured by these indiscreet and horrid
Metaphor-mongers. And when they thus blaspheme the
God of Heaven by such unhallowed expressions; to make
amends, they will put you in an " As it were " forsooth ! or
" As I may so say," that is, they will make bold to speak
what they please concerning GOD Himself, rather than omit
what they judge, though never so falsely, to be witty. And
then they come in hobbling with their lame submission, and
with their " reverence be it spoken " : as if it were not much
better to leave out what they foresee is likely to be inter-
preted for blasphemy, or at least great extravagancy; than
to utter that, for which their own reason and conscience tell
them, they are bound to lay in beforehand an excuse.

To which may be further subjoined, that Metaphors, though
very apt and allowable, are intelligible but to some sorts of
men, of this or that kind of life, of this or that profession.

For example, perhaps one Gentleman's metaphorical knack
of preaching comes of the sea ; and then we shall hear of
nothing but "starboard" and "larboard," of "stems,"
"sterns," and "forecastles," and such salt-water language:
so that one had need take a voyage to Smyrna or Aleppo,
and very warily attend to all the sailors' terms, before I shall
in the least understand my teacher. Now, though such a
sermon may possibly do some good in a coast town; yet

upward into the country, in an inland parish, it will do no
more than Syriac or Arabic.

Another, he falls a fighting with his text, and makes a
pitched battle of it, dividing it into the Right Wing and
Left Wing; then he *rears* it! *flanks* it! *intrenches* it! *storms* it!
and then he *musters* all again! to see what word was lost or
lamed in the skirmish: and so falling on again, with fresh
valour, he fights backward and forward! charges through
and through! routs! kills! takes! and then, "Gentlemen!
as you were!" Now to such of his parish as have been in
the late wars, this is not very formidable; for they do but
suppose themselves at Edgehill or Naseby, and they are not
much scared at his doctrine: but as for others, who have not
had such fighting opportunities, it is very lamentable to consider how shivering they sit without understanding, till the
battle be over!

Like instance might be easily given of many more discourses, the metaphorical phrasing whereof, depending upon
peculiar arts, customs, trades, and professions, makes them
useful and intelligible only to such, who have been very well
busied in such like employments.

Another thing, Sir, that brings great disrespect and mischief
upon the Clergy, and that differs not much from what went
immediately before, is their *packing their sermons so full of
Similitudes*; which, all the World knows, carry with them but
very small force of argument, unless there be *an exact agreement with that which is compared*, of which there is very seldom
any sufficient care taken.

Besides, those that are addicted to this slender way of
discourse, for the most part, do so weaken and enfeeble their
judgement, by contenting themselves to understand by
colours, features, and glimpses; that they perfectly omit all
the more profitable searching into the nature and causes of
things themselves. By which means, it necessarily comes
to pass, that what they undertake to prove and clear out to
the Congregation, must needs be so faintly done, and with
such little force of argument, that the conviction or persuasion
will last no longer in the parishioners' minds, than the
warmth of those similitudes shall glow in their fancy. So
that he that has either been instructed in some part of his

duty, or excited to the performance of the same, not by any judicious dependence of things, and lasting reason; but by such faint and toyish evidence: his understanding, upon all occasions, will be as apt to be misled as ever, and his affections as troublesome and ungovernable.

But they are not so Unserviceable, as, usually, they are Ridiculous. For people of the weakest parts are most commonly overborn with these fooleries; which, together with the great difficulty of their being prudently managed, must needs occasion them, for the most part, to be very trifling and childish.

Especially, if we consider the choiceness of the authors out of which they are furnished. There is the never-to-be-commended-enough LYCOSTHENES. There is also the admirable piece [by FRANCIS MERES] called *the Second Part of Wits Commonwealth* [1598]: I pray mind it! it is the *Second Part*, and not the *First*! And there is, besides, a book wholly consisting of Similitudes [? JOHN SPENCER's *Things New and Old, or a Storehouse of Similies, Sentences, Allegories, &c.*, 1658] applied and ready fitted to most preaching subjects, for the help of young beginners, who sometimes will not make them hit handsomely.

It is very well known that such as are possessed with an admiration of such eloquence, think that they are very much encouraged in their way by the Scripture itself. "For," say they, "did not our blessed Saviour himself use many metaphors and many parables? and did not his disciples, following his so excellent an example, do the like? And is not this, not only warrant enough, but near upon a command to us so to do?"

If you please, therefore, we will see what our Saviour does in this case. In *St. Matthew* he tells his disciples, that "they are the salt of the earth," that "they are the light of the world," that "they are a city set on a hill." Furthermore, he tells his Apostles, that "he sends them forth as sheep in the midst of wolves;" and bids them therefore "be as wise as serpents, and harmless as doves." Now, are not all these things plain and familiar, even almost to children themselves, that can but taste and see; and to men of the lowest education and meanest capacities!

I shall not here insist upon those special and admirable

reasons for which our Saviour made use of so many parables. Only thus much is needful to be said, namely, that they are very much mistaken, that, from hence, think themselves tolerated to turn all the world into frivolous and abominable similitudes.

As for our Saviour, when he spoke a parable, he was pleased to go no further than the fields, the seashore, a garden, a vineyard, or the like; which are things, without the knowledge whereof, scarcely any man can be supposed to live in this world.

But as for our Metaphorical- and Similitude-Men of the Pulpit, these things to them, are too still and languid! they do not rattle and rumble! These lie too near home, and within vulgar ken! There is little on this side the moon that will content them! Up, presently, to the *Primum Mobile*, and the Trepidation of the Firmament! Dive into the bowels and hid treasures of the earth! Despatch forthwith, for Peru and Jamaica! A town bred or country bred similitude is worth nothing!

"It is reported of a tree growing upon the bank of Euphrates, the great river Euphrates! that it brings forth an Apple, to the eye very fair and tempting; but inwardly it is filled with nothing but useless and deceiving dust. Even so, dust we are; and to dust we must all go!"

Now, what a lucky discovery was this, that a man's Body should be so exactly like an Apple! And, I will assure you that this was not thought on, till within these few years!

And I am afraid, too, he had a kind of a hint of this, from another who had formerly found out that a man's Soul was like an Oyster. For, says he in his prayer, "Our souls are constantly gaping after thee, O LORD! yea, verily, our souls do gape, even as an oyster gapeth!"

It seems pretty hard, at first sight, to bring into a sermon all the Circles of the Globe and all the frightful terms of Astronomy; but I will assure you, Sir, it is to be done! because it has been. But not by every bungler and ordinary text-divider; but by a man of great cunning and experience.

There is a place in the prophet *Malachi*, where it will do very nicely, and that is chapter iv. ver. 2, "But unto you, that fear my Name, shall the Sun of Righteousness arise with healing in his wings." From which words, in the first place, it plainly appears that our Saviour passed through all the twelve signs of the Zodiac; and more than that too, all proved by very apt and familiar places of Scripture.

First, then, our Saviour was in *Aries*. Or else, what means that of the Psalmist, "The mountains skipped like rams, and the little hills like lambs!"? And again, that in Second of the *Kings*, chap. iii. ver. 4, "And MESHA, King of Moab, was a sheep master, and rendered unto the King of Israel an hundred thousand lambs," and what follows, "and an hundred thousand rams, with the wool!" Mind it! it was the King of Israel!

In like manner, was he in *Taurus*. *Psalm* xxii. 12. "Many bulls have compassed me! Strong bulls of Bashan have beset me round!" They were not ordinary bulls. They were *compassing* bulls! they were *besetting* bulls! they were *strong Bashan* bulls!

What need I speak of *Gemini*? Surely you cannot but remember ESAU and JACOB! *Genesis* xxv. 24. "And when her days to be delivered were fulfilled, behold there were Twins in her womb!"

Or of *Cancer*? when, as the Psalmist says so plainly, "What ailed thee, O thou sea, that thou fleddest? thou Jordan! that thou wast driven back?" Nothing more plain!

It were as easy to shew the like in all the rest of the Signs.

But instead of that, I shall rather choose to make this one practical Observation. That the mercy of GOD to mankind in sending His Son into the world, was a very *signal* mercy. It was a *zodiacal* mercy! I say it was truly zodiacal; for CHRIST keeps within the Tropics! He goes not out of the Pale of the Church; but yet he is not always at the same distance from a believer. Sometimes he withdraws himself into the *apogæum* of doubt, sorrow, and despair; but then he comes again into the *perigæum* of joy, content, and assurance; but as for heathens and unbelievers, they are all arctic and antarctic reprobates!"

Now when such stuff as this, as sometimes it is, is vented in a poor parish, where people can scarce tell, what day of the month it is by the Almanack? how seasonable and savoury it is likely to be!

It seems also not very easy for a man in his sermon to learn [*teach*] his parishioners how to dissolve gold, of what, and how the stuff is made. Now, to ring the bells and call the people on purpose together, would be but a blunt business; but to do it neatly, and when nobody looked for it, that is the rarity and art of it !

Suppose, then, that he takes for his text that of *St. Matthew*, " Repent ye, for the Kingdom of GOD is at hand." Now, tell me, Sir, do you not perceive the gold to be in a dismal fear! to curl and quiver at the first reading of these words ! It must come in thus, " The blots and blurs of our sins must be taken out by the *aqua-fortis* of our tears ; to which *aqua-fortis*, if you put a fifth part of *sal-ammoniac*, and set them in a gentle heat, it makes *aqua-regia* which dissolves gold."

And now it is out ! Wonderful are the things that are to be done by the help of metaphors and similitudes ! And I will undertake that, with a little more pains and considerations, out of the very same words, he could have taught the people how to make custards, or marmalade, or to stew prunes !

But, pray, why " the *aqua-fortis* of tears ? " For if it so falls out that there should chance to be neither Apothecary, nor Druggist at church, there is an excellent jest wholly lost !

Now had he been so considerate as to have laid his wit in some more common and intelligible material; for example, had he said the " blots of sin " will be easily taken out " by the soap of sorrow, and the fullers-earth of contrition," then possibly the Parson and the parish might all have admired one another. For there be many a good-wife that understands very well all the intrigues of pepper, salt, and vinegar, who knows not anything of the all-powerfulness of *aqua-fortis*, how that it is such a spot-removing liquor !

I cannot but consider with what understanding the people sighed and cried, when the Minister made for them this metaphysical confession :

Omnipotent All ! Thou art only ! Because Thou art all, and because Thou only art ! As for us, we are not ; but we seem to be ! and only seem to be, because we are not! for we be but Mites of Entity, and Crumbs of Something!" and so on.

As if a company of country people were bound to understand SUAREZ, and all the School Divines!

And as some are very high and learned in their attempts; so others there be, who are of somewhat too mean and dirty imagination.

Such was he, who goes by the name of Parson SLIP-STOCKING. Who preaching about the grace and assistance of GOD, and that of ourselves we are able to do nothing, advised his "beloved" to take him this plain similitude.

"A father calls his child to him, saying, 'Child, pull off this stocking!' The child, mightily joyful that it should pull off father's stocking, takes hold of the stocking, and tugs! and pulls! and sweats! but to no purpose: for stocking stirs not, for it is but a child that pulls! Then the father bids the child to rest a little, and try again. So then the child sets on again, tugs again; but no stocking comes: for child is but a child! Then the father taking pity upon his child, puts his hand behind and slips down the stocking; and off comes the stocking! Then how does the child rejoice! for child hath pulled off father's stocking. Alas, poor child! it was not child's strength, it was not child's sweating that got off the stocking; but yet it was the father's hand that slipped down the stocking. Even so——"

Not much unlike to this, was he that, preaching about the Sacrament and Faith, makes CHRIST a shopkeeper; telling you that "CHRIST is a Treasury of all wares and commodities," and thereupon, opening his wide throat, cries aloud,

"Good people! what do you lack? What do you buy? Will you buy any balm of Gilead? any eye salve? any myrrh, aloes, or cassia? Shall I fit you with a robe of Righteousness, or with a white garment? See here! What is it you want? Here is a choice armoury! Shall I shew you a helmet of Salvation, a shield, or breastplate of Faith? or will you please to walk in and see some precious stones? a jasper, a sapphire, a chalcedony? Speak, what do you buy?"

Now, for my part, I must needs say (and I much fancy I speak the mind of thousands) that it had been much better

for such an imprudent and ridiculous bawler as this, to have
been condemned to have cried oysters or brooms, than to discredit, after this unsanctified rate, his Profession and our
Religion.

It would be an endless thing, Sir, to count up to you all
the follies, for a hundred years last past, that have been
preached and printed of this kind. But yet I cannot omit
that of the famous Divine in his time, who, advising the
people in days of danger to run unto the LORD, tells
them that "they cannot go to the LORD, much less run,
without feet;" that "there be therefore two feet to run
to the LORD, Faith and Prayer."

"It is plain that Faith is a foot, for, 'by Faith we
stand,' 2 *Cor.* i. 24; therefore by Faith, we must run
to the LORD who is faithful.

" The second is Prayer, a spiritual Leg to bear us
thither. Now that Prayer is a spiritual Leg appears from
several places in Scripture, as from that of JONAH speaking of *coming*, chap. ii. ver. 7, 'And my prayer *came* unto
thy holy temple.' And likewise from that of the Apostle
who says, *Heb.* iv. 16, 'Let us therefore *go* unto the
throne of grace.' Both intimating that Prayer is a
spiritual Leg : there being no *coming* or *going* to the
LORD without the Leg of Prayer."

He further adds, " Now that these feet may be able to
bear us thither, we must put on the Hose [*stockings*] of
Faith; for the Apostle says, ' Our feet must be shod with
the preparation of the Gospel of Peace.' "

The truth of it is, the Author is somewhat obscure : for,
at first, Faith was a Foot, and by-and-by it is a Hose,
and at last it proves a Shoe! If he had pleased, he could
have made it anything!

Neither can I let pass that of a later Author; who telling
us, "It is Goodness by which we must ascend to heaven,"
and that "Goodness is the Milky Way to JUPITER's Palace";
could not rest there, but must tell us further, that "to
strengthen us in our journey, we must not take morning
milk, but some morning meditations :" fearing, I suppose,
lest some people should mistake, and think to go to heaven
by eating now and then a mess of morning milk, because the
way was "milky."

Neither ought that to be omitted, not long since printed upon those words of St. JOHN, "These things write I unto you, that ye sin not."

The Observation is that " it is the purpose of Scripture to drive men from sin. These Scriptures contain Doctrines, Precepts, Promises, Threatenings, and Histories. Now," says he, " take these five smooth stones, and put them into the Scrip of the heart, and throw them with the Sling of faith, by the Hand of a strong resolution, against the Forehead of sin : and we shall see it, like GOLIATH, fall before us."

But I shall not trouble you any further upon this subject : but, if you have a mind to hear any more of this stuff, I shall refer you to the learned and judicious Author of the *Friendly Debates* [*i.e.*, SIMON PATRICK, afterwards Bishop of ELY, who wrote *A Friendly Debate between a Conformist and a Nonconformist*, in two parts, 1669] : who, particularly, has at large discovered the intolerable fooleries of this way of talking.

I shall only add thus much, that such as go about to fetch blood into their pale and lean discourses, by the help of their brisk and sparkling similitudes, ought well to consider, Whether their similitudes be true ?

I am confident, Sir, you have heard it, many and many a time, or, if need be, I can shew you it in a book, that when the preacher happens to talk how that the things here below will not satisfy the mind of man ; then comes in, " the round world which cannot fill the triangular heart of man ! " whereas every butcher knows that the heart is no more triangular than an ordinary pear, or a child's top.   But because *triangular* is a hard word, and perhaps a jest ! therefore people have stolen it one from another, these two or three hundred years ; and, for aught I know, much longer ! for I cannot direct to the first inventor of the fancy.

In like manner, they are to consider, What things, either in the heavens or belonging to the earth, have been found out, by experience, to contradict what has been formerly allowed of ?

Thus, because some ancient astronomers had observed that both the distances as well as the revolutions of the planets were in some proportion or harmony one to another : therefore people that abounded with more imagination than skill,

presently fancied the Moon, Mercury, and Venus to be a kind
of violins or trebles to Jupiter or Saturn; that the Sun and
Mars supplied the room of tenors, and the *Primum Mobile*
running Division all the tune. So that one could scarce heaı
a sermon, but they must give you a touch of "the Harmony
of the Spheres."

Thus, Sir, you shall have them take that of St. PAUL, about
"faith, hope, and charity." And instead of a sober instructing of the people in those eminent and excellent graces, they
shall only ring you over a few changes upon the three words;
crying, "Faith! Hope! and Charity!" "Hope! Faith! and
Charity!" and so on: and when they have done their peal,
they shall tell you that "this is much better than the
Harmony of the Spheres!"

At other times, I have heard a long chiming only between
two words; as suppose Divinity and Philosophy, or Revelation and Reason. Setting forth with Revelation first.
"Revelation is a Lady; Reason, an Handmaid! Revelation
is the Esquire; Reason, the Page! Revelation is the Sun;
Reason, but the Moon! Revelation is Manna; Reason is but
an acorn! Revelation, a wedge of gold; Reason, a small
piece of silver!"

Then, by and by, Reason gets it, and leads it away,
"Reason indeed is very good, but Revelation is much better!
Reason is a Councillor, but Revelation is the Lawgiver!
Reason is a candle, but Revelation is the snuffer!"

Certainly, those people are possessed with a very great
degree of dulness, who living under the means of such en-
lightening preaching, should not be mightily settled in the
right notion and true bounds of Faith and Reason.

No less ably, methought, was the difference between the
Old Covenant and the New, lately determined. "The Old
Covenant was of Works; the New Covenant, of Faith. The
Old Covenant was by MOSES; The New, by CHRIST. The
Old was heretoforè; the New, afterwards. The Old was
first; the New was second. Old things are passed away:
behold, all things are become new." And so the business
was very fundamentally done.

I shall say no more upon this subject, but this one thing,
which relates to what was said a little before. He that has
got a set of similitudes calculated according to the old

philosophy, and PTOLEMY's system of the world, must burn his commonplace book, and go a-gleaning for new ones ; it being, nowadays, much more gentle and warrantable to take a similitude from the Man in the Moon than from *solid* orbs : for though few people do absolutely believe that there is any such Eminent Person there ; yet the thing is possible, whereas the other is not.

I have now done, Sir, with that imprudent way of speaking by Metaphor and Simile. There are many other things commonly spoken out of the pulpit, that are much to the disadvantage and discredit of the Clergy ; that ought also to be briefly hinted. And that I may the better light upon them, I shall observe their *common method of Preaching*.

[**1.**] Before the text be divided, a *Preface* is to be made.

And it is a great chance if, first of all, the Minister does not make his text to be *like something or other*.

For example. One, he tells you, " And now, methinks, my Text, like an ingenious [*clever*] Picture, looks upon all here present : in which, both nobles and people, may behold their sin and danger represented." This was a text out of *Hosea*. Now, had it been out of any other place of the *Bible*; the gentleman was sufficiently resolved to make it like " an ingenious Picture."

Another taking, perhaps, the very same words, says, " I might compare my Text to the mountains of Bether, where the LORD disports Himself like a young hart or a pleasant roe among the spices."

Another man's Text is " like the rod of MOSES, to divide the waves of sorrow " ; or " like the mantle of ELIJAH, to restrain the swelling floods of grief."

Another gets to his Text thus, " As SOLOMON went up six steps to come to the great Throne of Ivory, so must I ascend six degrees to come to the high top-meaning of my Text."

Another thus, " As DEBORAH arose, and went with BARAK to Kadesh ; so, if you will go with him, and call in the third verse of the chapter, he will shew you the meaning of his Text."

Another, he fancies his Text to be extraordinarily like to " an orchard of pomegranates ; " or like " St. MATTHEW

sitting at the receipt of custom;" or like "the dove that
NOAH sent out of the Ark."

I believe there are above forty places of Scripture, that
have been "like RACHEL and LEAH": and there is one in
Genesis, as I well remember, that is "like a pair of compasses
stradling." And, if I be not much mistaken, there is one,
somewhere else, that is "like a man going to Jericho."

Now, Sir, having thus made the way to the Text as smooth
and plain as anything, with a *Preface,* perhaps from ADAM,
though his business lie at the other end of the *Bible* : in the
next place; [2] he comes *to divide the Text.*

> *Hic labor, hoc opus*
> *Per varios casus, per tot discrimina rerum,*
> *Silvestrem tenui.*

Now, come off the gloves! and the hands being well chafed
[*rubbed together*]; he shrinks up his shoulders, and stretches
forth himself as if he were going to cleave a bullock's head,
or rive the body of an oak!

But we must observe, that there is a great difference of
Texts. For all Texts come not asunder alike! For sometimes the words naturally *fall* asunder! sometimes they *drop*
asunder! sometimes they *melt*! sometimes they *untwist*! and
there be some words so willing to be parted that they *divide
themselves*! to the great ease and rejoicing of the Minister.

But if they will not easily come to pieces, then he falls to
hacking and hewing! as if he would make all fly into shivers!
The truth of it is, I have known, now and then, some knotty
Texts, that have been divided seven or eight times over!
before they could make them *split* handsomely, according to
their mind.

But then comes the Joy of Joys! when the Parts jingle!
or begin with the same Letter! and especially if in Latin.

O how it tickled the Divider! when he got his Text into
those two excellent branches, *Accusatio vera: Comminatio
severa* : "A Charge full of Verity: A Discharge of Severity."
And, I will warrant you! that did not please a little, viz.,
"there are in the words, *duplex miraculum; Miraculum in modo*
and *Miraculum in nodo.*"

But the luckiest I have met withal, both for Wit and

Keeping of the Letter, is upon these words of *St. Matthew* xii. 43, 44, 45 : " When the unclean spirit is gone out of a man, he walketh through dry places, seeking rest and finding none. Then he saith I will return," &c.

In which words, all these strange things were found out. First, there was a *Captain* and a *Castle*. (Do you see, Sir, the same letter!) Then, there was an *ingress*, an *egress* ; and a *regress* or *reingress*. Then, there was *unroosting* and *unresting*. Then, there were *number* and *name*, *manner* and *measure*, *trouble* and *trial*, *resolution* and *revolution*, *assaults* and *assassination*, *voidness* and *vacuity*. This was done at the same time, by the same man ! But, to confess the truth of it ! it was a good long Text ; and so, he had the greater advantage.

But for a short Text, that, certainly, was the greatest *break* that ever was ! which was occasioned from those words of *St. Luke* xxiii. 28, " Weep not for me, weep for yourselves ! " or as some read it, " but weep for yourselves ! "

It is a plain case, Sir ! Here are but eight words ; and the business was cunningly ordered, that there sprang out eight Parts. " Here are," says the Doctor, " eight Words, and eight Parts !

1. Weep not !
2. But weep !
3. Weep not, but weep !
4. Weep for me !
5. For yourselves !
6. For me, for yourselves !
7. Weep not for me !
8. But weep for yourselves !

That is to say, North, North-and-by-East, North-North-East, North-East and by North, North-East, North-East and by East, East-North-East, East and by North, East."

Now, it seems not very easy to determine, who has obliged the world most ; he that found out the Compass, or he that divided the fore-mentioned Text ? But I suppose the cracks [*claps*] will go generally upon the Doctor's side ! by reason what he did, was done by undoubted Art and absolute industry : but as for the other, the common report is that it was found out by mere foolish fortune. Well, let it go how it will ! questionless, they will be both famous in their way, and honourably mentioned to posterity.

Neither ought he to be altogether slighted, who taking that of *Genesis* xlviii. 2 for his text; viz., "And one told JACOB, and said, 'Behold, thy son JOSEPH cometh unto thee!'" presently perceived, and made it out to his people, that his Text was " a spiritual Dial."

"For," says he, "here be in my Text, twelve words, which do plainly represent the twelve hours. *And one told JACOB, and said, 'Thy son JOSEPH cometh unto thee!'* And here is, besides, *Behold*, which is the Hand of the Dial, that turns and points at every word of the Text. *And one told JACOB, and said, 'Behold, thy son JOSEPH cometh unto thee!'* For it is not said, *Behold JACOB!* or *Behold JOSEPH!* but it is, *And one told JACOB, and said, Behold, thy son JOSEPH cometh unto thee.* That it is say, Behold *And*, Behold *one*, Behold *told*, Behold *JACOB*. Again Behold *and*, Behold *said*, and also Behold *Behold*, &c. Which is the reason that this word *Behold* is placed in the middle of the other twelve words, indifferently pointing to each word.

" Now, as it needs must be One of the Clock before it can be Two or Three; so I shall handle this word *And*, the first word of the Text, before I meddle with the following.

"And *one told JACOB*. The word *And* is but a particle, and a small one: but small things are not to be despised. *St. Matthew* xviii. 10, *Take heed that you despise not one of these little ones.* For this *And* is as the tacks and loops amongst the curtains of the Tabernacle. The tacks put into the loops did couple the curtains of the Tent and sew the Tent together: so this particle *And* being put into the loops of the words immediately before the Text, does couple the Text to the foregoing verse, and sews them close together."

I shall not trouble you, Sir, with the rest: being much after this witty rate, and to as much purpose.

But we will go on, if you please, Sir! to [3] the cunning *Observations, Doctrines, and Inferences* that are commonly made and raised from places of Scripture.

One takes that for his Text, *Psalm* lxviii. 3, *But let the righteous be glad.* From whence, he raises this doctrine, that "there is a Spirit of Singularity in the Saints of GOD : but let the righteous—" a doctrine, I will warrant him ! of his own raising; it being not very easy for anybody to prevent him!

Another, he takes that of *Isaiah* xli. 14, 15, *Fear not, thou worm JACOB ! &c. . . . thou shalt thresh the mountains.* Whence he observes that " the worm JACOB was a threshing worm ! "

Another, that of *Genesis* xliv. 1. *And he commanded the Steward of the house, saying, Fill the men's sacks with food, as much as they can carry :* and makes this note from the words.

That " great sacks and many sacks will hold more than few sacks and little ones. For look," says he, " how they came prepared with sacks and beasts, so they were sent back with corn ! The greater, and the more sacks they had prepared, the more corn they carry away ! if they had prepared but small sacks, and a few ; they had carried away the less ! "

Verily, and indeed extraordinarily true !

Another, he falls upon that of *Isaiah* lviii. 5, *Is it such a fast that I have chosen ? A day for a man to afflict his soul ? Is it to bow down his head like a bulrush ?* The Observation is that " Repentance for an hour, or a day, is not worth a bulrush ! " And, there, I think, he hit the business !

But of these, Sir, I can shew you a whole book full, in a treatise called *Flames and Discoveries*, consisting of very notable and extraordinary things which the inquisitive Author had privately observed and discovered, upon reading the Evangelists ; as for example :

Upon reading that of *St. John*, chapter ii. verse 15, *And when he had made a scourge of small cords, he drove them all out of the Temple ;* this prying Divine makes these discoveries. " I discover," says he, " in the first place, that in the Church or Temple, a scourge may be made, *And when he had made a scourge.* Secondly, that it may be made use on, *he drove them all out of the Temple.*" And it was a great chance that he had not discovered a third thing ; and that is, that the scourge was made, before it was made use of.

Upon *Matthew* iv. 25, *And there followed him great multitudes of people from Galilee*, "I discover," says he, "when JESUS prevails with us, we shall soon leave our Galilees! I discover also," says he, "a great miracle, viz.: that the way after JESUS being straight, that such a multitude should follow him."

Matthew v. 1. *And seeing the multitude, he went up into a mountain.* Upon this, he discovers several very remarkable things. First, he discovers that "CHRIST went *from the multitude.*" Secondly, that "it is safe to take warning at our eyes, for *seeing the multitude, he went up.*" Thirdly, "it is not fit to be always upon the plains and flats with the multitude : but, *if we be risen with CHRIST, to seek those things that are above.*

He discovers also very strange things, from the latter part of the fore-mentioned verse. *And when he was set, his disciples came unto him.* 1. CHRIST is not always in motion, *And when he was set.* 2. He walks not on the mountain, but sits, *And when he was set.* From whence also, in the third place, he advises people, that "when they are teaching they should not move too much, for that is to be *carried to and fro with every wind of doctrine.*" Now, certainly, never was this place of Scripture more seasonably brought in.

Now, Sir, if you be for a very short and witty discovery, let it be upon that of *St. Matthew* vi. 27. *Which of you, by taking thought, can add one cubit unto his stature?* The discovery is this, that "whilst the disciples were taking thought for a cubit; CHRIST takes them down a cubit lower!"

Notable also are two discoveries made upon *St. Matthew* viii. 1. 1. That "CHRIST went down, as well as went up. *When he came down from the mountain.*" 2. That "the multitude did not go 'hail fellow well met!' with him, nor before him; for *great multitudes followed him.*"

I love, with all my heart, when people can prove what they say. For there be many that will talk of their Discoveries and spiritual Observations ; and when all comes to all, they are nothing but pitiful guesses and slender conjectures.

In like manner, that was no contemptible discovery

that was made upon *St. Matthew* viii. 19. *And a certain Scribe came and said, " Master, I will follow thee wheresoever thou goest."* " A *thou* shall be followed more than a *that. I will follow* thee *wheresoever thou goest.*

And, in my opinion, that was not altogether amiss, upon *St. Matthew* xi. 2. *Now when* JOHN *had heard in prison the works of* CHRIST, *he sent two of his disciples.* The discovery is this. That " it is not good sending single to CHRIST, *he sent two of his disciples.*"

Some also, possibly may not dislike that upon *St. Luke* xii. 35. *Let your loins be girded.* " I discover," says he, " there must be a holy girding and trussing up for heaven."

But I shall end all, with that very politic one that he makes upon *St. Matthew* xii. 47. *Then said one unto him " Behold thy mother and thy brethren stand without, desiring to speak with thee." But he answered and said, " Who is my mother ? and who are my brethren ? "* " I discover now," says he, " that JESUS is upon business."

Doubtless, this was one of the greatest Discoverers of Hidden Mysteries, and one of the most Pryers into Spiritual Secrets that ever the world was owner of. It was very well that he happened upon the godly calling, and no secular employment : or else, in good truth ! down had they all gone ! Turk ! Pope ! and Emperor ! for he would have discovered them, one way or another, every man !

Not much unlike to these wonderful Discoverers, are they who, choosing to preach on some Point in Divinjty, shall purposely avoid all such plain Texts as might give them very just occasion to discourse upon their intended subject, and shall pitch upon some other places of Scripture, which no creature in the world but themselves, did ever imagine that which they offer to be therein designed. My meaning, Sir, is this.

Suppose you have a mind to make a sermon concerning Episcopacy, as in the late times [*the Commonwealth*] there were several occasions for it, you must, by no means, take any place of Scripture that proves or favours that kind of Ecclesiastical Government ! for then the plot will be discovered ; and the people will say to themselves, " We know where to find you ! You intend to preach about Episcopacy ! "

But you must take *Acts*, chapter xvi. verse 30, *Sirs, what must I do to be saved?* An absolute place for Episcopacy! that all former Divines had idly overlooked! For *Sirs* being in the Greek Κύριοι, which is to say, in true and strict translation, *Lords*, what is more plain than, that of old, Episcopacy was not only the acknowledged Government; but that Bishops were formerly Peers of the Realm, and so ought to sit in the House of Lords!

Or, suppose that you have a mind to commend to your people, Kingly Government: you must not take any place that is plainly to the purpose! but that of the Evangelist, *Seek first the Kingdom of GOD!* From which words, the doctrine will plainly be, that Monarchy or Kingly Government is most according to the mind of GOD. For it is not said, "seek the *Parliament* of GOD!" "the *Army* of GOD!" or "the *Committee of Safety* of GOD!" but it is "seek the *Kingdom* of GOD!" And who could expect less? Immediately after this [*i.e., this argument*], the King came in, and the Bishops were restored [1660 A.D.].

Again, Sir (because I would willingly be understood), suppose you design to preach about Election and Reprobation. As for the eighth chapter to the *Romans*, that is too well known! but there is a little private place in the *Psalms* that will do the business as well! *Psalm* xc. 19, *In the multitude of my thoughts within me, thy comforts delight my soul.*

The doctrine, which naturally flows from the words, will be that amongst *the multitude of thoughts*, there is a great thought of Election and Reprobation; and then, away with the Point! according as the preacher is inclined.

Or suppose, lastly, that you were not fully satisfied that Pluralities were lawful or convenient. May I be so bold, Sir? I pray, what Text would you choose to preach up against non-residents? Certainly, nothing ever was better picked than that of St. *Matthew* i. 2. ABRAHAM *begat* ISAAC. A clear place against non-residents! for "had ABRAHAM not resided, but had discontinued from SARAH his wife, he could never have begotten ISAAC!"

But it is high time, Sir, to make an end of their preaching, lest you be as much tired with the repetition of it, as the people were little benefited when they heard it.

I shall only mind you, Sir, of one thing more ; and that is [4] the ridiculous, senseless, and unintended use which many of them make of *Concordances.*

I shall give you but one instance of it, although I could furnish you with a hundred printed ones.

The Text, Sir, is this, *Galatians* vi. 15, *For in* CHRIST *JESUS neither Circumcision nor Uncircumcision avail anything; but a new creature.* Now, all the world knows the meaning of this to be, that, let a man be of what nation he will, Jew or Gentile, if he amends his life, and walks according to the Gospel, he shall be accepted with GOD.

But this is not the way that pleases them ! They must bring into the sermon, to no purpose at all ! a vast heap of places of Scripture, which the *Concordance* will furnish them with, where the word *new* is mentioned.

And the Observation must be that "GOD is for *new* things. GOD is for *a* new *creature. St. John* xix. 41, *Now in the place where he was crucified, there was a garden ; and in the garden a* new *sepulchre, wherein was never man yet laid. There they laid JESUS.* And again *St. Mark* xvi. 17. CHRIST tells his disciples that they that are true believers, shall cast out devils, and speak *with* new *tongues.* And likewise, the prophet teaches us, *Isaiah* xlii. 10, *Sing unto the LORD a* new *song, and his praise to the end of the earth.*

" Whence it is plain that CHRIST is not for *old* things. He is not for an *old sepulchre.* He is not for *old tongues.* He is not for an *old song.* He is not for an *old creature.* CHRIST is for a *new creature ! Circumcision and Uncircumcision availeth nothing, but a new creature.* And what do we read concerning SAMSON ? *Judges* xv. 15. Is it not that he slew a thousand of the Philistines with one *new* jawbone ? An *old* one might have killed its tens, its twenties, its hundreds ! but it must be a *new* jawbone that is able to kill a thousand ! GOD is for the *new creature !*

" But may not some say, ' Is GOD altogether for new things ? ' How comes it about then, that the prophet says, *Isaiah* i. 13, 14, *Bring no more vain oblations ! &c. Your new Moons, and your appointed Feasts, my soul hateth !* And again, what means that, *Deuteronomy* xxxii. 17, 19, *They sacrificed unto devils, and to new gods, whom they knew*

> *not, to new gods that came newly up. . . . And when*
> *the LORD saw it, He abhorred them!* To which I
> answer, that GOD indeed is not for *new moons*, nor for
> *new gods*; but, excepting *moons* and *gods*, He is for the
> *new creature*."

It is possible, Sir, that somebody besides yourself, may be
so vain as to read this *Letter*: and they may perhaps tell
you, that there be no such silly and useless people as I have
described. And if there be, there be not above two or three
in a country [*county*]. Or should there be, it is no such complaining matter : seeing that the same happens in other
professions, in Law and Physic : in both [of] which, there be
many a contemptible creature.

Such therefore as these, may be pleased to know that, if
there had been need, I could have told them, either the book
(and very page almost) of all that has been spoken about
Preaching, or else the When and Where, and the Person that
preached it.

As to the second, viz. : that the Clergy are all mightily
furnished with Learning and Prudence ; except ten, twenty,
or so ; I shall not say anything myself, because a very great
Scholar of our nation shall speak for me : who tells us that
"such Preaching as is usual, is a hindrance of Salvation
rather than the means to it." And what he intends by
"usual," I shall not here go about to explain.

And as to the last, I shall also, in short, answer, That if the
Advancement of true Religion and the eternal Salvation of a
Man were no more considerable than the health of his body
and the security of his estate ; we need not be more solicitous
about the Learning and Prudence of the Clergy, than of the
Lawyers and Physicians. But we believing it to be otherwise,
surely, we ought to be more concerned for the reputation
and success of the one than of the other.

I COME now, Sir, to the Second Part that was
designed, viz. : *the Poverty of some of the Clergy*.
By whose mean condition, their Sacred Profession
is much disparaged, and their Doctrine undervalued.
What large provisions, of old, GOD was pleased to make

for the Priesthood, and upon what reasons, is easily seen to any one that but looks into the *Bible*. The Levites, it is true, were left out, in the Division of the Inheritance; not to their loss, but to their great temporal advantage. For whereas, had they been common sharers with the rest, a Twelfth part only would have been their just allowance; GOD was pleased to settle upon them, a Tenth, and that without any trouble or charge of tillage: which made their portion much more considerable than the rest.

And as this provision was very bountiful, so the reasons, no question! were very Divine and substantial: which seem chiefly to be these two.

First, that the Priesthood might be altogether at leisure for the service of GOD: and that they of that Holy Order might not be distracted with the cares of the world; and interrupted by every neighbour's horse or cow that breaks their hedges or shackles [*or hobbled, feeds among*] their corn. But that living a kind of spiritual life, and being removed a little from all worldly affairs; they might always be fit to receive holy inspirations, and always ready to search out the Mind of GOD, and to advise and direct the people therein.

Not as if this Divine exemption of them from the common troubles and cares of this life was intended as an opportunity of luxury and laziness: for certainly, there is a labour besides digging! and there is a true carefulness without following the plough, and looking after their cattle!

And such was the employment of those holy men of old. Their care and business was to please GOD, and to charge themselves with the welfare of all His people: which thing, he that does it with a good and satisfied conscience, I will assure he has a task upon him much beyond them that have for their care, their hundreds of oxen and five hundreds of sheep.

Another reason that this large allowance was made to the Priests, was that they might be enabled to relieve the poor, to entertain strangers, and thereby to encourage people in the ways of godliness. For they being, in a peculiar manner, the servants of GOD, GOD was pleased to entrust in their hands, a portion more than

ordinary of the good things of the land, as the safest
Storehouse and Treasury for such as were in need.

That, in all Ages therefore, there should be a continued
tolerable maintenance for the Clergy: the same reasons, as
well as many others, make us think to be very necessary.
Unless they will count money and victuals to be only Types
and Shadows! and so, to cease with the Ceremonial Law.

For where the Minister is pinched as to the tolerable conveniences of this life, the chief of his care and time must be
spent, not in an impertinent [*trifling*] considering what Text
of Scripture will be most useful for his parish; what instructions most seasonable; and what authors, best to be
consulted: but the chief of his thoughts and his main business must be, How to live that week? Where he shall have
bread for his family? Whose sow has lately pigged?
Whence will come the next rejoicing goose, or the next
cheerful basket of apples? how far to Lammas, or [Easter]
Offerings? When shall we have another christening and
cakes? and Who is likely to marry, or die?

These are very seasonable considerations, and worthy of a
man's thoughts. For a family cannot be maintained by
texts and contexts! and a child that lies crying in the
cradle, will not be satisfied without a little milk, and perhaps
sugar; though there be a small German *System* [*of Divinity*]
in the house!

But suppose he does get into a little hole over the oven,
with a lock to it, called his Study, towards the latter end
of the week: for you must know, Sir, there are very few
Texts of Scripture that can be divided, at soonest, before
Friday night; and some there be, that will never be divided
but upon Sunday morning, and that not very early, but
either a little before they go, or in the going, to church. I
say, suppose the Gentleman gets thus into his Study, one
may very nearly guess what is his first thought, when he
comes there—viz., that the last kilderkin of drink is nearly
departed! that he has but one poor single groat in the house,
and there is Judgement and Execution ready to come out
against it, for milk and eggs!

Now, Sir, can any man think, that one thus racked and

tortured, can be seriously intent, half an hour, to contrive anything that might be of real advantage to his people?

Besides, perhaps, that week, he has met with some dismal crosses and most undoing misfortunes.

There was a scurvy-conditioned mole, that broke into his pasture, and ploughed up the best part of his glebe. And, a little after that, came a couple of spiteful ill-favoured crows, and trampled down the little remaining grass. Another day, having but four chickens, sweep comes the kite! and carries away the fattest and hopefullest of the brood. Then, after all this, came the jackdaws and starlings (idle birds that they are!), and they scattered and carried away from his thin thatched house, forty or fifty of the best straws. And, to make him completely unhappy, after all these afflictions, another day, that he had a pair of breeches on, coming over a perverse stile, he suffered very much, in carelessly lifting over his leg.

Now, what parish can be so inconsiderate and unreasonable as to look for anything from one, whose fancy is thus checked, and whose understanding is thus ruffled and disordered? They may as soon expect comfort and consolation from him that lies racked with the gout and the stone, as from a Divine thus broken and shattered in his fortunes!

But we will grant that he meets not with any of these such frightful disasters; but that he goes into his study with a mind as calm as the evening. For all that; upon Sunday, we must be content with what GOD shall please to send us! For as for books, he is, for want of money, so moderately furnished, that except it be a small Geneva *Bible* (so small, as it will not be desired to lie open of itself), together with a certain *Concordance* thereunto belonging; as also a Latin book for all kind of Latin sentences, called *Polyanthæa*; with some *Exposition* upon the *Catechism*, a portion of which, is to be got by heart, and to be put off for his own; and perhaps Mr. [JOSEPH] CARYL *upon* [JOHN] PINEDA [*these two authors wrote vast Commentaries on the Book of Job*]; Mr. [JOHN] DOD upon the *Commandments*, Mr. [SAMUEL] CLARKE's Lives of famous men, both in Church and State (such as Mr. CARTER of Norwich, that uses to eat such abundance of pudding): besides, I say, these, there is scarcely anything to be found, but a budget of old stitched sermons hung up

behind the door, with a few broken girths, two or three yards
of whipcord; and, perhaps, a saw and a hammer, to prevent
dilapidations.

Now, what may not a Divine do, though but of ordinary
parts and unhappy education, with such learned helps and
assistances as these ? No vice, surely, durst stand before
him! no heresy, affront him!

And furthermore, Sir, it is to be considered, that he that
is but thus meanly provided for: it is not his only infelicity
that he has neither time, mind, nor books to improve himself
for the inward benefit and satisfaction of his people ; but also
that he is not capable of doing that outward good amongst
the needy, which is a great ornament to that holy Profession,
and a considerable advantage towards the having the doctrine
believed and practised in a degenerate world.

And that which augments the misery; whether he be able or
not, it is expected from him, if there comes a *Brief* to town,
for the Minister to cast in his mite will not satisfy! unless he
can create sixpence or a shilling to put into the box, for a
stale [*lure*], to decoy in the rest of the parish. Nay, he that
hath but £20 or £30 [=£60 *to* £90 *now*] *per annum*, if he bids
not up as high as the best in the parish in all acts of charity,
he is counted carnal and earthly-minded; only because he
durst not coin! and cannot work miracles!

And let there come ever so many beggars, half of these,
I will secure you! shall presently inquire for the Minister's
house. "For GOD," say they, "certainly dwells there, and
has laid up for us, sufficient relief!"

I know many of the Laity are usually so extremely tender
of the spiritual welfare of the Clergy, that they are apt to
wish them but very small temporal goods, lest their inward
state should be in danger! A thing, they need not much fear,
since that effectual humiliation by HENRY VIII. "For,"
say they, "the great tithes, large glebes, good victuals and
warm clothes do but puff up the Priest! making him fat,
foggy, and useless! and fill him with pride, vainglory, and
all kind of inward wickedness and pernicious corruption!
We see this plain," say they, "in the Whore of Babylon
[*Roman Catholic Church*]! To what a degree of luxury and
intemperance, besides a great deal of false doctrine, have

riches and honour raised up that strumpet! How does she
strut it! and swagger it over all the world! terrifying Princes,
and despising Kings and Emperors!

"The Clergy, if ever we would expect any edification from
them, ought to be dieted and kept low! to be meek and
humble, quiet, and stand in need of a pot of milk from their
next neighbour! and always be very loth to ask for their
very right, for fear of making any disturbance in the parish,
or seeming to understand or have any respect for this vile
and outward world!

"Under the Law, indeed, in those old times of Darkness
and Eating, the Priests had their first and second dishes,
their milk and honey, their Manna and quails, also their
outward and inward vestments: but now, under the Gospel,
and in times of Light and Fasting, a much more sparing diet
is fitter, and a single coat (though it be never so ancient and
thin) is fully sufficient!"

"We must look," say they, "if we would be the better for
them, for a hardy and labouring Clergy, that is mortified to
[the possession of] a horse and all such pampering vanities!
and that can foot it five or six miles in the dirt, and preach
till starlight, for as many [5 or 6] shillings! as also a sober
and temperate Clergy, that will not eat so much as the
Laity, but that the least pig, the least sheaf, and the least of
everything, may satisfy their Spiritualship! And besides, a
money-renouncing Clergy, that can abstain from seeing a
penny, a month together! unless it be when the Collectors
and Visitationers come. These are all Gospel dispensations!
and great instances of patience, contentedness, and resignation of affections [in respect] to all the emptinesses and
fooleries of this life!"

But cannot a Clergyman choose rather to lie upon feathers
than a hurdle; but he must be idle, soft, and effeminate!
May he not desire wholesome food and fresh drink; unless he
be a cheat, a hypocrite, and an impostor! And must he
needs be void of all grace, though he has a shilling in his
purse, after the rates be crossed [off]! and full of pride and
vanity though his house stands not upon crutches; and
though his chimney is to be seen a foot above the thatch!

O, how prettily and temperately may half a score of children
be maintained with *almost* £20 [=£60 *now*] *per annum*!

What a handsome shift, a poor ingenious and frugal Divine
will make, to take it by turns, and wear a cassock [*a long
cloak*] one year, and a pair of breeches another! What a
becoming thing is it for him that serves at the Altar, to fill
the dung cart in dry weather, and to heat the oven and pull
[*strip*] hemp in wet! And what a pleasant thing is it, to see
the Man of GOD fetching up his single melancholy cow from
a small rib [*strip*] of land that is scarcely to be found without
a guide! or to be seated upon a soft and well grinded pouch
[*bag*] of meal! or to be planted upon a pannier, with a pair
of geese or turkeys bobbing out their heads from under his
canonical coat! as you cannot but remember the man, Sir,
that was thus accomplished. Or to find him raving about
the yards or keeping his chamber close, because the duck
lately miscarried of an egg, or that the never-failing hen has
unhappily forsaken her wonted nest!

And now, shall we think that such employments as these,
can, any way, consist with due reverence, or tolerable respect
from a parish?

And he speaks altogether at a venture that says that "this
is false, or, at least it need not be so; notwithstanding the
mean condition of some of the Clergy." For let any one make
it out to me, which way is it possible that a man shall be
able to maintain perhaps eight or ten in his family, with £20
or £30 *per annum*, without a intolerable dependence upon
his parish; and without committing himself to such vileness
as will, in all likelihood, render him contemptible to his people.

Now where the income is so pitifully small (which, I will
assure you, is the portion of hundreds of the Clergy of this
nation), which way shall he manage it for the subsistence of
himself and his family?

If he keeps the glebe in his own hand (which he may
easily do, almost in the hollow of it!) what increase can he
expect from a couple of apple trees, a brood of ducklings, a
hemp land, and as much pasture as is just able to summer a
cow?

As for his tithes, he either rents them out to a layman;
who will be very unwilling to be his tenant, unless he may
be sure to save by the bargain at least a third part: or else,
he compounds for them; and then, as for his money, he
shall have it when all the rest of the world be paid!

But if he thinks fit to take his dues in kind, he then either demands his true and utmost right; and if so, it is a great hazard if he be not counted a caterpillar! a muck worm! a very earthly minded man! and too much sighted into this lower world! which was made, as many of the Laity think, altogether for themselves: or else, he must tamely commit himself to that little dose of the creature that shall be pleased to be proportioned out unto him; choosing rather to starve in peace and quietness, than to gain his right by noise and disturbance.

The best of all these ways that a Clergyman shall think fit for his preferment, to be managed (where it is so small), are such as will undoubtedly make him either to be hated and reviled, or else pitifully poor and disesteemed.

But has it not gone very hard, in all Ages with the Men of GOD? Was not our Lord and Master our great and high Priest? and was not his fare low, and his life full of trouble? And was not the condition of most of his disciples very mean? Were not they notably pinched and severely treated after him? And is it not the duty of every Christian to imitate such holy patterns? but especially of the Clergy, who are to be shining lights and visible examples; and therefore to be satisfied with a very little morsel, and to renounce ten times as much of the world as other people?

And is not patience better than the Great Tithes, and contentedness to be preferred before large fees and customs? Is there any comparison between the expectation of a cringing bow or a low hat, and mortification to all such vanities and fopperies; especially with those who, in a peculiar manner, hope to receive their inheritance, and make their harvest in the next life?

This was well thought of indeed. But for all that, if you please, Sir, we will consider a little, some of those remarkable Inconveniences that do, most undoubtedly, attend upon the Ministers being so meanly provided for.

First of all, the holy Men of GOD or the Ministry in general, hereby, is disesteemed and rendered of small account. For though they be called Men of GOD: yet when it is observed that GOD seems to take but little care of

them, in making them tolerable provision for this life, or
that men are suffered to take away that which GOD was
pleased to provide for them ; the people are presently apt to
think that they belong to GOD no more than ordinary folks,
if so much.

And although it is not to be questioned but that the
Laying on of Hands is a most Divine institution: yet it is
not all the Bishops' hands in the world, laid upon a man, if
he be either notoriously ignorant or dismally poor, that can
procure him any hearty and lasting respect. For though we
find that some of the disciples of CHRIST that carried on and
established the great designs of the Gospel, were persons of
ordinary employments and education: yet we see little
reason to think that miracles should be continued, to do
that which natural endeavours, assisted by the Spirit of
GOD, are able to perform. And if CHRIST were still upon
earth to make bread for such as are his peculiar Servants
and Declarers of his Mind and Doctrine; the Laity, if they
please, should eat up all the corn themselves, as well the
tenth sheaf as the others: but seeing it is otherwise, and
that that miraculous power was not left to the succeeding
Clergy ; for them to beg their bread, or depend for their
subsistence upon the good pleasure and humour of their
parish, is a thing that renders that Holy Office very much
slighted and disregarded.

That constitution therefore of our Church was a most
prudent design, that says that all who are ordained shall be
ordained to somewhat, not ordained at random, to preach in
general to the whole world, as they travel up and down the
road; but to this or that particular parish. And, no question,
the reason was, to prevent spiritual peddling ; and gadding up
and down the country with a bag of trifling and insignificant
sermons, inquiring "Who will buy any doctrine?" So that
no more might be received into Holy Orders than the Church
had provision for.

But so very little is this regarded, that if a young Divinity
Intender has but got a sermon of his own, or of his father's ;
although he knows not where to get a meal's meat or one
penny of money by his preaching: yet he gets a Qualification
from some beneficed man or other, who, perhaps, is no more
able to keep a curate than I am to keep ten footboys ! and so

he is made a Preacher. And upon this account, I have known an ordinary Divine, whose living would but just keep himself and his family from melancholy and despair, shroud under his protection as many Curates as the best Nobleman in the land hath Chaplains [*i.e.*, *eight*].

Now, many such as these, go into Orders against the sky falls! foreseeing no more likelihood of any preferment coming to them, than you or I do of being Secretaries of State. Now, so often as any such as these, for want of maintenance, are put to any unworthy and disgraceful shifts; this reflects disparagement upon all that Order of holy men.

And we must have a great care of comparing our small preferred Clergy with those but of the like fortune, in the Church of Rome : they having many arts and devices of gaining respect and reverence to their Office, which we count neither just nor warrantable. We design no more, than to be in a likely capacity of doing good, and not discrediting our religion, nor suffering the Gospel to be disesteemed : but their aim is clearly, not only by cheats, contrived tales, and feigned miracles, to get money in abundance ; but to be worshipped, and almost deified, is as little as they will content themselves withal.

For how can it be, but that the people belonging to a Church, wherein the Supreme Governor is believed never to err (either purely by virtue of his own single wisdom, or by help of his inspiring Chair, or by the assistance of his little infallible Cardinals ; for it matters not, where the root of not being mistaken lies) : I say, how can it be, but that all that are believers of such extraordinary knowledge, must needs stand in most direful awe, not only of the aforesaid Supreme, but of all that adhere to him, or are in any ghostly authority under him ?

And although it so happens that this same extraordinary knowing Person is pleased to trouble himself with a good large proportion of this vile and contemptible world : so that should he, now and then, upon some odd and cloudy day, count himself *mortal*, and be a little mistaken ; yet he has chanced to make such a comfortable provision for himself and his followers, that he must needs be sufficiently valued and honoured amongst all. But had he but just enough to

keep himself from catching cold and starving, so long as he
is invested with such spiritual sovereignty and such a peculiar
privilege of being infallible; most certainly, without quarrel-
ling, he takes the rode [?] of all mankind.

And as for the most inferior priests of all, although they
pretend not to such perfection of knowledge: yet there be
many extraordinary things which they are believed to be able
to do, which beget in people a most venerable respect towards
them: such is, the power of "making GOD" in the Sacrament, a thing that must infallibly procure an infinite admiration of him that can do it, though he scarce knows the *Ten
Commandments*, and has not a farthing to buy himself bread.
And then, when "CHRIST is made," their giving but half of
him to the Laity, is a thing also, if it be minded, that will
very much help on the business, and make the people stand
at a greater distance from the Clergy. I might instance,
likewise, in their Auricular Confession, enjoining of Penance,
forgiving sins, making of Saints, freeing people from Purgatory, and many such useful tricks they have, and wonders
they can do, to draw in the forward believing Laity into a
most right worshipful opinion and honourable esteem of
them.

And therefore, seeing our holy Church of England counts
it not just, nor warrantable, thus to cheat the world by
belying the *Scriptures*; and by making use of such falsehood
and stratagems to gain respect and reverence: it behoves us,
certainly, to wish for, and endeavour, all such means as are
useful and lawful for the obtaining of the same.

I might here, I think, conveniently add that though many
preferments amongst the Clergy of Rome may possibly be as
small as some of ours in England; yet are we to be put in
mind of one more excellent contrivance of theirs: and that
is, the denial of marriage to Priests, whereby they are freed
from the expenses of a family, and a train of young children,
that, upon my word! will soon suck up the milk of a cow or
two, and grind in pieces a few sheaves of corn. The Church
of England therefore thinking it not fit to oblige their Clergy
to a single life (and I suppose are not likely to alter their
opinion, unless they receive better reasons for it from Rome
than have been as yet sent over): he makes a comparison
very wide from the purpose, that goes about to try the livings

here in England by those of the Church of Rome; there being nothing more frequent in our Church than for a Clergyman to have three or four children to get bread for, by that time, one, in theirs, shall be allowed to go into Holy Orders.

There is still one thing remaining, which ought not to be forgotten (a thing that is sometimes urged, I know, by the Papist, for the single life of the Priests) that does also much lessen the esteem of our Ministry; and that is the poor and contemptible employment that many children of the Clergy are forced upon, by reason of the meanness of their father's revenue.

It has happened, I know, sometimes, that whereas it has pleased GOD to bestow upon the Clergyman a very sufficient income: yet such has been his carelessness as that he hath made but pitiful provision for his children: and, on the other side, notwithstanding all the good care and thoughtfulness of the father, it has happened, at other times, that the children, beyond the power of all advice, have seemed to be resolved for debauchery.

But to see Clergymen's children condemned to the walking [*holding*] of horses! to wait upon a tapster! or the like; and that only because their father was not able to allow them a more genteel education: these are such employments that cannot but bring great disgrace and dishonour upon the Clergy.

But this is not all the inconvenience that attends the small income that is the portion of some Clergymen: for besides that the Clergy in general is disesteemed, they are likely also to do but little good in their parish. For it is a hard matter for the people to believe, that he talks anything to the purpose, that wants ordinary food for his family; and that his advice and exposition can come from above, that is scarcely defended against the weather. I have heard a travelling poor man beg with very good reason and a great stream of seasonable rhetoric; and yet it has been very little minded, because his clothes were torn, or at least out of fashion. And, on the other side, I have heard but an ordinary saying proceeding from a fine suit and a good lusty title of honour, highly admired; which would not possibly have been hearkened to, had it been uttered by a meaner person : yet, by all means, because it was a fancy of His Worship's, it must be counted high ! and notably expressed !

If, indeed, this world were made of sincere and pure beaten virtue, like the gold of the first Age, then such idle and fond prejudices would be a very vain supposal ; and the doctrine that proceeded from the most battered and contemptible habit [clothes] and the most sparing diet would be as acceptable as that which flowed from a silken cassock [cloak] and the best cheer. But seeing the world is not absolutely perfect, it is to be questioned whether he that runs upon trust for every ounce of provisions he spends in his family, can scarce look from his pulpit into any seat in the church but that he spies somebody or other that he is beholden to and depends upon ; and, for want of money, has scarce confidence to speak handsomely to his Sexton : it is to be questioned, I say, whether one, thus destitute of all tolerable subsistence, and thus shattered and distracted with most necessary cares, can either invent with discretion, or utter with courage, anything that may be beneficial to his people, whereby they may become his diligent attenders and hearty respecters.

And as the people do almost resolve against being amended or bettered by the Minister's preaching, whose circumstances as to this life are so bad, and his condition so low : so likewise is their devotion very cool and indifferent, in hearing from such a one the *Prayers* of the Church.

The *Divine Service*, all the world knows ! is the same, if read in the most magnificent Cathedral or in the most private parlour ; or if performed by the Archbishop himself, or by the meanest of his priests : but as the solemnity of the place, besides the consecration of it to GOD Almighty, does much influence the devotion of the people ; so also the quality and condition of the person that reads it. And though there be not that acknowledged difference between a Priest comfortably provided for, and him that is in the thorns and briars ; as there is between one placed in great dignity and authority and one that is in less : yet such a difference the people will make, that they will scarce hearken to what is read by the one, and yet be most religiously attentive to the other. Not, surely, that any one can think that he whose countenance is cheerly and his barns full, can petition

heaven more effectually, or prevail with GOD for the forgive-
ness of a greater sin, than he who is pitifully pale and is not
owner of an ear of corn: yet, most certainly, they do not
delight to confess their sins and sing praises to GOD with
him who sighs, more for want of money and victuals,
than for his trespasses and offences. Thus it is, and will
be! do you or I, Sir, what we can to the contrary.

Did our Church indeed believe, with the Papists, every
person rightfully ordained, to be a kind of GOD Almighty,
working miracles and doing wonders; then would people
most readily prostrate themselves to everything in Holy
Orders, though it could but just creep! But as our Church
counts those of the Clergy to be but mortal men, though
peculiarly dedicated to GOD and His service; their behaviour, their condition and circumstances of life, will
necessarily come into our value and esteem of them. And
therefore it is no purpose for men to say "that this need not
be, it being but mere prejudice, humour, and fancy: and that
if the man be but truly in Holy Orders; that is the great
matter! and from thence come blessings, absolution, and
intercession through CHRIST with GOD. And that it is not
Philosophy, Languages, Ecclesiastical History, Prudence,
Discretion, and Reputation, by which the Minister can help
us on towards heaven."

Notwithstanding this, I say again, that seeing men are
men, and seeing that we are of the Church of England and
not of that of Rome, these things ought to be weighed and
considered; and for want of being so, our Church of England
has suffered much.

And I am almost confident that, since the Reformation,
nothing has more hindered people from a just estimation of a
Form of Prayer and our holy *Liturgy* than employing a company
of boys, or old illiterate mumblers, to read the *Service*. And
I do verily believe, that, at this very day, especially in Cities
and Corporations, which make up the third part of our nation,
there is nothing that does more keep back some dissatisfied
people from Church till *Service* be over, than that it is read
by some £10 or £12 man, with whose parts and education
they are so well acquainted, as to have reason to know that
he has but skill enough to read the *Lessons* with twice con-
ning over. And though the office of the Reader be only to

read word for word, and neither to invent or expound: yet people love he should be a person of such worth and knowledge, as it may be supposed he understands what he reads.

And although for some it were too burdensome a task to read the *Service* twice a day, and preach as often; yet certainly it were much better if the people had but one sermon in a fortnight or month, so the *Service* were performed by a knowing and valuable person, than to run an unlearned rout of contemptible people into Holy Orders, on purpose only to say the *Prayers* of the Church, who perhaps shall understand very little more than a hollow pipe made of tin or wainscoat.

Neither do I here at all reflect upon Cathedrals, where the *Prayers* are usually read by some grave and worthy person. And as for the unlearned singers, whether boys or men, there is no complaint to be made, as to this case, than that they have not an all understanding Organ, or a prudent and discreet Cornet.

Neither need people be afraid that the Minister for want of preaching should grow stiff and rusty; supposing he came not into the pulpit every week. For he can spend his time very honestly, either by taking better care of what he preaches, and by considering what is most useful and seasonable for the people : and not what subject he can preach upon with most ease, or upon what text he can make a brave speech, for which nobody shall be the better ! or where he can best steal, without being discovered, as is the practice of many Divines in private parishes. Or else, he may spend it in visiting the sick, instructing the ignorant, and recovering such as are gone astray.

For though there be churches built for public assemblies, for public instruction and exhortation ; and though there be not many absolutely plain places of Scripture that oblige the Minister to walk from house to house : yet, certainly, people might receive much more advantage from such charitable visits and friendly conferences, than from general discourses levelled at the whole world, where perhaps the greatest part of the time shall be spent in useless Prefaces, Dividings, and Flourishings. Which thing is very practicable ; excepting some vast parishes : in which, also, it is much better to do good to some, than to none at all.

There is but one calamity more that I shall mention, which
though it need not absolutely, yet it does too frequently, ac-
company the low condition of many of the Clergy : and that
is, it is a great hazard if they be not *idle, intemperate,* and
scandalous.

I say, I cannot prove it strictly and undeniably that a man
smally beneficed, must of necessity be dissolute and
debauched. But when we consider how much he lies subject
to the humour of all reprobates, and how easily he is tempted
from his own house of poverty and melancholy : it is to be
feared that he will be willing, too often to forsake his own
Study of a few scurvy books ; and his own habitation of darkness where there is seldom eating or drinking, for a good
lightsome one where there is a bountiful provision of both.

And when he comes there, though he swears not at all; yet
he must be sure to say nothing to those that do it by all that
they can think of. And though he judges it not fit to lead
the Forlorn in vice and profaneness : yet, if he goes about to
damp a frolic, there is great danger, not only of losing his
Sunday dinner, but also all opportunities of such future
refreshments, for his niceness and squeamishness !

And such as are but at all disposed to this lewd kind of
meetings ; besides the Devil, he shall have solicitors enough !
who count all such revelling occasion very unsavoury and unhallowed, unless they have the presence of some Clergyman
to sanctify the ordinance : who, if he sticks at his glass, bless
him ! and call him but "Doctor !" and it slides presently [*i.e.,
the Clergyman drinks*].

I take no delight, I must confess, to insist upon this : but
only I could very much wish that such of our Governors as
go amongst our small preferred Clergy, to take a view of the
condition of the Church and Chancel ; that they would but
make inquiry, Whether the Minister himself be not much out
of repair ?

HAVE now done, Sir, with the Grounds of that Disesteem that many of the Clergy lie under, both by
the *Ignorance* of some, and the *extreme Poverty* of
others. And I should have troubled you no further,
but that I thought it convenient not to omit the particular

Occasions that do concur to the making of many of our Clergy so pitifully poor and contemptible.

The first thing that contributes much to the Poverty of the Clergy is *the great scarcity of Livings.*

Churches and Chapels we have enough, it is to be confessed, if compared with the bigness of our nation : but, in respect of that infinite number that are in Holy Orders, it is a very plain case, that there is a very great want. And I am confident, that, in a very little time, I could procure hundreds that should ride both sun and moon down, and be everlastingly yours ! if you could help them but to a Living of £25 or £30 a year.

And this, I suppose, to be chiefly occasioned upon these two accounts : either from *the eagerness and ambition* that some people have, of going into Orders ; or from *the refuge of others* into the Church, who, being otherwise disappointed of a livelihood, hope to make sure of one by that means.

First, I say, that which increases the unprovided-for number of the Clergy, is people posting into Orders before they know their Message or business, only out of a certain pride and ambition. Thus some are hugely in love with the mere title of Priest or Deacon : never considering how they shall live, or what good they are likely to do in their Office ; but only they have a fancy, that a cassock, if it be made long, is a very handsome garment, though it be never paid for ; that the Desk is clearly the best, and the Pulpit, the highest seat in all the parish ; that they shall take place [*precedence*] of most Esquires and Right Worshipfuls ; that they shall have the honour of being spiritual guides and counsellors ; and they shall be supposed to understand more of the Mind of GOD than ordinary, though perhaps they scarcely know the Old Law from the New, nor the *Canon* from the *Apocrypha.* Many, I say, such as these, there be, who know not where to get two groats, nor what they have to say to the people : but only because they have heard that the office of a Minister is the most noble and honourable employment in the world ; therefore they (not knowing in the least what the meaning of that is), Orders, by all means, must have ! though it be to the disparagement of that holy function.

Others also there be who are not so highly possessed with

the mere dignity of the office and honourableness of the employment; but think, had they but licence and authority to preach, O how they could pay it away! and that they can tell the people such strange things, as they never heard before, in all their lives! That they have got such a commanding voice! such heart-breaking expressions! such a peculiar method of Text-dividing! and such notable helps for the interpreting all difficulties in Scripture! that they can shew the people a much shorter way to heaven than has been, as yet, made known by any!

Such a forwardness as this, of going in Holy Orders, either merely out of an ambitious humour of being called a Priest; or of thinking they could do such feats and wonders, if they might be but free of the Pulpit, has filled the nation with many more Divines than there is any competent maintenance for in the Church.

Another great crowd that is made in the Church is by those that take in there only as a place of shelter and refuge. Thus, we have many turn Priests and Deacons, either for want of employment in their profession of Law, Physic, or the like; or having been unfortunate in their trade, or having broken a leg, or an arm, and so disabled from following their former calling; or having had the pleasure of spending their estate, or being (perhaps deservedly) disappointed of their inheritance. The Church is a very large and good "Sanctuary"; and one Spiritual shilling is as good as three Temporality shillings. Let the hardest come to the hardest! if they can get by heart, *Quid est fides? Quid est Ecclesia? quot sunt Concilia Generalia?* and gain Orders; they may prove Readers or Preachers, according as their gifts and opportunities shall lie. Now many, such as these, the Church being not able to provide for (as there is no great reason that she should be solicitous about it) must needs prove a very great disparagement to her; they coming hither, just as the old heathens used to go to prayers. When nothing would stop the anger of the gods, then for a touch of devotion! and if there be no way to get victuals; rather than starve, let us Read or Preach!

In short, Sir, we are perfectly overstocked with Professors of Divinity: there being scarce employment for half of those who undertake that office. And unless we had some of the

Romish tricks, to ramble up and down, and cry Pardons and
Indulgences; or, for want of a living, have a good store of
clients in the business of Purgatory, or the like, and so make
such unrighteous gains of Religion : it were certainly much
better if many of them were otherwise determined. Or unless we have some vent [*export*] for our Learned Ones, beyond
the sea; and could transport so many tons of Divines yearly,
as we do other commodities with which the nation is overstocked; we do certainly very unadvisedly, to breed up so many
to that Holy Calling, or to suffer so many to steal into Orders :
seeing there is not sufficient work and employment for them.

The next thing that does as much to heighten the misery of
our Church, as to the *poverty* of it, is the Gentry's designing,
not only the weak, the lame, and usually the most ill-favoured
of their children for the office of the Ministry; but also such as
they intend to settle nothing upon for their subsistence :
leaving them wholly to the bare hopes of Church preferment.
For, as they think, let the Thing look how it will, it is good
enough for the Church ! and that if it had but limbs enough
to climb the pulpit, and eyes enough to find the day of the
month, it will serve well enough to preach, and read *Service* !

So, likewise, they think they have obliged the Clergy very
much, if they please to bestow two or three years' education
upon a younger son at the University : and then commend
him to the grace of GOD, and the favour of the Church ;
without one penny of money, or inch of land !

You must not think, that he will spoil his eldest son's estate, or
hazard the lessening of the credit of the family, to do that which
may, any way, tend to the reputation and honour of the Clergy!

And thus it comes to pass, that you may commonly ride
ten miles, and scarce meet with a Divine that is worth
above two spoons and a pepper box, besides his living or
spiritual preferments. For, as for the Land, that goes
sweeping away with the eldest son, for the immortality of
the family ! and, as for the Money, that is usually employed
for to bind out [*apprentice*] and set up other children ! And
thus, you shall have them make no doubt of giving £500 or a
£1,000 [=£1,500 *or* £3,000 *now*] for a stock [*capital*] to them :
but for the poor Divinity son, if he gets but enough to buy
a broad hat at second-hand, and a small *System of Faith* or
two, that is counted stock sufficient for him to set up withal.

U
7

And, possibly, he might make some kind of shift in this
world, if anybody will engage that he shall have, neither
wife nor children: but, if it so fall out, that he leaves the
world, and behind him either the one or the others : in what
a dismal condition are these likely to be! and how will their
sad calamities reflect upon the Clergy! So dismal a thing
is this commonly judged, that those that at their departure
out of this life, are piously and virtuously disposed, do
usually reckon the taking care for the relief of the poor Ministers' widows, to be an opportunity of as necessary charity as
the mending the highways, and the erecting of hospitals.

But neither are spiritual preferments only scarce, by reason
of that great number that lie hovering over them ; and that
they that are thus on the wing, are usually destitute of any
other estate and livelihood : but also, when they come into
possession of them, they finding, for the most part, nothing
but a little sauce and Second Course (pigs, geese, and
apples), must needs be put upon great perplexities for the
standing necessaries of a family.

So that if it be inquired by any one, How comes it to pass,
that we have so many in Holy Orders that understand so
little, and are able to do so little service in the Church?
if we may answer plainly and truly, we may say, "Because
they are fit for nothing else!"

For, shall we think that any man that is not cursed to
uselessness, poverty, and misery, will be content with £20 or
£30 a year? For though, in the bulk, it looks, at first, like
a bountiful estate ; yet, if we think of it a little better, we shall
find that an ordinary bricklayer or carpenter (I mean not
your great undertakers [*contractors*] and master workmen) that
earns constantly but his two shillings a day, has clearly a
better revenue, and has certainly the command of more
money. For that the one has no dilapidations and the like,
to consume a great part of his weekly wages; of which you
know how much the other is subject unto.

So that as long as we have so many small and contemptible livings belonging to our Church, let the world do what
it can! we must expect that they should be supplied by
very lamentable and unserviceable Things. For that nobody
else will meddle with them! unless, one in an Age abounding
with money, charity, and goodness, will preach for nothing!

For if men of knowledge, prudence, and wealth have a fancy against a Living of £20 or £30 a year; there is no way to get them into such an undertaking, but by sending out a spiritual press [*press gang*]: for that very few volunteers that are worth, unless better encouraged, will go into that Holy Warfare! but it will be left to those who cannot devise how otherwise to live!

Neither must people say that, "besides Bishoprics, Prebendaries, and the like, we have several brave benefices, suffice to invite those of the best parts, education, and discretion." For, imagine one Living in forty is worth £100 [=£300 *now*] a year, and supplied by a man of skill and wholesome counsel: what are the other thirty-nine the better for that? What are the people about Carlisle bettered by his instructions and advice who lives at Dover? It was certainly our Saviour's mind, not only that the Gospel should be preached to all nations at first; but that the meaning and power of it should be preserved, and constantly declared to all people, by such as had judgement to do it.

Neither again must they say, that "Cities, Corporations, and the great trading towns of this nation, which are the strength and glory of it, and that contain the useful people of the world, are usually instructed by very learned and judicious persons." For, I suppose that our Saviour's design was not that Mayors, Aldermen, and merchants should be only saved: but also that all plain country people should partake of the same means; who (though they read not so many *Gazettes* as citizens; nor concern themselves where the Turk or King of France [*LOUIS XIV.*] sets on next) yet the true knowledge of GOD is now so plainly delivered in Scripture, that there wants nothing but sober and prudent Offerers of the same, to make it saving to those of the meanest understandings. And therefore, in all parishes, if possible, there ought to be such a fixed and settled provision as might reasonably invite some careful and prudent person, for the people's guide and instruction in holy matters.

And furthermore, it might be added, that the revenue belonging to most of the Corporation Livings is no such mighty business: for were it not for the uncertain and humorsome contribution of the well-pleased parishioners, the Parson and his family might be easily starved, for all the lands and income that belong to the Church. Besides, the great mischief that such kind of hired Preachers have done in the World—which I shall not stay here, to insist upon.

And as we have not churches enough, in respect of the great multitude that are qualified for a Living: so, considering the smallness of the revenue and the number of people that are to be the hearers, it is very plain that we have too many.

And we shall, many times, find two churches in the same yard, when as one would hold double the people of both the parishes. If they were united for the encouragement of some deserving person, he might easily make shift to spend, very honestly and temperately, the revenue of both.

And what though churches stand at a little further distance? People may please to walk a mile, without distemperating themselves; when as they shall go three or four to a market, to sell two pennyworth of eggs.

But suppose they resolved to pretend that they shall catch cold (the clouds being more than ordinarily thick upon the Sunday; as they usually are, if there be religion in the case); and that they are absolutely bent upon having instruction brought to their own town, Why might not one sermon a day, or (rather than fail) one in a fortnight, from a prudent and well-esteemed-of Preacher, do as well as two a day from him that talks, all the year long, nothing to the purpose; and thereupon is laughed at and despised?

I know what people will presently say to this, viz., that "if, upon Sunday, the Church doors be shut, the Alehouses will be open! and therefore, there must be somebody (though never so weak and lamentable!) to pass away the time in the Church, that the people may be kept sober and peaceable."

Truly, if religion and the worship of GOD consisted only in *negatives*, and that the observation of the Sabbath, was only *not* to be drunk! then they speak much to the purpose: but if it be otherwise, very little. It being not much unlike, as it is the fashion in many places, to the sending of little children of two or three years old to a School Dame, without any design of learning one letter, but only to keep them out of the fire and water.

Last of all, people must not say that "there needs no great store of learning in a Minister; and therefore a small Living may answer his deserts: for that there be *Homilies* made on purpose by the Church for young beginners and slow inventors. Whereupon it is, that such difference is made between giving Orders, and License to Preach : the latter being granted only to such, as the Bishop shall judge able to make sermons."

But this does not seem to do the business. For though it be not necessary for every Guide of a parish to understand all the Oriental languages, or to make exactly elegant or profound discourses for the Pulpit ; yet, most certainly, it is very requisite that he should be so far learned and judicious as prudently to advise, direct, inform, and satisfy the people in holy matters; when they demand it, or beg it from him. Which to perform readily and judiciously requires much more discretion and skill, than, upon long deliberation, to make a continued talk of an hour, without any great discernible failings. So that were a Minister tied up, never to speak one sentence of his own invention out of the pulpit in his whole lifetime ; yet doubtless many other occasions there be, for which neither wisdom nor reputation should be wanting in him that has the care and government of a parish.

I shall not here go about to please myself with the imagination of all the Great Tithes being restored to the Church ; having little reason to hope to see such days of virtue. Nor shall I here question the almightiness of former Kings and Parliaments, nor dispute whether all the King HENRIES in the world, with ever such a powerful Parliament, were able to determine to any other use, what was once solemnly dedicated to GOD, and His service. By yet, when we look over the Prefaces to those *Acts of Parliament* whereby some Church revenues were granted to HENRY VIII., one cannot but be much taken with the ingenuity of that Parliament ; that when the King wanted a supply of money and an augmentation to his revenue, how handsomely, out of the Church they made provision for him, without doing themselves any injury at all !

For, say they, *seeing His Majesty is our joy and life; seeing that he is so courageous and wise; seeing that he is so very tender of, and well affected to, all his subjects; and that he has been at such large expenses, for five and twenty whole years, to defend and protect this his realm: therefore, in all duty and gratitude, and as a manifest token of our unfeigned thankfulness, We do grant unto the king and his heirs for ever, &c.*

It follows as closely as can be, that because the king has been a good and deserving king, and had been at much trouble and expense for the safety and honour of the nation, that therefore all his wants shall be supplied *out of the Church*! as if all the charges that he had been at, were upon the account only of his Ecclesiastical subjects, and not in relation to the rest.

It is not, Sir, for you or I to guess, which way the whole Clergy in general, might be better provided for. But, sure it is, and must not be denied, that so long as many Livings continue as they now are, thus impoverished; and that there be so few encouragements for men of sobriety, wisdom, and learning: we have no reason to expect much better Instructors and Governors of parishes, than at present we commonly find.

There is a way, I know, that some people love marvellously to talk of; and that is a just and equal levelling of Ecclesiastical preferments.

"What a delicate refreshment," say they, "would it be, if £20,000 or £30,000 a year were taken from the Bishops, and discreetly sprinkled amongst the poorer and meaner sort of the Clergy! how would it rejoice their hearts, and encourage them in their Office! What need those great and sumptuous palaces, their city and their country houses, their parks and spacious waters, their costly dishes and fashionable sauces? May not he that lives in a small thatched house, that can scarcely walk four strides in his own ground, that has only *read* well concerning venison, fish, and fowl: may not he, I say, preach as loud and to as much purpose as one of those high and mighty Spiritualists? Go to, then! Seeing it hath pleased GOD to make such a bountiful provision for His Church in general, what need we be solicitous about the emending the low condition of many of the Clergy, when as there is such a plain remedy at hand, had we but grace to apply it?"

This invention pleases some mainly well. But for all the great care they pretend to have of the distressed part of the Clergy, I am confident, one might easily guess what would please them much better! if (instead of augmenting small benefices) the Bishops would be pleased to return to them, those lands purchased in their absence [*i.e., during the Commonwealth, which were restored to the Bishoprics at the Re-*

storation]: and then, as for the relieving of the Clergy, they would try if they could find out another way!

But, art thou in good earnest? my excellent Contriver! Dost thou think that if the greatest of our Church preferments were wisely parcelled out amongst those that are in want, it would do such feats and courtesies? And dost thou not likewise think, that if ten or twenty of the lustiest Noblemen's estates of England were cleverly sliced among the indigent; would it not strangely refresh some of the poor Laity that cry "Small Coal!" or grind scissors! I do suppose if GOD should afterwards incline thy mind (for I fancy it will not be as yet, a good while!) to be a Benefactor to the Church; thy wisdom may possibly direct thee to disperse thy goodness in smaller parcels, rather than to flow in upon two or three with full happiness.

But if it be my inclination to settle upon one Ecclesiastical person and his successors for ever, a £1,000 a year [=£3,000 *now*] upon condition only to read the *Service* of the Church once in a week; and you take it ill, and find fault with my prudence and the method of my munificence, and say that "the stipend is much too large for such a small task": yet, I am confident, that should I make thy Laityship heir of such an estate, and oblige thee only to the trouble and expense of spending a single chicken or half a dozen larks once a year, in commemoration of me; that thou wouldst count me the wisest man that ever was, since the Creation! and pray to GOD never to dispose thy mind, to part with one farthing of it for any other use, than for the service of thyself and thy family.

And yet so it is, that, because the Bishops, upon their first being restored [in 1660], had the confidence to levy fines, according as they were justly due; and desired to live in their own houses, if not pulled down! and to receive their own rents: presently, they cry out, "The Churchmen have got all the treasure and money of the nation into their hands."

If they have, let them thank GOD for it! and make a good use of it. Weep not, Beloved! for there is very little hope that they will cast it all into the sea, on purpose to stop the mouths of them, that say "they have too much!"

What other contrivances there may be, for the settling

upon Ministers in general, a sufficient revenue for their subsistence and encouragement in their office; I shall leave to
be considered of, by the Governors of Learning and Religion.

Only thus much is certain, that so long as the maintenance of many Ministers is so very small, it is not to be
avoided, but that a great part of them will want learning,
prudence, courage, and esteem to do any good where they live.

And what if we have (as by all must be acknowledged)
as wise and learned Bishops as be in the world, and many
others of very great understanding and wisdom; yet (as was
before hinted) unless there be provided for most towns and
parishes some tolerable and sufficient Guides, the strength of
Religion, and the credit of the Clergy will daily languish
more and more.

Not that it is to be believed that every small country
parish should be altogether hopeless as to the next life,
unless they have a HOOKER, a CHILLINGWORTH, a HAMMOND,
or a SANDERSON dwelling amongst them: but it is requisite,
and might be brought about, that somebody there should be,
to whom the people have reason to attend, and to be directed
and guided by him.

I have, Sir, no more to say, were it not that you find
the word *Religion* in the Title: of which in particular I have
spoken very little. Neither need I! considering how nearly
it depends, as to its glory and strength, upon the reputation
and mouth of the Priest.

And I shall add no more but this, viz., that among those
many things that tend to the decay of Religion, and of a due
reverence of the *Holy Scriptures*, nothing has more occasioned it than the ridiculous and idle discourses that are
uttered out of pulpits. For when the Gallants of the world
do observe how the Ministers themselves do jingle, quibble,
and play the fool with the Texts: no wonder, if they, who are
so inclinable to Atheism, do not only deride and despise the
Priests; but droll upon the *Bible*! and make a mock of all
that is sober and sacred!

I am, Sir, Your most humble servant,

T. B.

August 8, 1670.

FINIS.

ISAAC BICKERSTAFF
[*i.e.*, RICHARD STEELE].

The miseries of the Domestic Chaplain, in 1710.

[*The Tatler.* No. 255. Thursday, 23 Nov. 1710.]

To the Censor of Great Britain.

SIR,

 *AM at present, under very great difficulties; which is not in the power of any one besides yourself, to redress. Whether or not, you shall think it a proper Case to come before your Court of Honour, I cannot tell: but thus it is.*

I am Chaplain to an honourable Family, very regular at the Hours of Devotion, and I hope of an unblameable life: but, for not offering to rise at the Second Course, I found my Patron and his Lady very sullen and out of humour; though, at first, I did not know the reason of it.

At length, when I happened to help myself to a jelly, the Lady of the house, otherwise a devout woman, told me "It did not become a Man of my Cloth, to delight in such frivolous food!" But as I still continued to sit out the last course, I was yesterday informed by the butler, that "His Lordship had no further occasion for my service."

All which is humbly submitted to your consideration, by,

Sir,

Your most humble servant, &c.

The case of this Gentleman deserves pity, especially if he loves sweetmeats; to which, if I may guess by his letter, he is no enemy.

In the meantime, I have often wondered at the indecency of discarding the holiest man from the table, as soon as the most delicious parts of the entertainment are served up: and could never conceive a reason for so absurd a custom.

Is it because a licorous palate, or a sweet tooth (as they call it), is not consistent with the sanctity of his character?

This is but a trifling pretence! No man of the most rigid virtue, gives offence by any excesses in plum pudding or plum porridge; and that, because they are the first parts of the dinner. Is there anything that tends to *incitation* in sweetmeats, more than in ordinary dishes? Certainly not! Sugar-plums are a very innocent diet; and conserves of a much colder nature than your common pickles.

I have sometimes thought that the Ceremony of the *Chaplain flying away from the Dessert* was typical and figurative. To mark out to the company, how they ought to retire from all the luscious baits of temptation, and deny their appetites the gratifications that are most pleasing to them.

Or, at least, to signify that we ought to stint ourselves in the most lawful satisfactions; and not make our Pleasure, but our Support the end of eating.

But, most certainly, if such a lesson of temperance had been necessary at a table: our Clergy would have recommended it to all the Lay masters of families; and not have disturbed other men's tables with such unreasonable examples of abstinence.

The original therefore of this *barbarous custom*, I take to have been merely accidental.

The Chaplain retired, out of pure complaisance, to make room for the removal of the dishes, or possibly for the ranging of the dessert.   This, by degrees, grew into a duty; till, at length, as the fashion improved, the good man found himself cut off from the Third part of the entertainment: and, if the arrogance of the Patron goes on, it is not impossible but, in the next generation, he may see himself reduced to the Tithe or Tenth Dish of the table.   A sufficient caution not to part with any privilege we are once possessed of !

It was usual for the Priest, in old times, to feast upon the sacrifice, nay the honey cake; while the hungry Laity looked upon him with great devotion: or, as the late Lord ROCHESTER describes it in a very lively manner,

And while the Priest did eat, the People stared.

At present, the custom is inverted.   The Laity feast while the Priest stands by as an humble spectator.

This necessarily puts the good man upon making great ravages on all the dishes that stand near him; and upon distinguishing himself by voraciousness of appetite, as knowing that "his time is short."

I would fain ask these stiff-necked Patrons, Whether they would not take it ill of a Chaplain that, in his grace, after meat, should return thanks for the whole entertainment, with an exception to the dessert?   And yet I cannot but think that in such a proceeding, he would but deal with them as they deserved.

What would a Roman Catholic priest think (who is always helped first, and placed next the ladies), should he see a Clergyman giving his company the slip at the first appearance of the tarts or sweetmeats?   Would he not believe that he had the same antipathy to a candid orange or a piece of puff paste, as some have to a Cheshire cheese or a breast of mutton?

Yet to so ridiculous a height is this foolish custom grown, that even the Christmas Pie, which in its very nature is a kind of consecrated cate and a badge of distinction, is often forbidden to the Druid of the family.

Strange! that a sirloin of beef, whether boiled or roasted, when entire, is exposed to his utmost depredations and incisions; but if minced into small pieces and tossed up with plums and sugar, it changes its property; and, forsooth, it is meat for his Master!

In this Case, I know not which to censure [blame], the Patron or the Chaplain! the insolence of power, or the abjectness of dependence!

For my own part, I have often blushed to see a Gentleman, whom I knew to have more Wit and Learning than myself, and who was bred up with me at the University upon the same foot of a liberal education, treated in such an ignominious manner; and sunk beneath those of his own rank, by reason of that character which ought to bring him honour.

This deters men of generous minds from placing themselves in such a station of life; and by that means frequently excludes Persons of Quality from the improving and agreeable conversation of a learned and obsequious friend.

Mr. OLDHAM lets us know that he was affrighted from the thought of such an employment, by the scandalous sort of treatment, which often accompanies it.

Some think themselves exalted to the sky,
If they light in some noble family :
Diet, a horse, and Thirty pounds a year;
Besides th'advantage of his Lordship's ear,
The credit of the business, and the State ;

Are things that in a youngster's sense sound great.
Little the unexperienced wretch does know,
What slavery he oft must undergo!
Who, though in silken scarf and cassock drest,
Wears but a gayer livery, *at best.*
When dinner calls, the Implement must wait,
With holy words to consecrate the meat :
But hold it, for a favour seldom known,
If he be deigned the honour to sit down!
Soon as the tarts appear, " Sir CRAPE, *withdraw !*
These dainties are not for a spiritual maw !
Observe your distance ! and be sure to stand
Hard by the cistern with your cap in hand !
There, for diversion, you may pick your teeth
Till the kind Voider comes for your relief."

Let others who, such meannesses can brook,
Strike countenance to every Great Man's look :
I rate my freedom higher !

The author's raillery is the raillery of a friend, and does
not turn the Sacred Order into ridicule : but it is a just
censure on such persons as take advantages from the necessities of a Man of Merit, to impose upon him hardships that
are by no means suitable to the dignity of his profession.

NESTOR IRONSIDE
[*i.e.*, *RICHARD STEELE*].

*Another description of the miseries of the
Domestic Chaplain, in 1713, A.D.*

[*The Guardian.* No. 173. Thursday, 17 Sept. 1713.]

 HEN I am disposed to give myself a day's
rest, I order the *Lion* to be opened [*i.e.,
a letter-box at* BUTTON'S *Coffee-house*], and
search into that magazine of intelligence
for such letters as are to my purpose.
The first I looked into, comes to me
from one who is Chaplain to a great
family.

He treats himself, in the beginning of it, after such a manner
as I am persuaded no Man of Sense would treat him. Even
the Lawyer, and the Physician to a Man of Quality, expect
to be used like gentlemen; and much more, may any one of
so superior a profession!

I am by no means encouraging that dispute, Whether the
Chaplain, or the Master of the house be the better man, and
the more to be respected? The two learned authors, Dr. HICKS

and Mr. COLLIER (to whom I might add several others) are
to be excused, if they have carried the point a little too high
in favour of the Chaplain : since in so corrupt an Age as that
we live in, the popular opinion runs so far into the other
extreme.

The only controversy between the Patron and the Chaplain
ought to be, Which should promote the good designs and
interests of each other most ? And, for my own part, I think
it is the happiest circumstance in a great Estate or Title, that
it qualifies a man for choosing, out of such a learned and
valuable body of men as that of the English Clergy, a friend,
a spiritual guide, and a companion.

The letter which I have received from one of this Order, is
as follows :

Mr. Guardian,

 *HOPE you will not only indulge me in the liberty of two
or three questions ; but also in the solution of them.*

*I have had the honour, many years, of being
Chaplain in a noble Family ; and of being accounted*
the highest servant *in the house : either out of respect to my
Cloth, or because I lie in the uppermost garret.*

*Whilst my old Lord lived, his table was always adorned with
useful Learning and innocent Mirth, as well as covered with
Plenty. I was not looked upon as a piece of furniture, fit only to
sanctify and garnish a feast ; but treated as a Gentleman, and
generally desired to fill up the conversation, an hour after I had
done my duty* [i.e., said grace after dinner].

*But now my young Lord is come to the Estate, I find I am
looked upon as a* Censor Morum, *an obstacle to mirth and talk :
and suffered to retire constantly with* "Prosperity to the Church!"
in my mouth [i.e., after drinking this toast].

*I declare, solemnly, Sir, that I have heard nothing from all the
fine Gentlemen who visit us, more remarkable, for half a year,
than that one young Lord was seven times drunk at Genoa.*

I have lately taken the liberty to stay three or four rounds [i.e., of the bottle] *beyond [the toast of]* The Church ! *to see what topics of discourse they went upon : but, to my great surprise, have hardly heard a word all the time, besides the Toasts. Then they all stared full in my face, and shewed all the actions of uneasiness till I was gone.*

Immediately upon my departure, to use the words of an old Comedy, " I find by the noise they make, that they had a mind to be private."

I am at a loss to imagine what conversation they have among one another, which I may not be present at : since I love innocent Mirth as much as any of them ; and am shocked with no freedoms whatsoever, which are inconsistent with Christianity.

I have, with much ado, maintained my post hitherto at the dessert, and every day eat a tart in the face of my Patron : but how long I shall be invested with this privilege, I do not know. For the servants, who do not see me supported as I was in my old Lord's time, begin to brush very familiarly by me : and they thrust aside my chair, when they set the sweetmeats on the table.

I have been born and educated a Gentleman, and desire you will make the public sensible that the Christian Priesthood was never thought, in any Age or country, to debase the Man who is a member of it. Among the great services which your useful Papers daily do to Religion, this perhaps will not be the least : and it will lay a very great obligation on

Your unknown servant,

G. W.

Benjamin Franklin.

Poor Richard improved, Being an Almanac, &c., for the year of our Lord 1758.

Richard Saunders. Philom.

Philadelphia.

Courteous Reader.

 HAVE heard that nothing gives an author so great pleasure as to find his works respectfully quoted by other learned authors. This pleasure I have seldom enjoyed. For though I have been, if I may say it without vanity, an *eminent* author of

Almanacs annually, now a full quarter of a century, my brother authors in the same way, for what reason I know not, have ever been very sparing in their applauses; and no other author has taken the least notice of me: so that did not my writings produce me some solid Pudding, the great deficiency of Praise would have quite discouraged me.

I concluded at length, that the people were the best judges of my merit; for they buy my works: and besides, in my rambles, where I am not personally known, I have frequently heard one or other of my Adages repeated, with "as *Poor RICHARD* says!" at the end of it. This gave me some satisfaction, as it shewed, not only that my Instructions were regarded, but discovered likewise some respect for my Authority. And I own, that to encourage the practice of remembering and repeating those wise Sentences: I have sometimes *quoted myself* with great gravity.

Judge, then, how much I must have been gratified by an incident I am going to relate to you!

I stopped my horse lately, where a great number of people were collected at a Vendue [*sale*] of Merchant's goods. The hour of sale not being come, they were conversing on the badness of the Times: and one of the company called to a clean old man, with white locks, "Pray, Father ABRAHAM! what do you think of the Times? Won't these heavy taxes quite ruin the country? How shall we be ever able to pay them? What would you advise us to?"

Father ABRAHAM stood up, and replied, "If you would have my advice; I will give it you, in short; for *a word to the wise is enough*, and *many words won't fill a bushel*, as *Poor RICHARD* says."

They all joined, desiring him to speak his mind; and gathering round him, he proceeded as follows:

"Friends" says he, "and neighbours! The taxes are indeed very heavy; and if those laid on by the Government were the only ones we had to pay, we might the more easily discharge them: but we have many others, and much more grievous to some of us. We are taxed twice as much by our IDLENESS, three times as much by our PRIDE, and four times as much by our FOLLY: and from these taxes, the Commissioners cannot ease, or deliver us by allowing an abatement. However let us hearken to good advice, and something may be done for us. *GOD helps them that help themselves*, **as** *Poor RICHARD* says in his *Almanac* of 1733.

It would be thought a hard Government that should tax its people One-tenth part of their TIME, to be employed in its service. But Idleness taxes many of us much more; if we reckon all that is spent in absolute sloth, or doing of nothing; with that which is spent in idle employments or amusements that amount to nothing. Sloth, by bringing on diseases, absolutely shortens life. *Sloth, like Rust, consumes faster than Labour wears; while the used key is always bright,* as *Poor RICHARD* says. But *dost thou love Life? Then do not squander time! for that's the stuff Life is made of,* as *Poor RICHARD* says.

How much more than is necessary do we spend in sleep? forgetting that *the sleeping fox catches no poultry;* and that *there will be sleeping enough in the grave,* as *Poor RICHARD* says. If Time be of all things the most precious, *Wasting of Time must be* (as *Poor RICHARD* says) *the greatest prodigality;* since, as he elsewhere tells us, *Lost time is never found again;* and what we call *Time enough! always proves little enough.* Let us then up and be doing, and doing to the purpose: so, by diligence, shall we do more with less perplexity. *Sloth makes all things difficult, but Industry all things easy,* as *Poor RICHARD* says: and *He that riseth late, must trot all day; and shall scarce overtake his business at night.* While *Laziness travels so slowly, that Poverty soon overtakes him,* as we read in *Poor RICHARD;* who adds, *Drive thy business! Let not that drive thee!* and

> *Early to bed, and early to rise,*
> *Makes a man healthy, wealthy, and wise.*

So what signifies *wishing* and *hoping* for better Times! We may make these Times better, if we bestir ourselves! *Industry need not wish!* as *Poor RICHARD* says; and *He that lives on Hope, will die fasting. There are no gains without pains.* Then *Help hands! for I have no lands;* or if I have, they are smartly taxed. And as *Poor RICHARD* likewise observes, *He that hath a Trade, hath an Estate,* and He that *hath a Calling, hath an Office of Profit and Honour:* but, then, the Trade must be worked at, and the Calling well followed, or neither the Estate, nor the Office, will enable us to pay our taxes.

If we are industrious, we shall never starve, for, as *Poor RICHARD* says, *At the working man's house, Hunger looks in; but dares not enter.* Nor will the Bailiff, or the Constable enter: for *Industry pays debts, while Despair increaseth them,* says *Poor RICHARD.*

What though you have found no treasure, nor has any rich relation left you a legacy, *Diligence is the Mother of Goodluck,* as *Poor RICHARD* says; and *GOD gives all things to Industry.* Then

> *Plough deep, while sluggards sleep;*
> *And you shall have corn to sell and to keep,*

says *Poor DICK.* Work while it is called to-day; for you know not, how much you may be hindered to-morrow : which makes *Poor RICHARD* say, *One To-day is worth two To-morrows,* and farther, *Have you somewhat to do to-morrow ? do it to-day !*

If you were a servant, would you not be ashamed that a good master should catch you idle? Are you then your own Master? *Be ashamed to catch yourself idle !* as *Poor DICK* says. When there is so much to be done for yourself, your family, your country, and your gracious King; be up by peep of day ! *Let not the sun look down, and say, " Inglorious, here he lies !"* Handle your tools, without mittens ! Remember that *The cat in glove catches no mice !* as *Poor RICHARD* says.

'Tis true there is much to be done; and perhaps you are weak handed; but stick to it steadily ! and you will see great effects, For *Constant dropping wears away stones,* and *By diligence and patience, the mouse ate in two the cable,* and *little strokes fell great oaks ;* as *Poor RICHARD* says in his *Almanac,* the year I cannot, just now, remember.

Methinks, I hear some of you say, " Must a man afford himself no leisure ? "

" I will tell thee, my friend ! what *Poor RICHARD* says.

> *Employ thy time well, if thou meanest to gain leisure !* and
> *Since thou art not sure of a minute, throw not away an hour !*

Leisure is time for doing something useful. This leisure the diligent man will obtain; but the lazy man never. So that, as *Poor RICHARD* says, *A life of leisure, and a life of laziness are two things.*. Do you imagine that Sloth will afford you more comfort than Labour? No! for as *Poor RICHARD* says, *Trouble springs from idleness, and grievous toil from needless ease. Many without labour, would live by their Wits only; but they'll break, for want of Stock* [*i.e.*, Capital]. Whereas Industry gives comfort, and plenty, and respect. *Fly Pleasures! and they'll follow you! The diligent spinner has a large shift,* and

> *Now I have a sheep and a cow*
> *Everybody bids me " Good morrow."*

All which is well said by *Poor RICHARD*.

But with our Industry; we must likewise be Steady, Settled, and Careful: and oversee our own affairs *with our own eyes,* and not trust too much to others. For, as *Poor RICHARD* says,

> *I never saw an oft removed tree,*
> *Nor yet an oft removed family,*
> *That throve so well, as those that settled be.*

And again, *Three Removes are as bad as a Fire*; and again *Keep thy shop! and thy shop will keep thee!* and again, *If you would have your business done, go! if not, send!* and again,

> *He that by the plough would thrive;*
> *Himself must either hold or drive.*

And again, *The Eye of the master will do more work than both his Hands*; and again, *Want of Care does us more damage than Want of Knowledge*; and again, *Not to oversee workmen, is to leave them your purse open.*

Trusting too much to others' care, is the ruin of many. For, as the *Almanac* says, *In the affairs of this world, men are saved, not by faith, but by the want of it.* But a man's own care is profitable; for, saith *Poor DICK, Learning is to the Studious,* and *Riches to the Careful*; as well as *Power to the Bold,* and *Heaven to the Virtuous.* And further, *If you would have a faithful servant, and one that you like; serve yourself!*

And again, he adviseth to circumspection and care, even in

the smallest matters; because sometimes, *A little neglect may breed great mischief*: adding, *For want of a nail, the shoe was lost; for want of a shoe, the horse was lost; and for want of a horse, the rider was lost*; being overtaken, and slain by the enemy. All for want of care about a horse-shoe nail.

So much for Industry, my friends! and attention to one's own business; but to these we must add FRUGALITY, if we would make our industry more certainly successful. *A man may*, if he knows not how to save as he gets, *keep his nose, all his life, to the grindstone; and die not worth a groat at last. A fat Kitchen makes a lean Will*, as Poor RICHARD says, and

> *Many estates are spent in the getting,*
> *Since women, for Tea, forsook spinning and knitting;*
> *And men, for Punch, forsook hewing and splitting.*

If you would be healthy, says he in another *Almanac, think of Saving, as well as of Getting! The Indies have not made Spain rich; because her Outgoes are greater than her Incomes.*

Away, then, with your expensive follies! and you will not have so much cause to complain of hard Times, heavy taxes, and chargeable families. For, as Poor DICK says,

> *Women and Wine, Game and Deceit,*
> *Make the Wealth small, and the Wants great.*

And farther, *What maintains one vice, would bring up two children.*

You may think perhaps, that, a *little* tea, or a *little* punch, now and then; diet, a *little* more costly; clothes, a *little* finer; and a *little* entertainment, now and then; can be no great matter. But remember what Poor RICHARD says, *Many a Little makes a Mickle*; and farther, *Beware of little expenses! a small leak will sink a great ship*; and again, *Who dainties love; shall beggars prove!* and moreover, *Fools make feasts, and wise men eat them.*

Here are you all got together at this Vendue of Fineries and knicknacks! You call them Goods: but if you do not take care, they will prove Evils to some of you! You expect they will be sold cheap, and perhaps they may, for less than they cost; but if you have no occasion for them, they must be *dear* to you! Remember what Poor RICHARD says! *Buy*

*what thou hast no need of, and, ere long, thou shalt sell thy
necessaries!* And again, *At a great pennyworth, pause a while!*
He means, that perhaps the cheapness is apparent only, and
not real; or the bargain by straitening thee in thy business,
may do thee more harm than good.   For in another place,
he says, *Many have been ruined by buying good pennyworths.*

Again, *Poor* RICHARD says, *'Tis foolish, to lay out money in
a purchase of Repentance:* and yet this folly is practised every
day at Vendues, for want of minding the *Almanac.*

Wise men, as *Poor* DICK says, *learn by others' harms; Fools,
scarcely by their own:* but *Felix quem faciunt aliena pericula
cautum.*   Many a one, for the sake of finery on the back,
has gone with a hungry belly, and half starved their families.
Silks and satins, scarlet and velvets, as *Poor* RICHARD says, *put
out the kitchen fire!* These are not the necessaries of life; they
can scarcely be called the conveniences: and yet only because
they look pretty, how many *want* to have them!   The artificial wants of mankind thus become more numerous than the
natural; and as *Poor* DICK says, *For one* poor *person, there are
a hundred* indigent.

By these, and other extravagances, the genteel are reduced
to poverty, and forced to borrow of those whom they formerly
despised; but who, through Industry and Frugality, have
maintained their standing.   In which case, it appears plainly
that *A ploughman on his legs is higher than a gentleman on his
knees,* as *Poor* RICHARD says.   Perhaps they have had a small
estate left them, which they knew not the getting of.   They
think *'tis day! and will never be night!*; that *a little to be spent
out of so much! is not worth minding* (*A Child and a Fool,* as *Poor*
RICHARD says, *imagine Twenty Shillings and Twenty Years can
never be spent*): but *always taking out of the meal tub, and never
putting in, soon comes to the bottom.*   Then, as *Poor* DICK says,
When the well's dry, they know the worth of water! but this they
might have known before, if they had taken his advice.   *If
you would know the value of money; go, and try to borrow some!*
For, *he that goes a borrowing, goes a sorrowing!* and indeed, so
does he that lends to such people, *when he goes to get it in
again!*

Poor DICK further advises, and says

> *Fond Pride of Dress is, sure, a very curse!*
> *Ere Fancy you consult; consult your purse!*

And again, *Pride is as loud a beggar as Want, and a great deal more saucy!* When you have bought one fine thing, you must buy ten more, that your appearance may be all of a piece; but *Poor DICK* says, *'Tis easier to suppress the First desire, than to satisfy All that follow it.* And 'tis as truly folly, for the poor to ape the rich; as for the frog to swell, in order to equal the ox.

> *Great Estates may venture more;*
> *But little boats should keep near shore!*

'Tis, however, a folly soon punished! for Pride that *dines on Vanity, sups on Contempt*, as *Poor RICHARD* says. And in another place, *Pride breakfasted with Plenty, dined with Poverty, and supped with Infamy.*

And, after all, of what use is this Pride of Appearance? for which so much is risked, so much is suffered! It cannot promote health or ease pain! It makes no increase of merit in the person! It creates envy! It hastens misfortune!

> *What is a butterfly? At best*
> *He's but a caterpillar drest!*
> *The gaudy fop's his picture just.*

as *Poor RICHARD* says.

But what madness must it be, to *run into debt* for these superfluities?

We are offered, by the terms of this Vendue, Six Months' Credit; and that, perhaps, has induced some of us to attend it, because we cannot spare the ready money, and hope now to be fine without it. But, ah, think what you do, when you run in debt? *You give to another, power over your liberty!* If you cannot pay at the time, you will be ashamed to see your creditor! You will be in fear, when you speak to him! You will make poor pitiful sneaking excuses! and, by degrees, come to lose your veracity, and sink into base downright lying! For, as *Poor RICHARD* says, *The second vice is Lying, the first is Running into Debt:* and again, to the same purpose, *Lying rides upon Debt's back.* Whereas a free born Englishman ought not to be ashamed or afraid to see, or speak to any man living. But Poverty often deprives a man of all spirit and virtue. *'Tis hard for an Empty Bag to stand upright!* as *Poor RICHARD* truly says. What would you think of that Prince, or the Government, who should issue an Edict for-

bidding you to dress like a Gentleman or Gentlewoman, on
pain of imprisonment or servitude. Would you not say that
" You are free! have a right to dress as you please! and that
such an Edict would be a breach of your privileges! and such
a Government, tyrannical!" And yet you are about to put
yourself under that tyranny, when you run in debt for such
dress! Your creditor has authority, at his pleasure, to
deprive you of your liberty, by confining you in gaol for life!
or to sell you for a servant, if you should not be able to pay
him! When you have got your bargain; you may, perhaps,
think little of payment, but *Creditors* (Poor RICHARD tells us)
have better memories than Debtors; and, in another place, says,
*Creditors are a superstitious sect! great observers of set days and
times*. The day comes round, before you are aware; and the
demand is made, before you are prepared to satisfy it: or, if
you bear your debt in mind, the term which, at first, seemed
so long, will, as it lessens, appear extremely short. TIME
will seem to have added wings to his heels, as well as
shoulders. *Those have a short Lent*, saith Poor RICHARD, *who
owe money to be paid at Easter*. Then since, as he says, *The
Borrower is a slave to the Lender, and the Debtor to the Creditor*;
disdain the chain! preserve your freedom! and maintain
your independency! Be *industrious* and *free!* be *frugal* and
free! At present, perhaps, you may think yourself in thriving
circumstances; and that you can bear a little extravagance
without injury: but

> *For Age and Want, save while you may!*
> *No morning sun lasts a whole day,*

as *Poor RICHARD* says.
Gain may be temporary and uncertain; but, ever while you
live, Expense is constant and certain: and *'tis easier to build
two chimneys than to keep one in fuel*, as Poor RICHARD says.
So *rather go to bed supperless, than rise in debt!*

> *Get what you can! and what you get, hold!*
> *'Tis the Stone that will turn all your lead into gold!*

as *Poor RICHARD* says. And when you have got the Philosopher's Stone, sure, you will no longer complain of bad times,
or the difficulty of paying taxes.

This doctrine, my friends! is Reason and Wisdom! But, after all, do not depend too much upon your own Industry, and Frugality, and Prudence; though excellent things! For they may all be blasted without the Blessing of Heaven: and, therefore, ask that Blessing humbly! and be not uncharitable to those that at present, seem to want it; but comfort and help them! Remember, JOB suffered, and was afterwards prosperous.

And now to conclude. *Experience keeps a dear school; but Fools will learn in no other, and scarce in that!* for it is true, *We may give Advice, but we cannot give Conduct,* as *Poor RICHARD* says. However, remember this! *They that won't be counselled, can't be helped!* as *Poor RICHARD* says: and farther, that, *If you will not hear reason, she'll surely rap your knuckles!*"

Thus the old gentleman ended his harangue. The people heard it, and approved the doctrine; and immediately practised the contrary, just as if it had been a common sermon! For the Vendue opened, and they began to buy extravagantly; notwithstanding all his cautions, and their own fear of taxes.

I found the good man had thoroughly studied my *Almanacs*, and digested all I had dropped on those topics during the course of five and twenty years. The frequent mention he made of me, must have tired any one else; but my vanity was wonderfully delighted with it: though I was conscious that not a tenth part of the wisdom was my own, which he ascribed to me; but rather the gleanings I had made of the Sense of all Ages and Nations. However, I resolved to be the better for the Echo of it; and though I had, at first, determined to buy stuff for a new coat; I went away resolved to wear my old one a little longer. Reader! if thou wilt do the same, thy profit will be as great as mine.

I am, as ever,

Thine, to serve thee!

July 7, 1757.   RICHARD SAUNDERS.

INDEX

Edinburgh : Printed by T. and A. CONSTABLE